T0314188

BLOOD AND DIAMONDS

BLOOD

AND

DIAMONDS

GERMANY'S IMPERIAL AMBITIONS IN AFRICA

STEVEN PRESS

Harvard University Press

Cambridge, Massachusetts
London, England

2021

First printing

Library of Congress Cataloging-in-Publication Data

Names: Press, Steven, author.
Title: Blood and diamonds : Germany's imperial ambitions in Africa / Steven Press.
Description: Cambridge, Massachusetts : Harvard University Press, 2021. |
Includes bibliographical references and index.
Identifiers: LCCN 2020043311 | ISBN 9780674916494 (cloth)
Subjects: LCSH: Diamond industry and trade—Africa, Southern—History. |
Diamond industry and trade—Germany—History. | Diamond industry and trade—
United States—History. | Conflict diamonds—History. | Herero (African
people)—History. | Nama (African people)—History. | Germany—Colonies—Africa. |
Germany—Politics and government.
Classification: LCC HD9677.G32 P73 2021 | DDC 338.2 / 782096881—dc23
LC record available at https://lccn.loc.gov/2020043311

For Miriam

◈

CONTENTS

BLOOD AND DIAMONDS

INTRODUCTION

◆ Start walking inland from Lüderitz, the southernmost coastal town in the African state of Namibia. Go a few miles and you will enter the Namib, a desert that, to the uninitiated, seems like sand, sand, and more sand. The portion of the Namib to the south and east of Lüderitz is known as the Forbidden Zone (*Sperrgebiet*). Despite amounting to just 3 percent of Namibia's overall land, the Forbidden Zone's 10,000 square miles of terrain approximate the size of Massachusetts.[1]

Many of Lüderitz's roughly 12,000 inhabitants work in the Forbidden Zone, a place that induces fear beyond that attending most wildernesses. Signs on the area's outskirts warn trespassers of arrest and hefty fines. But anyone authorized to enter the Forbidden Zone—the "Zone," for short—knows that it is nigh-impossible to survive it without assistance. Natural fresh water sources do not exist there, despite the ground's contiguity with the cold, powerful waves of the Southern Atlantic. Annual rainfall averages a quarter of an inch. Droughts have lasted as long as six years.[2] And, while thick morning fog provides enough moisture to keep ants and beetles alive, humans are not so lucky.

Nights in the Zone often turn freezing. Daytime temperatures can surpass 120 degrees Fahrenheit, sometimes reaching 140 in canyons. Vegetation cannot tolerate such extremes, rendering the ground barren and lunar-like. Only the wind has staying power, whipping up dust without apparent pause. Sand gets in the throats and eyes of human travelers, stinging the flesh. Imperceptibly at first, then absolutely, sand even lodges under shoe soles as if in an attempt to escape.

Climate is one reason why the Zone figures in travel guides as an eerie corner of the globe. But one must recall, too, that a man-made prohibition has *forbidden* the place. Clinging to an orange-brown expanse of rock, beneath shifting dunes that can reach several hundred feet in height,

A view in 2017 from an abandoned German colonial bungalow at Kolmanskop, Namibia, located at a remove of ten kilometers from the coastal town of Lüderitz. The sand of the Namib Desert has reclaimed the bungalow floor.

the history of the Zone's prohibition lies buried amid the ruins of the lost empire that created it. Today one finds traces of that empire scattered across an uninhabited patchwork of decrepit bungalows, rusted machinery, signposts bearing Gothic script, and abandoned ditches filled with unidentified skeletons. Tying it all together are millions of tiny stones that, because prized by the world, contributed to a long domination of this African land by Europeans.

The territory that became the Zone won little attention until 1908, when railroad workers found troves of diamonds beside some track under repair. At the time, Namibia did not exist as a sovereign state; instead, Germany ruled it as a colony named Southwest Africa. The diamond strike thus originally promised to benefit not Indigenous people but German colonizers. The Germans claimed ownership of what were, by some accounts, then the richest diamond deposits in history. "Their" reserves doubled what India and Brazil had produced in centuries of mining, even approaching the equivalent weight of all diamonds extracted by humans prior to the twentieth century.[3]

After 1908, Southwest Africa's German occupiers worried about protecting the mineral wealth from perceived interlopers. As a result, colonial authorities sealed off much of the Namib from the public, reclassifying the affected area as the Forbidden Zone. The Zone had the potential to change an array of fortunes: for consumers, who coveted diamonds for jewelry; for bankers, who aimed to monetize dubious deeds of ownership; for officials, who tried to elevate their second-rate posting; for prospectors, who hoped to strike it rich; for stockjobbers, who built a speculative house of cards atop diamond fantasies; and, not least, for Imperial Germany's political elites, who dreamt of attaining the global influence enjoyed by Britain.[4]

◆　　　◆　　　◆

This book charts the rise and fall of Germany's colonial diamonds as a means to reassess Germany's overseas empire, one of a ramshackle agglomeration of experiments undertaken in Africa, the Pacific, and China. Lasting roughly from 1884 to 1918, the German overseas empire amounted to an area five times the size of Imperial Germany proper.[5]

The Germans' inaugural and signature overseas holding was Southwest Africa. Before 1908, when diamonds began turning up in droves, the colony faced deep problems: administrative corruption, economic stagnation, inadequate European settlement, and the aftershocks of a brutal military campaign that nearly annihilated two entire groups of Indigenous people. Southwest Africa's problems figured as an indictment of Germany's broader colonial project, about which scandals proliferated and for which apologists struggled to excuse parlous budgets. Germany was a fledgling colonizer, having joined in on Africa's partition later than did rivals France and Britain. That said, Germany was also a mighty scientific and industrial nation the value of whose exports topped out at 10 billion marks annually before 1914.[6] It thus seemed difficult to explain the country's perceived "underperformance" in colonies like Southwest, as it was known.

Standard accounts stress how, despite Imperial Germany's prowess, its overseas colonies disappointed economically. It is said that they never met more than .5 percent of Germany's raw material needs or provided a steady market for German exports. Goods from the colonies also never contributed more than a marginal .5 percent of total German exports to the world. Diverse critics have reiterated these statistics from the turn of the century, leading historians to regard German colonialism as economically inconsequential.[7] But such an interpretation rests on two problematic assumptions: first, that colonies' official export numbers accurately reflected real exports; and second, that colonial economics existed in a linear relationship between metropole and colony.

In fact, German colonialism contributed vastly more exports than was officially acknowledged. Moreover, German colonialism had major effects on global circuits of labor and capital, as well as on commodity chains. This book will demonstrate each of those effects by tracing the transatlantic web that supplied diamond jewelry in the early 1900s—a substantial, if mysterious, market in which Germans came to control between a fifth and a fourth of global production before the First World War.[8]

Imperial Germany, as a suddenly powerful stakeholder in the diamond trade, generated hundreds of millions of marks simply from mining and exporting rough stones between 1908 and 1914. Germans had reason to dream about earning more riches by muscling in on the lucrative stages of the diamond business that came after extraction: cutting, polishing, and shipping. Additionally, in a less obvious twist, diamonds gave Germany an economic weapon against the British Empire. By drawing on its colonial supplies, Germany could produce more or less exactly the number of carats that the United States, the world's biggest buying pool, could absorb. Should the Germans decide to flood the market with their diamonds, then British South Africa and the British-dominated diamond industry faced peril.

Inside Germany, diamonds' economic potential, real and imagined, brought significant consequences in the age of imperialism. State officials reckoned that diamonds, because sold abroad for foreign currency, could help to fill worrisome gaps in the domestic balance of payments. Legal disputes related to private colonial diamond ownership also put billions of marks at stake, minting millionaires and occasioning court battles over who could benefit from the stones' sale and consumption.[9] Diamonds even played an overlooked role for German investors, with company shares tied to African claims determining multiple swings of the stock market.

While colonial economics has received scant historical attention in studies of Imperial German politics, it is worth revisiting.[10] Tracing the path of diamonds from discovery to consumption reveals how colonial economics influenced social and foreign policy debates and highlighted evolving cultural phenomena, such as anti-Semitism. Diamonds reinforced and sharpened domestic divides over the concentration of wealth. Finally, diamonds caused upheavals with implications not confined to the compact duration, or geographically distant location, of formal German colonialism.

In 1902, the British economist J. A. Hobson published *Imperialism: A Study,* arguing that colonies and colonial wars did metropolitan taxpayers more harm than good. Debates about Hobson's findings have lasted for decades and drawn in, among others, Vladimir Lenin. In the spirit of Peter Cain and Antony Hopkins, two historians who revised Hobson to focus on "gentlemanly capitalism" as a driving force for British imperial expansion, I propose to reexamine the financial dynamics at work in German imperialism. Here it is necessary but insufficient to ask whether imperialism paid the nations that supported it. Likewise, it is necessary but insufficient to note that imperialism often had the result of funneling public money into private hands.[11] Building on such inquiries, I will follow international transfers of capital and labor that stretched beyond Germany's formal imperial boundaries, asking whom German imperialism benefited, and also how, when, and with what results particular segments of society bought into the idea that imperialism *would* benefit them.[12]

For Germans to champion overseas colonies, their government and propagandists had to engage in the skillful creation and maintenance of demand at particular junctures. Diamonds—themselves the subject of intense and often dishonest marketing—figured in this process. Over more than three decades of existence, from 1884 to 1918, promoters of German imperialism dangled the prospect of diamonds in Southwest Africa to justify taxpayer expenditures and the destruction of Indigenous lives. When diamonds at last materialized, Germans expected a huge appreciation in colonial value through enhanced national standing or the creation of new wealth for the masses.

Neither appreciation occurred. Diamonds harvested in Germany's colonial realm profited only select constituencies: companies that controlled mineral rights, merchants who defrauded gullible buyers, mine owners who coerced African labor, or bankers who engaged in rigged stockjobbing. German diamonds, like the German overseas empire itself, did not so much create wealth for average citizens as channel it away from, and around, them. Such a flow of capital was another colonial effect, albeit a subtle one.

•   •   •

It is tempting to view diamonds as a fixed part of life. In our time they represent a ubiquitous luxury, an incessantly advertised object, and, to many, a classic symbol of love and wealth. Owners of a diamond have a sense that it emerges in stages: by nature, by a miner's labor, and then by a cutter's skill. Less appreciated is how a diamond is an *invented* product.[13]

Outside of limited and relatively recent industrial uses, a diamond's consumption historically has much more to do with prestige than with utility. Arguably no place on earth better illustrates that principle than does Namibia, formerly the colony known as German Southwest Africa. For hundreds of years, Namibia's Indigenous people had little use for diamonds, regarding them as objects to which they attached no value and which they generally let sit in the sand. Outsiders often proved similarly indifferent, absent the aid of marketing. In the late nineteenth century, when Europeans combed the Namib Desert hoping to find a diamond consistent with the image of jewelry glamorized in the West, they ignored millions of rough diamonds that, in an unaltered state, resembled shards of glass and thus carried no social weight.

The diamond's prestige could neither have grown so pervasive, nor lasted so long, without European imperialism. From the 1870s on, as Africans under duress extracted unprecedented supplies, European colonizers helped to maintain an illusion abroad that diamonds were scarce and therefore valuable. Simultaneously, European powers, including Germany, expanded their political control into African territories thought to contain most of the world's extant diamonds. Without these linked processes, the diamond market as we know it today would not exist. The partition of Africa would likely have looked different. And the political economies of multiple twenty-first-century African states, including Namibia, would lack their primary point of orientation.

The ascent of the diamond could not have occurred without rapidly expanding consumption, above all in the United States. It is no secret that Americans came to embrace mass-marketed diamond engagement rings. But it is poorly understood how Americans did so concurrently with the extension of European empires overseas. By 1908, the United States accounted for 75 percent of world diamond demand, followed distantly by Britain, Germany, and France.[14] Although rich and middle-class citizens buying a ring in New York City or Chicago did not imagine themselves fueling a colonial engine in Africa, their purchases subsidized European violence in militarized zones extending from the deep mining pipes of Kimberley to the harsh Namib. To this extent, American materialism enabled European empire in Africa, with the beautiful luxuries adorning American fingers metaphorically tarnishing their owners with the stain of overseas exploitation and war. Americans became consumers of "blood" or "conflict" diamonds, well before such concepts existed.

By the early 1900s, diamonds tied Africa to the rest of the world and vice versa. At the time, a diamond's typical journey began with people unjustly written out of its history and advertising: Pedi, Tsonga, Swazi, Sotho, Herero, Nama, San, and Ovambo laborers who struggled in difficult conditions to leverage stones they extracted into improvement or maintenance of life. Upon leaving Africa, a diamond passed through the hands and minds of various Anglo-Europeans: white-collar bankers who hyped stock shares based on mining claims; salespeople in the American Midwest who exploited ignorance about what gave diamonds "value" and how "value" accrued over time; and, not least, rich Manhattanites who wore gaudy rings in what Thorstein Veblen famously termed conspicuous consumption.

As diamonds circulated in Europe and the United States, each stone's interactions contributed to economic globalization, a process in which Germany's participation then arguably trailed only that of Britain.[15] Like railroads and steam engines, diamonds became a node in the spread of capitalism. One dark side of that spread was that, in Europe and America, marketers of empire convinced swathes of average people to buy into an illusion that empire-building was profitable for all. But an infinitely uglier aspect could be found in the Forbidden Zone of Southwest Africa, where Germans building an empire overseas ensured the diamond's prestige in part through ruthless exploitation and killing of thousands of African miners.

•   •   •

At the turn of the twentieth century, the Herero and Nama peoples of Southwest Africa lived under an increasingly oppressive order imposed by German colonists. Starting in the 1880s, Germans stole land, cattle, and dignity from Southwest's true, Indigenous owners, with indebtedness and disease inducing immense suffering besides. In 1904, the Herero and Nama rose up to deal the vaunted German military a series of humiliating defeats. Over the next four years, German soldiers responded with a series of reprisals that included indiscriminate extermination orders, mass starvation, and concentration camps intended to break those resisters who remained.[16]

The most notorious concentration camp was located at Shark Island, a peninsula abutting today's town of Lüderitz and the adjacent Forbidden Zone. So many murders were carried out at Shark Island that the staff ran out of room to bury corpses. Between just mid-1906 and early 1907, 1,203 out of 2,000 prisoners perished.[17] Some bodies washed out to sea and became food for sharks. The German military carted other remains into the desert, away from the nearby town and into a largely uninhabited terrain that would be featured in headlines about fabulous diamond strikes in 1908.

Since the 1960s the slaughter of the Herero and Nama, once relatively ignored by scholars, has emerged alongside German colonialism as an important chapter in history. Cultural studies have told us much about German colonial fantasies of power and domination. So, too, have historians interested in gender, anthropology, race, memory, sociology, and transnational movements of ideas. Perhaps the liveliest ongoing exchanges, however, concern possible legacies of German overseas colonialism in the Third Reich. Debates on this subject have resulted in a scholarly consensus that German violence in Southwest Africa was genocidal. That consensus has in turn prompted interrogations of German military culture and the racialist foundations of later Nazi rule in Europe, albeit with divergent conclusions.[18]

A riddle remains between the lines of this rich literature. German colonialism is rightly judged to have had profound impacts, both on Indigenous peoples and on Germans. Contemporaneously, though, German colonialism is assumed to have had little economic basis, with virtually all historians accepting that Germans irrationally pumped their money into a colonial foray that failed to reward them. Why did Germans waste so much cash and life trying to colonize Africa, when that pursuit brought them less than nothing? The riddle looms larger when one travels to present-day Namibia's Forbidden Zone, where African workers have been mining diamonds since the days of German occupation. For more than 112 years, Europeans have continually shipped Namibian diamonds to the United States and other countries around the world.

We know a great deal about *how* German violence unfolded in the country that became Namibia. But the history of the Forbidden Zone adds to our understanding of *why* Germans pursued such brutal routes to colonial power. Diamonds, a valuable commodity from an arid region with few other marketable commodities, were a catalyst for German formal colonization and the subsequent maneuvers and actions of this foreign power. Diamonds, as a result, shaped the German outlook on overseas imperialism and globalization before the First World War.

The field of colonial studies has at times lacked a strong perspective from the relatively moribund field of colonial economics. This book forges links between the two, demonstrating how German ambitions and the realities of the Forbidden Zone's surrounding mineral wealth influenced German colonial history. To capture the spirit of that undertaking, I have titled my book *Blood and Diamonds,* a coupling whose wording is akin to phrases familiar in German historiography. Perhaps the most famous such phrase came from a Prussian budget committee meeting in 1862, when Bismarck told members of parliament that German unification must occur on the strength of "iron and blood." In the intervening century and a half, scholars have played on Bismarck's moment for assorted purposes. John Maynard Keynes gave us "coal and iron," pointing to mastery of these commodities as the source of Germany's nineteenth-century rise. Fritz Stern submitted "gold and iron," a reminder of the mechanisms by which Bismarck's banker financed a Prussian military machine. Eckart Kehr's "rye and iron" summarized the influential alliance of industrial and agrarian interest groups. More recently, Niall Ferguson's "paper and iron" reassessed the relationship between monetary policy and economic might.[19]

Adding "blood and diamonds" to this litany will tell us new things about German imperialism, but the phrase also helps us to reimagine the global role of Germany in four ways. It speaks to genocidal violence and diamonds as the defining traits of Germany's short-lived overseas colonies. It refers to a highly uneven distribution among Germans of colonial loot, as well as a political battle at home over its meaning. It represents a plea to evaluate the impact of German colonial economics transnationally and globally, rather than strictly in relation to the German metropole. And, finally, the association of blood and diamonds establishes a connection between German colonial violence and an everyday process of consumption that predominantly emerged, and endures, in the United States.

Chapter 1 begins with a cautionary tale of the so-called founder of German Southwest Africa, Adolf Lüderitz. Lüderitz schemed to steal lands where he believed enormous quantities of diamonds might be found. Even after his untimely demise, his ambitions and deceptions continued to determine developments in Southwest. The actions of Lüderitz's heirs hampered the colonial economy, which committed itself to agriculture and mining despite inadequate resources, and tensions between Indigenous groups and colonists grew intractable, leading to a brutal war and to a campaign for reform led by Bernhard Dernburg, a brilliant but unlikeable banker.

Conventional accounts state that Germans discovered diamonds in Southwest Africa in 1908, during Dernburg's tenure as secretary of colonial affairs and shortly after the genocidal campaign ended.[20] But to say Germany made "discoveries" that year is misleading, as I will demonstrate in Chapter 2. Starting in 1884, consistent with the ambitions of Lüderitz, the German military and adventurers gathered geologic clues pointing to major diamond deposits in the colony. Germany imagined that once these deposits turned up in Southwest Africa, the colony would enjoy success similar to that of South Africa. The global impact of South African gold and diamonds was so far-reaching that historians refer to it as a mineral revolution. The problem was that Germans in Southwest did not understand where Southwest's diamonds came from, let alone the functioning of the world's diamond trade and the artificial mechanisms underpinning it. Into the 1900s, these subjects remained shrouded in secrecy.

Chapter 3 explores how that changed in 1908. In the shadow of Indigenous people's graveyards, Germans at last found the diamonds they coveted near railroad tracks in the Namib Desert. As a mania took hold, divergent accounts of a German mineral revolution emerged, depending on whether one was an army colonel, a royal, a Berlin-based stock analyst, a dissolute prospector, a run-of-the-mill machinist, or a young woman settling into colonial stenographic work. With the tap of wealth beginning to flow from the arid Namib to Germany, debates erupted among Germans about which segments of society should control it. Bernhard Dernburg, head of the country's colonial affairs, controversially resolved the uncertainty by turning most of the Namib into the Forbidden Zone.

The German colonial state had to monetize its diamonds before a growing, voracious public sphere. Doing so involved a collision with De Beers, one of the world's most powerful multinationals. Chapter 4 examines the ways in which, not long after his hoped-for diamond boom commenced, Dernburg addressed espionage by De Beers. To keep German diamonds away from De Beers, Dernburg issued decrees to restrict trade and traffic in diamonds to a handful of mining companies backed by large German banks. Not all Germans accepted his measures. In an era of intellectual battles over oligarchies and monopolies, aggrieved parties voiced their displeasure in colonial town halls, metropolitan newspapers, colonial courts, and even the German parliament. Dernburg, so critics alleged, had picked winners and losers among Germans with the kind of Social-Darwinian spirit supposedly reserved for colonial theaters.

In a quest to compete further with De Beers, Dernburg worked to transform the nature of diamond consumption in the United States, which was emerging as the world's largest market by far for such luxuries. Owing to qualities unique to gemstones from Southwest Africa, Germany helped to make the diamond engagement ring accessible to broader segments of American society than ever before. A partner in this transformation was the city of Antwerp, whose connections with Germany and the United States form the subject of Chapter 5. Antwerp's diamond cutters enjoyed unique access to American consumers. As a result, Dernburg selected Antwerp as the exclusive distributor of products from the Namib's Forbidden Zone, where diamond extraction was strictly controlled.

Unhappily for German leadership in Berlin, the Antwerp connection offended an array of Germans. They alleged that trade in Antwerp served as an example of crony capitalism and was insufficiently nationalistic.

Southwest Africa's Herero and Nama, ravaged in the years preceding 1908, gained access to diamonds only insofar as it was convenient for their oppressors. When Germans sought to remove colonial diamonds in large quantities, they tried to cobble together a workforce but, in the wake of genocide, found Nama and Herero unwilling or unable to participate. Chapter 6 tracks the "solution" developed by Bernhard Dernburg and Germany: the importation of thousands of Ovambos into diamond fields from an area far to the Namib's north, considerably outside colonial control.

Migrant Ovambos traveled south, hoping they could send their wages home to those in desperate need. Once arrived, though, the Ovambos met with nightmarish conditions, contractual fraud, and extraordinarily high death rates. The diamond fields reified the relationship between colonial trade and colonial violence. In addition, a surge of arriving Ovambo workers outnumbered local Nama and Herero, a development that would have long-range consequences for Southwest Africa's political future.

In 1909 and 1910, a fever for colonial investment gripped stock exchanges across Imperial Germany. Chapter 7 follows how traders drove up share prices of German colonial companies with diamond business—and even some sham colonial companies with *no* business. An astonished consultant, inspecting the fields of Southwest Africa, assured bankers that they could expect billions of marks' profit in return for virtually no effort. Such breathless reporting, stoked by self-interested promoters and scant regulation, created a stock bubble. By the time that bubble burst, some Germans had made fortunes. Countless more had lost money through criminal enterprises and bad faith.

The losers in this upheaval did not remain passive. Nor did the Germans legally excluded from Southwest Africa's mineral rush. A torrent of illicit Namibian diamonds flowed into major international markets. This practice embarrassed Germany and Dernburg, the colonial secretary. It threatened to ruin the improving revenues of its colonies and, more ominously, functioned as fodder for anti-Semitism in fin-de-siècle politics. Chapter 8 follows investigations of the illicit activity conducted by a clandestine network of German detectives. The investigations revealed that a growing underworld thrived on a current of resentment among white settlers in Southwest Africa. A big ingredient in crime, it turned out, was ordinary Germans' ambivalence about the laws of colonial plunder.

In Berlin, while Germany continued to contest the disposition of diamond spoils, one of parliament's most ambitious members turned to examining the legal rights of German colonial miners. Starting in 1910, Matthias Erzberger enhanced his reputation by attacking the German Colonial Corporation for Southwest Africa, a powerful business entity. In addition to making millions from diamond extraction, the Corporation claimed partial sovereign rights over the Forbidden Zone and people inside it. Chapter 9 is an account of how Erzberger mobilized public hatred of the Corporation in order to impact domestic politics, not least through the ouster of his rival, Bernhard Dernburg. How the populism attending Dernburg's removal eventually hurt Germany's diamond industry and affected its role in the world forms the subject of Chapter 10.

Germans struggled to harness diamonds to their advantage in the First World War. These tiny supplies from the colonies played an outsized role in the development of the German war machine, as I show in Chapter 11, as well as in the fortunes of a vulnerable German currency and in the loss of faith by Germans in their government. As a result, when Dernburg, Erzberger, and other diplomatic figures gathered around Paris to sort out a new international order starting in 1918, control of the world's diamonds formed an important addendum to the agenda. By then Germany's once-lucrative overseas empire had fallen apart, its former settlers disaffected, and its memory housed largely in the custody of right-wing nationalists who hated the European peace.[21]

With *de facto* sovereignty over Southwest Africa having fallen into the hands of South Africa during the war, German diamond companies looked to reduce their risk by selling off *de jure* property claims before international law sorted the wreckage. Amid this fraught atmosphere, an overlooked alliance emerged between German businessmen, South African politicians, and the American interests of J. P. Morgan and Herbert Hoover. On the strength of their maneuvering, Ernest Oppenheimer, an outsider, acquired ownership of Germany's colonial diamond mines.

In the 1920s and 1930s, South Africa struggled to curtail smuggling, and Ernest Oppenheimer leveraged his grip on seemingly limitless mineral wealth in Southwest Africa to take over De Beers. Oppenheimer, using infrastructure and legal architecture created by Imperial Germany, gave the world an unchallenged diamond cartel and an infamous marketing campaign: "Diamonds Are Forever." But Oppenheimer did nothing to reform the Namib's horrifying legacies and its Forbidden Zone, allowing blood and diamonds to mix anew. Meanwhile, although engagement rings remained a fixture largely specific to the United States, Nazi Germany stoked its own illusions of colonial value to win over voters, foment anti-Semitism, and make the case for another world war.

RULERS

◈   Otto von Bismarck, unified Germany's first imperial chancellor, never liked the idea of formal German colonies. Upon overseeing the creation of the German Empire in 1871, Bismarck rejected countless schemes to acquire non-European parts of the world. Between 1882 and 1885, however, he visibly modified his stance and set his country on a course to seize territories overseas. Germany became a major power in Africa, occupying lands that comprise today's Namibia, Cameroon, Togo, and Tanzania. Bismarck separately authorized German expansion in the Pacific Ocean, where Germans rushed to grab much of what are now independent states in Samoa, Papua New Guinea, Nauru, Palau, and the Marshall Islands.[1]

Although the reasons for Bismarck's move remain disputed, it is clear that he regarded colonial expansion as a source of domestic political success. Intending to broaden his base of popular support, Bismarck pledged to back German colonists with "protection": visits from the German navy to subdue Indigenous peoples, as well as diplomatic support against diverse European rivals. Bismarck qualified his commitment to "protect" with the caveat that merchants, not state-appointed bureaucrats, must administer Germany's new colonies and pay the bulk of associated costs. Thus, precisely as the chancellor initiated German colonialism, he sought to mitigate its risks. He imagined powers like Britain would take less offense at private German rivals than they would at direct German colonization.[2] He also hoped to limit the impact of colonial protection on German state budgets, the passage of which forced him to deal with more parliamentary scrutiny than he wished. Accordingly, he eschewed use of the word "colonies" to describe Germany's new commitments. He called them "protectorates."

Germany and its colonies
1914

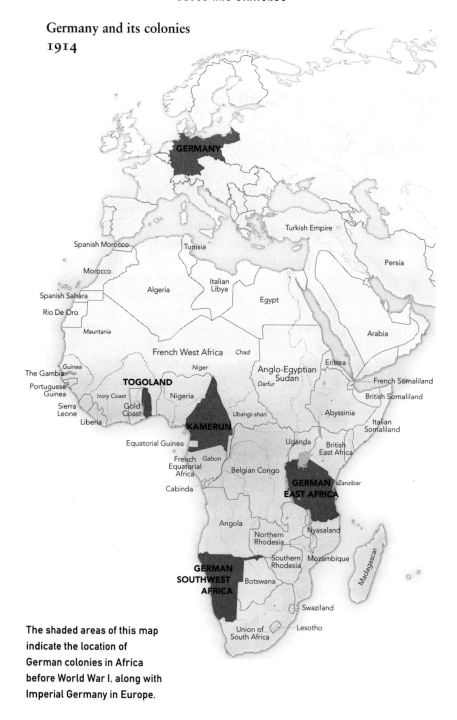

The shaded areas of this map indicate the location of German colonies in Africa before World War I, along with Imperial Germany in Europe.

Throughout 1884 and 1885, Bismarck commissioned a select group of merchants to form German "East India Companies." He assigned these companies certain rudimentary political functions in the protectorates: creating armies, keeping order among traders, and ruling the inhabitants loosely "protected" by Germany. To entice the companies into performing such costly governing work, Bismarck guaranteed them monopolies over vast lands in the protectorates, as well as over potential mineral finds there. By contrast, the chancellor defined his role as that of a facilitator. He would create a small colonial bureaucracy and occasionally arrange state subsidies for the German "East India Companies" through the German federal parliament. While the companies would do the hard work, a clever Bismarck would monitor their board meetings.[3] In the interim, he planned to bask in the support of German nationalists seeking glory in overseas expansion.

Bismarck's limited-liability colonial empire proved illusory.[4] Each year, the chancellor found himself doing what he had aimed to avoid: requesting new funds from parliament for colonial development; getting the German military bogged down in armed conflicts with Indigenous peoples; and subjecting an expanding aspect of his foreign policy to third-party political scrutiny. Arguably, Bismarck's colonial vision failed most spectacularly in Southwest Africa. Southwest became a fiasco partly because of Bismarck's mistakes, but also owing to myriad deceptions surrounding the colony's other founder: Adolf Lüderitz.

.   .   .

Entering the 1880s, no European power claimed to control the coast of Southern Africa between Portuguese Angola and the British-dominated Cape Colony. Geographers referred to this intermediate, uncolonized area as Southwest Africa. So, too, did Adolf Lüderitz, a Bremen-based adventurer. In 1882 Lüderitz focused his attention on Angra Pequeña, a natural harbor along the Southwest African coast. Though known for choppy currents and persistent fog, Angra Pequeña formed an entrance to the Namib Desert, beyond which two often-warring Indigenous populations, the Nama and Herero, had recently resumed fighting over control of cattle and grazing territory.[5] Seeking to capitalize on the disarray attending such wars, Lüderitz plotted to colonize first Angra Pequeña and then all of Southwest Africa.

Greed, in addition to ego, motivated his quest. Small islands near Angra Pequeña contained guano, a highly marketable fertilizer. Moreover, the harbor itself, by virtue of proximity to wars, offered Lüderitz a post from which to sell European weapons to Indigenous peoples—a trade from which German Rhenish missionaries already profited. Still more tantalizing was the geologic connection between Southwest Africa and neighboring South Africa's Griqualand West, where digging in the 1870s had revealed vast deposits of diamonds. Like many adventurers, Lüderitz hoped to participate in this broader mineral rush.[6] His case, though, was unique, insofar as he won backing for his business venture from Bismarck's German Empire.

In early 1883 an agent working for Lüderitz landed at Angra Pequeña and trekked 124 miles across the Namib to the eastern interior, arriving at a town named Bethanie. In Bethanie, Lüderitz's agent met with Josef Frederiks, the chief of a regional Nama clan. Supposedly in exchange for gold valued at £100 and two hundred loaded rifles, Frederiks signed a contract in which he committed to sell Lüderitz not only Angra Pequeña but roughly twenty-five square miles of desert abutting the harbor. Later in 1883, Lüderitz's agent returned to Bethanie to sign a second contract that represented a massive extension in scope and scale. This time, in exchange for £500 and sixty more rifles, Frederiks supposedly sold Lüderitz sovereignty, or political control, over roughly 10,000 total square miles in Southwest Africa.

Lüderitz prepared, offered, advertised, and interpreted his contracts with Josef Frederiks in bad faith. To be sure, Frederiks affixed his mark of "x" to paper documents supplied by Lüderitz's agent. And Frederiks did not mind selling a strip of land the Nama regarded as desert. But Frederiks could not read the text of the documents Lüderitz asked him to sign. Nor did Frederiks rule, or own, as much territory as the contracts purported to transfer. Indeed, while Lüderitz styled Frederiks as "King of the Nama," Frederiks was really just one chief among several Nama clans. Finally, while Frederiks did agree orally to sell Lüderitz some land, Frederiks did not agree to sell so much land or any political control. According to later investigations and his own private correspondence, Lüderitz's agent misled Frederiks during negotiations into thinking the sales' parameters were smaller than what was detailed in the signed contracts. Lüderitz instructed his agent in this deception from Bremen, Germany.[7]

Bismarck rightly suspected that Lüderitz was a swindler. But Bismarck was a master of *Realpolitik* who, at the time, saw economic and political potential in Lüderitz's colonial project. To this end, Bismarck helped to arrange the notorious Berlin Conference in late 1884: a gathering of European diplomats who, while agreeing to rules for carving up Africa, also legitimized Lüderitz's bogus claims. In Berlin, Bismarck committed to interpret the purchase contracts with Frederiks as "treaties" transferring sovereignty from an Indigenous ruler to a German subject. Bismarck even recognized Lüderitz as the new ruler of "Lüderitzland," an immodestly named portion of Southwest Africa with an estimated population of 40,000.[8]

Able to shut out European rivals from Southwest Africa with the German navy's backing, Adolf Lüderitz turned Angra Pequeña into a foothold to produce more dubious treaties supposedly purchasing territory from Nama and Herero leaders farther to the north. Bismarck assured Germans that Lüderitz was an upright pioneer managing an embryonic state under loose protection from German Emperor Wilhelm I. In fact, Lüderitz cared more about his own aggrandizement than about colonial governance. Hastily devoting his energy to conducting mineral surveys in the Namib, he failed to pay what little he owed to Josef Frederiks, "King of the Nama," who subsequently became a broken alcoholic.[9]

Lüderitz, struggling to fund engineering projects and turn up minerals, soon flirted with financial ruin. In early 1885, he sought to raise cash by selling the ruling powers he claimed to have bought from Josef Frederiks and various other leaders in Southwest. Asking for a price astronomically higher than what he had paid, Lüderitz brazenly promised to sell to the highest bidder, even if that bidder happened to be British. Bismarck felt cheated. Were it not for his intercession in 1884, Lüderitz's generous basket of "rights" would have remained illegitimate paper claims without worth in the eyes of rival Europeans. Bismarck had vouched for Lüderitz diplomatically, antagonizing Britain in the process. In a further complication, Bismarck had pledged to extend the German sphere of influence in Southwest Africa well to the north of Lüderitzland, in areas farther afield. Lüderitz's disloyalty left Bismarck to worry not only about the prospect of losing a German "national" claim, but about a blow to German prestige.[10]

At Bismarck's request, a consortium of wealthy Germans stepped in to buy out Lüderitz as the "sovereign" ruler of Southwest Africa. In short order, the consortium transferred its holdings to a new legal entity, the German Colonial Corporation for Southwest Africa. Extant records show that the Corporation's shareholders included heavy hitters from the business world: Bismarck's personal banker, Gerson Bleichröder, and the mining tycoon Hugo zu Hohenlohe-Öhringen. In letters, these men spoke of their venture as a favor to Bismarck and a patriotic gesture. But other archived documents indicate that shareholders of the Corporation anticipated finding major mineral wealth in Southwest Africa. In a later, confidential discussion, Paul von Schwabach, the head of Germany's Bleichröder banking house, acknowledged this dynamic and asserted that the Corporation's interests were "identical" with those of large German banks, which invested in the Corporation and expected profits.[11] Similar ambitions could be read into the actions of Adolf Lüderitz, who quietly reinvested some of his sale proceeds into the Corporation.[12]

In 1886, while digging for precious stones in the Orange River about 160 miles to the south of Angra Pequeña, Adolf Lüderitz drowned. Upon succeeding Lüderitz, the German Colonial Corporation continued his pattern of deception. The Corporation knew Lüderitz had cheated the Bethanie Nama; stone boundary markers placed by the Nama proved as much. Still, the Corporation cynically insisted on enforcing Lüderitz's expansive interpretation of control in order to increase access to Kubub, a rare source of fresh water. In Germany, the Corporation assured Bismarck it would build roads, develop trade ports, and build an army. But in Southwest, the Corporation delayed formal acceptance of these duties and showed only passing interest in them. The Corporation's first concern was to make sure it enjoyed tax-exempt status in Germany.[13] Once classified as a nonprofit, the Corporation deployed its capital toward the hunt for minerals, with its principal achievement in "governance" being the opening of an office for processing all mining activity in the colony.

Struggling to generate revenues, the Corporation traded with Nama and Herero, who bought weapons to use against each other and the Germans. To appease Bismarck, the Corporation reluctantly hired a few dozen mercenaries to build an "army." Mostly, though, the Corporation sat idle, daring Bismarck to pay bills for colonizing Southwest Africa. Seeking to ameliorate the disappointing news, the Corporation wrote to the German emperor touting "mineral treasures," which it predicted would soon prove "of importance" to the broader German economy.[14]

Top officials declared the Corporation hopeless in 1889. By then, groups of Herero had concluded that it was incapable of fulfilling treaty obligations to "protect" either warring clans or their German trading partners. When a revolt by Herero led the Corporation's tiny army to disband, the few German colonists living in Southwest also fled. Bismarck, despite having subsidized the Corporation repeatedly, had to worry anew about a loss of prestige and a collapse of investor confidence in colonies. Reluctantly, he took steps toward colonization, crushing the Herero uprising with German troops and enlarging his staff of colonial bureaucrats to deal with existential questions like courts. Southwest Africa thus started to resemble a colony more than a protectorate. Worse still for Bismarck, Germany's success in quelling an Indigenous challenge was greeted with new threats from the absentee Corporation, which entered into talks (just as Lüderitz once had) to sell its rights to a consortium of British businessmen. Bismarck, disillusioned but afraid to see his colonial failure exposed, used state money to buy some of Lüderitz's passed-on "rights"— at a premium. The Corporation booked a considerable profit from this sale, on which it paid no taxes. Further, the Corporation retained monopoly rights over areas where precious minerals were thought likely to appear soon. Bismarck concealed key details from the public.[15]

Southwest's struggles mirrored those of Germany's other colonial forays. In 1884 and 1885, news of Bismarck's colonial turn met with palpable domestic enthusiasm even in areas normally skeptical of the young federal government's policies. But such excitement gave way to fractured support by 1890, when Bismarck fell from power.[16] A substantial German colonial lobby remained active, notably in the form of the Pan-German League, a group founded in 1891 to pressure the government into enhancing protectorates and seizing yet more control in Africa. Colonialism, though, lost its popularity and enjoyed less relevance among the middle class than did the related, but distinct, cause of navalism. Working-class Germans also fretted about the profitability, morality, and utility of colonies. To these skeptical ranks one could even add Wilhelm II, who became emperor of Germany in 1888.[17]

When launching his colonial foray in 1884, Bismarck had correctly concluded that the colonial ventures he was supporting were deceitful. Within less than a decade, though, Bismarck—himself a would-be swindler hoping to use colonies for election gains—became a dupe of select business promoters who promised to do heavy colonial lifting and delivered none. Bismarck did not win sympathy from the public or Emperor Wilhelm II for his mistakes. Instead, as Bismarck identified himself as the victim of "colonial fraud" and complained about German colonialism's only achievement being the "aggrandizement of million-aires," he lost his office.[18]

In hindsight, it is apparent that Bismarck and many other Germans were deceived in part by the psychological appeal of imperialism.[19] A herd mentality predisposed a large portion of the German population to "get in" on a great colonial deal for fear of missing out. After all, the posses-sion of colonies supposedly accompanied the achievement of a certain ma-turity or prestige in the life of people and nations.

Actors at the elite level were no more immune to colonies' allure than German citizens and consumers. While some financiers rightly denied that they were consciously perpetrating a "colonial fraud" on the public, others encouraged particular campaigns of colonial expansion under pre-texts they did not recognize as dubious. For their part, the German gov-ernment supported colonial treaties known to be tainted with dishonesty in the belief that they were putting one over on less sophisticated dupes in other parts of the world. The dupes were supposed to be Africans, Chi-nese, and Pacific Islanders. And the dupers were supposed to enrich themselves or their national cause.[20]

Whether the perceived gain was one of money or prestige is immate-rial. Nearly every actor in the chain, because complicit in colonialism, was not only a potential victimizer but an easy victim. European colo-nialism infamously reinforced ideas of Social Darwinism, with putative winners among European states being divided into camps of the more and less strong. That same rule held for diverse "European" actors at and below the level of a state like Germany.[21]

By the 1890s, with this dynamic starting to reveal itself, German co-lonial promoters responded to a national mood of disappointment by saying that Bismarck's colonies were better than no colonies. This claim usually appeared in reference to Southwest Africa. To most critics, how-ever, Southwest remained the *Schmerzenskolonie,* or the "painful colony." Struggling to find the place on a map, characters in a German play de-bated whether it looked more like a veal cutlet or a goat's horn. No one "would have dared to recommend its acquisition," a future colonial gov-ernor added, "had he been able to foresee" the toll. Die-hards believed statesmen when they called Southwest a "good, but poor" colony. How-ever, impartial observers deemed its settlers second rate, and their home simply poor.[22]

Little development took place in "German" Southwest Africa until the mid-1890s. At one point, the German Colonial Corporation abandoned its offices at Angra Pequeña, which it had renamed "Lüderitz Bay." In 1893, Leo von Caprivi, Bismarck's successor as chancellor, declared that Southwest Africa must become a settler colony, with an economy based on farming and ranching. To open up land for this purpose, Germany expanded its direct colonial presence. Doing so involved merging "Lüderitzland" with other, northern territories German agents had purported to acquire via treaties signed with Nama and Herero. Attempting to convert paper claims into real control, German colonial troops further antagonized Indigenous populations and sparked fresh violence. In 1894, Germany stationed its first military garrison in the colony at Lüderitz Bay, still the legal home of the Corporation.[23]

By 1900, Southwest counted just 1,200 settlers, of which the majority were not farmers but soldiers and bureaucrats.[24] A more traditional colonial state was emerging, but it looked top-heavy. In a further complication, potential investors struggled to determine how much power the German Colonial Corporation retained. On paper, the Corporation continued at times to assert itself as a semi-sovereign, even placing legal obstacles in the way of colonization. In 1897, for instance, the German colonial state began to build Southwest's first railroad in the wake of a rinderpest epidemic that ravaged oxen used for commerce, transit, and food. This railroad construction met with threats of lawsuits from the Corporation, which jealously guarded its monopoly right to build railroads in Southwest despite making no use of that right.[25] Construction was completed only after the state steered some additional money and preference toward the Corporation in exchange for acquiescence.

The Corporation's lack of investment posed its own challenges to settlement. Throughout the 1890s and into the 1900s, the Corporation held onto ownership of a vast portion of terrain abutting and including the Namib Desert. But the Corporation was so lax there that local European settlers—upset over inadequacies in schools, infrastructure, hospitals, transport, and police—likened themselves to "stepchildren." In many cases, the Corporation practiced inaction in the hope that property values would rise and allow it to cash out its holdings on favorable terms. Through 1908, it leased or sold just 3 percent of its land in Southwest while leaving the remaining portion untouched. Yet, according to various estimates, the German Colonial Corporation and related concessionary companies owned as much as 38 percent of the land in the colony, with marked predominance over areas thought most likely to yield gold or diamonds.[26]

The German government in Berlin felt unable to address the imbalance without suffering humiliation. The architects of Southwest Africa's founding in 1884 had behaved disgracefully, even in the context of European imperialism. If fully disclosed, their actions would also have damaged the reputation of Bismarck, Leo von Caprivi's predecessor as chancellor and still a hero to many. "We have Southwest Africa," Caprivi remarked to the German parliament in 1893. "I shall avoid retrospective consideration as to how we got it and whether it was a good thing."[27]

While Caprivi understandably proved reluctant to probe history, many contemporary politicians did not. "The German Colonial Corporation," opined the liberal president of the state parliament in Schaumburg-Lippe, represented "the great economic error" of Bismarck's tenure. The Catholic Center Party and the Social Democratic Party agreed, calling for the Corporation's dissolution. These diverse critics looked justified in deeming the Corporation a "thoroughly failed" experiment. Legal documents had guaranteed the Corporation spectacular control. Yet in the 1890s and 1900s that very control, meant to spur a German scramble for wealth in minerals, undermined a scramble for wealth in settlement. In this context, a major confrontation between colonists and Indigenous peoples was also brewing.

●　　　●　　　●

Starting around 1893, Germany's inchoate colonial state in Southwest, reluctant to push the elites who ran the Corporation, tried to foster economic development by opening up space for settler farms. In theory, the plan made some sense. Southwest consisted of a vast but sparsely peopled territory, with a less forbidding climate than most sub-Saharan destinations. When people surveyed the nearly one million square miles of African territory that Germany claimed in the 1880s, Southwest seemed like the only plausible site for Germany's surplus population. Since the 1840s, millions of Germans seeking opportunity had famously migrated to the Americas—with the last big wave lasting from 1880 through the mid-1890s. Many of those who stayed in Germany worried about a crowded future full of social strife.[28] Propagandists assured Germans that Southwest, if settled, could address both problems.

Germany employed diverse tactics to attract settlers. State-sponsored advertisements spoke about Southwest's dry air as ideal for people suffering from tuberculosis. More tangibly, Germany subsidized land purchases and granted land in Southwest to ex-soldiers willing to take up farming. By 1908, though, such efforts had led to the creation of just 440 privately owned farms. Europeans broadly had settled a paltry 2 percent of the colony, and a significant portion of these arrivals were not Germans but Boers.[29]

Here again, the Corporation frustrated state attempts at development. The Corporation's agents sold plots of land to would-be small farmers without divulging that the plots in question lacked a water source. In an added complication, the Corporation's leadership sometimes sold mineral and land rights to areas over which it exercised no control, and to which it held bogus legal claims even by colonial standards.[30]

The German colonial state forged ahead. It sold land directly to concessionary companies and to settlers, with the caveat that the state's title to this land needed to come about through dispossession of Indigenous inhabitants. By the mid-1890s, in areas far outside the Corporation's paper control, state bureaucrats asserted state ownership of "unoccupied" land—that is, land without a clearly identifiable property deed. Because European notions of private property were foreign to pastoralist communities of Nama and Herero, few such deeds existed in Southwest. Confiscations grew more frequent.[31]

Within a decade of the push for settlement, the German colonial state had stripped Southwest's Herero and Nama of 100,000 square miles of earth. Land seizures, along with settler chauvinism and dishonest trading, contributed to the deterioration of already-fraught relations between newly arriving Germans and the Indigenous people with whom they shared space. In the early 1880s, the Nama and Herero had been the joint owners of Southwest Africa. Two decades later, these two groups retained undisputed claims to just one-third of Southwest's land. They had also lost much of their cattle, their main source of wealth.[32]

The ranching business Germans hoped to control in Southwest constantly wrestled with diseases. Foremost among these was rinderpest, a viral infection. In about four short years from late 1896 through roughly 1900, it struck down 95 percent of the herds in the colony—a pandemic stretching across southern Africa that devastated Herero, frustrated German development projects, and heightened the already considerable antagonism between German settlers and Indigenous peoples. Even by 1908, when the colony's head veterinarian declared rinderpest extinguished, he did not fully understand its causes and reckoned with a likely resurgence.[33]

German Southwest Africa, 1914

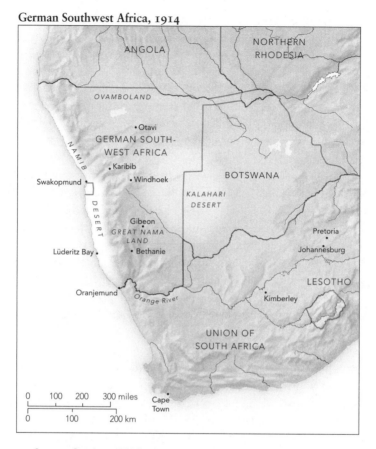

German Southwest Africa in a regional setting, c. 1914, alongside
South Africa. Note the path of the Orange River from Kimberley to
the Atlantic coast abutting Southwest Africa and Lüderitz Bay.

German colonists attempting to maintain ranches or farms in Southwest Africa required water but struggled to meet this basic need. The
problem was apparent throughout the colony but remained especially
stark around Lüderitz Bay, set between a salty ocean and the Namib
Desert, which lacked detectable springs or streams. Throughout the 1890s
and into the 1900s, Lüderitz Bay imported barrels of fresh water by boat
from Cape Town, a nearly 500-mile journey. Some of these imported barrels stayed in Lüderitz Bay. Others made their way into the colony's inte-

rior via pack animals—all of whom required their own stocks of fresh water.[34]

The rest of Lüderitz Bay's water came from three underwhelming sources. First, there was rain, which fell in minute quantities perhaps twice a year on average. Second, there were groundwater supplies from a spring in Garub and from the Orange River, respectively located across sixty- and two-hundred-mile stretches of dangerous terrain. Third, there were coal-powered steam engines that condensed and desalinated seawater pumped in from the ocean.[35]

While German engineers struggled to develop the first two options, people complained about the third. Nonetheless, the condensation method's slowly, crudely manufactured water was necessary to keep Southwest Africa's main harbor alive while German officials opened a new port at Swakopmund, roughly 280 miles to the north. In addition to having a stale odor, condensed drinking water around Lüderitz Bay was unhealthy. Scientific tests showed this water contained excessive levels of chlorine and bromine—the latter of which corroded human tissue.[36] Another problem was capacity. The machines could not supply enough water to meet basic drinking needs, let alone those of sanitation.

To conserve resources was not an ethic that German settlers brought to Southwest; they needed to learn it on the spot. Local laws criminalized the waste of water used to rinse or clean. Hoteliers instilled a conservation ethic by placing one canister of all-purpose water in a guest room each day, along with a note that clarified the shortage and listed prices for extra quantities. Few people planted trees or flowers, as more than one desolate cemetery attested. Barely able to maintain hydration, as mounds of discarded mineral water bottles indicated, settlers also made painful economies when it came to laundry and bathing.[37]

German Southwest Africa relied on the British Empire for imported water to make ends meet. That reliance represented a strategic problem. The colonial state sought funds for dams, wells, and irrigation, but it modernized slowly; indeed, towns like Lüderitz Bay would install underground pipes for a water supply system only in 1910. In the interim, old-fashioned imports of water from the Cape grew larger and more necessary amid growing settler populations and heightened consumption. The Cape, and thus the British Empire, could cease sending materials to Southwest at any point. And that kind of weapon was something British naval planners had appreciated from the 1880s, given their own historic fears about Britain's dependency upon materials imported from overseas.[38]

Water shortages in Southwest reflected and reinforced another vulnerability: food scarcity. Just over half—55 percent—of Southwest Africa's
land is arid or extremely arid; the rest is a mixture of savannah and wood-
lands, much of which remained inaccessible to early German colonists.
As of 1900, just 1 percent of Southwest was arable. Nama and Herero
had demonstrated that ranching was viable in places. However, in addition to lacking regular water access beyond unreliable groundwater, the
colonial state could not convince enough Indigenous people to work as
laborers on farms or ranches. German farmers struggled or declined to
feed workers properly, causing armed confrontations. Separately, many
early settlers chose not to take up farming at all and met their nutritive
needs through imported wheat, oats, and vegetables.[39]

Further imports went to feed livestock, which a disproportionate
number of settlers chose to raise because it proved more lucrative than
crop growing. But startup costs in that business were high, and cattle
needed food and water, too. These tendencies left Southwest unable to
nourish itself and under threat from Britain, which could have devastated
the colony by cutting off supplies. Imported food burdened Southwest's
economy. Acquiring nourishment from abroad entailed heavy, often inflated costs. It also tied up money outside the colony that might have benefited of the colonial economy, with major multiplier effects. The food
deficit smarted acutely around 1906, when economic recession left colonists struggling to finance existing operations and to secure credit for new
ones. Southwest's economy remained in a slump for years, with farmers
particularly desperate.[40]

In time, Germans hoped that the colonial state would invest in irrigation, which would power the thriving agrarian and ranching economy
desired by colonial lobbyists. Southwest might produce enough corn, beef,
potatoes, and meat to feed itself. Next, Southwest would export its surplus to Germany, itself facing a dependency on other countries for food
imports. If properly developed, the desert sands of this colony, the German
state imagined, could help to feed an empire and reverse the fortunes of
settler farmers simultaneously.[41]

Trying to realize these fantasies, colonial officials wrangled with Indigenous groups over the few viable water holes in the colony, often by
insisting on dubious written documents supplied by the colony's founding
"ruler," Adolf Lüderitz. An impetus to find water reinforced and accelerated the process of kicking Herero and Nama off their land—either by
force, or by making Indigenous landholding dependent on forced labor.[42]

Dispossession of this kind was familiar throughout sub-Saharan Africa, whether in Boer, British, Belgian, Portuguese, or French territory. In the German case, however, violence attending the dispossession reached an unprecedented extreme. Between 1904 and 1908, in a manner historians now agree was genocidal, Germany attempted to annihilate Indigenous people as a race.

In 1904, as German seizures of land and water sources proliferated in Southwest Africa, the Herero attempted to break free from an increasingly harsh colonial regime. When bands of Herero killed approximately 150 German settlers, Berlin began sending reinforcements in droves. Operating under the command of the notorious General Lothar von Trotha, some 14,000 incensed German soldiers carried out reprisals, which culminated in the issuance of "extermination orders" and the use of the colony's first concentration camps.[43] The Nama, initially allied with the Germans against the Herero, later revolted, only to meet with similarly grim fates. Before the outbreak of major violence, the Herero and Nama populations numbered 80,000 and 20,000, respectively. By 1908, the totals had dropped to 15,000 and 10,000.

Racially motivated as the German military's slaughter of Nama and Herero was, it had economic dimensions, too. Armed conflict gave the German colonial state a convenient pretext for finalizing the confiscation of Indigenous wealth: cattle, land, and water. Meanwhile, the colonial state's violence also enabled a continued pattern of dysfunctional, deceptive capitalism among Germans. For example, when troop supplies and land contracts circulated through the colony's southern half, they often passed through Lüderitz Bay, which the Corporation still controlled. The label accompanying the provisions sold by the Corporation read "SWG": an acronym meant to correspond with part of the Corporation's German name (*Süd-Westafrika-Gesellschaft*). Insiders, though, joked that "SWG" stood for *Sand-Wucher-Gesellschaft,* or "Sand Profiteering Society." In fact, as money poured into Southwest, the German Colonial Corporation experienced its first stretch of sustained strong earnings, not just in goods and shipping, but in side businesses such as colonial banking and small land sales.[44] Unprecedented fighting in Southwest allowed the long-idle Corporation to book considerable profits and pay a dividend to shareholders.

Back in Germany, where some prominent critics spoke out against the genocidal violence in Southwest, the colony remained notorious for its unpredictable weather, its troublesome soil, and its enormous

A view in 2017 of Shark Island, also known as the "island of death." Between 1904 and 1908, the German colonial army used Shark Island—actually a peninsula two kilometers from the center of what was then the town of Lüderitz Bay—as the base for one of the world's first concentration camps. Today, Shark Island has a memorial plaque to commemorate victims, but otherwise serves as a camping ground.

geographical remove. Another source of odium was the colony's settler population, which disproportionately consisted of castoffs from the German army. Southwest Africa's settlers displayed extraordinarily high rates of lawbreaking, with an average of one in two facing criminal prosecution annually as of 1908. That tendency, combined with a litigiousness that brought each white resident to court an average of four times per year, forced the colonial state to spend relatively large sums on "justice" despite according virtually none to Africans.[45]

Those sums were one of several reasons why Southwest became an embarrassing drain on the German treasury. Up to and including the genocidal campaign between 1904 and 1908, Germany committed roughly 750 million marks to the colony's offices, infrastructure, and, most substantially, military occupation. To finance this lethal campaign, the German government in Berlin asked parliament to approve swelling budgets. This the parliament did, to the lament of a minority who surmised that increased funding would only induce Southwest's colonial state to devour capital and lives more rapidly.[46]

The troubles in Southwest mirrored those in German colonial holdings broadly. First, the volume of trade for Germany's colonies proved meager prior to 1904, and German banks made no significant investments. Second, emigration to colonies failed to materialize in the expected quantity. Third, while German propagandists cast their colonial officials as gentlemen, the record of German rule was replete with sexual slavery, burned villages, drunken killings of servants, and head-taking familiar to readers of Conrad's *Heart of Darkness*. Even in Togo, a place politicians deemed Germany's "model colony," scandals abounded. A contemporary joke said a colonial bureaucrat had simple duties: to remain silent about atrocities when they occurred, and to leak documents about those atrocities years later.[47]

•   •   •

Conflict over German colonial funding eventually grew intractable enough that Emperor Wilhelm II and his chancellor, Bernhard von Bülow, looked for radical solutions. In September 1906, these men put Bernhard Dernburg, a banker, in charge of fixing not just bloody Southwest Africa but the entire German colonial empire. At the time, a fragile parliamentary coalition supporting the German government showed signs of crumbling. The appointment of Dernburg was meant to shore up this coalition's credibility with progressives, also known as left liberals. Dernburg, as an informal member of the left-liberal ranks, carried strong business credentials and went on to support the causes of women's suffrage and world peace. Though he had no advanced education beyond an honorary doctorate—a title he clung to by signing every letter as "Dr. Dernburg"—he understood restructuring projects. He had served on dozens of corporate boards and in the upper management of two German "D"-Banks, Deutsche and Darmstädter. He had also co-founded Germany's steel syndicate.[48]

While jostling for a government post in early 1906, Dernburg had ramped up his attendance around Berlin at lectures on the colonies, positioning himself as the person to reform Germany's colonial affairs.[49] Dernburg styled himself an African expert—going so far as to mount an enormous map of Africa behind his office desk—and key governmental advisors believed him. They had reason to do so. Though a lazy student in secondary school, Dernburg became an adult workaholic. He once reported to a banking job during a blizzard, then did everyone else's tasks in an empty building for an entire day. During ocean voyages he toiled into the night on letters and presentations, emerging from his cabin only for meals. The loudest commotions did not disturb his focus.[50]

Whereas Dernburg's predecessors were older lawyers and army aristocrats, he was a bourgeois capitalist of forty-two years upon entering office. To be sure, his injection of private-sector acumen into German government's higher ranks was not unprecedented. But he was relatively youthful, and his personality proved flamboyant enough to move the colonies front and center in relation to parliament and the public. His ascension looked like a step of modernization in a country where nobility had dominated the government and seldom mixed with other segments of society.[51]

Media outlets lavished Dernburg with praise in part because his father worked as the editor of a major newspaper, with allies among Germany's most influential journalists. The press grew enthused about Dernburg's years spent working in New York City, the accent of which popped up in English-language talks he gave abroad. "Dr. Dernburg knows everything," raved one reporter, "that is to be known about America in general and about Wall Street in particular." Peers were said to regard Dernburg as a genius when it came to finance, hailing him as a "captain of industry" and "the Morgan of Germany." He was reported to possess an astonishing memory and to easily process complex economic problems.[52] He also had a reputation for expertise in modern, "American" management techniques then in vogue.

The emperor, Bülow, and diverse German politicians expected Dernburg to run the country's colonies efficiently. He would supposedly transform the colonies into a profitable concern, ending a boondoggle marked by a brutal army, absentee landlords, and profligacy. Hence, upon taking office, Dernburg quickly tried to root out corruption. After identifying graft and waste identified during a scandal over arrangements for colonial troop supplies, he voided several contracts between the government and high-profile war profiteers. Then he went further, selling off his stock portfolio and resigning his board memberships to ensure propriety after accepting a major cut in pay by taking a government job. Finally, in public finance, he brought heightened oversight by deploying staff from the office of Prussian budget management to the colonies.[53]

Dernburg next turned to the project of modernizing colonial bureaucracy. Without regard for tradition, he introduced typists to overcome cumbersome internal communications; he encouraged the use of telephones for long-distance correspondence; he mandated regular working hours from nine in the morning to six at night; and he required officials deployed to colonies to undergo regular medical evaluation. Elsewhere, Dernburg revamped colonial trial procedure and sentencing policies. And he inaugurated studies of customary African laws, to be pursued by an institute in Hamburg that would instruct current and future colonial officials in a more "scientific" approach to public administration. Over time, such officials would take on legislative and judicial functions formerly assumed by colonial governors from military or aristocratic backgrounds.[54]

Dernburg promised not just reform but élan. He traveled around the world promoting Germany's overseas colonial project. Then he did something no predecessor had done and toured the colonies composing that project. Dernburg's remit, so he told embedded journalists and photographers, was not just to improve civil servants and end widespread corruption. Rather, Dernburg wanted to cultivate public trust when it came to colonies, then convert that trust into major capital investment.[55]

Owing to Dernburg's efforts, colonies attained a higher level of prestige in Imperial Germany. After 1907, colonial affairs no longer came under the purview of the Imperial Foreign Office, where they had languished in relative neglect since the 1890s. Instead, management of colonial affairs fell to a new, discrete Colonial Office, an institution theoretically commensurate with the colonies' rising share in overall German budgets and bureaucratic personnel.[56] Dernburg, head of the office, became the first state secretary for colonies.

At the height of his popularity, Dernburg criticized conditions in Southwest Africa. Dernburg, a liberal imperialist, argued that Germans needed to develop a modus vivendi with the Africans they would govern. Accordingly, he pushed for some measures to improve African living standards in the belief that Germany would only succeed as a colonizer if it could coexist with the people needed for labor. Though a champion of Weltpolitik, the contemporary doctrine that called for German foreign policy to stake out a "place in the sun," Dernburg noted that science thought most Europeans physically unsuited for tropical life. In addition, he dismissed as irrational those Germans who talked solely about using colonies as spaces to which Germany should steer migrants, instead of about how these colonies might bring Germany raw materials and profits. Dernburg, who fancied himself thoroughly rational, insisted that German colonialism needed to turn Africans into productive laborers for agriculture and mining. Germany would use the wealth generated to support investment in colonial resources—especially land cultivation—with which to improve settler and Indigenous life. In exchange for African contributions, Dernburg's Germany supposedly would deliver "its higher civilization, its moral values, and its better technical methods."[57]

None of this talk qualified Dernburg as a humanitarian, and he retained much in common with the German military planners who enacted genocidal policies. "In the process of civilization," he once told an audience, "some native tribes, just like some animals, must be destroyed if they are not to degenerate and become encumbrances on the state." Dernburg was guilty of much abuse himself. During a visit to East Africa he condoned the whipping of his porters, who carried bags each marked with a tag reading "His Excellency." Later, in an effort to placate settlers, Dernburg commissioned the repression of accurate reports about their violence. Last, and perhaps most damningly, Dernburg's "reform" plans failed to include substantive revisions of laws concerning the treatment of Africans.[58]

Still, there *was* a logic to Dernburg's view of colonies, insofar as he recognized that German policy needed to include Africans. One could hardly take that stance for granted when reviewing the exterminationist streak of German colonialism, and that was why Dernburg struck many contemporary observers in Germany as one who might bring progress in Southwest. His approach, as intended, convinced left liberals in the German parliament in 1906 that their country was headed in the right direction overseas. Thinking that Europeans and Africans must forge a working "solidarity" seemed to represent a step up from the policies of Dernburg's predecessors, though a bridge too far in the eyes of some critics. Among the latter figured military officers and plantation owners, who balked when Dernburg resisted their calls to legislate the compulsory labor of all Indigenous peoples. Dernburg, so complaints ran, "favored one-sidedly the natives."[59]

Dernburg's top priority in office was to finish railroad construction. The bills had started to pile up after 1897, when the first track was laid in Southwest. Advisors claimed railroads would unlock the colony's economic potential in multiple ways: increased access to world markets; improvement of troop movement to nullify potential coordinated uprisings; replacement of oxen as a means of transport; curbing of epidemics.[60] A functional railway would also indicate to the colony's German settlers the solidity of their bond to the mother country.

Germany laid more track in Southwest than in any other colony. But when railroads kept returning more bills than expected, the German government in Berlin struggled to convince parliament to pass their budgets. It hardly helped matters that rail projects, once funded, experienced delays until costs ballooned well beyond estimates. Physical conditions posed challenges, too. Heavy winds in the sandy Namib meant constant maintenance just to keep train tracks from disappearing under dunes. Those same tracks, laid atop shifting ground, often collapsed. Hence, in 1906, when a conflict over colonial budgets culminated with the dissolution of parliament by Emperor Wilhelm II, a *causa proxima* was the lopsided defeat of a bill authorizing renewed funding of a dinky narrow-gauge railroad in the Southern Namib, running from Lüderitz Bay to the colony's interior.[61]

As Dernburg sprinted to finish faltering railroad projects, more Europeans arrived to work in the vicinity of the original Lüderitzland. Many of the migrants hunted diamonds, a commodity that Adolf Lüderitz had sought unsuccessfully in the 1880s. But what exactly was a diamond? Where did it come from, and why did it appeal to humans? In the early 1900s, Germans could find answers only in South Africa.

CHAPTER 2

RICHES

◈ Joseph Conrad opens his novel *Victory* by telling the reader that "there is, as every schoolboy knows in this scientific age, a very close chemical relation between coal and diamonds."[1] The chemical relation to which Conrad refers started as long ago as three billion years. Inside the earth's mantle and at depths approaching 100 miles below sea level, extreme pressure and high temperatures converted carbon atoms into complex allotropes. Diamonds, as the most glamorous of these allotropes became known, bore a complex crystal, tetrahedral structure.

At some point, magma erupted to push the diamonds closer to the earth's surface in a pipe structured like a funnel. When the pressure below the surface grew extraordinary, explosions distributed diamonds at distances many miles away. In the absence of such pressure, unexploded diamonds remained in the pipe to cool, as the earthen walls around them turned black. Inching upward in a measure indecipherable to human civilization, these diamonds seeped out from the surface. In some cases, they stayed right next to the pipe, despite the passage of time. In other cases, rivers and wind carried them far afield. The earth contains dozens of diamond pipes—under Northern Canada, South America, Africa, Australia, and Siberia.

The diamond found appeal by at least the fourth century BC, when Buddha's throne allegedly came to consist of a single carved diamond. In the West, poets like the Roman Marcus Manilius celebrated the stone as a talisman.[2] As of the fifteenth century, though, a diamond still had no scientifically identifiable function—that is, no use value, to use terminology familiar to readers of Karl Marx and Adam Smith's seminal *Wealth of Nations*. As a result, the diamond held a notable but relatively undistinguished position among precious stones, with emeralds and sapphires, among others, outclassing it.

Diamonds, Smith wrote in 1776, appeared "of no use but as ornaments." But by then their prices and prestige had risen considerably. To Smith, the question was how diamonds could bring so much in exchange value. Smith thought the discrepancy owed to labor, for it proved harder for people to take stones out of a mine than, say, to draw water from a river. A less respectable explanation had come earlier from the notorious economist John Law, who posited that while Europeans believed diamonds had a great deal of beauty when compared with other common gems, this beauty became "greatly enhanced" by diamonds' perceived scarcity. Humans certainly liked shiny items, particularly when they felt the possession of those shiny items indicated superiority. Europeans, for their part, especially prized shiny items from exotic locales: places like a mythic "valley of diamonds" where Aristotle was said to have told students they would find enormous riches guarded by serpents.[3]

Whether a diamond's luster indicated supernatural power was debated for a time, but ultimately judged irrelevant. During Europe's early modern era, a steady market emerged in which diamonds held considerable exchange value and functioned as stores of wealth. A European trader working in Golkonda or Goa—the world's foremost diamond supplier and market respectively through the end of the seventeenth century—might convert his locally amassed fortune into one or more "roughs," rather than risk losing it in larger, less fungible, or less transportable assets. This same trader could then take his roughs and the value they carried back from India to Europe, have the roughs cut and polished into an aesthetically pleasing shape, and finally sell them to wealthy courts, whose preference for ostentation stemmed from a wish to display and project power. Thomas "Diamond" Pitt, grandfather of the British prime minister William Pitt the Elder, earned his nickname through such a process.[4]

A diamond became more marketable in Europe after the late fifteenth century, when experiments showed that a cutter could use diamond dust to shape rough stones into attractive consumer products. Ownership by elites helped to foster the products' mystique, as did the fame of certain wearers. Use of the term, and perhaps the product, by royalty also constituted a kind of informal advertising campaign. Queen Victoria celebrated her "Diamond" Jubilee in 1897. And the run-up to George V's coronation in 1910 became "an important factor" in spiking demand for diamonds.[5]

Diamonds offered the wealthy tangible advantages over other asset classes. Owners could quickly obtain cash for diamonds in any city. By virtue of a diamond's durability, it also arguably retained its value better than did artwork, paper, or metal assets. Anyone could cut, clip, or melt a coin; a diamond seemed indestructible. Added to this, a diamond represented a lightweight load. Unlike with gold, silver, furs, and salt, a fortune in diamonds could be transported in a napkin. A final advantage was authenticity. Alchemists had their fool's gold, forgers their paintings and paper currency. But, notwithstanding that it proved almost impossible for an amateur to discern a real diamond from a fake, no one could yet synthesize a diamond. Lack of replicability distinguished this jewel from those that could be manufactured, such as rubies.[6]

India, having distributed rough diamonds throughout the world for ages, exhausted its supplies in the eighteenth century. Simultaneously, Portuguese colonists in the Brazilian settlement of *Arraial do Tijuco* (today's Diamantina) began shipping diamonds back home. From the late 1720s into the early 1800s, European supply spiked. Enough carats flowed out of Brazilian mines that the country's emperor leveraged them to make interest payments on state bonds. Between 1850 and 1870, on the strength of slave labor and further discoveries in Bahia, Brazil dominated the trade with renewed vigor. Decline soon followed, however, and by century's end annual Brazilian exports fell to a quarter of their peak levels.[7]

Then came South Africa. After a Boer farm boy found a glittering pebble along the banks of the Orange River in 1867, he passed his pebble on to others, including merchants, who suspected it was a diamond but struggled to authenticate it and explain its presence. Esteemed geologists, many of them British, at first dismissed the possibility that the Boer stone indicated significant diamond deposits in South Africa. Experts argued that the region's geologic formations were too different from those in India and Brazil—whose rivers, so the argument ran, represented the *only* possible sites for significant deposits.[8]

After two years of haggling, experts accepted the authenticity of the Boer youth's pebble. Prospectors looking to get rich descended on South African rivers and started digging, only to discover four diamond-bearing pipes of earth under farms, not rivers. These pipes soon became home to mining camps and a rush of new arrivals. Starting in 1871, diggers excavated the ground on a grand scale, centering their efforts around massive open-pit mines. The biggest of these, Kimberley, became the largest manmade hole in the world at thirty-five acres and eight hundred feet deep. Whereas Brazil, at its peak, produced 200,000 carats annually, the "Big Hole" yielded 1,000,000 carats per year in the early 1870s and quadrupled that output by 1888.[9] Thousands of African laborers worked in the mines, and a new city emerged that also took the name of Kimberley. Kimberley's ascent instantly rendered it South Africa's second-largest population center and first site for electric lighting.

The diamond market, flooded with South African stones, faced headwinds by 1873. Prices initially fell by as much as half, affected by intermittent economic recessions. There were enough diamonds circulating around the world for savvy businessmen to contemplate why anyone would care about them. Yet, on the whole, the unprecedented supply of stones coincided with unprecedented buying across the world. Virtually every Western country, but especially the United States, experienced an explosion of *nouveaux riches* in the 1870s. From New York City to San Francisco, strong demand kept diamond sales brisk, and South Africa sold its stones without causing a collapse of prices.[10]

In fact, the volume of diamond transactions grew so prodigious as to motivate the German Adolf Lüderitz's penetration into Southwest Africa. The territories Lüderitz claimed to purchase from Indigenous Nama leaders between 1883 and 1885 sat adjacent to the Orange River: the same site where scattered diamonds had turned up in the 1860s, as a prelude to enormous discoveries in the 1870s. Copper had been mined off and on in Southwest Africa. But missionary reports spoke of Nama land as containing even more valuable minerals. And other sources mentioned Indigenous people migrating from Southwest who circulated diamonds with qualities distinct from those found in South Africa. Hence, at the onset of his titular rule in Southwest, a confident Lüderitz invested heavily in mining equipment and surveys, with a focus on diamonds. Nama people trading around Lüderitz Bay nicknamed the hill overlooking town the "Diamond Mountain." This hill in turn became the geographic center around which the majority of German colonial administrative offices based themselves.[11]

Lüderitz was not wrong: Southwest contained hundreds of millions of carats in diamonds. Having spent so much in acquiring the land and goods to mine diamonds, though, Lüderitz walked past these riches in the sands of the Namib Desert. To explain such a failure, one must consider recency bias. In the late nineteenth century, conventional wisdom posited, erroneously, that significant diamond deposits could exist only in two settings: either in a river (as in India and Brazil), or buried far beneath the surface in ancient volcanic pipes (as in South Africa). Accordingly, when Lüderitz arrived to inspect Southwest in 1884, he fixated on the idea that he must, in his words, open up a "colossal mine" centered around an enormous "hole"—in essence, a second Kimberley. That vision led Lüderitz to hunt blue ground, a specific type of igneous rock understood to sit atop the four major diamond pipes in South Africa. In the process, he ignored much atypical earth in front of him in Southwest, where diamonds lay scattered in the sand in a pattern no geologist had encountered.[12]

A second explanation for Lüderitz's failure to find diamonds is that he and his heirs, the German Colonial Corporation, lacked assistance from more than a handful of people. African and European migrants sporadically identified diamonds in the desert surrounding Lüderitz Bay, first in the 1850s, then in 1884, 1898, 1903, 1906, and 1907. Unhappily for German colonists, though, such parties either did not try to convince skeptical merchants of the stones' provenance or failed when so attempting.[13] Even after German occupation, Southwest remained a sparsely populated land whose global trade connections extended less widely and deeply than South Africa's. This disparity meant relatively fewer opportunities for inhabitants of Southwest to aid mineral searches through individual discoveries, and fewer opportunities for experts to corroborate them.

Making matters worse, Lüderitz and the Corporation unwittingly locked many who traveled in their wake into a kind of confirmation bias. For example, days into an inspection of Lüderitz Bay's surroundings in 1884, a German naval lieutenant approached Lüderitz's deputy with glee at having found dozens of small diamonds in dunes. The deputy dismissed the news, insisting that if any diamonds existed in the area, Lüderitz and his team of engineers would already have found them. The lieutenant, convinced of his own ignorance, left the stones behind and omitted the incident from his letters home.[14]

A related problem was that, when untouched by man, rough diamonds in Southwest Africa looked inconspicuous to passersby. Unlike the jewels with which Europeans were familiar—polished gemstones adorning necklaces and rings—a diamond sitting atop the Namib Desert did not necessarily sparkle. Nor did such a diamond always possess properties associated with cut diamonds, the common permutations of which humans had honed in order to better reveal symmetry, to better reflect light, and to better exploit a diamond's cellular properties as a rhombic dodecahedron. Finding a diamond in the Namib could thus prove more difficult than imagined, even when (or precisely because) many specimens lay at one's feet. As if to further confuse, the desert's gravelly sand contained plenty of agates, feldspar, and quartz. These other types of crystals glowed just as strongly as the diamonds that often sat alongside them.[15]

After Adolf Lüderitz died and Southwest was inherited by the better-funded German Colonial Corporation, searching for diamonds remained a frustrating process in which natural danger represented a final inhibiting factor. "Hundreds of wagons passed over the ground," remarked a visiting chemist, "yet everyone looked to the journey's end, never scanning the ground with a seeing eye." Because the dunes a few kilometers outside of Lüderitz Bay gave way to harsh desert, few employees of the Corporation moved from one area to the next, and when they did so they moved as quickly as possible because no water sources existed for humans or pack animals. Fear began to mount about a half mile into the desert. Marked roads were constantly overtaken by dunes, and sketched routes often proved impassable. One's life seemed at stake in each expedition.[16]

After leaving Lüderitz Bay for the interior, a contemporary team could take as many as twenty-five days to cross the Namib Desert and reach the other side. There were no trees visible for stretches of eighty miles. People could hardly trust sight, anyway, because the Namib Desert's terrain would confuse the eye's ability to distinguish between near and far, or to make out large objects, let alone a diamond. Two members of the colonial army lost each other and their sense of direction while out on a patrol. One eventually perished of thirst, the other of a self-inflicted gunshot meant to avoid the agony of a slow death.[17]

. . .

In the early 1870s, South Africa witnessed a struggle for political control of diamond wealth. The main contenders were the Boer Republics, the British Cape Colony, and the Griqua, an Indigenous group of mixed Khoisan and European ancestry. Over the next decade, the British steadily took control of Kimberley. The Cape Colony prospered as a result, allowing for investments in infrastructure that powered major economic growth. In the 1880s, discoveries of the world's greatest gold supply in the Rand dramatically accelerated the rise of South Africa as a force in the global economy and reinforced divisions between Boers and Britons, who competed with each other for imperialist claims to land, labor, and minerals.

In Kimberley, success made it difficult to conceal that diamonds were no longer rare. So many mining operations littered the landscape that people started boasting that diamonds were as common as dirt. True, it was hardly bad if these commodities existed in sufficient supply to encourage jewelers to sell lower-priced stones that more buyers could afford. That said, if diamonds no longer appeared exclusive, they might lose so much prestige that buyers would cease to covet them. A key component of any jewel's appeal, as theorized by the contemporary sociologist Georg Simmel, was how people could wear it as a way to transmit their putatively unique personality to those around them, and to see that personality valued by beholders. If everyone achieved this goal through diamonds, then the objects would lose popularity among wealthy and poor alike. "No one," John Maynard Keynes noted, "would want diamonds if they were cheap."[18]

Even slightly diminished esteem could threaten an industry built on taste. A diamond still lacked a tangible function or purpose in the 1800s—much like the ostrich plumes South Africans also exported as luxuries. A virtually limitless diamond supply awaited human extraction, and each diamond coming into the world never went away. By the time Kimberley shook up the market, consumers had already stored millions of diamonds in safety deposit boxes and safes.[19]

No one understood this dynamic better than the Englishman Cecil Rhodes, a ruthless empire builder who arrived in South Africa amid the great diamond rush in 1871. Aware of the profusion of diamonds occurring in Kimberley's wake, Rhodes made it his mission to preserve the appearance of diamonds' rarity. Lest people fixate on why diamonds had value, Rhodes proposed a monopoly of production sufficient to keep diamonds scarce in accordance with demand, supply, and culture. Over the course of the 1870s, he worked to realize this vision by amalgamating rivals around the De Beers mine, one of the three diamond-bearing pipes about a mile from Kimberley.[20] In the 1880s, Rhodes successfully applied his tactics to Kimberley itself, buying out or merging with rivals before ultimately folding his diamond assets into a new company, De Beers Consolidated Mines.

A general observer could be forgiven for thinking that De Beers was a rugged concern run by Boers like the De Beer family, whose eponymous farm became the site of the first diamond mine Rhodes controlled. In reality, De Beers was a British imperial venture that exemplified the kind of industrial concentration common in late nineteenth-century Europe. Rhodes put De Beers together with financing from two British sources: first, N. M. Rothschild; second, a syndicate of London-based, German-Jewish businessmen who had mostly emigrated from Germany after the "Hungry Forties" and functioned as middlemen working in the diamond business. Leveraging the financial backing of these individuals to buy up South African production, Rhodes held back supply to keep prices high. In the process, De Beers became, or so Rhodes boasted, "the richest, the greatest and the most powerful company the world has ever seen."[21]

By the early 1900s, 95 percent of the world's known diamond deposits could be found either in De Beers' home, the Cape Colony, or in the two adjoining Boer Republics. These three states would merge in 1910, thus creating a Union of South Africa. In terms of industry dominance, that meant De Beers' only real peer was Standard Oil. Both companies sabotaged competitors and launched price wars. But it was De Beers that struck observers as resembling a state more than it did a business. Nor was this impression inconsistent with the high degree of control the company's founders exercised over people's lives. Starting in 1885, Rhodes forced nominally "free" African diamond workers to live in closed compounds, without the ability to leave or move unmonitored for the duration of their contracts. Joining them in confinement were thousands of convicts whom a pliant Cape Colony loaned out for cheap labor.[22]

De Beers terrorized rival miners in large part because of Rhodes. He came to dominate not just diamonds but gold, Southern Africa's other juggernaut mineral industry. In diamond matters, Rhodes's management bought up weaker competition, achieved output quotas, and released or withheld diamonds as world demand and economic conditions warranted. But Rhodes also maintained a diverse portfolio, with revenue streams from another company, Gold Fields of South Africa, financing his extraordinary schemes throughout the continent, not least the Cape-to-Cairo Railway. It was not enough that Rhodes dominated the Cape Colony's politics into the late nineteenth century, becoming finance minister in 1884 and prime minister in 1890. To the north, he exerted further influence through his control over the British South Africa Company, an imitator of the East India Company that exercised sovereign powers in an area then known, in customarily immodest fashion, as Rhodesia. With such muscle behind him, Rhodes did not confine his ambition to the British sphere of influence. In the mid-1890s, he predicted that the Cape Colony would eventually swallow all of Southern Africa. To accelerate the transition, Rhodes advocated forcing Southwest out of German hands.[23]

Along with interlocking forces of arms and politics, a mystique clung to De Beers even upon Rhodes's death in 1902. The company's specter lurked wherever diamonds turned up, the assumption being that De Beers would ruin anyone who tried to challenge its near-monopoly. De Beers' finances continued to look robust, buoyed by a surge in demand from the United States, as well as by favorably low American tariffs on the importation of cut stones. Diamonds had long figured as a preferred jewel among America's wealthy. Recently, though, the United States had seen such tremendous wealth generation that the country's richest citizens dwarfed the likes of the Rothschilds and Krupps in purchasing power. There was "a superabundance of money for luxuries" in America, as one analyst later put it. In 1905, for example, it was not remarkable for Jane Stanford to travel to Hawaii carrying $75,000 worth of jewelry, mostly diamonds, in her luggage.[24]

At the same time, ably marketed jewelry adorned bourgeois and working-class bodies in America with increasing regularity. It was also because of this second phenomenon that, by the first decade of the 1900s, the United States accounted for 75 percent of world diamond consumption. To grasp the imbalance, consider that whereas annual British consumption of jewelry came to around 400,000 pounds sterling in this era, De Beers' London headquarters exported diamond parcels worth that much in a month's time. The United States' appetite proved so insatiable that, according to estimates from 1908, the country licitly imported $593,000 worth of cut diamonds each week. While the parameters of the world diamond market were expanding elsewhere, consumers in the United States without question drove the business.[25]

American consumer habits formed another part of the puzzle surrounding diamonds. Asked in 1883 to explain what was then a new trend, the "engagement ring," a major jeweler in New York City said, "there is no fashion in them particularly." Diamonds, he confirmed, were the most expensive stone placed in "engagement rings," but turquoise, pearls, and amethysts dotted many a fiancée's finger. Starting in the

1890s, this dynamic changed. American couples overwhelmingly bought engagement rings with diamonds set in them. By the early 1900s, diamonds came to make up 90 percent of the country's sales in precious stones.[26]

Attempting to explain the diamond's near-ubiquity, German colonial secretary Bernhard Dernburg identified women as a driving force. "The fairer sex," he once told the Reichstag to their amusement, "is not entirely innocent in this sensational and interesting development." Here the colonial secretary seconded some British counterparts: Lord Randolph Churchill, who declared that the diamond industry derived from "woman's vanity and its gratification"; and the magazine *The Spectator,* which credited feminine "weakness." This sexism mirrored the copy found in American jewelers' catalogs, which contained such statements as "woman is consumed with a passion for the cold, white brilliant gem."[27]

What these authors left unexplored was invented tradition: the social entrenchment, especially in America, of a notion that the giving of a diamond ring was "customary." "Custom decreed," said a representative advertisement in South Carolina, the purchase of a diamond ring specifically when it came to engagements. To think of using another stone for this purpose, added a jeweler in Missouri, was to consider "substitution" where supposedly timeless ways dictated otherwise. Insofar as these and similar American etiquette guides identified a *diamond* engagement ring as necessary for "traditional" courtship, modern relationships could stall or falter over an imagined lack of compliance. A fin-de-siècle bride in European nations like Germany typically exchanged only wedding rings with her husband. By contrast, in the United States virtually every couple's marriage was celebrated with two rounds of jewelry for two "purposes." Crucially, too, buyers outside of America who purchased engagement rings proved more comfortable with variety when choosing stones for their rings.[28]

American law played its own role in the diamond's approach toward ubiquity. Around the turn of the century, courts struggled with "breach of promise" suits: whether and how to compensate a bride manqué with damages for lost opportunity and for emotional harm. Concerns about potential gold-digging and insincerity were common; the "custom" of premarital engagements had grown more frequent; marriages across ethnic lines tested traditions; and religious bodies were increasingly absent from sorting romantic relations in an age of secularization. With the advent of diamond engagement rings, however, the courts' work to sift through these issues became somewhat easier. The possession of a diamond engagement ring not only signified a clear, mutual consent to marry, it was acceptable as an "insurance" policy for a fiancée in case her intended jilted her. The ring could easily be resold for cash in a world where nearly everyone valued diamonds. Tax assessors did their part to substantiate this notion; Nebraska, for example, required residents to register diamonds in their possession because of diamonds' ascribed status as cash equivalents.[29]

Throughout the rise of diamonds in America, De Beers shared power with a London-based syndicate. Like Rhodes, the syndicate's members wanted to keep the price of diamonds stable. But they also wanted to remain the exclusive channel for diamond sales and marketing. In 1887, the syndicate unofficially attached this condition to its financing of Rhodes, requiring De Beers to sell its production through London, where syndicate members would evaluate and set the price for each stone. In practice, several syndicate members would serve on the De Beers board of directors; but the syndicate's actions were not those of De Beers *per se,* and the occasionally anti-Semitic Rhodes did have his disagreements with the predominantly Jewish syndicate.[30] By partnering with De Beers for exclusive supply, the syndicate came to exercise a near-monopoly on evaluating and pricing the world's diamond production. Anyone wanting to bring a diamond to the rest of the world essentially had to go through the syndicate offices in London, located at Number Two Charterhouse Street.

German colonists in Southwest Africa knew that, should they ever discover diamond wealth, they would likely have to work within or against the system of De Beers and the London syndicate. De Beers occupied a supreme position for diamond production, controlling 95 percent of world output and 98 percent of South Africa's. If the Germans attempted to challenge De Beers, the company could try to break them by selling diamonds at a rock-bottom price and mobilizing the enormous financial resources of the syndicate to wait out the storm. Those resources included a final invention by Rhodes designed to overcome nature's unpredictability and strengthen De Beers' grip on the market. This idea was a "secret reserve": an enormous stockpile to be kept in a safe under the syndicate offices in London. As the 1890s gave way to the 1900s, De Beers continued to supply the syndicate with all sorts of rough diamonds, enjoying the bonus of no government import tax on stones sent from the

Cape Colony into England.[31] The syndicate paid De Beers for shipments, then strategically placed certain kinds and quantities of diamonds in "the safe." Thereafter, whenever De Beers and the syndicate wanted to influence the world's dealers, rival producers, or consumers, they could open the safe, distributing or withholding precisely those stones whose release most behooved De Beers and the syndicate.

In the ecosystem dominated by De Beers, the process of manufacturing a diamond's retail price looked labyrinthine. It involved between five and nine stages of "adding value." In the initial stage, at De Beers' offices, bureaucrats arrived at a production quota for their mines by using birth statistics to predict the number of engagements between the sexes likely to take place in upcoming months. Planners also looked to the calendar, where the most popular months for American couples' engagements—September and March—became the most popular months for engagement ring buying.[32] Once De Beers tallied its numbers, it sold a shipment of rough diamonds to the syndicate, whose interests remained at any given time either coextensive with those of De Beers or closely allied. In London, the syndicate evaluated the roughs they received from South Africa for color, clarity, and size.

The syndicate's next move was to host "sight-holders" for secret auctions, placing a 15–20 percent markup onto the price De Beers had just charged. The sight-holders consisted of diamond brokers near Amsterdam, Antwerp, Paris, and (to a lesser extent) New York City.[33] The brokers themselves were not especially global, being Europeans or of recent European descent. However, because they held the exclusive privilege of buying from the syndicate, they practically distributed diamonds to the world.

At roughly ten-week intervals, sight-holders wrote the syndicate and asked for a buying appointment; the syndicate then fixed a nonnegotiable meeting time. The eventual meeting involved no bargaining. Sight-holders accepted "lots" and prices chosen for them in advance, with assortments that included choice items, such as those of very large caratage, but also stones that were harder to sell and less profitable. Should a sight-holder protest by asking to choose certain stones in accordance with retail customers' demand, the syndicate would insist on all or nothing, then probably blacklist the sight-holder. "You buy on their terms," a Manhattan merchant said ruefully, "or you don't buy at all."[34]

Such leverage allowed the syndicate to demand full payment in cash at each appointment, netting a fortune. The syndicate set diamond prices throughout the world. When those prices changed on a more or less monthly basis—increasing five times in 1906 alone—the syndicate determined in what measure, for only by its restrictions was the supply and mystique of the diamond managed. Over time the price of a diamond unmistakably crept up, outpacing inflation in other sectors by a considerable margin. Aware of this trend, jewelers in the United States proceeded to feature it as a virtue, as when an advertisement in rural Tennessee assured readers "your real estate, stocks, and bonds may come down, but diamonds will not only not come down but will steadily increase in value."[35]

Sight-holders, having no choice but to purchase their lots from the syndicate in London or risk exclusion and return home empty-handed, generally routed their rough diamonds to continental European cutting factories. Highly skilled workers there shaped and polished stones to render them aesthetically pleasing—and yet more expensive.[36] Cutters ultimately sold their refined, cut products to importers, who shipped them to places like the United States, slapping another markup on a diamond's price.

The final stage in "adding value" to diamonds took place with retail jewelers. These jewelers might be sight-holders, or they might purchase diamonds wholesale from an importer. In New York City, America's premier market, several prominent retailers sat cheek by jowl in Manhattan. There was the rarefied Tiffany and Co. There was Cartier, which opened its Manhattan branch in 1909. And there was Black, Starr, and Frost, America's oldest jeweler, which unveiled a new Italian Renaissance–inspired salon on Fifth Avenue in 1912 in the hope of remaining close to rich customers.[37]

Notwithstanding such time-honored institutions, a relatively new American channel had emerged by 1908. Diamonds could be delivered by mail from firms like the Chicago-based Loftis Bros. and Sears, Roebuck, and Company. In its contemporary catalog, Sears devoted four pages to diamond rings, pledging to sell "diamonds on the same basis as we sell the commonest household necessity, on the same small percentage of profit." The catalog presented options ranging from a simple diamond, to a diamond with mounting, to a diamond with mounting and setting. Every conceivable variation and caratage appeared itemized and adjoined to a serial number, with the guarantee that products arrived in a plush-covered case.[38]

*   *   *

Not long after Adolf Lüderitz arrived in Southwest Africa in 1884, he imagined himself becoming a German counterpart to Cecil Rhodes: part diamond magnate, part ruler. Lüderitz even envisioned "his" colony as a challenger to South Africa for regional supremacy. Time quickly revealed both notions as chimerical, for while South Africa's diamond and gold wealth rendered Rhodes world-famous by the 1890s, Lüderitz died in obscurity and Southwest Africa's colonists toiled in relative poverty. The German Colonial Corporation, guarding its expansive rights, employed a team of geologists in its territory but otherwise discouraged research by taxing third-party prospectors heavily. The German colonial state, desperate for revenue streams outside the Corporation's control, saw no choice but to charter more large concessionary companies to look for minerals farther to the north in Southwest. In keeping with German experience in the colony, the new companies made grand promises on which they lacked the capital to deliver.[39]

Substantial copper deposits did materialize in Southwest. These, however, fell into the possession of a concessionary company dominated by British backers. Eager to make a splash, German colonial officials hoped for more valuable minerals, with the latter always seeming imminent but never quite surfacing. Prospectors claimed to enter the Namib and walk out with diamond-stuffed gear; separately, African shepherds and a Portuguese railway worker engaged in the traffic of rough diamonds from the colony. Engineers assured the German government that they could, for a fee, locate the source of such stones. Officials, already struggling with budgets, declined to pay.[40]

Nonetheless, in 1901, a major geographical conference in Germany reviewed presentations concluding that authorities should "not rule out the possibility" of major diamond recovery in Southwest Africa. One year later, an audience in Halle listened to optimistic reports from some of Germany's top geologists. In the following year, a leading German trade journal stated with "high probability" that Southwest contained diamond deposits rivaling those found in Kimberley, South Africa.[41]

The main reason for confidence was "blue ground," a specific type of igneous rock that Europeans understood to accompany major diamond deposits. Contemporary maps of Southwest Africa noted fifteen spots containing "blue ground." Propagandists assumed that, once diamond pipes had been found beneath this blue ground, money would flow and the settlement of the colony would take care of itself. Betting that diamonds would turn up first at specific blue ground sites in the northern mainland of Southwest, Cecil Rhodes had De Beers invest in the concessionary company holding mineral rights there. The German government denounced Rhodes's cheek. In private, though, the colony's governor surmised that if De Beers had involved itself, diamonds must sit somewhere nearby.[42]

Germans digging around Southwest's "blue ground" sites never revealed pipes like those discovered around Kimberley. This puzzled numerous observers, from experienced scientists to curious officials. Southwest's terrain looked "incoherent and without rules" compared to South African mines, from which Europeans presumed they had gleaned immutable truths about the origin of diamonds. For skeptical financiers, it became possible to dismiss a few diamonds popping up in Southwest as "small white stones embedded in sand on top of a rock which contains nothing."[43]

Many experts saw Southwest as having "nothing in common with" Kimberley and therefore unlikely to yield many diamonds. Others insisted that the Namib would eventually prove just like South Africa, replete with gold and diamonds. In the end, the blue ground in Southwest proved less relevant than did the colony's connection to the Orange River, which ran from the interior of South Africa across the southern edge of Southwest. Eons ago, an explosion from the volcanic pipes beneath Kimberley dispersed tons of diamonds into the nearby Orange. At that ancient time, the river extended well into the terrain that later became the Namib Desert, ultimately draining into the Atlantic. The vagaries of time, water, and wind had given Southwest diamonds in a way no German expected. That deviation explained why German prospectors testing fields in Southwest Africa sometimes found one or two choice stones in otherwise empty tracts of sand.[44]

While Germans lacked advanced geologic knowledge about the Namib in the late 1800s and did not confirm large diamond deposits there until 1908, they were hunting for them across Southwest Africa starting in 1884. Further, archived documents attest that the Germans were looking in places and ways that exacerbated tensions with Indigenous populations. In 1896, Henning von Burgsdorff, a military officer and administrative head of a district that included the town of Gibeon, urged the German colonial governor to assert more control over Gibeon *because* the town's environs were "almost certain" to yield diamonds. Diamonds, wrote Burgsdorff, formed "the decisive reason" for an advance. A handful of official papers from 1898 records that some of the diamonds Burgsdorff anticipated did appear around Gibeon, and that the stones were confirmed as authentic by an investment group tied to Emperor Wilhelm II. Of course, for Germans to seek more control over Gibeon meant heightened risk of conflict with the Nama, whose leading figure at the time, Hendrik Witbooi, had his power base in the town.[45]

In 1901, German forces around Gibeon identified "blue ground," which was on the mind of a member of the military high command when he later made a local inspection. True, the diamonds around Gibeon remained very limited in quantity. But this dearth prompted German authorities, convinced that foreign agents had hidden the source of the stones, to weigh criminalizing the concealment of further information. Following reports of another modest find at Gibeon in 1903, the government even opened an expansive file regarding "legal measures to secure diamond extraction."[46]

On September 16, 1904, with the German army having cut off retreating Herero in the Omaheke Desert, and with Jacob Morenga already leading small contingents of Nama against the Germans, Chancellor Bernhard von Bülow reported to Emperor Wilhelm II about the likelihood of imminent diamond strikes to the south, in Gibeon. Having pondered Bülow's presentation, Wilhelm II issued a decree designed to expedite diamond prospecting.[47] About two weeks later, General Lothar von Trotha issued his "extermination order," which effectively promised to kill all Herero unless they exited the colony. While Trotha's order initially concerned only Herero, it strengthened the will to revolt among certain contingents of Nama who had so far remained loyal to the Germans. On October 3, 1904, Nama contingents, under chief Hendrik Witbooi, fired the shots that opened up another front in the Indigenous uprising. The Nama's first target was Henning von Burgsdorff, the German district officer responsible for running Gibeon and promoting its diamond prospects.

There is no proof that the German emperor knew in advance about Lothar von Trotha's extermination order. There is evidence, though, that the emperor both delayed rescinding the order and ultimately sanctioned it. To these caveats one might add that, as the emperor pondered military policy in Southwest, Bülow's presentation about diamond riches in October was unlikely to have faded from the emperor's memory. The very people Trotha pledged to annihilate figured as obstacles to a perceived fountain of mineral wealth. Promoters had promised German leadership that diamond extraction could commence only on the condition that the uprisings be brought to an end "with all possible haste."[48]

Between 1904 and 1907, as German military spending mounted, planners noted that contemporary diamond exports from neighboring South Africa brought in between 80 and 100 million marks annually. The colonial state's quest for diamonds formed the subject of newspaper articles directly adjoining reports on military developments. Finally, an official publication of the German Foreign Office spoke of a "responsibility" to search Southwest until there was a preponderance of evidence that the colony contained no major diamond deposits, as opposed to insufficient evidence that it did.[49]

With large-scale military campaigns against Herero and Nama underway and the German government searching for reasons to justify the costs, a major financial paper cited diamonds as among the reasons to consider Southwest Africa "worth" fighting for. In 1906, another small deposit of diamonds turned up on small islands off the coast of Lüderitz Bay. In 1907, the official mouthpiece of Germany's colonial lobby expressed renewed "confidence" that Nama country's diamond riches would reward the German people.[50]

Because German officials had manifold indications that diamonds *would* surface in Southwest, and because Germans were actively searching for mineral wealth, it is necessary to consider more than land and labor as economic motives for German violence against the Nama and Herero.

The Nama lived on, and were rightful owners of, terrain conclusively proven to contain blue ground and already shown to contain some pockets of diamonds. German planners repeatedly bet on diamonds to rescue their colonial project. And it was the German military campaign against the Nama from 1904 that hastened the construction of a railroad along whose tracks the hoped-for major diamond deposits actually lay waiting. As this railroad was being built by imprisoned Nama and Herero, German diamond prospectors complained that the uprising of Indigenous freedom fighters was holding up work. In the prospectors' depiction, the "problem" of the uprising needed to be dealt with before the Germans could access diamond wealth. One could even ask whether this attitude contributed to a later wartime dynamic, in which German authorities attempted to lure some fleeing Herero back into Southwest as workers but continued to prefer "extinction" when it came to Nama.[51]

The German most associated with genocidal violence, Lothar von Trotha, had not witnessed diamond strikes when he departed the colony in late 1905. Nonetheless, the turning of the German military eye to the stretch abutting Lüderitz Bay improved the odds of large-scale diamond discovery and created a new momentum toward it. For a sustained period, thousands of German soldiers and attendant personnel traversed ground that harbored rich deposits. Furthermore, military operations against the Nama bled into the quest for major diamond finds. Into early 1908, politicians in Berlin inquired about the welfare of *current* Nama prisoners at Lüderitz Bay's Shark Island, which lay just a few miles from diamond riches. Throughout and after 1908, when news of fabulous diamond strikes spread, the German army continued rounding up and murdering bands of Nama—including the Bethanie clan that lived nearest the finds.[52]

The Nama of Bethanie remained Josef Frederiks's people. As heirs to the parties originally defrauded by Adolf Lüderitz, they had, if alive, a strong legal case against German ownership of the Namib and against any mining that would base itself on this alleged German ownership. A file about preparations for a system of "diamond exploitation" was created in December 1906, while the concentration camp at Shark Island counted the Nama leader Cornelius Frederiks, Josef's militant successor, among its prisoners.[53]

In military operations, German troops sometimes took an interest in diamond finds, with one participating soldier going on to produce a dissertation about Germany's incipient diamond industry. Prospectors in the vicinity of confirmed deposits acknowledged engaging in armed reprisals against nomadic San peoples thought to know the location of more diamonds near their home. Similarly, a major in the army had his men patrol for Nama at a site he knew contained blue ground. Prospective diamond riches and violence, in other words, reinforced one another. When Trotha spoke of "streams of blood and money" that would "destroy" Southwest Africa's Indigenous peoples, the money he referenced was not exclusively cash. And the streams flowed not only from Germany into Southwest Africa, but also in reverse.[54]

•   •   •

In 1907, a European prospector reported diamondiferous strata along the coast of Southwest Africa and won an audience with Bernhard Dernburg, the German colonial secretary. Dernburg, eager to tout the news before he could verify the claim, announced to the Reichstag that the unearthing of big diamond deposits in Southwest Africa was imminent. Among those stirred by the announcement was Johannes Semler, chief spokesperson on colonial affairs for the national liberal party. Diamond wealth, Semler predicted, would change the course of Southwest's history.[55]

Semler was right, but Dernburg's announcements about diamond finds in 1907 proved premature. When no tangible progress materialized by late 1907, and as the military campaign in Southwest decelerated, people in Germany dismissed Dernburg's rosy predictions. This lukewarm reception of Dernburg's diamond claim owed much to his character. Alfred von Tirpitz, the head of the German navy, dismissed him as a "hot-air artist." Numerous other contemporaries expressed similar doubts. Dernburg's keys to promotion were often, noted close associates, "big bluffs and high-sounding talk," or projections that seamlessly mixed fantasy with realism.[56]

Despite his successes in reforming colonial management, it was fair to wonder whether Dernburg hyped shreds of evidence for diamonds in order to spotlight his own colonial dynamism. Dernburg had a reputation as a publicity hound and self-promoter. The actress Hedwig Pringsheim complained that he navigated life as if in an "endless advertisement." He came from a wealthy, prominent bourgeois family that included a brother who was a famous architect and a father who had belonged to Emperor Friedrich III's entourage. Displaying a capacity to distort reality, Dernburg was known to have published pseudonymous celebrations of his achievements in life. He ensured that when foreign journalists toured Berlin, he "accidentally" encountered them everywhere. It was typical when, after he had given a lecture declaring that he preferred "half-truths" to "brutal truth," he quickly released a long-winded press statement defending the remark.[57]

Dernburg's style hardly proved more sympathetic than his personality. At age forty, he was a tall, potbellied, broad-shouldered man, his arms flabby, his cheeks pale, his nose long and bulbous. Beneath the black top hat he wore unfailingly when outdoors, his unkempt beard stretched up so far that it almost touched his blue eyes. Those eyes in turn told a story: shot full of blood from overwork, they sat amid unruly brows, inflamed lids, and multiple folds of skin that resembled bags on bags. Photographs could do little to hide the problem.[58]

In the office, Dernburg struck peers as a "sitting giant": he looked in control when parked behind his desk but bedraggled once he stood up.

Bernhard Dernburg, c. 1910. Between 1906 and 1910, Dernburg headed Germany's colonial affairs.

At social functions, whether in Europe or in Southwest Africa, he acted like a nervous wreck. He did not know where and when to stand, or how to wear his napkin. The loose-fitting black coat and white collared shirt in which he regularly dressed could not conceal his deficient hygiene, inducing acquaintances to call him "chingachgook" behind his back, in a sardonic allusion to James Fenimore Cooper's "noble savage." Sticklers for etiquette likened Dernburg to a cow and to Grobian, patron saint of the vulgar. Upon meeting him, one general grumbled about this "most ill-mannered brute I have ever met in high places."[59]

Dernburg's detractors knocked him as vain, reckless, and wont to shirk blame. They dinged him as a colossal egotist convinced his name was on everyone's lips. Dernburg admittedly found it difficult to keep his mouth shut when circumstances required, proving impatient in conversations and unable to filter his statements for offensive remarks. Such flaws had at times threatened to block his ascent in the banking world, only to give way in consideration of his prodigious talents. "He can think as hard as he likes," said the German-American banker Jacob Schiff, "but he should not talk."[60]

Although his announcement about diamonds in 1907 did not bear fruit immediately, Dernburg soon had good reason to talk. In April 1908, Germany at last realized its precious mineral dreams when railroad workers happened upon dunes full of diamonds in the Namib Desert. Fantastic reports about riches trickled into not only Dernburg's office, but that of De Beers—a double blow for the latter, given that De Beers had bet on diamonds being found in the half of Southwest Africa opposite the strikes. De Beers executives heard about ragtag German operations loading up coal scuttles and wastebaskets with rough diamonds. South African parliamentarians mused about inexperienced Germans combing through sands by hand and collecting nearly two hundred diamonds in two hours' time.[61]

Fittingly, Dernburg went to see for himself.

CHAPTER 3

RUSH

◆ On June 23, 1908, German officials made a public announcement confirming rumors of diamond strikes in Southwest Africa. People spent the next month flooding into Lüderitz Bay, the town nearest the diamonds and, until that month, home to about 300 European civilians.[1]

On the afternoon of July 25, 1908, Colonial Secretary Bernhard Dernburg personally inspected fledgling diamond fields in the desert adjacent to Lüderitz Bay. Dernburg had arrived that morning at the town's best hotel—a revived barracks whose windows overlooked rocks full of discarded trash and glass shards. He made his field trip with the industrialist Walther Rathenau: his roommate, interlocutor, and fellow traveler. Both men, in an effort to educate themselves, had recently toured De Beers' grand operations in neighboring South Africa. Conferring with executives and foremen at Kimberley, the Germans had even taken an automobile drive around the "Big Hole."[2]

In Southwest Africa, Dernburg and Rathenau proceeded to examine the fields of one man, August Stauch. Stauch was an instant millionaire credited with discovering diamonds in the colony between April and June 1908. His mystique rested on a few fabrications, foremost among them that his genius lay behind recent finds. In fact, the more important figure had been Zacharias Lewala, an African migrant from the Cape with experience in mines. While shoveling sand around construction on the rail line from Lüderitz Bay, Lewala identified a one-quarter carat stone for his foreman, only to see the foreman relay the news to Stauch, an asthmatic engineer hired to maintain train tracks. Contemporary diamond experts acknowledged Lewala's contribution—as did Stauch, who discreetly hired him as his valet. But the white public of Southwest Africa took a different approach, choosing to valorize Stauch and other German frontiersmen around Lüderitz Bay as the colony's mineral pioneers.[3]

Like German soldiers who traversed the Namib before him, Stauch struggled to distinguish diamonds from agates and so frequently grabbed anything in the vicinity of the railroad that resembled a precious stone. The crucial factor was Stauch's business acumen, which induced him to seek scientific examination of his stones. This was an important step that previous claimants had not taken because they tended to be itinerants or hapless. Despite his apparent ignorance of banks and dislike of big-city ways, Stauch proved shrewd. Far from striking out on his own without support from big capitalists, he told Lenz & Co., his employer on the railroad, about his diamonds.[4] While Stauch awaited scientific results for authentication—the process took about two months—he quietly bought up mineral rights near the train tracks using loans from Lenz & Co., which was effectively a subsidiary of a big German bank friendly with Bernhard Dernburg.

In June 1908, just before rumors of Southwest's diamond riches were confirmed by the state, Stauch rapidly extended the scope of his claims in the desert. Carving out sixty-three fields for himself—each field running between 100 and 150 square kilometers—he became the local leader in production. Weeks later, once his stones had been authenticated, he walked around Lüderitz Bay handing out diamonds as charity and socializing with all classes, encouraging German settlers to seek their fortunes in the nearby desert. Within months, Stauch and a motley group of associates controlled even more of the colony's mining claims, which tended to remain small and numbered in the hundreds. Stauch had become a frontier tycoon.[5] A self-educated transplant to the colonies, he was a hard-working father of two who turned Lewala's diamond into a fortune of wealth and admiration from fellow colonists.

To Bernhard Dernburg, Stauch's remained an amateur operation, its "Diamond-King" hardly worth discussing. In part this derision owed to the fact that, by the time of Dernburg's visit in July 1908, the colonial secretary was ill-disposed toward the local environment. Travel to Southwest precipitated an outbreak of eczema and nerve pain in his arms and legs, which he attributed to unusually heavy use in climbing some rocks to get to the higher streets in Lüderitz Bay. Accustomed to physical inactivity, Dernburg ordered a special four-wheel drive Mercedes manufactured for his trip. But when that plan stalled, he had to ride around Lüderitz Bay in a partly enclosed mule-cart, with the dust from wind irritating his labored breathing. As Dernburg toured Stauch's diamond fields, his discomfort grew greater. In a bit of publicity designed to illustrate Namibian diamonds' abundance, Stauch encouraged Dernburg and press members in attendance to place their stomachs on the hot desert floor, then dig through the sand for stones. Thirty minutes later, amid a dozen other diggers, an exasperated Dernburg crouched on his knees, clutching a rough diamond but evidently straining to retain his composure before cameras.[6]

While touring Stauch's operations, Dernburg saw primitive mining technique, disorganized boundaries, and scant security. "Wild and indiscriminate pegging," recalled one engineer, "was going on all over." And this, insiders reported, in a place where diamonds lay strewn about "like apples under a shaken tree" that one had "simply to stoop down to pick up." Further cause for concern came during dinner on the evening of Dernburg's visit, when local merchants assured him over beer that they had the exploitation of diamonds "in hand." It was impossible for an egotist like Dernburg to delegate the management of mineral wealth that promised to render him a successful state secretary. In addition to his aesthetic shortcomings and self-aggrandizing, he did not work well with others. He terrorized subordinates, offended peers, and dripped sarcasm. He demanded that he unilaterally make all "important" decisions. He turned his back on discussants in the middle of conversations. On one occasion, he even telegrammed a meeting's outcome while waiting for the meeting to start. "No one with self-respect," rued a former associate, "could possibly work with this man."[7]

Dernburg later snickered when describing Stauch and Southwest's other businessmen. "Not one of these gentlemen," he said, "was able, a year ago, to distinguish between a diamond and a lump of sugar." In Dernburg's estimation, such locals sold diamonds in a way that mixed ignorance and irresponsibility. Sometimes they used rough diamonds to buy a drink in Lüderitz Bay. More often, they dumped their diamonds to agents for Amsterdam cutters, or even for De Beers, with the experienced buyers taking advantage of their green counterparts.[8]

Dernburg was not wrong. Naïve sellers around Lüderitz Bay lacked connections to premier diamond cutters and marketers based in Europe's Low Countries. Without major investors, sellers around Lüderitz Bay also had no machinery to evolve the German diamond industry away from plucking stones out of the sand. Perhaps most important, local sellers were ignorant of the diamond market's dependency on scarcity and thus put downward pressure on the price of rough stones, disturbing confidence in the diamond as a commodity. In September 1908, a detective working for De Beers purchased a parcel of 2,687 carats in Lüderitz Bay at a price of fifty-six marks per carat. Presented with a similar parcel one month later, the same agent lowered his offer price to twenty-one marks per carat. Aware of this trend and frightened by the amateurism he associated with Stauch, Dernburg spent his remaining time in Lüderitz Bay imparting financial knowledge in a publicity event. Among those gathered to listen were Stauch admirers prospecting so haphazardly in the desert that maps of their oft-conflicting claims resembled Venn diagrams.[9]

Not every local around Lüderitz Bay was an ignoramus, nor every ignoramus a local. But extant maps confirm Dernburg's belief that Southwest's diamond claims needed more regulation. So, too, do diaries. Consider that, on another visit in the early weeks of the boom, the commander of German military forces in Southwest Africa, Ludwig von Estorff, stopped at land he did not own outside Lüderitz Bay. Though he had no permit to prospect there, Estorff collected ten diamonds in as many minutes. After quickly selling some of the stones back in town, he returned to Germany with some special gifts for the ladies in his life, (presumably) none taxed and none reported.[10]

Unlike Dernburg, the amiable, energetic Stauch was a dogged optimist who talked of his love for Southwest Africa's people and climate. He nurtured visions of prosperity less for Germany than for its colony. Stauch was no simpleton, either, becoming a fourfold millionaire within months of the discoveries—and improbably placing his net worth slightly ahead of the more accomplished Dernburg's. Starting in 1909, Stauch lived large. He bought a lakeside villa in a posh Berlin suburb, Grunewald, not far from Dernburg's own home. Surrounded by a forest of tall conifers, Stauch kept a large staff and threw elegant parties. He outfitted his rapidly expanding family with silks, lace, and handfuls of toys. He joined the yacht club. For good measure, he secured a second mansion. As Stauch became rich he spent more time in Germany. He also cunningly kept associates from shares of wealth he had promised them. Nevertheless, he remained one of German Southwest Africa's most popular figures—and so formed a considerable threat, in Dernburg's assessment.[11]

On the strength of Stauch's fields, many of the colony's European settlers—whose ranks rose to 15,000 within the next five years—hoped for empowerment through diamonds. Dernburg reckoned these people would exercise scant restraint if rewarded with large revenues up front, and the proof was the cheeky Stauch. Stauch already consumed as much as did Dernburg—who fancied "luxury" as "alien to his temperament," and who frequently implored settlers to moderate their spending. For their part, Southwest's settlers resented such big banks as had made Dernburg rich. After all, the big banks, according to inaccurate local lore, had refused to offer Stauch assistance only to have him prove them wrong with his diamonds.[12]

Settlers' budding sympathy for Stauch sprang partly from this lie, but also from his supposed example of colonial self-sufficiency. Before long, Stauch's loose consortium refashioned itself as a publicly traded company headquartered in Lüderitz Bay.[13] By contrast, most owners of land and prospecting rights in the Namib were located far away, in metropolitan German areas like Berlin. To the uninitiated, Stauch looked like a relative paragon of virtue. His diamond riches not only inspired hope and encouraged settlement in a dispirited colony, they also promised, in theory, to turn a backwater into a global presence under local control.

◆   ◆   ◆

Just a year before Dernburg's visit to Southwest Africa in 1908, Lüderitz Bay's future looked tenuous. Between 1904 and 1907, German soldiers had patronized the town as a base. Starting in 1908, though, these soldiers began shipping out in a trend that would see their ranks drop from 10,000 to 2,500.[14] Not everything went away with the army: an electrical power network, the first such development in the colony's history, stayed in place, along with a fresh railway connection approaching completion. But the railway project—pushed by Dernburg—perversely drained more commerce than it added, rendering the town unfruitful to most Germans who remained.

Just before Stauch's diamond finds, Lüderitz Bay was left with a non-military European population of perhaps 300 people. Lüderitz Bay's skyline consisted of three government buildings, with architects and engineers struggling to break through massive rock deposits whenever they scraped together funds.[15] The town appeared, to quote a dismissive South African, "little more than a forlorn collection of corrugated iron huts clustering around one or two of the more important buildings, dignified by the names of 'hotel,' 'store', and 'customs house.'" No proper physician was a permanent resident—a problem when typhus broke out. Wildlife, consisting of ravens and hyenas, appeared only sporadically, and the main dock had been chewed away by shipworm, with the water beneath silting up from the Atlantic's peculiar current. In these and other ways nature disadvantaged Lüderitz Bay—a harbor between an ocean and a desert. To European visitors, it was a dingy, boring place through which one passed reluctantly.[16]

The diamond rush in 1908 reversed this reputation. Lüderitz Bay was now in the big leagues. Within a few months of Stauch's rise, Lüderitz Bay saw its European population rocket from 300 to 1,121, of whom 836 were Germans. The town received a new dock as one of 121 projects pushed through by engineers in a remarkably busy season. An infusion of diamond wealth promptly occasioned five times as much building in town as had occurred during the height of wartime spending. Though the journey from one construction site to another remained arduous, with winds blowing sand over one's ankles and craggy masses forcing life-threatening detours, plots of land in town began to line up on a grid. Houses looked sturdier, too, as reinforced concrete replaced corrugated iron sheets. So alive was the transformation that, miles out to sea, one heard construction cranes—along with foghorns and whistle buoys to alleviate the exceedingly difficult, and increasingly busy, process of pulling into port. People heard change in town, too, in offices that vibrated with the constant clacking of typewriter keys.[17]

An increase in commerce accompanied an increase in international prestige. When Britain appointed its first consul to German Southwest Africa, Lüderitz Bay became his base. Notices about the town started to appear in global financial centers, from Geneva to San Francisco. German professional journals dripped with hype. So, too, did educational materials such as an astronomy textbook that helped students understand longitude by telling them how Görlitz lay more or less on the same line as Lüderitz Bay. People could sense a corresponding uptick in cultural esteem for the larger colony around Lüderitz Bay. Popular author Clara Brockmann spoke of Southwest as a "new Germany on African soil," and Prince-Regent Luitpold of Bavaria purchased paintings depicting Stauch's diamond fields.[18]

In lockstep with the diamond boom, more ships arrived in Lüderitz Bay at shorter intervals. Engineers pitched the port as a future hub of traffic between London and Johannesburg. In October 1909, for the first time in what was the living memory of local residents, a British warship even anchored in Lüderitz Bay for an official visit, landing a party whose

A view from atop the hills of Lüderitz Bay. c. 1909. In the background at left, one can see Shark Island.

stated purpose was to meet the famous Stauch. Moritz Bonn, a German economics professor close to Dernburg, had ridiculed Southwest Africa's copper deposits. But now Bonn urged scientific study of the colony's diamonds.[19]

In February 1909, Lüderitz Bay got its own newspaper—a weekly published every Sunday. The paper's editors credited "increasing trade and traffic" with birthing their project. Telephone activity between Lüderitz Bay and the rest of Southwest Africa began, surpassing expectations and expanding into the adjacent desert. A project for a streetcar line also came to fruition, along with a slaughterhouse and an enhanced electrical grid. These moves, viewed at the time in global perspective, fostered wild dreams of growth. San Francisco, it was said by German colonists, had once been home to a few hundred Europeans, but a large-scale transformation of that area took just a few years after its own mineral rush commenced.[20]

Closer to home, residents of Lüderitz Bay looked to the example of South Africa. Through the middle of the nineteenth century, South Africa was a place not so different from Southwest. Aside from the Cape, mid-century Europeans saw most of South Africa as a colonial waste: its soils largely infertile, its governance problematic, its thirst unending. Then a spectacular infrastructure network emerged in a relatively short time following the onset of mineral extraction in the 1870s. It was as part of this process that, by 1895, German investors had contributed one-fifth of all foreign investment in the Boer-controlled South African Republic. Educated Germans did not think it unreasonable to expect that diamonds would cause such rapid prosperity in Southwest, or even lead to a ten-fold increase in its settler population.[21]

Progress could look ugly. Runoff from construction flowed into the harbor at Lüderitz Bay with regularity, mixing with seaweed to muddy waves that naturally ran deep blue. By late 1908, three smokestacks over-looked the town, behind rows of brightly painted homes. In daylight, so much coal dust and sand got in one's eyes—and so little greenery dotted the land—that the place often resembled gray on gray. Further evidence of transition abounded socially, with a severe housing crunch greeting the arrival of bakers, butchers, mechanics, watchmakers, and hoteliers. Within a short time, ten tailors competed against each other in Lüderitz Bay; Windhoek, the colony's capital and home to a much larger popula-tion, counted half as many.[22]

"The discovery of diamond deposits," reported the Roman-Catholic Parisian daily *L'Univers,* "infused a new life" into Southwest Africa. But "new life" meant new careers, cultures, and consumer price inflation. "A storm of newcomers," lamented one fortune-seeker, was "overwhelming" Lüderitz Bay. So, too, was turnover among residents. Ships went unloaded on account of dockworkers heading to the desert to prospect. A sizeable group of police quit to seek their fortunes. Business owners unable to capitalize on diamonds simply shut down their operations without no-tice. Military veterans slotted for farming careers instead launched ex-peditions with rented camels.[23]

Struggling to adapt, the colonial state started losing resources and time to the boom: first, by buying up prospecting permits on the sec-ondary market in the hope of creating a new revenue stream; second, by having to replace civil servants and military attachés who defected to di-amond ventures; third, by agonizing over how to subsidize pay in the face of Lüderitz Bay's high cost of living. Some town clerks kept their jobs but speculated in diamond claims while working, precisely as the state tested laws to prohibit such activity. In other cases, soldiers bought stakes in diamond ventures with the bonus that a loophole exempted them from income tax in Germany if they had "official" business in Southwest. Low pay likely contributed to an exodus from the public sector; compared with peers in other colonies, Southwest's bureaucrats and soldiers received a lower salary.[24]

"New life" also intersected with social concerns. Repeat visitors to Lüderitz Bay noted streets that looked more cosmopolitan, with a freshly built Masonic Lodge and a "colorful population from all nations and classes." Diversity was a logical consequence of more ships arriving with fortune-seekers. However, in addition to intracolonial arrivals from Windhoek, Swakopmund, or South Africa, migrants entered town direct from Europe—mostly British, but also Russians, Czechs, Italians, Norwegians, Romanians, Poles, and Portuguese. A still more important shift came with a spike in the local African population. In 1908, Lüderitz Bay counted 839 nonwhite residents. Within a year, this total rose to 1847, not including another 1,195 living at nearby diamond fields.[25]

Partly because of the diamond boom and its attendant jobs—building docks, assisting police, extending narrow-gauge railroad track into the Namib—ethnic Germans became a more distinct minority in Lüderitz Bay and the surrounding country. But perception of this change was exacerbated, not begun, by diamonds. When major military operations in Southwest ended in 1907, the future district officer at Lüderitz Bay, Rudolf Böhmer, already referred to his jurisdiction as retaining little space that was "really German." In 1908, with diamonds on everyone's mind, the colony's leading newspaper warned of a "stream of suspicious elements" pouring in. The paper also worried about unsuccessful prospectors washing out in the desert and returning to farms destitute and unemployed.[26]

Such anxiety resonated in Germany. One of the richest men in Lüderitz Bay was Paul Weiss, a Pole who emigrated to the colony shortly before the diamond finds. Weiss made his money selling beer, spirits, and flasks for use on diamond expeditions. By contrast, the popular fiction of Hans Grimm valorized Germans immune from diamonds' allure. And the pan-Germans railed against foreigners "living like dogs" in a colony that was sacrificing its "German-ness" to profit motives.[27]

Foreign visitors to Lüderitz Bay wisecracked about pedestrians who "experienced a thrill on catching a gleam from the dirt of the pavement, which, on investigation, proved to be from the fragment of a broken bottle." German farmers who supported brutal subjugation of Indigenous peoples separately worried about an "epidemic" of "diamond fever."

Diamonds were "robbing everyone of reason and deliberation," one complained, and in so doing were causing Africans to "lose respect for the white man." A Braunschweig-based geographer complained of men who, consumed by visions of diamond wealth, "degenerated into half animals." Less crudely, a Catholic priest sent letters back to Germany denouncing diamond stock as having "destroyed family happiness" with "enticing, but spurious prospects." Perhaps diamonds truly did, as the author Clara Brockmann complained, "corrupt character" in those who sought them.[28]

Against this backdrop, residents in Lüderitz Bay grumbled about a corresponding rise in the fortunes of groups perceived as parasites: lawyers paid to litigate the hunt for diamond claims; notaries taking fees to stamp papers that proved worthless; mapping bureaus controlling access to cartographic knowledge; and private detectives advertising background-check services. It now seemed impossible for a lay person to make sense of the various local industries and their red tape. Of the latter there was plenty, for the town had 4,000 documents notarized in 1909. It was also difficult to make sense of people. Carl Reinshagen, a notary public who certified diamond claims, worked in four other capacities: as a lawyer defending certain diamond companies; as the head of the local racetrack; as a traveling representative for Lüderitz Bay commerce; and as a stockholder investing in diamonds. Reinshagen always made share purchases under the name of his assistant, in order, he admitted confidentially, "to appear objective in my dealings as notary."[29]

Religion played its own role in this miniature culture war around diamonds. Nineteenth-century modernization coincided with a "secularizing European mind," to borrow a paradigm from Owen Chadwick. In European colonies like Southwest, one could argue that economic modernization contributed to a sense of urgency on the part of colonial religionists to prevent further losses. Shortly into the diamond boom, accordingly, a Catholic missionary order opened a prefecture extending from Windhoek through the southern Namib. Outside of the roughly 180 European Catholics living in Lüderitz Bay—another number that attested major diversification in a territory dominated by Rhenish Protestants—the prefecture targeted African youths imported from Togo to work in such service industries as the post office.[30]

Each diamond field in Southwest Africa, already contested by businessmen, witnessed religious battles that unfolded more or less absent such order as Dernburg thought was missing. Protestant and Catholic missions both dispatched catechists to the diamond fields to greet migrant African workers descending from Ovamboland, an area hitherto accessible only to Finnish missions. German missionaries even stalked Ovambos on their journey south, starting around Ondjiva and winding all the way to the vicinity of Lüderitz Bay.[31]

By the time of Bernhard Dernburg's visit to Lüderitz Bay in July 1908, missionaries and other arrivals found local housing in short supply, and hotels grew so overcrowded that people paid to sleep under billiard tables. This and other incidences of living cheek by jowl did not show up in statistical tables readily cited by officials. But Southwest Africa swarmed with would-be businessmen, prospectors, and even vacationers naively hoping to combine sunbathing with digging. Many of the people filling up Lüderitz Bay were itinerants without stable home lives or familiar politics, and the lack of housing compounded that condition. An army captain characterized the town's spirit as "gold-digging." Some of his compatriots deemed the transients in town ruinous, a "grave danger to Germanness."[32]

The select few colonists already made rich by diamonds held lavish masquerade balls and established a horse-racing club. Some of these tycoons even ostentatiously bathed in imported soda water. But most people in Lüderitz Bay bathed only rarely, and then with reused, malodorous water. And they struggled to cope when shops implemented outrageous mark-ups on items like tea, coffee, toothbrushes, milk, and meat. As the diamond rush raged, a German emigration office reported that Lüderitz Bay's cost of living grew twice as high as that of the average mainland German city. Prices for pack animals and digging equipment increased to ten times their pre-1908 levels. Raising bureaucrats' wages to keep up with this inflation became impossible. In some cases, civil servants refused transfers to the town.[33]

More broadly, difficulties making ends meet determined life. Café waiters scoffed at tips of less than fifteen percent, and members of the Catholic church congregation could not donate to the desired extent. German bankers partly blamed the lower rate at which residents collectively saved money; their counterparts in other colonial sites were more thrifty. In Lüderitz Bay, people certainly earned and spent rapidly, for consumption was a way of life. But poverty among local Europeans had deeper causes. While food and water were costly, the state's legal definition of minimum subsistence income for Europeans in the colony remained the same as in mainland Germany.[34]

German colonists to whom no diamond wealth fell understandably proved unenthusiastic about concomitant social changes. "Outsider" ethnicities ranging from East Asians to Galician Jews encountered redoubled discrimination and legal impediments to residency. Separately, Southwest Africa's struggling farmers begrudged the manner of consumption in Lüderitz Bay—the way people there shunned local "German" goods for foreign ones, and the way price inflation emanating from the town rendered colonial farms' already high start-up costs less tolerable.[35]

As diamonds started to predominate in, and alter, the German colonial imaginary, farmers hoped to grow their agricultural output and improve their lot. Inadequate access to fresh water had long proven a constraint on Southwest Africa's economic development. At the time of the diamond rush, no less than fifty-five separate digging projects were underway to look for water sources across the colony. As prices for land and water rose, however, settlers had to fight harder to irrigate their farms, hydrate their animals, and feed themselves in a land half composed of desert. Making matters worse, anemic rainfall totals had coincided with a global economic recession.[36]

In 1908, the year of Stauch's meteoric rise, the colonial state in Southwest unveiled duties on tobacco, matches, alcohol, and cosmetics—all hitherto untaxed. A further imposition came in the form of inaugural land taxes. Farmers felt the effects acutely. They lived largely on dwindling credit from Hamburg banks, which, like their counterparts in other German cities, had less gold on hand than usual and were showing less faith in international agreements in the wake of a financial crisis in 1907. The diamond rush did not relieve farmers' cash problems. To be sure, Bernhard Dernburg, the man responsible for policy, talked about promoting farmer irrigation projects. But he acted indifferently and forged ahead with measures that funneled wealth elsewhere, chiefly to further railway construction.[37]

Eyeing newfound minerals, farmers presumed to have found the means to drill enough wells to distribute fresh water to farms throughout Southwest. "We must," ran an increasingly familiar refrain, "turn our diamonds into water." By this plan, the colonial state needed to use revenues from diamond taxes in order to pay for more intensive drilling projects. An apparent transformation in water access had already taken place around the operations of August Stauch. Overhead costs at his biggest site, including labor, came to just 5 marks per carat extracted. By comparison, it cost four times as much money to extract a carat from De Beers' mines in South Africa, where diamonds lay deep underground.[38] Stauch thus had wide margins with which to accumulate cash, and he spent a good deal of it to provision drinking water for his European workers. As Stauch touted plans to drill wells deep under the desert floor, he paid for additional imports to sustain farming, ranching, and comforts hitherto unknown to the colony, including ice cream shops and bowling alleys.

Dernburg was dubious that Stauch's largesse foreshadowed a new era of hydration and comfort. Stauch's free spending left his diamond business ludicrously undercapitalized. More important, the diamond rush so increased the local population as to raise water prices to levels commonly seen in times of severe drought. In fact, Stauch's top-dollar payment for importation of drinking water drove up the rate for his competitors, some of whom had to spend themselves broke to hydrate their own workers.[39]

When German military patrols marched southward from Lüderitz Bay, they, too, drew on the town's frail water supplies. Yet, just months into the boom, those same supplies grew strained to the extreme by an unanticipated increase in demand accompanied by a failure at the main facility providing water for Lüderitz Bay. The combination heightened German dependence on water imports from the Cape. The colonial food supply faced its own pressure, because bakers exited the work force and pooled their meager resources to mount expeditions. Stories about how a pair of Europeans working ten miles outside Lüderitz Bay "had gathered 8000 carats, worth over \$300,000, in one afternoon" made food production look insufficiently remunerative.[40]

Months into the rush, heightened consumption of imported water became the main cause of skyrocketing living expenses around Lüderitz Bay. In 1907, before diamonds were discovered, the price of a cubic meter of fresh water in Lüderitz Bay hovered around forty marks. After the boom, the price per cubic meter rose to 264 marks, or 1 mark per gallon. To put that increase into perspective, consider that in Munich at this time, a gallon of beer cost 1 mark. This was not even to mention the discrepancy between Lüderitz Bay and the diamond fields dozens of miles to the south. There the price of fresh water could reach 1,000 marks per cubic meter, or four times as much as in Lüderitz Bay.[41]

•　　　•　　　•

In the decades after 1885, the German Colonial Corporation remained the major landlord in and around Lüderitz Bay. It was also the owner of the local water supply, as well as of water drilling equipment around town and in the adjacent diamond fields. The Corporation's idleness earned it the unique distinction of offending the military, conservatives, liberals, and workers simultaneously. All these groups accused the Corporation of sitting out the violent conquest of Southwest Africa only to profit from it, while average Germans shed blood and money to pay the colony's expenses.[42]

The Corporation's behavior was not only self-interested but, at times, farcical. Throughout Southwest's occupation by Germans, the Corporation mostly played down the governing responsibilities and privileges it had inherited from Adolf Lüderitz's estate. However, in a few instances where a trace of precious minerals re-emerged, the German Colonial Corporation asserted itself as a "sovereign" co-equal to the German colonial state. So it had been in 1887 and 1896, when reports about potential gold strikes induced the Corporation to announce that it was "ready to exercise its sovereign rights" and "create an army" in the vicinity of Lüderitz Bay. And so it was in 1907, when a team of international investors asked Germany to let a diamond-hunting expedition land at Lüderitz Bay, only to find that the Corporation denied them permission to do so.[43]

In 1907, Southwest's colonial state fought back. In a shot across the Corporation's bow, state officials announced they would sell parcels of state-owned land only to people who would actually work it. Separately, colonial municipalities turned to challenge the Corporation by taxing its real estate. Lüderitz Bay, for one, pressured the Corporation with a potential property-tax law. Hoping to avoid receiving such a bill, the Corporation commissioned public-relations newspaper articles to refute charges of avarice. That said, the Corporation also undertook negotiations to sell some holdings to municipal governments. In Lüderitz Bay, these holdings included streets, squares, and the court house.[44]

Prior to the materialization of diamond wealth in 1908, the Corporation's shareholders reckoned that, without a spike in land prices or some major strikes in precious minerals, Southwest was a losing proposition. The antagonism of colonists and bad publicity at home contributed to the Corporation's decision, in February 1908, to sell Germany its remaining governing and mining claims in Southwest Africa effective October 1 of that year.[45]

The diamond rush that occurred in mid-1908 suddenly rendered the Corporation's prospects robust. In the span of just a few months, August Stauch had proven that, across a desert the Corporation still dominated legally, diamonds lay strewn in enormous quantities. Indeed, it was the Corporation's board that had sold mining permits to Stauch and other prospectors between April and July 1908, when Dernburg visited Lüderitz Bay. In August 1908, therefore, the Corporation's directors experienced an epiphany when agents from De Beers arrived in Berlin to "discuss" diamonds with Dernburg. The Corporation's directors called a meeting and decided to reinvigorate their sleepy mining operations. Not only did the Corporation stop selling permits to third-party prospectors like Stauch, it took a firmer line in negotiations to sell tracts of land to municipalities. The Corporation's desire to drive a harder bargain for land threatened to impede other areas of economic development in Southwest Africa, such as railroads and agriculture. Finally, the Corporation began physically occupying more of the land to which it held ownership titles.[46]

Around the time of Dernburg's visit to Lüderitz Bay, the Corporation cabled the colonial secretary to discuss the agreement it had recently signed, whereby it was supposed to sell its residual governing and mining rights to Germany. The Corporation, wishing to continue in the exercise of these rights, alleged that earlier paperwork had never been notarized. As a result, the Corporation denied the validity of the sale. State officials in Southwest balked at the ploy, griping about the Corporation's "illusory" promises.[47]

In Berlin, however, Dernburg granted the Corporation's wish. During earlier negotiations, Dernburg had recognized that the Corporation owned the rights it later declined to sell. He did not want to look inconsistent. Besides, he knew that the Corporation had shareholders whose investment he needed to build Southwest Africa's infrastructure: Deutsche Bank; the Disconto Bank; Bleichröder; M. M. Warburg; and, not least, the Berliner Handelsgesellschaft, whose connections to German mining companies, German-born South African "Randlords," the Rothschilds, and Dernburg himself ran deep.[48]

After finishing his inspection of Lüderitz Bay, Dernburg crafted a platform to rein in Stauch and the local diamond rush, and to affirm the German Colonial Corporation's control. The keystone was a decree, issued on September 22, 1908, to convert most of the Namib Desert into what Dernburg called the Forbidden Zone. By law, this expanse of 10,000 square miles—about five-sixths the size of Belgium—would become accessible only to people with existing permits to dig for diamonds. Dernburg's stated goal in creating the Forbidden Zone was to stem a proliferation of unscrupulous diamond activity while allowing state officials time to sort out hundreds of overlapping prospecting operations and claims—a mayhem Dernburg derided as "unworthy of civilization."[49]

Prior to the creation of the Forbidden Zone, mining in the desert had theoretically been open to all European residents in Southwest Africa. Any colonist could purchase a permit from the owner of a given parcel of land. Dernburg's decree ended this free market in prospecting by prohibiting landowners from issuing new permits. Stauch and his frontier confederates were grandfathered by the decree because they had already secured permits. But their claims covered a small fraction of the Forbidden Zone. The remainder of the Zone's land was owned by the Corporation, which committed itself to mining diamonds in an environment where it did not need permission. The Zone thus became an area from which prospectors other than the Corporation were barred, and in which the Corporation could extract diamonds without significant interference or competition.[50]

With his decree, Dernburg swiftly achieved consolidation of production in an economic sector—a fairly extreme result even in 1908, the heyday of trusts. As a by-product, Dernburg appeared to make progress toward replacing scattered, inconsistent decision-making with a more uniform policy: his own. Beyond following the dictates of his ego, however, he also hoped that the Zone would attract more investment to Southwest Africa. German banks already had sent, and were sending, a great deal of capital abroad. Between 1870 and 1913, the country's share of total global foreign investment came to 13 percent.[51] In comparison, Germans gave the German colonies a paucity. But perhaps, as the owners of a rich territory in Southwest that they alone could harvest, the large German banks behind the Corporation would find assurance of stability and invest in the broader colony. Perhaps, too, the German banks would mobilize their capital reserves to mount a viable challenge to De Beers, the British company that otherwise enjoyed near-complete domination over the world diamond supply.

Dernburg's Forbidden Zone conformed to expectations held within the German banking industry, not just about the diamond business, but about economics. Writing a handful of years earlier, then-banker Hjalmar Schacht condemned the idea of efficient markets by reference to the history of diamond mining. It was incumbent upon the state and technocrats, Schacht argued, to transform the planless economy seen early in a diamond rush into a "systematic harmony." Dernburg, in his blunt way, obliged. Before returning from Southwest Africa to Germany, he gave another fair-sized crowd of settlers some impromptu if verbose remarks about how diamonds would further the legacy of the colony's founder, Adolf Lüderitz. Later, back in Berlin, Dernburg railed against business practices in Southwest and issued further decrees to streamline the colony's diamond production.[52] In the process, he ignited a debate about the beneficiaries, and legality, of colonial economics.

CHAPTER 4

CONFLICT

◈ When he created the Forbidden Zone in late 1908, Colonial Secretary Bernhard Dernburg saw it as a necessary evil, in view of the administrative mess and ignorance attending haphazardly run claims around Southwest's diamond fields. Colonial settlers disagreed, associating Dernburg with a policy they perceived as villainous. Still, he forged ahead. "He was not," recalled a friend, "among those people who lose faith in themselves."[1]

To start, Dernburg could defend his decision by referencing legal precedent. Within Germany, restrictions on free mining in large areas had recently emerged. In 1905, Prussia's diet had passed the so-called *lex Gamp*—a law developed out of fear that large private companies were amassing monopolistic control over potash and coal supplies. From 1906, the *lex Gamp* prohibited, for two years and throughout the kingdom of Prussia, any new acquisitions of potash and coal claims.[2]

In technology, Dernburg found a second powerful argument to justify the Forbidden Zone. In the frenzied early months of the diamond rush, numerous amateur miners around Lüderitz Bay stripped their claims of stones easily picked from the sand. A sense soon spread, recorded the writer Clara Brockmann, that "the diamond blessing" was "becoming scarce." Surface stones glimmered in the moonlight so that an African laborer crawling flat on his stomach could either pick them up or finagle them on the point of a butter knife by turning over a patch of earth. When surface stones became elusive, workers ran seawater through a series of sieves that separated diamonds from unearthed blocks of sandy composite. Here, however, the peculiar climate of the Forbidden Zone interfered, with morning mists caking the sand and clogging up the sieves.[3]

Amateurs without expertise tended to cherry pick the most visible diamonds in the sand, and typically the largest. Because diamond yields tended to decline over time, cherry picking threatened to make long-term digging unsustainable. Dernburg knew as much. So he urged the Germans in Southwest to mine to average yield, and to dig into thicker grains of sand at depths of several meters, where geologists still hoped pipes full of diamonds awaited discovery—along with the real money, or so it was thought by reference to the example of Kimberley.[4]

The key to Dernburg's proposed transition was machine-based digging. De Beers did not rely on a few shovels to pull up sediment from Kimberley's "Big Hole," which ran 800 feet underground. Instead, De Beers perfected the process of extraction with hoisting machines that could raise six loads of composite 1,000 ft. in forty-five seconds.[5] Steel cars brought such loads to a factory floor in Kimberley, where De Beers ran different-size grains through more machines calculated precisely to extract diamonds, the most dense material. Kimberley's operations also proceeded night and day, thanks to hundreds of electric lamps and an abundance of water secured by De Beers.

Establishing the Forbidden Zone would help Germany catch up to De Beers in a hurry while mechanization got underway. Large German banks could afford the estimated 200 million marks' worth of machinery needed to excavate the desert's diamond-bearing sand in the long term. The banks also had sufficient capital to supplement their investment in technology with a rapid expansion in coverage throughout an enormous terrain. As of early 1909, August Stauch's company controlled roughly sixty-three fields and had a capitalization in the tens of thousands of marks. By contrast, the Deutsche Diamanten-Gesellschaft, a vehicle of the Corporation and thus the banks, worked 600 fields and had a capitalization running into the millions.[6]

German bankers, sympathetic to Dernburg's logic but aware of his dependency on their resources, made their participation in his incipient diamond industry contingent upon his toleration of the German Colonial Corporation's questionable legal claims. These claims stretched back to the time of Adolf Lüderitz, and they included a literal "sovereign right" to rule over matters inside the former Lüderitzland, which had now become the Forbidden Zone. In exchange for tolerating the Corporation's "sovereign right" claim, which the banks behind the Corporation had made inconsistently since Lüderitz's death, Dernburg received the banks' financial support to begin major diamond production in Southwest.[7] Dernburg's measure to transform Southwest Africa's prospective diamond fields into a restricted zone thus occurred in partnership with the Corporation and the giants of the German banking industry.

In the fine print of Dernburg's decree creating the Forbidden Zone, he announced that, until 1911, the Zone would "be reserved to the Corporation for exclusive prospecting and extraction." When the German public eventually learned about the Corporation's involvement in crafting this decree, Dernburg found it difficult to defend the arrangement. Plenty of defense was advisable, however, because thousands of Germans in Southwest Africa expecting to strike it rich considered themselves robbed of easy money.[8]

In Lüderitz Bay, protests against Dernburg called for him to spread the wealth by letting average people dig inside the Zone. He conceded nothing. A month after creating the Forbidden Zone, which made it legally impossible for more settlers to prospect in the desert, Dernburg had the temerity to warn against a "get-rich-quick" mentality. Then he banned all unlicensed travelers from even entering the Zone. In part, the colonial secretary justified his additional measures by citing a high rate of criminality among the colonial settler population. He also argued that, so long as August Stauch and his ilk kept collecting tiny claims, De Beers might move in and buy them out, thus checking the rise of the German diamond industry before it began in earnest.[9]

As small-timers in the colony seethed about wealth legally outside their reach, Dernburg announced that the semi-sovereign Corporation, rather than public organs, would control the process of surveying land situated inside the Forbidden Zone. Beginning in March 1909, expeditions for this purpose located new deposits that typically yielded larger-carat stones than did those nearest Lüderitz Bay. Dernburg bragged at a banquet in Berlin that this fresh diamond wealth was even more prodigious than publicly acknowledged. Meanwhile, although some prospecting permits previously issued by the Corporation for the land that became the Zone remained available on a makeshift secondary market, these permits changed hands only for sums as high as 100 times above face value. Incredibly, the Corporation also reserved the prerogative to terminate secondary-market permits if their use was not a matter of public record.[10]

Many would-be prospectors looked to avoid red tape by hunting diamond deposits in Southwest Africa that lay outside the Forbidden Zone.

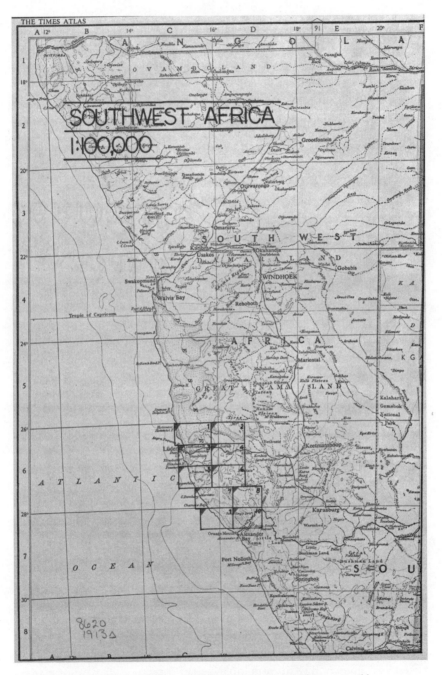

The Forbidden Zone in Southwest Africa, 1913. The ten boxed areas roughly approximate the boundaries of the Zone.

Such ventures brought civilians farther into the desert, to both the north and south. But to move into the distant, shifting dunes of the Namib was to court death, even if one wore a helmet, glass goggles, and a respirator to keep sand out. Harried Europeans periodically climbed seventy-foot-high cliffs along a southern path that hugged the coast to avoid drowning. Such an expedition could easily extend two hundred miles away from Lüderitz Bay, taking as long as thirty-three days round trip and leaving a trail of deserted pack animals, spooky campsites, scorpion bites, and corpses.[11]

As members of expeditions risked their lives for diamonds outside the Zone, they drew into their orbit residents who had previously worked in Southwest Africa as carpenters, salesmen, or photographers. Initial optimism soon gave way to despair. Ship captains traveling along the coast reported seeing men huddled together on beaches, their clothes in tatters and their supplies exhausted, clinging to the delusion that they would imminently locate a fortune. When such unfortunates returned to Lüderitz Bay with no use for wooden posts they had purchased to mark out diamond deposits, they used them for firewood. Other prospectors showed up in town to register hard-fought claims tested over several months inside the Zone, only to hear that such claims conflicted with ones made by the Corporation and were therefore invalid.[12]

Space in Lüderitz Bay, amid Dernburg's measures, remained squeezed. Lüderitz Bay had turned overcrowded and expensive, and an apparent means to resolve that inequality lay close by. The Corporation guarded a vast domain that, in the words of a foreign consul, "might have supported a great population." Settlers with modest means lived at the crowded bottom of Lüderitz Bay's topography. The offices of the powerful German companies the Corporation represented sat higher up, away from the din and with plenty of space to expand. At this remove, the Corporation corresponded with large German banks that had begun selling mortgage-backed securities whose collateral was real estate in Lüderitz Bay. The thinking went that, with diamonds turning up everywhere, such real estate would appreciate even in a worst-case scenario. A by-product, though, was that more settlers struggled to purchase land because officials had begun to add value to most property assessments on the assumption that diamonds would turn up there.[13]

Their lives on hold, a majority of the Europeans seeking diamond riches in Lüderitz Bay idled in crowded, Prussian-style dwellings that

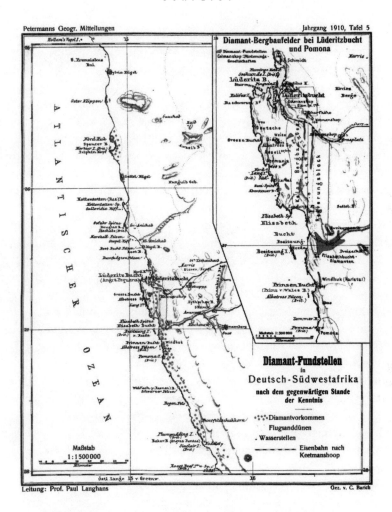

Petermanns Geogr. Mitteilungen

Jahrgang 1910, Tafel 5

Diamant-Bergbaufelder bei Lüderitzbucht und Pomona

Diamant-Fundstellen
in
Deutsch-Südwestafrika
nach dem gegenwärtigen Stande
der Kenntnis

Diamantvorkommen
Flugsanddünen
Wasserstellen
Eisenbahn nach
Keetmanshoop

Maßstab
1:1500000

Leitung: Prof. Paul Langhans Gez. v. C. Barich

Dots indicate the spots where significant diamond deposits had been
found in Southwest Africa as of mid-1909.

came to define the town. Small windows, if any, were to be found. Insufficient ventilation could not handle the heat from a cooked meal. On a
summer night, claustrophobic bedrooms sometimes registered a ther-
mometer reading of 110 degrees Fahrenheit. Despite flashy technological
advances like telephones, the town still lacked sewerage. So people threw
their waste out into the street, only to see it rendered more putrid by
heat and, in some cases, whipped up by wind into open mouths. As

overcrowding and lack of water for handwashing exacerbated shoddy sanitation, gastroenteritis became endemic. Typhus cases also increased by seventeen times in the first year of the rush.[14]

Days of waiting proved tedious, with the desert and the Forbidden Zone limiting walking possibilities to a tiny radius. One of the few routes for a stroll involved a gruesome trek past the tin shacks of the Shark Island concentration camp, where German authorities continued to string up corpses of Nama and Herero accused of rebellion. As for the town streets proper, they remained sandy and narrow. But now they teemed with horses and streetcars that had to run through the backyards of poor people's dwellings.[15]

Resentment surrounding Dernburg's rules was evident in the creation of Lüderitz Bay's newspaper in early 1909. Local residents paid the editors' wages, and their work unwaveringly defended against perceived threats, not least the Corporation. The paper's first editorial criticized how the Corporation forced white residents to live in a "state of medieval feudalism." Evidently unaware of longstanding colonial trends dating to Bismarck, the authors complained that Dernburg threatened to turn Southwest into "the object of exploitation by foreign companies gifted with monopolies."[16]

In Southwest, or so many settlers argued, an incipient diamond standard supported by fat cats stifled industry. An apposite parallel lay with France, where, from 1907, riots broke out in the Midi over luxury commodities, owing to a coalition of minor wine growers and diverse workers decrying the rules of an uncaring state. But the most relevant point of comparison lay in Prussia, the dominant state in the German Empire. In Prussia, as in Southwest, money meant not only power but superior legal access, such that the votes of the richest citizens counted more than did those of the less well-off. In 1909, potential further democratization of this unequal voting system arguably constituted Germany's most important question. Hence, on the occasion of a presentation Dernburg was to give in Germany about colonial diamonds, he found his way clogged by 8,000 demonstrators who turned his policies into a platform to protest against Prussia's three-class franchise.[17]

A distant Dernburg assured Germany and colonists that the Forbidden Zone would end in 1911. But there were whispers that the Corporation planned to delay this transition. For now, Dernburg appeared to have made up his mind that the greatest spoils of German colonialism would belong to heavy hitters behind the Corporation—and not to farmers, let alone to bakers, locksmiths, or veterans who became failing prospectors.[18]

Local officials and town elders in Lüderitz Bay tried to intervene by hounding the Corporation with litigation. When such efforts stalled, a prominent doctor decried the Corporation's "rape" of Southwest at a town hall meeting. Later, in a similar setting, a revered farmer complained that the colony had been "gifted" to the Corporation, which was taking out "millions from our land without any concern" for churches, schools, or culture, and without paying any local taxes.[19]

As public anger mounted over inequality, the Corporation took refuge in private tennis courts, contesting lawsuits until plaintiffs could not afford legal fees. But the dispute over colonial diamond access gained traction in the politics of Imperial Germany, where "the spirit of *nouveau riche,*" to quote one historian, was in the ascendant, and where the chancellor had just encouraged more economy and less luxury.[20] Against this backdrop, as Dernburg tussled with commentators interrogating the social justice of the Corporation's Forbidden Zone, he had to consider how Germany would compete with De Beers in selling diamonds.

•   •   •

In late 1908, Dernburg delivered a characteristically long-winded report to the Reichstag, Germany's lower house of parliament. In this, Dernburg's first major public address about diamonds, he touted future prospects for the colonies. But he stressed a need for sobriety around Lüderitz Bay, where settlers did not know enough to allow for proper development. Dernburg accused Germans who sold a diamond without sufficient financial acumen of undermining the national interest. Not only, he argued, did they jeopardize the tax revenue Berlin hoped to derive from mining; they subverted his initiative to develop a horizontally integrated German diamond industry.[21]

By combining colonial mineral wealth with German technocracy, Dernburg proposed to poach business from the world's chief diamond producer, De Beers. In fact, Dernburg planned to reshape the global trade by turning German interests in Southwest into "a second De Beers." At the moment, De Beers and the London syndicate dominated the global diamond trade. But history suggested it was possible to challenge this dominance, for, prior to South Africa's meteoric rise and Brazil's attendant decline, Paris, not London, had functioned as the site through which the majority of the world's diamonds had to pass for sale and marketing.[22] Other sites had claimed power over diamonds, too. Antwerp and Amsterdam had specialized in cutting and polishing, for example, along with towns in France's Jura Mountains.

The dominance of De Beers and London had already motivated Amsterdam to approach Dernburg about buying German output. In Antwerp, too, significant opportunities had popped up, including Eastern European émigrés with connections to the *Leipziger Messe*—an important link to buyers inside the Austro-Hungarian Empire, especially Cracow.[23] Clearly, many parties were discontented with a diamond business that had come to look more like a map of the British Empire with an appendix in Continental Europe.

As Dernburg noted, other threats to De Beers' supremacy had emerged in the early 1900s. To start, complaints about the company's beneficial tax arrangements had prompted a formal hearing before the British House of Lords. Although De Beers formally incorporated itself in South Africa— holding its board meetings in Kimberley and claiming immunity from British laws, which were more aggressive in taxing business income—the Lords ruled that De Beers' peculiar governing structure meant it was *controlled* from London. De Beers, therefore, owed considerable back taxes to British authorities. In future, the company would have to pay far more than the 10 percent of net earnings to which it had grown accustomed.[24]

Besides its tax woes, De Beers faced heightened competition from Premier, a rival South African miner that, starting in 1903, controlled its own diamond pipe near Pretoria, in the Transvaal. As of 1908, Transvaal was a piece in the British Empire but still a distinct unit from the Cape Colony. The Transvaal government, which held 60 percent of Premier's shares, remained outside the jurisdiction of the Cape.[25] Premier, accordingly, had a means to refuse cooperation with De Beers in price-fixing and output management at given times.

In October 1907, a full-blown financial panic seized the United States. World diamond demand and rough diamond prices proved highly sensitive to American turbulence, moving down in direct proportion to American equities. Into early 1908, worried Americans bought so much less jewelry than usual that four of New York City's leading diamond importers collapsed. De Beers' share price plummeted, and the company's managers agonized over keeping dividend payments steady. Stories about De Beers' troubles soon found accompaniment in reports on the rise of

German Southwest. "A lot of damned fools," fumed the outgoing Cape prime minister, Leander Starr Jameson.[26]

Midway through 1908, De Beers resolved to form a cartel with Premier, causing prices for diamonds to climb upward from their 1907 lows. Contemporaneously, though, De Beers struggled to address new German output. One competitive advantage for Southwest Africa was that its initial production costs were exceedingly low. Namibian wind had split and scattered diamonds across the desert, facilitating an easier retrieval of stones for the Germans. Whereas South African workers needed to plumb the bowels of the earth in Kimberley, German diamond workers proceeded first through light digging, and later through mining no more than several dozen feet deep. No wonder, then, that German overhead amounted to a quarter of what was necessary in South Africa.[27]

On average, German diamonds also ran considerably smaller in size than those mined in South Africa. While 43 percent of South African diamonds weighed more than one carat, 99 percent of German stones were one carat or less, often about the size of green peas, hazelnuts, or hemp seeds. This disparity provided the Germans with an opportunity. As of early 1908, just before German production in Southwest Africa ramped up, high-quality stones weighing less than a carat represented just 3.1 percent of the world's annual output.[28]

Because nearly all the small German diamonds proved of high quality, Dernburg believed that Germany could extract enough such material to let it determine prices for stones of this size. The class of stones that predominated in Southwest Africa—commonly referred to at the time as mêlées (4–16 per carat)—were soft, easily worked on, and ideal for popular "brilliant" cuts. Mêlées required very little alteration, as opposed to the somewhat rougher stones De Beers mined. This difference looked crucial to Dernburg because a normal cutting process for diamonds wasted 60 percent of a rough's mass. The German stones also looked aesthetically superior to many coming out of South Africa. Perception of beauty, in this case, owed to the pure whiteness of German diamonds, so unlike their typically yellowish South African counterparts. German diamonds had high "limpidity," or clarity, making them more likely to sparkle to a consumer without heavy alteration. An estimated 85 percent of German stones proved naturally suited for jewelry.[29]

Easily cut stones from Southwest Africa promised to affect the business globally. They would reduce the commissions that jewelers needed to pay to cutters by as much as 27 percent, thereby raising the jewelers' profit margins. Higher margins, in turn, would allow jewelers to retail their diamond wares at slightly lower prices, attracting less affluent customers seeking modestly sized engagement rings. Even a modest reduction in price was critical for many consumers.[30]

That left Dernburg with the question of marketability. Diamond production generated patriotic sentiment inside Germany, such that a notable in Mannheim bragged about having secured for himself, a "virtuous citizen," the "largest stone yet extracted" in Southwest Africa.[31] Even outside the fatherland, though, diminutive German stones had a fighting chance because they proved very accessible to buyers of the American middle class—in whose willingness to purchase lay the future of diamonds, broadly speaking.

As of 1908, about 50 percent of diamond buying in the United States was still an activity of the richest 10,000 Americans. But the other half of the market was growing in importance, and it favored smaller stones. Of course, Americans typically considered bigger as better. Still, from the turn of the century, retailers in Manhattan reported demand being strongest for stones running 1 carat or less, but of a high quality. In good times, then, as the pool of American middle-class consumers expanded, German stones would likely move in greater quantity than would large and expensive diamonds, whose pool of potential buyers remained limited.[32]

Sensing a threat, De Beers resorted to spying. Well before Dernburg gave his speech to the Reichstag, the company instructed its agents to visit Lüderitz Bay and secretly learn more about conditions, only to run into the problem of the Forbidden Zone. De Beers' proxies visited bureaucrats at the Colonial Office in Berlin, cabling back information about whom De Beers might bribe. Francis Oats, the chairman of De Beers, attempted to undermine Dernburg's scheme by suggesting an alliance between the two powers. A second De Beers executive tried to ingratiate himself with Dernburg by sending along fruit baskets and contorting his schedule in accordance with the whims of the haughty German colonial secretary.[33]

De Beers also engaged in corporate espionage by buying up stocks of diamonds being sold by naive or venal Germans active in Southwest Africa. In 1909, police in Berlin raided the villa of one of August Stauch's chemists, Georg Heim. The police found a large parcel of diamonds ready for shipment to London. Subsequent investigation confirmed that De Beers had paid Heim to smuggle multiple shipments of diamonds out of

Stauch's fields. De Beers, prior to putting Heim's stones in its safe, studied them to infer the general quality, size, and yield of diamond fields in Southwest. Heim, for his part, profited an estimated $75,000 in the deal—a veritable fortune.[34]

Upon arrest in Berlin, Heim claimed to have found the 4,500 carats in his possession in the Orange River, just south of the Forbidden Zone. Not long after, he attempted to jump out of a window. This ignominious end humiliated Dernburg's enemies in Southwest: August Stauch, other small producers, and settlers. Subsequent press revelations exposed rank amateurism on their part, with a security performance lagging behind that of the German Colonial Corporation and the big miners established by banks. Stauch and the managers who hired Heim were aware of his ill repute; their hope was to save the money needed to hire someone with a clean record. Nor was Heim's circumvention of his managers sophisticated: he mainly baked diamonds into the side of clay pots that he shipped back to Germany undetected.[35]

As the Heim affair unfolded in newspapers, it reinvigorated the specter of De Beers' stockpile. In theory, De Beers could strategically release or withdraw diamonds whose circulation most affected Germany: those whose weight was one carat or less. Such a move could cause a collapse in the price of small stones and leave Germany's diamond industry in distress. For now, De Beers declined to use its weapon, preferring to keep prices of small stones steady to avoid eroding the confidence of the masses. However, the London syndicate now made sure that its sight-holders, at every sale, received parcels that mixed in many small diamonds alongside the prized larger stones. London's modified "offer" to buy was in fact a demand that sight-holders could not refuse, unless they wished to forfeit access to rough diamonds from South Africa. Duress aside, the new offer from London had the advantage of being something the Germans could not match, given the relative lack of larger stones in Southwest.[36]

Dernburg retaliated with a pledge to clamp down on smuggling and to educate gullible settlers in Southwest about how to protect the German diamond industry from De Beers' incursions. Settlers resented the lecture, but Dernburg proved correct about De Beers' bad intentions. Undeterred by its failure with Heim, De Beers began discreetly to buy up stock shares of small German diamond mining companies from multiple accounts and in amounts calculated to avoid raising the eyebrows of German officials.[37]

When Dernburg learned of De Beers' stock-buying tactics, he faced two unattractive alternatives. On the one hand, he could refuse to allow sales of German colonial diamond companies' stock to foreigners. On the other hand, he could let De Beers buy up such shares and risk De Beers' taking over the German diamond industry from the inside out. Instead, Dernburg creatively forced the German companies targeted by De Beers to dilute the shareholdings De Beers had already purchased.[38] The German Colonial Corporation, for example, soon issued an additional two million marks' worth of stock, with large German banks buying up the new shares at specially authorized low prices.

Unfortunately for small producers, they, too, became victims of Dernburg's response. In a move that thwarted De Beers but rankled settlers in Southwest Africa, large German banks themselves bought up any available shares of small German producers. The large banks then rapidly used those shares to take control of small mining operations and to merge them with a handful of larger German miners. By 1912, just six firms accounted for 96 percent of overall German diamond production in Southwest Africa.[39]

Buoyed by German stones' competitive advantages, Dernburg planned to fight back further against De Beers by imitating its structure. According to another decree Dernburg wrote and then had an excited emperor promulgate in January 1909, Southwest Africa's diamond industry would run through a central selling organization known as the Regie. Originally defined as a company with eighteen board members representing seventeen German banks and the German Colonial Corporation, the Regie would promote the consolidation of production in Southwest by forcing an output quota on each miner operating inside the Forbidden Zone.[40]

Dernburg augmented the Regie's power by defining as illicit several practices otherwise assumed permissible. Travelers from Lüderitz Bay to the Forbidden Zone now required written authorization from a diamond company for steps they took inside the Zone. On pain of imprisonment, authorized travelers could not stop during their journey without permission. As a corollary, possession of diamonds in Southwest that were not registered with the Regie became a crime. Dernburg reinforced this policy by levying fines of up to 100,000 marks per unregistered stone, as well as imprisonment for a year. The draconian threat perplexed residents of the colony who might innocently buy a stone from a merchant without sufficient paperwork, or who might plausibly have a stone fall into their shoe in a stretch of desert outside the Forbidden Zone.[41]

Dernburg's criminalization of unlicensed diamond traffic, radical though it seemed in Southwest, represented as much an adaptation as an innovation. The Cape Colony had put a succession of similar measures into effect between 1877 and 1895, in the form of a "Diamond Trade Act."[42] But while the Cape government mostly harassed black Africans, Dernburg targeted white settlers. He also pushed policies that settlers viewed (rightly) as tailored to financiers in the German metropole.

The Regie's composition infuriated excluded parties, among them frontier entrepreneurs like August Stauch. Hoping to foster compliance with the Regie's output quotas, Dernburg encouraged the creation of a new Chamber of Mines at Lüderitz Bay. As a sop, he offered to let small producers in Southwest name a representative in Berlin to argue for their interests in a vague advisory capacity. In the meantime, the Regie's favored miner—a subsidiary company consisting of 50 percent investment from the German Colonial Corporation and 50 percent from a consortium of large German banks—received the highest output quota.[43]

Production was not the Regie's only remit. The Regie reserved the right to "evaluate"—that is, to price—every diamond from Southwest. To this end, each stone from Southwest needed to carry a tag identifying its producer and provenance from the moment of extraction. Moreover, despite taking advance fees from producers for every evaluation, the Regie reserved the right to refuse to process certain stones—including those whose tags bore the mark of an ostracized producer. In a final coup, the Regie enjoyed prerogatives to order stockpiling; to arbitrarily cut or raise producer quotas; to control marketing; to choose to whom and how diamonds would be sold for cutting; and, not least, to negotiate unilaterally with governments and organizations like De Beers on behalf of the whole German diamond industry. Tying it all together was a private spy network initiated by the Regie for the purpose of ensuring compliance.[44]

A series of additional slights led to disgruntlement in Southwest. After evaluation and sale of diamonds, the Regie sent producers in the colony an invoice detailing their share of takings, minus evaluation costs and a 33.33 percent export toll paid to the colonial state. But the Regie sent the invoice only at the close of each business year, wreaking havoc on the ledger books of many inexperienced firms. Fringe diggers who needed their money quickly could secure an advance payment—at 6 percent interest. The Regie resolved billing disputes "in the best interests of producers," with the proviso that officials from Dernburg's Colonial Office could visit to make inspections of the inventory from time to time.[45]

Dernburg lent the force of law, not just to the Regie's ruthless monopoly, but to the incorporation of virtually the entire German Empire within the Regie's territory. The Regie thus functioned as a state-approved, national cartel. To be sure, the Imperial German state's tolerance of cartels was a fact of life in domestic coal, steel, electrical, and potash markets. Nevertheless, the German diamond cartel proved even more ambitious than its model, De Beers. Unlike De Beers, the German version was not a response to overproduction or crisis. Rather, the German diamond cartel entered the world at the same time as, and coterminously with, the German colonial diamond industry. The state's creation of the cartel further distinguished the Regie from De Beers, which came about only after initial governmental ambivalence. In an additional twist, Dernburg's state joined in the cartel as one of the Regie's profit-sharing participants.[46]

There were larger issues at stake here than the fate of Southwest Africa's colonists. In terms of foreign policy, Dernburg's quest to compete with De Beers figured as part of an effort to contest, and curtail, Britain's global power. In terms of domestic policy, the relationship between the state and market seemed at issue, for while powerful bankers praised Dernburg, skeptics identified the Regie as a sign of the state's embrace of monopoly capitalism. By the early 1900s a bevy of German institutions, including the Imperial Supreme Court, held that cartels were a legal form of organization that could enforce binding contracts for output. A Bavarian court even advanced the opinion that cartels were a moral good.[47]

The co-creator of the Regie was the industrialist Walther Rathenau, who had traveled to Lüderitz Bay with Dernburg and who later became the foremost architect of the German war economy. With this link in mind, one should not overlook how the Regie previewed wartime developments and, in Dernburg's words, "how our economy may look in the future." Rathenau, like Dernburg, appreciated the fungibility of statehood and corporations. That was why Rathenau advocated for a German-dominated European customs union. And it was why he unsuccessfully lobbied between 1911 and 1914 for a state-sanctioned and -directed monopoly on electricity that would be run by a consortium of participating large businesses. Dernburg achieved Rathenau's vision early, through the Regie. In the process, Dernburg illustrated how colonies functioned as laboratories of modernity, because his example inspired powerful figures to think about forming a public-private cartel in Germany in other sectors.[48]

Like colonialism *and* cartels, the diamond system erected by Dernburg was an economic experiment. It came about amid a backdrop of heated debate over what cartels were; over how powerful they ought to grow; and, not least, over whether their economic power was inherently a threat to the state. This was a debate most famously associated with Rudolf Hilferding's *Das Finanzkapital* (1910), whose author's assumptions about economics looked confirmed by diamond developments in Southwest Africa. Predictably, the controversy over the diamond system spilled over into a slew of contemporary theses and academic examinations on the German economy.[49]

. . .

Historians of German colonialism have noted the diamond strikes in Southwest Africa but drastically underestimate their size and impact. One scholar has written that, between 1908 and 1913, Southwest Africa exported 52 million marks worth of diamonds in total. However, in transcripts from a South African parliamentary investigation held in 1913, a director of De Beers testified that Southwest Africa's licit diamond exports *in 1912 alone* came to 50 million marks in value. In 1913, the annual figure actually rose to 59 million marks—meaning the Germans shipped out more in value from their colony that year than the Belgians did from their notorious regime in the Congo.[50]

Between 1908 and 1914, Germany disposed over as many as 1.5 million carats of annual diamond production. In an additional complication, smuggling out of Southwest Africa proved so rampant that real diamond exports outstripped reported levels by twofold or more.[51] Extrapolating from such facts about illicit activity, one might credibly consider the true export value of Southwest's diamonds in 1913 to have approximated 118 million marks.

On the strength of these data, it becomes necessary to recalculate trade statistics for German colonies in the aggregate. A recent secondary article speaks of a lowly 57 million marks in combined export value for the German colonies in 1913. Extant primary sources actually indicate a higher total just for Southwest Africa, when taking into consideration its diamonds and assorted goods. Of course, one also needs to add in Germany's other colonies, including Tsingtao, and doing so yields an export value total for German colonialism somewhere between 243 and

302 million marks, depending on the inclusion of illicit diamond figures. In view of this revised math, what is assumed to have been a pathetic colonial share of .5 percent in Germany's overall exports of 10 billion instead becomes 2.4–3 percent. That distinction hardly means Germany's colonies proved as important economically as France's or Britain's. But it suggests a need to reexamine the anatomy of the German colonial economy. There was more money motivating this colonial regime, and more money generated from its exploitation of Indigenous peoples, than has been acknowledged in curt dismissals.[52]

To grasp these dynamics completely, one has to look not only beyond the German nation in Europe but beyond German colonies overseas. In the years preceding 1914, nearly all of the world's uncut, "rough" diamonds came from South and Southwest Africa, where colonial merchants assessed and priced stones before exporting them to Europe. Most rough diamonds were subsequently cut in Antwerp or Amsterdam, after which their price jumped from an average of around fifty German marks per carat to an average of 100. In roughly 75 percent of cases, the cut diamonds then departed Europe for the United States, where their price per carat again rose upon arrival, now to an average of around 150 marks. Ultimately, by the time each diamond found its way into display cases of American retail jewelry shops, prices had risen to as much as twenty times the value assigned at the moment of extraction from Africa.[53]

Determining how much wealth this process captured is fundamental to understanding the allure that diamonds held for German colonialism, whose biggest potential customers after 1908 lived in the United States. Around the turn of the twentieth century, reputable international observers alleged that statistics issued by European governments concealed the amounts of money at stake in the global diamond trade. In keeping with that repression of information, diamond merchants declined to publish the number of carats the United States imported. Still, a trade association of diamond cutters in the United States estimated their country's annual consumption in 1913 at 1,140,000 carats in weight. Working on the basis of knowledge about the value chain, it is conceivable that in that year, Americans transferred more than 1.14 billion marks' worth of money in exchange for retail diamonds. Assuming similar machinations took place in the remaining 25 percent of the global market, one can surmise that the diamond business yielded something approaching 1.4 billion marks in revenue in 1913.

A sum of 1.4 billion marks in 1913 easily surpassed what Germany was said to have spent cumulatively on its colonial governing expenses since 1884. Further, 1.4 billion marks in 1913 matched the combined cash value from annual sales of Germany's two leading exports: machines and iron wares. Colonial diamonds meant serious, and significant, money. Like sugar, slavery, and cotton, diamonds attested to the impact the "periphery" of the global economy had on the "center" of the world economy in modern history.[54] Germany, as a suddenly powerful stakeholder in the diamond trade, had the ability to take in hundreds of millions of additional marks per annum simply from mining and exporting rough stones. But Germany had reason to dream about earning still more riches by muscling in on the lucrative stages of the diamond business that came after extraction: cutting, polishing, and retailing.

CHAPTER 5

MARKETS

◈ "In Bernhard Dernburg," cracked the German satirical magazine *Kladderadatsch,* "diamonds found their Homer." This assessment, made in jest, had merit: when Dernburg promoted diamonds,
the glittering objects generated popular interest in Germany's colonies.
After 1908, the colonies' political administration experienced wider
scrutiny in part because of Southwest's fortune-making potential. The
Reichstag spent several sessions discussing adjustments to the Regie. A
celebrity impersonator targeted Dernburg. Even on a train of ski vacationers headed to the Harz mountains, people could not escape discussion about Southwest's mineral wealth.[1]

Dernburg taxed diamond exports heavily, using those revenues to
finish colonial railroads. Yet, such revenues immediately faced a challenge
from De Beers, which threatened to cut off any diamond retailers who
bought stones from Germany. Crucially, De Beers controlled the world's
supply of medium- and large-sized diamonds, whatever the German
abundance of mêlées. Dernburg needed to address this problem, and his
first option was to sign a contract that allowed Germany to function as
an independent producer selling diamonds to the London syndicate,
which would market the stones to sight-holders and retailers. In this way,
London had already accommodated Premier, the company that became
De Beers' largest South African competitor upon acquiring major diamond deposits in the Transvaal. But Premier did not evaluate or price its
own stones, instead letting the syndicate do such work. Thus, Premier
lost considerable sums that might have allowed for additional research,
development, and glory. Dernburg, an egotist, wanted it all.[2]

His next option was to task the big German banks who ran the
German Colonial Corporation, as well as the Regie, with selling German
diamonds to retailers around the world. But the bankers protested that

they lacked experience in marketing such a unique commodity.[3] So Dernburg, again proving creative, approached European merchants in Antwerp, a city with a grudge against De Beers and London. The diamond link Dernburg forged with Antwerp proved highly profitable between 1909 and 1914. That said, the location and nature of the profits generated further unrest—both among Southwest Africa's settlers and among metropolitan Germans.

•   •   •

"The world is a ring and Antwerp the diamond within." The truth was more contingent than this Renaissance-era saying indicated. Starting in the fifteenth century, when Portuguese and Dutch travelers imported the art of diamond cutting from the Indian subcontinent to Europe, the city of Antwerp became the principal beneficiary.[4] Antwerp's innovation was to perfect not just cutting, but a process in which diamond dust, a kind of powder made from grinding crushed diamond fragments, smoothed each rough stone. This method of polishing proved so commercially successful that before long, diamonds needed to claim an Antwerpian link to achieve maximum value and esteem in Europe.

Antwerp's diamond sector blossomed during the early 1870s, when a spike in supply from South Africa required more workers to do more cutting and polishing. Nevertheless, Antwerp fell on relatively hard times by century's end, as some of its cutting jobs relocated to Amsterdam, a competitor since Antwerp's sacking by the Spanish in 1584. Amsterdam's diamond workforce expanded twentyfold between 1870 and 1880, ultimately overtaking Antwerp's in 1885. Antwerp continued to lose ground in the 1890s, owing partly to De Beers' strong-arm tactics and partly to successful local workers' strikes that frightened investors. By 1904, Antwerp employed 3,000–4,000 diamond cutters to Amsterdam's 7,000–12,000.[5]

Antwerp's merchants worked to reverse the trend. In Amsterdam, headaches surrounded collective bargaining, which the Dutch diamond industry agreed to recognize as a perpetual process. As a result, some Amsterdam-based merchants put their stones to work in Antwerp, where high labor prices started to subside in the wake of a successful lockout by owners of cutting shops. Still, as of 1908, Antwerp could claim no steady rough diamond supply of its own, leaving too little work for cutters. Little wonder, then, that when a Southwest African railway worker

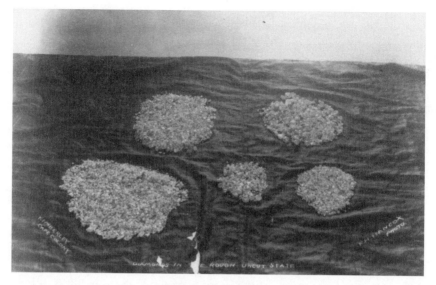

These uncut diamonds were gathered by five different mines in two days from Kimberley, South Africa, in the early twentieth century.

showed up in Antwerp in 1909 with 1,200 illicit carats to sell, he found himself nearly trampled by eager buyers.[6]

For valid reasons, Dernburg chose to sell German stones through the Regie to Antwerp. Despite Antwerp's setbacks, the city retained sufficient cash to buy Germany's entire annual diamond production—with the caveat that the price was somewhat discounted relative to what the syndicate in London cynically offered. In late 1909, with Dernburg's assent, an Antwerp syndicate contracted with the Regie, hoping thereby to challenge the London syndicate's dominance and recast Antwerp, not just as the world's foremost diamond-cutting center, but as a destination for rough stones and finished diamond marketing. By allying with Germany, this new Antwerp would not have to settle for taking London's allotments, which included an array of stones that ranged from lucrative to lackluster. Instead, Antwerp would liberate itself from London and develop its own sight-holders, including Germany's jewelers, while pocketing some additional premiums.[7]

In the wake of its agreement with the Regie, Antwerp succeeded mightily. The city's cutting population quickly rose to 16,000, more than doubling Amsterdam's. With Antwerp routing perhaps 25 percent of all world output through its factories for cutting and polishing, the city also won the status of the world's preeminent polished diamond buying center. Within a few years, Antwerp extended its operations to conduct more such business than the rest of Europe combined. Accordingly, Antwerp's merchants reaped handsome rewards.[8]

To Dernburg's credit, the Regie's arrangement with Antwerp brought large, guaranteed sales. German authorities in Southwest taxed those sales via a 33.33 percent export tariff, boosting state finances. Aside from taxes, the German state made more money by taking a slice of the profits generated by the Regie when it sold to Antwerp. The risk regarding Antwerp, however, lay not so much with metrics of revenue as with German public opinion. Dernburg and the system he oversaw experienced fierce criticism. Settlers in Southwest Africa protested that unloading German production to a Belgium-based syndicate entailed accepting less money than diamonds might fetch on the open market. Here Dernburg had rejoinders ready: that his arrangement with Antwerp was only for a year, with an option to renew or cancel; and that the "open market" was controlled by De Beers and the London syndicate, which was willing to overpay in the short term to suppress German production in the long term.[9]

A more trenchant criticism came from Germany's Social Democratic Party, whose representatives questioned Dernburg's preference for Antwerp over an infant cutting industry developing at home, in the Hessian city of Hanau.[10] Hanau, its diamond industry under construction since 1874, appeared suited to handle diamonds from Southwest Africa. The relative clout of Antwerp and Amsterdam had long forced Hanau's cutters to accept batches of trifling stones that the larger cutting centers could not process economically. In response, Hanau specialized in stones like the quarter- and half-carat ones Germany now produced.

Hanau saw the diamond rush around Lüderitz Bay and hoped for golden days. Under Dernburg's Antwerp plan, however, Hanau and mainland Germany would mostly get money, not jobs. Hanau saw a fivefold expansion in its commissioned work after 1908, but only relative to very modest statistics reported previously. Hanau otherwise missed out on the revenues reaped by Antwerp, whose diamonds merchants earned millions of marks annually, then generated lots of secondary and tertiary activity in their local economies. This disparity, so complained Social Democrats, represented a dereliction of duty by Dernburg: a privileging of dirty competition over long-term goals such as those maintained by De Beers, the organization that should have been Germany's model. Yes, Antwerp could offer Dernburg higher prices than Hanau's potential German buyers.[11] But Dernburg's acceptance of a deal with Antwerp to maintain horizontal integration of the German diamond industry—so the argument went—kept him from achieving vertical integration, and thus ultimately limited the success that Germany could hope to achieve on the world market.

By leaving cutting to foreigners, the connection between Antwerp and Germany would deprive the German state of additional potential diamond tax revenues that ran into the tens of millions annually. Social Democrats also had a point when they claimed that the reason Antwerp could offer better prices than Hanau was that Antwerp exploited its workers more. One could argue that Hanau's superior treatment of workers would have yielded higher-quality work and a better polished stone—eventually fetching a higher price with consumers and delivering more net profits to Germany.[12]

Rancor over Antwerp spread beyond Social Democrats to several German political parties. When Hanau's mayor traveled to Berlin to appeal his city's lot, he met with such a rude reception from Dernburg that he later received a public apology. Antwerp, its industry already powerful, got 98 percent of German diamonds. The remaining 2 percent found their way to Hanau. While Antwerp's cutters expanded, Hanau's largest cutting and polishing firm worked on a paltry 20,000 carats a year—some of which came via smugglers. Hanau's Reichstag deputy complained of a "crisis" of unemployment in which Hanau's streets were full of victims who had "no bread on account of its being stolen by the Regie." Anti-Belgian literature concerning diamonds reached the desk of the German State Secretary of the Interior.[13]

Dernburg justified Hanau's underwhelming fate partly by reference to popular confusion about motives. The German state, he conceded, had obligations to diverse constituents. But the state's commitment to fiscal health trumped calls to function as an "office for social politics." Cheap labor costs for Antwerp's cutters vis-à-vis German rivals represented a significant advantage.[14] Another factor was Antwerp's friendliness to jewelers seeking to buy on credit—a process facilitated, with an unprecedented ease and breadth, by the Banque Générale Belge. Finally, whatever the rhetoric of nationalists, Dernburg knew that Antwerp was becoming increasingly "German" in the years overlapping with Southwest's diamond boom. By 1912, the number of the city's German residents rose to 30,000, or about 10 percent of its population. As important, Antwerp formed the center of German commercial interests in Belgium, with roughly 70 percent of German steel exports traveling through the city in a typical year.

Dernburg's decision *against* Hanau also was affected by questions about domestic capacity. The German government's unification of weights and measures in 1871 had neglected to address the status of the carat— which by 1908 not only persisted as an anomaly relative to the metric system but even continued to represent multiple weights in such different locations of the German Empire as Hamburg and Berlin. A similarly detectable difference lay in the domestic German diamond market, which had never grown large and did not have a culture of engagement rings. In a contemporary article on diamonds, for instance, Germany's most-read periodical, *Die Gartenlaube,* mentioned nothing about betrothal but spoke of brooches and dress pins as equals to rings in terms of German diamond consumption.[15]

In Dernburg's view, Hanau found itself disadvantaged by German society's tepid interest in diamonds. As of 1909, German consumers purchased 200,000 carats annually. By comparison, consumers in the United States bought well over 3 million carats. Between 1908 and 1914, German Southwest Africa came to claim between 20 and 25 percent of licit world diamond production. With German cutters claiming just 4 percent of world cutting capacity at the *end* of that six-year period, there is no question that, had Dernburg planned to funnel Southwest's stones through Hanau, he would have faced a serious lag in the time to market of cut and polished stones. In so doing, he would have delayed gratification for the colonies, the Reichstag, and his own career.[16]

This was not even to mention the problem of replicating the London syndicate's "sight-holder" model—after which Germany, at least early on, attempted self-consciously to style its diamond operations. The Regie controlled stones typically weighing 1 carat or less; in fact, its contributions doubled at one stroke the world's supply of such items. This surfeit meant that the Regie needed a partner like Antwerp, for Antwerp also processed larger-sized diamonds with which smaller German stones could be combined to compose a mix that retailers would have to buy.[17] By contrast, if Berlin picked Hanau, and Hanau developed an overstock of mêlées, nothing could keep retailers from taking advantage of Hanau's one-dimensionality and, by extension, that of the Regie.

German Social Democrats were still right when they alleged Dernburg could have tried harder to find another way. He might, for one, have

created a massive cash reserve fund with which to pay off Southwest producers and put small-time German cutters to work in the short term.
Thereupon, Dernburg might have created a national stockpile of "roughs"
so as to avoid overproduction, then drawn on stockpiles of cut stones at
the most favorable times to fetch high sale prices.[18]

Here a kind of path dependence prevailed. The German Empire had
no history with rough diamond sales. And Germany was entering into a
business De Beers and London had run for decades. Germany, as a relatively new and ineffective colonial power, desired quick profits to show
to banking investors as well as other participants at multiple levels: the
farmers, the small-time miners, and the public generally. Further, in order
to make money in diamonds, Dernburg thought Germany needed to draw
on international advantages and flows of trade. This perceived interdependence paralleled circumstances in German Togoland, where Germans'
attempts to grow cotton induced them to recruit African-American experts to the colony in the hope that these consultants would transfer
knowledge to Indigenous peoples.[19]

From 1909, the Belgian-German diamond connection featured in
booths at international trade shows. When financial returns resulting
from the first sales to Antwerp proved superb, studies from the newly
founded Hamburg Colonial Institute went on to endorse Dernburg's
course. German ambassadors abroad could tout the Regie's supply of diamonds to Antwerp as proof that their country's brand of colonialism—
unlike, say, the French variant—subscribed to principles of free trade.
Equally important, Dernburg could boast that, despite expanding the
world's diamond supply considerably, his system increased the price of
each diamond Germany sold in its initial years of production.[20]

•   •   •

The Antwerp connection paid off above all because the city's diamond
merchants, unlike foreign competitors, had made inroads into the highly
lucrative American market. From the 1880s, in a process that peaked
around 1907, a wave of immigrants from the Austro-Hungarian and Russian Empires passed through Antwerp on their way to the United States.
Exploiting such pathways, a leading Belgian diamond cutter, Louis Coetermans, set up a network of transatlantic agents. Hence, after 1908,
rough diamonds shipped by the Regie to Antwerp fit into established
distribution routes in cities like New York City and Cincinnati, where

Antwerp embedded its own agents as importers—thus, to some extent, cutting out middlemen between itself and retailers.[21]

Dernburg correctly anticipated that the small stones distributed by Antwerp would prove popular with the American diamond ring market, which was becoming more democratic insofar as it was expanding to include new sorts of buyers. "No diamond, no engagement" was a motto heard as much among America's lower and middle classes as among its elites. The diamond ring now dominated in a realm where it had once been one of many options, including less expensive stones like turquoise. In San Francisco, readers of the newspaper's society column heard that no diamond engagement ring was "too little"—it was a question of a "fiancée's pocketbook and not of his heart." Precisely for this reason, readers of modest means were given to believe that there *was* a diamond size right for them.[22]

In the Midwest, affluent consumers still spent several thousand dollars apiece on large diamond engagement rings. But, in and around cities like St. Louis, traveling diamond salesmen also went door to door hawking rings nestled in tissue paper beneath vest-pocket wallets. The region's conventional jewelers reported an increase in small-carat ring buying, with newspaper advice sections indicating waxing conformity among financially insecure youths, some of whom believed that it was impossible to get engaged without a ring. "In many poor families," remarked the *Wall Street Journal,* bread could now seemingly "be dispensed with, but [. . .] engagement rings will continue to be bought." A hospital in downtown Chicago felt it necessary to craft rules banning its nurses from wearing these baubles. Likewise, a contemporary social scientist in the Northeast did not consider it unusual that a working-class seventeen-year-old, employed as a washerwoman in a college dormitory, wore "a little diamond engagement ring."[23]

By 1909, the aggregate of average Americans' spending on diamond engagement rings overtook that by richer citizens. Observing that the mean amount of an engagement ring purchase *fell* in this era, a journalist quipped: "He may be earning only $20 a week, but she's got to have a diamond engagement ring, if the stone's no more than a quarter of a carat." A quarter of a carat was where many jewelers started. But the contemporary Sears catalog went further, featuring an entry-level option of a "third quality" one-eighth carat diamond ring, mounted and set, carrying a price of $9.59. Notably, of twenty-eight possible sizes of cut stones in the Sears catalog, twenty-one weighed in at one carat or less.

Such stones, it will be recalled, were a type in which German Southwest Africa specialized and De Beers lagged.[24]

To a unionized American baker earning thirty cents an hour and working around sixty hours a week, a one-eighth carat ring from Sears would cost half a week's wages. In Sears' hometown, Chicago, the ring's price represented the equivalent of a "nice little dinner discreetly arranged" at a hotel for a young couple. Such a palatable cost meant that, even when demand sometimes flagged for larger gems, sales of small ones remained steady. A dark side of this phenomenon was that the retail market drew in the sort of person who, in addition to having "no knowledge of diamonds that will permit him to value them correctly," as insiders noted, could ill afford to make a mistake. For Americans buying in shops, innovations nevertheless smoothed the way to participation. "Easy payment" installment programs required little money up front, promised "confidentiality," and encouraged participants to signal they were not "cheap" by taking on loans that could stretch out over several years.[25]

Marketing gimmicks helped, too. From Iowa to Maryland to Nevada, advertisements suggested that some of the least expensive engagement rings contained "perfect" diamonds. Not only did jewelers have rings "to suit all pockets." Advertisements promised the poorest of couples that a ring, however microscopic, could signify "perfection": a concept that carried no meaning for gemologists but flattered a couple's sense of their love's uniqueness. "Perfection in an engagement ring," even if obtained for $15 in rural Kansas, would "be a constant source of pleasure in years to come." As for wealthier consumers, they could strive for the "most perfect" stone. Or they could distinguish themselves anew by wearing rings with one larger stone set against several smaller ones.[26]

Evidence from this period suggests that many African Americans also started to figure among buyers of diamond engagement rings. Precisely as German producers came to inundate the world with small, high-quality diamonds, the *Chicago Defender* gave its readers instructions on so many questions of etiquette as to suggest an inchoate practice: on which finger to wear an engagement ring, how much to spend on this ring, and what to do with it in case of a broken promise. Jewelers queried by the *Defender* estimated that ninety-nine out of every hundred engagement rings sold were diamond solitaires, and that the outlier was an opal set inside a circle of thirteen tiny diamonds.[27] Consumers in America, including African Americans, thus helped to fund the German colonial apparatus, with that same apparatus correspondingly enabling American courtship rituals: sex, marriage, family. Desire in one sphere reinforced desire in the other.

Because of the entry of German stones into the market, South African miners had to work harder to keep their output consistent with engagements to marry in the United States, where the number of carats imported in 1913, for example, would exceed only thinly the number of that year's roughly 1,021,000 newlywed couples. By contrast, Germany, continuing to increase its output of diamonds, visibly inverted a dynamic much bemoaned in domestic politics: dependency on the United States for raw materials like cotton. In a time when Germany grappled with trade deficits owing to this and other dependencies, diamonds represented a flashy counterexample. Diamonds were a German export not needed at home that would bring in coveted foreign exchange when sold abroad.[28] They were easy.

Another entanglement lay in the realm of gender. In Dernburg's Germany, conservatives' sexism led them to complain about how diamonds stored a large amount of wealth on a woman's body, a supposedly unsafe place. Germany experienced no democratization of its diamond market, with domestic sales of small stones proving soft. By contrast, the more widespread diamond ring ownership became in the United States— thanks to an influx of German stones—the more American women participated in the receipt of rings that could empower them. Through a diamond ring, materially motivated women in a society that otherwise embraced sexual inequality might leverage a romance into wealth independent of marriage, wills, and families. The diamond ring allowed a woman to get a better sense of a man's finances, his willingness to spend money, and his honesty: she need only visit a jewelry store to confirm prices. It was because of this potential that numerous American court cases affirmed women's retention of engagement rings in the event of failed engagements.[29]

      •   •   •

By 1910, Dernburg's sale of stones through Antwerp became increasingly streamlined. In Lüderitz Bay, roughly once a week but sometimes more frequently, agents from the Regie set and paid a rate for parcels of diamonds received from the Forbidden Zone, whereupon the agents sent a package to Germany via a ship in the German East Africa Line. At Berlin, twenty times a year, such packages arrived at the Regie headquarters in the Behrenstraße, where clerks either stockpiled stones or repackaged them for sale to Antwerp.[30]

The Regie's diamond sales represented a source of pride for Germany's financial class. They also represented a coup for the proponents of the *Weltpolitik* that saw Germany take greater slices of Chinese, African, and world affairs around the turn of the century. In this context, Emperor Wilhelm II hosted Dernburg for skat games and hailed him as the second coming of Cecil Rhodes. Dernburg was rumored to be in line for ennoblement, with his position as state secretary more than assured. Wilhelm II spent a good deal of time raving about "Dernburg's diamonds," his expectations building with each account. The emperor even proposed elevating Dernburg to the position of chancellor.[31]

Beyond these considerations, evidence suggested that Dernburg's diamonds made a positive impact on German colonial economics. The record shows that, within five years, Dernburg delivered a diamond industry extracting around 1.5 million carats annually from Southwest. Yes, the German Colonial Corporation, the Regie, and Antwerp received a significant portion of the money generated after extraction. That said, the German state treasury received 64.5 percent of this money.[32]

The record confirms broader successes under Dernburg's leadership, which was powered by diamonds: near fourfold increases in colonial companies' capitalization, colonial production, and colonial trade respectively; and the approval of hundreds of million marks' worth of new railroad funding wrested from an otherwise difficult Reichstag. By leveraging diamond tax revenues and diamond prestige, Dernburg was able to complete railroad projects that had dragged on for years. Added to this, he facilitated a jump in colonial investment from private, nonstate sources. In Lüderitz Bay, knock-on effects were visible. With improvements underway to the water treatment facilities in and around town, the cost of a cubic meter of water eventually dropped from 264 marks to 30 marks, and then to 15.[33]

None of these metrics, though, could prevent popular opinion from starting to turn against Dernburg after his decision for Antwerp. One source of anger was the influential journalist Maximilian Harden, a former confidant of Dernburg's who became an enemy after feeling himself shunned by the colonial secretary during a prominent libel trial known as the Eulenburg Affair. Harden reminded readers that Dernburg had "preached to the Reichstag about a new Kimberley" and styled himself "the prophet of a new colonial diamond magnificence." But most of this talk, in Harden's view, owed to Dernburg's penchants for self-promotion and careerism. German Southwest was no "second British South Africa." If investors looked beyond impressive numbers and the "fairy-tale castle" Dernburg conjured, they would see the nation losing while a few wealthy bankers and Antwerp profited handsomely.[34]

Among Germany's anti-Semite political party, which hated Harden, similar criticisms emerged about the ethics and utility of a profitable diamond business. The anti-Semites accused Dernburg of an "exaggerated, one-sided, capitalistic colonial policy" that hurt Germans. For two reasons, this vitriol mattered. First, the anti-Semite party was a member of the parliamentary "Bloc" assembled by Chancellor Bülow in 1907.[35] Second, Dernburg, although born to a baptized Christian, was of Jewish ancestry. While the anti-Semites largely overlooked Dernburg's "Jewishness" in the early days of the Bloc, they changed course in the wake of diamond strikes and of news about Antwerp, threatening the stability of the chancellor's already-fragile alliance in parliament.

A majority of settlers in Southwest agreed with Germany's anti-Semites, regarding Jews as "bloodsuckers" and "foreign bodies." Even small-time diamond producers like August Stauch complained about "the nose of the colonial secretary," whose Christian faith they overlooked. The colonial community as a whole denigrated diamond tycoons based in Antwerp and thoroughly embedded within that city's Jewish community. They hated how the middleman between Germany and Antwerp was set to receive a commission on all the Regie's diamond sales in perpetuity.[36]

Nor did anti-Dernburg rhetoric remain the preserve of a few groups. A leading intellectual, Werner Sombart, fingered Antwerp as a source by which the "spirit of capitalism" and finance had penetrated Europe's legal system. Dernburg, so one agrarian-spirited newspaper alleged in an anticipation of Sombart, acted more "capitalistically than nationalistically" with his diamond policy. Adding to the furor was Egyptian activist Dusé Mohamed Ali. In his influential 1911 tract, *In the Land of the Pharaohs*, Ali castigated "diamond princes" as "a most ignoble band" who lied about imperialism's true purposes and beneficiaries—the latter of whom, so his argument went, honored civilizations less than they did materialism.[37]

Efforts to martial statistics to defend Dernburg's colonial diamond connection with Antwerp failed to appease multiple segments of the political spectrum in Germany. Dernburg, it turned out, did not adequately address heterogeneous cultural interpretations of colonialism. For every ardent proponent of diamonds in Southwest Africa, convinced of economic returns and value, there emerged die-hard Social Democratic opponents of colonialism alleging misappropriation and con jobs. Other opponents, including conservatives, preferred to focus on developing colonies as sources of national prestige, for arguably Westerners' colonies, like their diamonds, were less about a rational program of economic development than about doing something because peers like Britain and France were doing it. A culture of imitation, not efficient production of wealth, explained why contemporary theorists of German colonization described their dreams as a "German Hong Kong," "German Kimberley," or "German India."[38]

For many Germans, overseas colonies served a similar purpose to that attending the consumption of luxury goods. Thorstein Veblen's *Theory of the Leisure Class* (1899) spoke of luxuries as vehicles for economic elites to flaunt their power in public, while Max Weber identified luxuries as ways for feudal elites to reassert themselves amid economic rationalization and modernity.[39] A colony in the hands of a semifeudal empire like Germany might pull off both tricks: on the one hand, showing the superiority of the German state to alternative, more democratic models; on the other, allowing space to replicate a vanishing feudal way of life and reject any notion of accounting for its prestige. Status and power did not allow for neat measurement, of which Dernburg offered plenty.

Dernburg learned this lesson when his heavy-handed moves to monetize diamonds brought unprecedented resistance from German settlers in Southwest Africa. On the one hand, settler resistance ought not to have meant much: The population of Southwest was trifling. On the other hand, settler entrants into the colonial diamond debate—some farmers, but mostly ranchers—enjoyed a disproportionately large voice owing to powerful political champions. The governor of Southwest Africa, as well as metropolitan German conservatives, agrarians, and anti-Semites, all complained on behalf of settlers about how the diamond industry was allegedly operating to the detriment of other areas in colonial life.

Agricultural schemes to develop Southwest never appealed to mainstream German financiers and economists such as Dernburg, who defined colonies as a business venture. In the wake of the diamond boom, the idea of an economy based on small farms appeared especially erroneous,

European-controlled areas
1914

Spanish Morocco

Tunisia

Morocco

Spanish Sahara

Rio De Oro

Mauritania

Algeria

Italian Libya

Egypt

Turkish Empire

Persia

Arabia

FRENCH

French West Africa

Chad

BRITISH

Anglo-Egyptian Sudan

Darfur

Eritrea

French Somaliland

British Somaliland

Abyssinia

Italian Somaliland

The Gambia

Guinea

Portuguese Guinea

Togoland

Niger

Nigeria

Sierra Leone

Ivory Coast

Gold Coast

Liberia

Kamerun

Ubangi-shari

Equatorial Guinea

GERMAN

French Equatorial Africa

Gabon

Belgian Congo

Uganda

British East Africa

Zanzibar

German East Africa

Cabinda

Angola

PORTUGUESE

Nyasaland

Northern Rhodesia

Southern Rhodesia

Mozambique
PORTUGUESE

Madagascar

German Southwest Africa

Botswana

BRITISH

Swaziland

Union of South Africa

Lesotho

European colonies in Africa on the eve of World War I.

because many Germans had defected from farms across the colony and headed to Lüderitz Bay to pursue dreams of wealth in the diamond business. To Dernburg's critics, however, agriculture represented the real "financial future of Southwest." When settlers complained about Lüderitz Bay's political importance growing "overweight," the governor of Southwest agreed and warned that Dernburg's policy was turning the colony against Germany.[40] Looking over the papers of the German office for resettlement of emigrants in Southwest Africa, it is difficult not to conclude that they, too, took a side by discouraging applicants from seeking diamond fortunes.

As Dernburg managed a mineral rush, he grew less interested in the resettlement of German emigrants from Europe; higher-ups in the Colonial Office seldom discussed it. Instead, Dernburg's focus for colonization turned overwhelmingly to the development of railroads and mining. This shift induced many Germans to ask how much Southwest Africa's fate was going to mirror that of neighboring South Africa—itself the site of a long struggle between farmers and miners to establish dominance over the policies of the colonial state.[41]

In 1910, some 13,962 Europeans lived in Southwest Africa. While that number represented nearly double the total reported in 1907, not all growth seemed equal. At a time when German agriculture was coming to rely visibly on seasonal migrant labor from Polish sources in Austria-Hungary and Russia—as many as 750,000 people annually—hypernationalists in Germany reviled the way in which diamonds were rendering the demographics of Southwest less German. Agrarian politicians, for their part, feared a stream of non-German Europeans moving into the colony would buy up too much land and weaken the colony's cultural fabric.[42]

Southwest, which prior to the diamond finds had been a predominantly agricultural and military colony, was building itself on an industry that appeared to require too few Germans. Simultaneously, the colony was starting to look more diverse not just in its economy, but ethnically. A changing Southwest bothered pan-Germans because it had lots of "non-German" place names bestowed by Boer migrants and because it "allowed" Indigenous workers to speak pidgin German mixed with other foreign tongues. As sex between white and black became common in the colony, the German parliament took up debates over bans on mixed marriages in 1912.[43] Indeed, it was racial issues in the demographically fluctuating Southwest that helped to shape Imperial Germany's passage of a landmark citizenship law in 1913. A person's ethnic descent, not sustained residency inside German territory, became the primary legal criterion for inclusion as a German citizen.

While the ranks of European merchants and artisans attending Southwest's diamond business multiplied, other economic sectors such as farming fared comparatively poorly. To conservatives in Germany, the disparity augured a realignment of priorities in the German colonies overseas. A realignment, that is, away from a kind of land-based polity of farmers for which many in the Prussian elite harbored a nostalgia, and to whose "protection" nearly all Reichstag parties, from conservatives to liberals, pledged themselves in campaign programs.[44]

Arguably the whole motivation behind German imperialism, Joseph Schumpeter would soon argue by implication, was a desire by the Prussian elite to preserve land-based, militaristic, and likely atavistic ways of life in a new setting. To Schumpeter's point, aristocrats imagined Southwest, and the German colonies generally, as a trip back in time to a place where even rich, well-connected nonnobles had to enter the governor's mansion through a side door.[45] The Mark Brandenburg, like Southwest, had once figured as a wasteland prior to its internal conquest by Prussian rulers and their backers.

German colonies, or so this line of thinking ran, should provide outlets to replicate an outdated social order amid a sea change in Europe. Nowhere was that change more apparent than in Prussia, where urban wealth had risen to 64 percent of the country's total. Yet, Lüderitz Bay was no stranger to the changes taking place in Europe. A miniature industrial revolution around the diamond mines encouraged the development of classes and socioeconomic divides within a dwarf European community in Germany's sole settler colony. In 1909, European carpenters and masons in Lüderitz Bay staged the first workers' strike in the colony's history.[46]

Added to the seeming confirmation of the inevitability of Marxian class struggle in colonies was uncertainty about the location of power. In the metropole, an erratic emperor generally neglected to exercise his theoretically near-absolute prerogative over the colonies. Filling the vacuum, German parliament contested seemingly everything: whether the Reichstag's or Bundesrat's interpretations of laws would prevail in conflicts; whether colonial courts might draw from the Imperial German

constitution in adjudicating local disputes; whether parliamentariza-
tion in colonies might follow the course it took in Prussian history; and
whether the colonies were "domestic," "foreign," "neighboring," or "non-
German imperial" territory.[47]

Diamonds revealed that the rule of uncertain power held *within* Southwest, too. Farmers and ranchers predominated in the colony's north,
and particularly around Windhoek, where Germans composed 90 percent
of the European population. The north was a region that lay at a relatively high altitude, and a region that comprised perhaps as much square
mileage as Prussia. Accordingly, northern Southwest Africa and its
German residents' visions for the future had little to do with the sea-level
southern Namib, where diamonds were mined. On the contrary, the north
of the colony viewed investment in the south, or revenue that stayed there,
as a blow to the colony's core.[48]

Last but not least, the railroads Dernburg built in Southwest Africa
joined with his diamonds to challenge the colonial status quo, as if in a
nod to the optimist Émile Zola's dream of a "steam-engine of diamond"
representing the "most beautiful of things" in the late nineteenth century.
In 1904, Southwest counted just 480 kilometers of railway. Over the next
four years, that number quadrupled. Another four years later, buoyed by
the diamond find, the number rose to 3,900 kilometers.[49] If farming—
which was simultaneously losing its supreme role in the metropolitan
German economy—gave way in Southwest to railways, trade, and industry, then one might expect attendant effects of modernization. Perhaps the franchise in Southwest would expand to include more than
roughly 2,000 German male voters. Perhaps, too, civil liberties would expand to include more than just a small German cadre. Miners, foremen,
and the like would also incline to vote for Social Democrats.

Dernburg had an interest in managing the diamond wealth carefully,
with an eye toward the long term: competing against De Beers, bringing
in foreign exchange, improving the colonial balance sheet. Southwest African farmers did not share those foci. True, they saw some benefits
from increased state spending on agriculture in an economy rendered
more prosperous by diamonds. Overall, however, Southwest's German
farmers and their metropolitan German champions charged that, within
a few decades, the mineral treasure would be exhausted.[50] They also worried that intensification of diamond work meant heightened competition
for a pool of laborers that already looked thin: first, because few Ger-

mans had shown interest in emigrating to Southwest Africa; second, because Germany's military had ravaged the Herero and Nama in the previous years and had accelerated a railroad-building campaign with a thirst for workers.

Germany's agricultural lobby urged the colonial state to get as many diamonds out of the ground as possible, as quickly as possible, and promptly reinvest the proceeds into crop and livestock management—the only viable projects in Southwest, as they saw it. By this path the colony would, as one journalist advertised it, "repay Germany for the sacrifices she has made, not in the form of simple cash," but through the more spiritually important act of "satisfying the economic needs of the mother country": that is, supplying Germany with reliable flows of meat and produce necessary to sustain German growth. Food represented a crucial metropolitan desire, in view of what was then a rising German dependence on imported grain.[51]

In the early 1900s, there was little doubt that Southwest Africa would eventually push for autonomy, as the Union of South Africa had, and as one of its predecessors, the Cape Colony, had since receiving "responsible government" in 1853. In August 1908, Dernburg gave some lip service to the idea of enhanced colonial autonomy, in another case of his talking too freely. As diamond profits piled up, though, he made several fateful decisions that seemed autocratic in light of pro-autonomy sentiment.[52] His creation of the Forbidden Zone and the Regie demonstrated powerfully that he did not think the colony ready for a say in its affairs.

Even if colonial farmers succeeded in winning a larger voice, their priorities did not strictly align with those of Germany. That divergence became apparent after 1908, when farmers pressured the colonial government at Windhoek to lobby for state legalization of prostitution, only to meet with odium from Berlin. A further gap was evidenced in trade statistics that showed German colonies conducting more business with non-German parties than had been the case in the past. Many in Berlin, whatever their political persuasion, dreaded placing control of decades' worth of Southwest African diamonds in the hands of Southwest's settlers, because divergence between the colony and the metropole seemed likely to grow wider over time.[53]

Upon taking office, Dernburg had committed to some decentralization of colonial governance once the colonies proved capable of balancing their budgets and existing more or less as financial independents. So, too, had major opposition figures in the Reichstag. But the discovery of diamonds tested such pledges, with Dernburg fearing that Southwest Africa's push to exercise control around diamond matters was a lever by which to force greater autonomy in an unexpectedly short time. Dernburg characterized settlers' call to control diamonds as a potential step on a road to features of self-government: local control over legislation, over administration, and, not least, over budget subsidies from Berlin.[54]

At issue between the lines of conversations about autonomy was who would best keep, manage, and grow the pot of colonial wealth. When the inauguration of Southwest Africa's *Landesrat,* an elected council of notables, took place in 1910, the council focused on how to maximize diamond revenue, and how to make sure it stayed in the colony. Dernburg bristled at both inquiries.[55] It was one thing, he thought, to commit vaguely to increased autonomy in colonial settings. That was the order of the day, and even in the more restrictive German colonial holdings, 1911 would see a major step in this direction when the occupying government in Alsace-Lorraine gave the territory a constitution, complete with a bicameral legislature and universal manhood suffrage.

Africa was not Alsace. Germans in Southwest Africa resented the mother country increasingly in direct proportion to the growth of the diamond industry, which settlers perceived to be unfairly dominated by bankers and technocrats from a distant, indifferent metropole. A new motive and means for greater independence thus emerged in lockstep. Back in Germany, commentators sympathetic to Dernburg grew angry at the notion that Southwest should keep and manage diamond money internally. They stopped talking about Southwest's push for autonomy and employed a different term: treason.[56]

Three months after Dernburg's creation of the Regie, a district court in Southwest Africa declared the Regie illegal. Not long thereafter, the same colonial court refused to recognize one of Dernburg's decrees and acquitted some settlers prosecuted for violations. The district officer for Lüderitz Bay joined in by "bringing the attention" of the local population to the German Colonial Corporation's dubious role in the Forbidden Zone. Again without authorization from Dernburg, the municipality of Lüderitz Bay crafted measures to seek new tax payments from the Regie and the Corporation.[57]

In 1909, August Stauch and other mining dignitaries in Southwest Africa laid out dozens of settler objections in a pamphlet that they sent to the Reichstag. The pamphlet's authors demanded a parliamentary inquiry about reforming Dernburg's management of German colonial diamonds.[58] The Regie's executive board and directors, it was proposed, ought to yield half of their seats to small-producer control, with the addendum that half of the capital should be supplied by small producers. A second proposed change related to transparency. Stauch and his confederates asked that the Regie notify the public of details in its transactions with Antwerp. Every sale price and every inventory needed to emerge from Dernburg's shroud of secrecy.

•   •   •

As with issues of shifting demographics in Southwest Africa, settler offensives against Dernburg fit into a larger debate in which German agrarian lobbyists agitated against industrialism in the mother country. The Hansa Union, an organization founded in 1909 with funding from large banks and electrical firms, sought to fight back by winning over diverse middle-class groups and driving a wedge between land-holding elites and governmental policy. The Hansa Union tried to appeal to small shop-owners and artisans. It championed bureaucratic reforms so that people like Dernburg—whose merit, rather than his birth, formed the basis for his appointment—could take the place of less deserving aristocrats. Dernburg belonged to the Hansa Union, taking a hand in the structuring of its program.[59]

With the relationship between industrial development and state regulation already up for debate, Dernburg's diamonds helped to occasion unprecedented investigations into the possession and concentration of wealth in Imperial Germany. Critics knew that, of the 177 board seats occupied by financiers in Germany's largest industries, six banks controlled 123 seats. This consolidation of class power by a small coterie of bankers was one finding of Rudolf Martin's *Yearbook of Millionaires,* self-published serially between 1912 and 1914. Martin, lately an official of the German state, hoped to expose the precise worth, addresses, and tax obligations of Germany's 500 wealthiest citizens. Unsurprisingly, bankers won a disproportionate share of attention, with Dernburg appearing on page 49 carrying an estimated net worth of 3 million marks, despite his having taken a major pay cut to become a state secretary.

Martin did not have to do much homework to identify Dernburg, who, in addition to keeping his wife and six children in luxury, annually spent the equivalent of his official salary on suits and cigars.[60]

The diamond story in Southwest Africa seemed to prove that German state policies systematically favored large industry and the wealthy at the expense of diverse constituencies. First, despite being located in a place "paid for" by taxpayers and soldiers, Germany's nascent diamond business had clearly fallen under the domination of bankers. Second, Lüderitz Bay was being overrun by diamond-related businesses that seemed insufficiently German in comportment, and to this extent the town was losing the character and potential many pan-Germans, agrarians, and conservatives imagined it to have. Third, German jewelers resented having to traipse across the border to Antwerp to buy "German" diamonds. Fourth, allowing rich Belgian merchants to profit from Germany's colonial minerals in such direct terms inflamed German agrarian, anti-Semitic, and Social Democratic sentiment.[61]

Like most Germans, Southwest's local producers lacked reserves and diversified revenues. To the degree that both would struggle to wait out economic downturns, they saw themselves disadvantaged in an unfree market. Whom the German public would favor in the matter of Dernburg against Southwest was thus predetermined. No one could deny that the assembly of the Regie by Dernburg had come about without democratic discussion of alternatives, to the immediate benefit of elites who were already very wealthy and to the exclusion of people who were poor. Having reviewed the closed records of the *Berliner Handelsgesellschaft*, a company historian later stated that the bank itself had really founded the Regie—of which it functioned as the largest shareholder, and in whose headquarters its board meetings took place.[62]

Meanwhile, back in Southwest Africa, Indigenous workers were witnessing first-hand the ruthlessness of the German diamond cartel Dernburg had created.

CHAPTER 6

LABOR

◆ Looking back on American media coverage of diamonds in the early 1900s, one is struck by the absence of information about Africans, the people whose work powered the industry. In periodicals published from New York City to Los Angeles, the American public heard much about geology and fashion. Sometimes they even read about De Beers. In no case, however, did Americans have to confront details about miners—who they were, where they came from, and how they toiled under duress. Popular accounts not only obfuscated the bloody history behind European colonial diamonds in South and Southwest Africa, but also kept consumers from grasping the implications of their purchases. Americans broadly did not understand that their engagement rings contained conflict diamonds, or perhaps they simply chose not to know.

Consider a brochure printed in 1904 by Loftis Bros., a Chicago-based jeweler. Its pages, while educating potential clients on "interesting facts about diamonds," effectively pretended that no Africans touched the stones so prized in the United States. As if to demonstrate the potential of the passive voice, the brochure does not once refer to humans removing diamonds from the earth. Diamonds "are found." Blue ground "is hauled to the surface." Mines "are worked." Methods "are employed."[1]

When examining the people who extracted Germany's diamond wealth, one has first to understand who did not. A census in 1913 counted 7.6 million Africans living in German East Africa; German Cameroon and Togo had 2.65 million and 1.03 respectively. German Southwest lagged far behind, its African population no higher than 80,000 and perhaps as low as 50,000. The colony's sparsely peopled landscape represented an extreme example of a sub-Saharan colonial trend in which European bureaucrats presumed to find too few willing wage-laborers.[2]

The German military's genocidal campaign in Southwest incalculably exacerbated this deficit, which only worsened after 1908, when August Stauch and the German Colonial Corporation struck it rich. Once Germans made major diamond finds in the colony, they learned about an unintended consequence of what historians called "the peace of the graveyard." The inhumanity and short-sightedness of the colonial regime left diamond businesses without enough labor to activate the mineral wealth they coveted.[3]

Of the Herero and Nama who survived, most of their 20,000 working-age males had already been forced into work on farms and railroads. As a response, German diamond companies targeted women, children, and frail adult males. Dernburg supported this push. Taking another page out of Cecil Rhodes's book, Dernburg imposed further restrictions on Nama and Herero cattle ownership, and he implemented a tax—payable only in cash—on members of Indigenous populations deemed reluctant to labor. Southwest's governor piled on with laws making it impossible for Nama or Herero to hunt game or seek employment outside of the district in which they currently resided. The colonial state might grant exemptions to work in diamond fields; otherwise, the colony's main Indigenous groups could neither exercise freedom of movement to search for food, nor win better terms in their occupation, nor organize as laborers.[4]

This German lawfare succeeded. In late 1908, just 100 Africans worked in the colony's diamond fields. By 1914, an engineer recorded 100 Nama working in a single field, with German clerks classifying each person as "property." Brutal as these arrangements were, however, they did not slake the colonial thirst for labor. Nama and Herero consistently frustrated state attempts to track them via a system of identification tokens intended to function as passports. Reports also spoke of Herero women forgoing pregnancy in the wake of social devastation. Compounding these acts of resistance (from the German perspective), there remained a problem of basic numbers. Even if state authorities forced every remaining Nama and Herero into diamond fields, the companies would eventually need several thousand more people to do low-wage work. By comparison, 52,000 Africans were staffing modernized diamond mines in the South African Rand, and 130,000 were digging gold.[5]

In Southwest, diamonds competed with agriculture not only for spiritual and political control, but also for workers. German farmers' designs, far from abating, were increasing in the wake of diamond finds. Hence, the colonial state expelled nomadic San people from areas desired for ranching and agricultural expansion, and officials forced the San eastward to "reservations." At the same time, in an attempt to placate two constituencies simultaneously, state officials stipulated that San found outside the yet-undefined reservation grounds must be sent to Lüderitz Bay.[6]

As the number of workers needed for diamond extraction continued to rise, Germany looked outside its colony to address a labor shortage, with officials opting to recruit migrant workers from the Cape. To this extent, the Germans paralleled, and competed with, their contemporaries in southern African mining sectors. Indeed, so pronounced was South Africa's own labor shortage that it prompted a series of legislative decrees culminating in the Natives Land Act of 1913, which effectively prohibited Indigenous peoples from owning land outside a few small areas. The act forced many holdouts into a wage-labor existence at mining compounds.[7]

Still, thousands of Africans departed the Cape for employment in German Southwest Africa. With a regional economic depression beginning around 1904, in the aftermath of the Second Anglo-Boer War, unemployment swept through Cape Town and devastated migrants from the eastern Cape who had shunned underground mines to seek higher wages in transport and railways. Food riots erupted throughout the Cape in 1906. More or less contemporaneously, most Nama and Herero violently exited the colonial labor force in German Southwest. Accordingly, a trend emerged in which imported Cape migrants, relatively well paid, worked in Southwest as stevedores, mail carriers, police assistants, and ranch hands.[8]

After 1908, the Cape workers in Southwest overwhelmingly transferred to the diamond sector, and James La Guma figured among them. Aged sixteen, La Guma was a leatherworking apprentice who moved to Lüderitz Bay upon seeing an advertisement touting the prospect of a rural experience denied to him at home. La Guma heard that German diamond "mines" were above ground—as opposed to the pits seen around Kimberley, where a German visitor remarked on the deathly ill appearance of African workers. On this basis, La Guma opted for Southwest, where average daily wages rose from 2.4 marks in 1910 to 4 marks in 1912, easily surpassing wages for equivalent work in South African mines.[9]

Within Southwest, the influx of Cape migrants brought social consequences. A Cape migrant could earn twice as much as did a female

European house servant, and this whiff of pay parity offended some of the more racist colonists. One of Southwest's newspapers, evidently responding to discontentment, felt the need to publish an announcement "from a well-informed source" that African wages on the diamond fields were "absolutely not higher than what was usual." Unconvinced, settlers complained about Cape migrants who returned home after short stints without spending any money in the colony. At one point, Lüderitz Bay's immigration commissioner rejected the admission of Cape workers he deemed too light-skinned. He endorsed a fear that their presence in diamond fields would confuse absolute lines of division between white and black.[10]

Cape laborers had no illusions that German diamond companies would allow them to settle down or ascend a social ladder in Southwest. Like bosses at the Cape and in the Transvaal, the Germans engaged in rank exploitation. People like La Guma saw that contracts signed with German recruiters frequently went unhonored in Southwest. Added to this, German colonial law allowed European employers to levy corporal punishment against Africans who "violated" contracts by contesting, or insisting on, the honoring of certain contractual provisions.[11]

German diamond companies eventually deemed Cape labor too expensive and problematic. This change coincided with an incident in which German soldiers gunned down Cape migrants who tried to stage a strike on a railroad construction project. By 1912, the majority of Cape workers in Southwest returned home to work in domestic mines. As a percentage of overall African workers in the diamond fields of Southwest, Cape migrants dropped to 30 percent.[12]

Authorities explored creative ways to fill the gap, with little success. Kru from Liberia, employed as migrant labor elsewhere in Southwest, seemed far too expensive for diamond work. Amid efforts to import Indian and Chinese "coolies," settlers also voiced fresh concerns about muddying the ethnic clarity supposedly in place throughout the colony. Less controversially, the colonial state tried first to convince a contingent of German miners to relocate from the Ruhr, and then to remove sixteen- and seventeen-year-old orphans from crowded cities to the open climes of Southwest. On the surface, there was some appeal to the former idea, for while a miner of coal in Dortmund would earn 4.8 marks on average per day during this period, a German diamond worker in Southwest earned between 8 and 12 marks. But a prospective raise looked less appealing when accounting for the high cost of colonial living, the heavy expense of ship passage, and the caveat that German workers in Southwest did not enjoy state-guaranteed access to sickness- or accident insurance.[13]

The Germans needed another solution.

· · ·

In 1908, Ovamboland was a region inside the nominal borders of German Southwest Africa but outside the *de facto* control of the German colonial state. Consisting of around 180,000 square kilometers, Ovamboland's southern border lay around 1,000 kilometers north of Lüderitz Bay. It was a consistently warm place where cold weather was unknown; its soil hardly resembled that of Hereroland, let alone of oft-foggy Namaland. Accordingly, Ovamboland's social contact with the latter two areas was minimal. Its economy largely ran on autarkic agrarianism. And its people possessed weaponry thought sufficient to repulse forcible German incursion.[14]

Shortly into the diamond boom, groups of Ovambos made the trek to Southwest's diamond fields, with roughly 200 arriving in January 1909. Thereafter the rate of migration grew steadily, such that, in 1910 alone, 5,000 Ovambos journeyed to the fields. By 1914, 6,300 migrant Ovambos held diamond jobs at a given time, with another 5,400 employed on Southwest's railway construction sites and farms. Because such labor movement dramatically outweighed what was seen in other German colonies, it was logical to ask why and how so many Ovambos made it happen.[15]

Following the genocide of 1904–1907, Ovamboland remained the largest Indigenous population within reach of the German colonial state in Southwest. Ovambo kingdoms, counting between 100,000 and 120,000 subjects, had surplus labor. Added to this, ecological forces had wrecked the Ovambo economy. Locusts and drought devastated Ovambo subsistence crops in 1907, to the extent that by mid-1908 there was massive local famine. Many Ovambo farms shut down, and violence broke out over much of the territory. That upheaval partly explained why, just as Germans came looking for diamond labor in 1908, Ovambo leaders identified 14,500 of their people as ready for migrant work in distant parts of Southwest Africa.[16]

Contemporaneously, domestic political crises ripened. The Cuanhama kingdom, lying in the north of Ovamboland in an area nominally claimed by Portuguese Angola, suffered devastating military defeats. In early 1908, King Kambonde kaMpingana died. A leader in Ondonga, a polity in the south of Ovamboland, he was also a determined resister of the Germans.[17] Ovamboland's upper class and remaining leaders started to look vulnerable, both to nonelites and to each other. The domestic climate grew so tumultuous that Kambonde kaNgula, who had once split control over Ondonga with kaMpingana into eastern and western halves, made a push for unification.

Between 1908 and 1909, Kambonde kaNgula and four other leaders signed protection treaties with Germany. kaNgula asked the Germans to station troops in Ondonga, believing that he could use them as a counterweight to Portuguese threats. This move for "protection," coinciding with a willingness to agree to treaties with the Germans, facilitated mass labor exportation. German negotiators, for their part, thought it unwise to invade Ovamboland but coveted its people to fix the labor deficit in Southwest Africa. Agents for the colonial state would withdraw their troop presence from Ovamboland in 1911, once labor arrangements with Ovambo leadership were in place and the viability of "protection" was assured.[18]

Earnings from diamond labor in Southwest proved welcome news for Ovambo kings. They bolstered their shaky finances by taxing remitted money; hard currency was necessary for an Ovambo economy growing more dependent on foreign trade. When Ovambo workers returned home after a season in the diamond fields, leaders also imported knowledge about what the Germans were up to—technologically, militarily, socially. Finally, Ovambo society availed itself of transregional connections, for by 1909 the area around Lüderitz Bay housed Nama, Herero, Basuto, Xhosa, Malagasy, and even West Indians who either worked in the mines or provided goods and services for the agglomerations of migrant laborers living in a nascent township later deemed the "Native Location."[19]

For their part, regular Ovambos used diamond wages to offset a hunger crisis among their families and bolster their households with foodstuffs purchased from German merchants. With flexibility to negotiate somewhat in view of the short labor supply, some Ovambos even ensured that their wages were paid in silver, rather than in German paper notes they believed likely to depreciate. This concession notwithstanding, German employers deemed the costs of Ovambo employment favorable. Ovambos would theoretically leave German-controlled areas when their contracts ended—thus freeing the Germans from having to deal with a multiethnic society. In addition, Germans paid Ovambos just half the average wage paid to Cape migrants.[20]

That said, asymmetries and misrepresentation characterized most exchanges between Ovambos and Germans in the diamond industry. For one, the colonial state did not properly vet or monitor labor recruiters. Despite German prohibitions on recruiting north of the Red Line (a sanitary cordon designed to prevent the influx of veterinary diseases from Ovamboland into the rest of Southwest Africa), enterprising souls flouted the system. The only real means of policing recruitment was for rival recruiters to tattle, as when a copper mining firm complained about a diamond agent pushing their man out of a particular village. A similar sentiment animated miners around Lüderitz Bay, who beseeched the German government at Windhoek to freeze out farmers from hiring people in Ovamboland. Some Ovambos astutely weaponized this dysfunction. When signing a contract to go mine diamonds, they falsified their names and home addresses with the goal of avoiding an employer's legal enforcement of the contract.[21]

Contracts signed by Ovambos usually did not feature precise language and clear terms—for example, assigning a worker a six-month stint in the south before they returned north. Instead, recruiters deliberately left undefined a number of crucial aspects, including just who a given Ovambo's employer was, whether his wages were fixed, and what the parameters of "work" were. This vagueness allowed for Ovambos to sign up thinking they were going to work at Tsumeb—a copper mine desirable for being closer to Ovamboland—only to find out their real destination was a diamond field outside Lüderitz Bay. German diamond recruiters also dangled signing bonus incentives they had no intention of honoring, on the assumption that the rewards outweighed the risks of fines from the colonial state. Hardly any German officials remained in or near Ovamboland to monitor the negotiations.[22]

Southwest's influx of Ovambo labor also functioned as a wage depressant. Over time, an increasingly higher disparity obtained between Ovambo and Cape-migrant pay. True, the German miners offered slightly higher wages to Ovambos who signed on for longer-term contracts. But to agree to these durations meant missing the harvest in Ovamboland, thus further eroding the economic and moral fabric of Ovambo society. A longer contract term also limited opportunities for marriage, the gathering of money for which was often a motive behind migrant work.[23]

Ovambos who returned home after six-month stints in the diamond fields generally brought back pittances relative to anticipated earnings. Some workers opened savings accounts in a Lüderitz Bay bank, only to find out months later that they had much less money than they expected. Predatory salesmen lurked in the colony, offering Ovambos baubles and costly goods alongside agents around the diamond fields who pushed alcohol sales and clothing at wild markups. A Finnish missionary reported that most Ovambo households, desperately awaiting the return of working males, had "nothing" to show from diamonds despite months of familial deprivation and undermanned harvests. As a result, diamond companies struggled to re-sign Ovambos who had finished their contracts and returned home for harvest season.[24]

Those were the workers lucky enough to survive the brutal conditions facing Ovambos on their southward journey from Ovamboland to the diamond fields. The first leg involved a two-week march of 400–500 kilometers on foot, after which Ovambos reached the nearest railroad. Then they were herded into suffocating compartments, where they had to reckon with harrowing spates of robberies along their way to Swakopmund, Germany's second colonial harbor.[25] The final leg involved travel on crowded ships from Swakopmund to Lüderitz Bay.

Upon arrival in the Forbidden Zone, some Ovambos, deprived of proper lodgings and forced to sleep on sand dunes, froze to death during the cold, windy nights. Often wearing only a breechcloth and kneepads as clothes, Ovambos had to make do with little more than a paper-thin sheet for bedding. Authorities in Lüderitz Bay cruelly denied the new arrivals permission to build fires for warmth. Ordinances also banned the creation of salubrious accommodations for the workers—houses with windows, doors, and wooden floors.[26]

With few exceptions, Ovambos toiled at the diamond fields for seven days a week. Forced to inch up on their hands and knees like swimmers, they dug through the sand haphazardly, placing stones they found in tin cans hung around their necks. Workers typically needed to wear goggles to see beyond the glare and keep the wind from blowing particles into their eyes. In some cases, masks were necessary to prevent choking on dust. Over time, this disarray gradually gave way to a more "modern" process with machines and production lines. Old-fashioned disease ran rampant throughout the years following 1908. Overworked Ovambos, given little to eat but rice, lacked proper nutrition and overwhelmingly suffered from scurvy. Added to this were pneumonia, enteritis, smallpox,

Unidentified African workers dig for diamonds outside Lüderitz Bay. 1908.

and tuberculosis—the latter, tellingly, more or less absent from areas in Southwest that were unconnected to diamonds. "One heard a lot of coughing," noted a pithy German visitor.[27]

A major vector for illness was the water supply. Even by the austere standards of Southwest Africa, Ovambos in diamond fields lacked adequate hydration. On many scorching desert days that left everyone sweating and struggling to quench their thirst, German employers allocated Ovambos between two and a half and five liters a day: a quantity that represented a small fraction of what European and Cape coworkers received, at twenty-five and ten liters respectively. Worse still, German employers did not allow Ovambos to access imported water or desalinated water, instead forcing Ovambos to drink the water used for pack animals. This inferior liquid came from local wells whose brackish contents included copious salt. It also contained between 8,165 mg and 37,630 mg of chlorine per liter. Even though scientists advised Europeans in Southwest to view 2,000 mg of chlorine per liter as a theoretical upper limit for human safety, the management of German diamond fields still allotted the dirty water to Ovambos. Small wonder that the workers consistently registered complaints about water quality, as well as persistent stomach pains and diarrhea.[28]

When Ovambos felt it necessary to use the bathroom, they did so in an iron pot close by, with no doors or covering so as to let German overseers detect potential smuggling. This was yet another indignity, but not the greatest. That came at the end of the day—or to be more precise, just before the next morning—when the exhausted workers, their immune systems compromised, returned to sleep in horribly overcrowded blocks, without any isolation for the sick. Hundreds of men climbed into several rows of concrete compartments, each one a horizontal box. The most generous of these amounted to the size, as the remaining architecture confirms, of a telephone booth. Others were even smaller: less than three by three by four feet, in the case of Stauch's company.[29]

Workers routinely faced another challenge: corporal punishment. Among migrant contingents interviewed in Ovamboland by an army captain, nearly all expressed shock about the frequency of violence near Lüderitz Bay. Behind each team of Ovambos in the fields stood European overseers, employed by the German company responsible for the area at a rate of roughly one European to a dozen Africans. An overseer brandished a whip and used it if people did not work "quickly." An overseer also deployed an anti-smuggling toolkit: enemas to flush out any swallowed stones, and gags to make sure workers did not insert stones in their teeth. The gag was to remain in place until every worker went to sleep in a nearby compound and had his entire body inspected by company officials.[30]

In 1911, a German government publication recorded an extraordinary prevalence of sickness among Ovambos in the diamond fields. An ordinance later that year sought to curtail excesses, requiring, among other things, that a doctor be stationed at fields with more than 200 workers. "The most precious resource in our colonies," admonished one physician, "is not diamonds [. . .] but the human." Ovambos may have been deemed "too valuable" to treat poorly, but most employers did so. In 1913, a government doctor—the second of exactly two posted to the Forbidden Zone—delivered another caustic report. Employers had changed nothing, and Ovambos continued to enjoy none of the benefits accorded their white counterparts: medical care, clean water, decent lodging, and medicine.[31]

Many Ovambo wives never again heard from husbands who went to work in the Zone. While no one today knows for sure what became of the dead, it is likely that firms buried corpses in mass graves several kilometers outside Lüderitz Bay—as the German military had done with countless Nama "resisters." Published statistics do not address the point reliably, and there is evidence that officials sought to suppress the compilation of such information. In any event, it would be difficult to learn more because of nondisclosure agreements put into effect by diamond

Ovambos work in a diamond field under the supervision of a German foreman on horseback.

companies. In the small print of contracts signed by fieldworkers—whether European or African—lurked riders prohibiting not only the reporting of information about the company's practices to third parties, but also any assistance with such reporting.[32]

When German dignitaries arranged visits to diamond fields, they saw a façade of progress, including colorfully painted colonial architecture. But the African workers whose labor underwrote it all were dying in droves. It was reported that 10 percent of the African workforce at Kolmanskop, one of the largest diamond fields, perished in a single year. Over a similar period, a separate government source recorded that, out of 2,200 Ovambo diamond workers, 331 did not survive.[33]

In fact, the true rates of mortality in Southwest were often worse. According to one confidential account, 45 percent of the African workers at the Kolmanskop field died in a single year. Over a similar span, the harsh conditions of the Phoenix Diamond Society claimed eighteen of two dozen employees. To put these death rates into perspective, consider that during the Second Anglo-Boer War, an annual civilian death rate of 12 percent in internment camps induced Lloyd George to suspect "a policy of extermination" on the part of administrators. Consider, too, that over nearly three years of concentration camp operations in Southwest, 45 percent of prisoners died.[34]

The pace of diamond deaths belied claims by German colonial propagandists that African workers "know their rights [. . .] very well." Likewise, the deaths contradicted the German government's public announcements of happy results in recruitment of labor. Oskar Hintrager, the colony's deputy governor, privately acknowledged that something needed to be done about the "truly high" mortality rates in the diamond fields. Back in Windhoek, the capital of Southwest Africa, suspicious officials weighed an intervention against diamond companies' labor abuses. The colonial state considered forcing the firings of abusive foremen and repeat offenders. The colonial state also lodged complaints about "diamond sorters" who were "continually striking the natives." Looming in the background was a justified fear that Ovambos returning home would instill a hatred for German rule, which had not yet fully reached Ovamboland.[35]

In principle, German colonial labor laws should have forced employers to provide Ovambo workers with some guarantees: for instance, the freedom to choose one's workplace; to have adequate shelter against the elements; and to have a sufficient supply of "African" food. Theoretically, too, the colonial state's intervention should have stood at the head of a reform movement led by people like Dernburg. In 1912, for example, the Reichstag passed a resolution against the imposition of forced labor in its colonies.[36]

The reality looked otherwise. None of the racism, cruelty, and ruthlessness contributing to genocide in Southwest Africa had vanished by the time the colony's mineral wealth appeared. These same forces contributed to mass death in the diamond fields, where treatment of labor proved as irrational as had the attempted extermination of Nama and Herero. The final days of genocide in the colony bled into the early days of the diamond boom. Thus, when German diamond companies awarded mining foremen "a certain right to punish" Ovambos so that discipline could "be upheld," they displayed a continuity with the manorial sentiment prevailing among German farmers and ranchers before 1904: the kind that designated Africans as all-but-formal slaves. As if to clinch the point, the German diamond companies stuffed their roster with members of the colonial army.[37] Reservists and retired lieutenants who had carried out genocide now supervised Ovambos looking for precious stones in "peacetime."

The bulk of reporting about employer abuses would necessarily have to come from Ovambo workers as witnesses. Yet, Ovambos encountered arbitrary beatings from sergeants at police stations when attempting to lodge complaints. Moreover, according to the longstanding racist policy of Southwest, courts did not allow African witnesses to take an oath. That practice effectively discounted African witnesses' statements. As a result, while Ovambos did sometimes speak with a magistrate, they seldom received credence in trials, thus allowing for a conspiracy of silence on the part of European employers and employees. Workers who witnessed also had to fear reprisals: sacking, corporal punishment, and diamond companies' false statements that the worker had "instigated" riots. In some cases, related fears led to collaboration in which workers offered highly improbable statements to assist a particular company's defense, with the company tacitly assuming that African witnesses in its favor would be given a credence denied to any antagonists.[38]

Because the site in which laborers worked was the Forbidden Zone, independent investigators found it difficult to ascertain the veracity of allegations. Defendants could easily dismiss the rare European who provided credible incriminating information as being "addicted to gossip." The law courts, or so confided the chief magistrate at Lüderitz Bay, consequently became "utterly useless" to check abuse. Only occasionally did a plaintiff obtain a conviction or a monetary fine. More broadly, some of Southwest's residents refused to accept the authority of local courts or officials when addressing African-European confrontations. Amid this disobedience, fines levied on the convicted "meant very little and did nothing," according to private correspondence of the governor.[39]

That is not to say no Africans fought back. Years into the diamond boom, German statistics estimated that Southwest desired about twice as many Ovambo laborers as it was taking in yearly. This gap owed partly to many Ovambos' refusal to return to the diamond fields, a form of passive resistance that manifestly contributed to employers' anxiety about German dependence on Ovamboland. It is likely that recruitment pressures induced employers, by 1914, to concede an unpaid day off for workers.[40]

Signs of direct resistance also appeared. In 1912, fifty Ovambos decamped from the fields to Lüderitz Bay to demand an inquest into the death of a colleague, a man whose exposed, bloodied chest a diamond company's staff doctor had diagnosed as a heart attack.[41] Then there were cases like that of Juvera, an Ovambo working for August Stauch's Koloniale Bergbaugesellschaft (Colonial Mining Company). In April 1911, Walter Vogel, a German overseer, alleged Juvera was rinsing diamonds too slowly and struck him on the shoulder with a cudgel. Juvera reported this abuse to a foreman, identifying it as part of a pattern in which Vogel beat Ovambo employees. Vogel retaliated the next day by hitting Juvera again, this time with special ferocity.

When a bloodied Juvera tried to defend himself, other German sorters joined Vogel to torture him. Using wooden planks, the Germans split open Juvera's left arm and delivered six blows to his head that penetrated to his skullcap. After spending six weeks in a tent, unable to work, Juvera filed a complaint with police. A judge convicted Vogel and his accomplices. But the sentence was appallingly light, mandating six months' imprisonment for Vogel and small fines for his accomplices. Even such nominally successful prosecutions resulted in appeals from diamond companies, which delayed the implementation of undesirable verdicts. Most judges, admitted an official, did "not know the conditions on the diamond fields, nay, perhaps had never seen one," on account of the exclusivity of the Forbidden Zone.[42]

A final force behind the perpetuation of worker abuse was public opinion, or lack thereof. Whereas the consumption of diamond wealth and potential colonial expansion sites remained hot topics, no significant international or metropolitan constituency addressed violence and abuses in the German diamond fields. As consumers, the American public seemed aloof, with nary a newspaper article on diamonds or fashionable rings talking about the violence that accompanied the extraction of glittering stones in Africa. The absence of American concern looms all the larger when thinking of the broad international concern voiced against King Leopold II's rule in the Congo. While an array of brilliant polemicists like Mark Twain and E. D. Morel spread the word about "red rubber," no literary talent of the day took up the theme of "red diamonds."

If newspaper pages and Reichstag debates are indicative, the German public also did not find conditions among colonial diamond laborers scandalous. Abuse of African workers hardly represented an exception to the rule in Southwest, where German farmers held seigneurial privileges and where violence was an everyday matter. Still, it is striking that no uproar emerged over Ovambo deaths, because it was certainly possible for contemporary Germans in the know to raise concerns. Social Democrats, the Catholic Center, and Bernhard Dernburg had all spoken out during the military campaign in Southwest, whether to protest General Lothar von Trotha's policy of extermination or to curb the pace of death in concentration camps.[43]

Apathy may be explained by Germans' lack of interest in purchasing diamonds, or else the secrecy surrounding the conditions of workers in Southwest Africa's Forbidden Zone. The flow of information from the Zone was highly restricted, and the discreetness of the German Colonial Corporation and German banks behind miners did not make for as flamboyant a villain as Leopold II. However, when scanning newspapers in the years between 1908 and 1914, one *does* find that colonial diamond scandal flourished in Germany—but only in relation to the distribution of material gains from sales.

●   ◆   ◆

When questioned by colonial officials about worker abuse in diamond fields, the German Colonial Corporation insisted on its autonomy within the Forbidden Zone, citing a contractual arrangement approved by Dernburg and the government in Berlin. While Germany did not fully concede this autonomy, litigation was pending and Dernburg did not want to antagonize the Corporation for fear of compromising the diamond industry or colonial investment from big banks. In the interim, the Corporation mostly shielded diamond companies from prosecution—whether companies its shareholders controlled or companies from whom the Corporation received rents. One such moment occurred when a company tied to the Corporation refused to allow a police inspector from Lüderitz Bay to examine an Ovambo worker's corpse. Here and in numerous other letters, top German officials in Berlin ordered the district commissioner and local judges to back off.[44]

The Corporation could offer a powerful argument when dealing with state officials investigating labor abuse: the diamond companies saved the German state the expense of governance. The companies helped to finance local police within their mining concessions. They fed, housed, and transported employees while building new infrastructure to assist in the extraction and processing of diamonds.[45] In the end, the almost total absence of official intervention in the lives of the diamond workers meant healthy savings for Berlin.

Dernburg and other German officials had not yet made up their minds regarding the parameters of the colonial state in Southwest Africa. It was unclear to what extent the colony should resemble its metropolitan companion in "state" matters such as policing, taxation, and schooling. To be sure, colonial bureaucrats deepened their reach into the personal lives of Africans in the early 1900s, out of what one historian calls a "madness for control" and "power fantasies" spurred by Indigenous people's frustrations of German plans. Nonetheless, the state did not introduce its first professional police force until 1907.[46]

In this context, the Germans struggled to arrive at regulations concerning life in the Forbidden Zone—especially because the Corporation still claimed autonomy on the basis of governing rights acquired from Adolf Lüderitz. Perhaps colonial state officials were responsible for monitoring wages, working hours, and safety standards for workers in the diamond fields; or perhaps that task should fall to the companies. No one yet knew. In an uneven archipelago of authority that saw towns, military barracks, and police stations dot the landscape but leave functionally "blank" spaces in between, diamond fields became another place where the colonial state was either not present, or not present at particular moments. The fields demonstrated, to borrow from Jeffrey Herbst, the "schizophrenic nature of colonial power in Africa."[47]

The German Colonial Corporation mirrored the German colonial state in that they sought to govern selectively, in accordance with whatever calculation appeared most economical. This dynamic had its parallel in the German domestic attitudes toward cartels. Consider the following early definition of cartels, only with "sovereignty" and "governance" as the object of the agreement between contracting parties, instead of a commodity like coal: "agreements made between producers in a particular line of production, with the object of eliminating to some extent unrestricted competition among themselves, and of regulating output more or less so as to adjust it at any rate approximately to demand; cartels aim specifically at avoiding overproduction."[48] "Overproducing" colonial governance proved a concern for Germany. In Southwest Africa, the colonial state and the Corporation wanted to ensure that they did not ruin *each other* with competition so that neither one could successfully carry out its goal of enriching itself.

The definitive era of cartels was the era of New Imperialism, chartered companies, indirect rule, and sovereignties split by contractual agreement, rather than purely by custom. Colonial rivals in Africa pooled governance, whether public, private, or in-between, while trying to limit ruinous competition. Hence, for years after 1908, the Corporation and companies under its umbrella asserted that investigations of diamond labor abuses would violate the Corporation's governing rights and activity. In 1912, for instance, the head of the Southwest African Mining Chamber, Emil Kreplin—a Hanseatic army veteran who doubled as the mayor of the town of Lüderitz Bay, a major shareholder in a diamond mining operation under the Corporation, and the director of the Kolmanskop mining company—concluded that "everything else" but a foreman's murder of an employee should fall outside the state's regulatory purview in the Forbidden Zone.[49]

This situation, as a colonial governor later put it, was "bad." But one would do better to help it "fade away," rather than to challenge it head-on. Bernhard Dernburg, the colonial secretary, determined that the solution was to negotiate a price at which to pay the Corporation to transfer its residual governing rights. Dernburg had to preside over this process without disturbing the confidence of domestic German investors that their "rights," even if not so extreme as the Corporation's, would never meet with confiscation. This matter was perceived as an issue of the rule of law, violations of which risked undermining Germany's prestige before the world and at home. Nor was it possible to forget that the very presence of German authority in Southwest Africa owed to the paper documents forged by Adolf Lüderitz in the 1880s. The colonial state periodically needed to recognize these documents as sacrosanct in order to justify their actions vis-à-vis Indigenous peoples. But the Corporation's claims also derived from these documents, putting a lot of weight on a shaky foundation.[50]

Aware that the government at last wanted to rid itself of the embarrassment of disputed colonial sovereignty, the Corporation pushed Dernburg for generous financial terms in negotiations. For Dernburg, the risks attending his efforts were considerable. First, suppose the colonial state replaced the Corporation and injected more police and oversight of labor into the Forbidden Zone. Such projects would bring scores of new people to fields laden with easily picked diamonds, likely triggering a rise in smuggling and creating headwinds for diamond prices. Second, suppose the colonial state began to insist on the enforcement of labor-law provisions against the claims of large diamond miners. This course might trigger a decline in production or a capital flight from Southwest Africa—if only as a bargaining tactic on the part of business. Either eventuality might deprive the cash-strapped colonial state of revenue that had begun to turn colonial red ink into black.[51] Finally, there was the specter of De Beers. To pierce the autonomy of the Corporation and the secrecy of diamond production might offer De Beers a new path through which to spy on German competition and conduct sabotage.

Dernburg found it difficult to suppress information about his negotiations with the Corporation. The German public took extraordinary interest in Southwest Africa, not least because Dernburg had worked to publicize colonial engagement through heavily reported trips to the colonies during his tenure. One journalist, reviewing secondary works, complained of an "increasingly mountainous literature" on diamonds. Media entrepreneurs also proved eager to capitalize on the public's growing appetite for information about colonial finances and businesses.[52]

Too much scrutiny of money-making in the colonies would heighten domestic struggles over the relationship between state and capitalism. Conflict was already materializing in heated debate over tax reform, which in turn was touching on tricky issues of where parliament's authority began and ended. The more Dernburg could keep himself and the Corporation out of such reckonings, the better.

CHAPTER 7

STOCKS

In early 1908 shares of German colonial companies figured among the least desired assets in Europe. German colonial stocks, unlike their successful British counterparts, never won recognition from brokerages as "investment grade." Instead, they figured as obscure objects of speculation. Prior to 1908, only two brokerages in Berlin bothered to deal in these products, whose cumbersome names— *Kolonialgesellschaftsanteile* and *Kolonialwerte*—would never have lasted if they traded regularly. By contrast, South African mining shares circulated frequently in Germany. German traders even nicknamed South African shares "Kaffirs," in a nod to the then-common racial epithet.[1]

Public demand for German colonial equities proved tepid throughout the inaugural decades of the country's overseas empire. A thin, elite stratum complained about holding onto colonial shares out of patriotic sacrifice, in a dynamic familiar to observers of French, Russian, and even British imperialisms. Owing to legal peculiarities, German colonial companies did not have to register in the usual way and offered potential stockholders less transparency than did most domestic businesses. Financial journalists therefore encouraged readers to remain filled with mistrust concerning colonial promotions. Undeterred, German officials sought to permit sales of colonial shares in increments as low as 100 marks—a level ten times lower than was typical. When these efforts, too, failed to attract investors, what little activity there was in colonial shares took place between private German banks.[2]

By the 1890s, as German state subsidies began to flow to the colonies, the outlook remained grim. In a single down year, thirty German colonial companies entered liquidation, costing many investors their savings. Those who held out also faced strain. Without large capital reserves, they could not afford to wait for long-term appreciation of risky, high-priced colonial shares or the sporadic and unpredictably sized dividends such shares paid. Many Germans desired dividends paid on time and at regular intervals, in the same manner as a state-issued bond provided.[3]

Germany's stock exchanges bustled in the years surrounding 1908. Per capita, domestic stock listings surpassed those seen in the United States and in France. German colonial stocks, not German stocks, were the problem. Unlike with normal public companies (a legally distinct classification known as *Aktiengesellschaften*), the duty of regulating shares in German colonial companies fell to Bernhard Dernburg's fledgling German Colonial Office—not to seasoned, better-resourced bureaucrats. The Colonial Office did very little regulating, so anyone buying or issuing a German colonial share operated under looser supervision than applied to other German shares.[4]

The risks of this looseness were not fully apparent as 1908 began. One reason was that domestic financial journals quoted share prices for colonial stocks in more or less the same way as they did for conventionally regulated ones. A second reason was that German colonial share certificates passed through familiar places. The shares did not trade *on* government-sanctioned stock exchanges in Berlin, Hamburg, Frankfurt, Dresden, Breslau, Magdeburg, and a dozen other cities. But, once the shares became popular, they traded *around* these exchanges, typically on the curb outside.[5]

Individual Germans technically could not purchase colonial shares directly but needed to go through licensed brokers. These intermediaries alone could legally quote sales prices. Yet, by law such intermediaries also remained free, not only from having to honor advertised prices at the moment of transfer, but from needing to quote prices at all before executing a trade. In an added risk to consumers, the bid (buy) and the ask (sell) prices for a German colonial share varied considerably more than for traditional stocks. One private bank quoted a spread of 13 percentage points for B-shares of the South Cameroon Company.[6]

Prices accessible to the public via newspapers appeared to provide a mechanism to combat high, or hidden, transaction costs. But newspapers proved of limited meaning when it came to actual colonial share purchases. Most sales of the shares occurred in bulk batches negotiated among banks owning large share blocks, creating a circumstance ripe for manipulation and self-interested arbitrage. Powerful financial institutions controlled the big colonial companies, as well as the big blocks of shares;

accordingly, they controlled access to most shares by potential investors. In this climate, prices quoted in daily newspapers did not prove reliable, let alone comprehensive. Besides, because of a law prohibiting public listings of colonial share prices in other fora than government organs, newspapers minimized their legal exposure by telling readers only about big winners or losers. Rather than receiving accurate information about a long list of stocks, a potential retail investor typically got a glimpse into a few standouts as if they represented the entire colonial sector.[7]

Brokers dealing with German colonial shares worked in divisions housed separately from the rest of banks' trading. Such makeshift operations came outfitted with names like "department for stock shares without an exchange notation." The paperwork bearing these names included confusing disclaimers about lack of liability. Hence, should colonial trading divisions become more numerous, legal loopholes would allow more opportunities for confusion and deception—on the part both of established brokers and of lesser-known ones with strange business descriptions.[8]

Potential investors living in German colonies faced their own difficulties. No officially licensed stock exchange existed in Southwest Africa; as a result, share buyers in the colony needed to secure physical share certificates from a stock exchange in Germany. To do so, colonists had to go through a notarial process that, in a place where little surplus capital existed, frequently proved cost-prohibitive. Furthermore, would-be colonial stockholders needed to have share certificates sent to them via insured postal delivery from Germany, in another considerable expense. Assuming a settler could pay these costs, their stock transactions had to run through an unregulated, oft-unethical intermediary—usually an insurance agent who offered to facilitate share deliveries. One such figure was Friedrich Knacke, a Lüderitz Bay–based jack-of-all-trades whose other jobs included running boat tours to the diamond fields and selling poorly cut South African diamonds he falsely advertised as "local."[9]

Dangers attending colonial investment tied into still other points of legal confusion. Would the German state, to cite one frequently asked question, tax its citizens' colonial share gains at the same rate as it did their domestic ones? And how would the German state treat stock holdings by Southwest African settlers, in whose colony taxes on European wealth were a novelty in 1908? In 1907, as Germany's federal government mulled how to tax colonial profits and how to apportion colonial debts, shares in the German Colonial Corporation for Southwest Africa dropped 10 percent in the few days surrounding such debates. Amid this volatility, one must note, Germany was already reorganizing stock-market accounting. Conservatives, in particular, had introduced legislation to raise taxes on stock transactions, with the idea that such a levy would reduce the need for potential taxes on inheritances and liquor. And the latter taxes drew inveterate opposition from the Agrarian League, the lobbying arm of East Elbian landholding elites.[10]

Colonial uncertainty did not end with German tax policy but extended to the commercial sphere. Literally, it proved difficult to weigh colonial commodities, for just as Germany put off standardization of laws between its colonies, so Germany delayed introducing standardized weights and measures inside the colonies. How uncertain units of measure complicated transactions became obvious in 1905, when marines arriving in Southwest Africa discovered that the local business community would not accept the five-mark German coins marines carried. A decree, though not widely publicized, soon obviated this particular embarrassment, but it did not include all colonies, nor obligate colonial merchants to quote prices in marks. Thus, some German customs officials kept taking English pounds sterling as currency and weighing in the Arabic *frasila*. Subsequent legislation also failed to address paper marks, which circulated widely despite not being legal tender. Entering 1908, creditors in Southwest did not have to accept paper money as payment for debts—and so compounded people's doubts about colonial transaction safety.[11]

Through the years, particular unease surrounded German colonial mining shares, which frightened Germans who had recently lost hundreds of millions of marks betting on stocks for miners in the Congo and South Africa. Many Germans regarded London, the world's leading market in mining stocks, as a place swamped with shell games, unscrupulous promotion, and inadequate regulation. If even the residents of a long-standing colonizing metropole remained amateurs when it came to colonial securities, then one could hardly expect different behavior from the Germans.[12]

◆   ◆   ◆

From the moment gates and checkpoints began to go up around Southwest's Forbidden Zone, a mania set in around the stock exchange in Berlin, then the world's third-largest equity trading site behind New York and London. In the case of the German Colonial Corporation, shares experienced a meteoric rise. The Corporation, largely unknown to the public in early 1908, became Germany's most coveted stock in the summer of 1909. Prior to August Stauch's diamond strikes, the Corporation's shares traded just under par. Post-discovery, and without any public statements yet as to Dernburg's policies, these same shares spiked to a 410 percent premium relative to face value. In the days following Dernburg's first speech to the Reichstag, diamonds climbed to 500 percent.[13]

To say the rise continued would be a gross understatement. By mid-1909, with Dernburg enforcing the Forbidden Zone and the Regie, traders drove up the Corporation's share price to 2,020 percent. This ascent looked astonishing when viewed in terms of the Corporation's market capitalization. Before diamond discovery, it stood at 2 million marks; afterward, it quickly reached 40 million marks.[14] At face value, a share of the Corporation still carried the price of 1,000 marks. But each share was now "worth" 20,200 marks on the open market.

As the Corporation began hunting for a newer, more prestigious headquarters in Berlin, experts set a price target of 30,000 marks per share, their optimism owing to correspondents who had reported large-scale projections for the monetization of Southwest's diamonds. One insider spoke of the Corporation controlling 30 million pounds sterling in diamond wealth. That was the equivalent of 600 million German marks, or about 1.2 times De Beers' market capitalization. A second projection delivered to the Rothschilds pegged the Corporation's diamond wealth at one billion marks. A third projection—confidentially distributed to the directors of the Colonial Corporation—came from an agent who, after inspecting some fields, pronounced himself "gobsmacked" and assured his superiors they could "comfortably expect billions" in marks from the "richness that lies around here." To put such numbers into proper relief, consider that the notorious national debts of the German Empire, amassed since the 1870s, amounted to 4 billion marks at this time.[15]

Spectacular projections would buoy not just the Corporation but other Southwest African diamond producers, two of which saw their share prices rise to double and triple face value in 1908, only to soar higher in 1909. Ancillary bounces took place in colonial companies generally. The South African Territories Ltd., a company that held lands at the extreme eastern reaches of Southwest where no diamonds existed, surged from 500 marks per share to 2,000. Shares of the South

West Africa Company, which had no business model, went public at 196 percent of face value and promptly earned consideration for listing on the Berlin stock exchange.[16]

Skeptics cautioned that this upward trend owed partly to scores of English buys, with De Beers in the lead. In fact, De Beers sold the few shares it owned in the Corporation early in the euphoria. The overwhelming majority of buyers for German colonial mining shares came from within the German Empire.[17] And one driver of their commitment was superb dividends.

Prior to the diamond boom, arguably the hottest stock in Germany was that of the Gelsenkirchen coal firm. It paid an 11 percent dividend, meaning that each Gelsenkirchen share brought its owner an extra payout corresponding to roughly 11 percent of the share price—say, 110 marks for each thousand-mark share. Compare that dividend to those handed out by the Koloniale Bergbaugesellschaft, a Southwest African diamond miner in which Stauch and his proxies held a majority stake. The Bergbaugesellschaft paid shareholders dividends of 1,300 percent in 1909, 2,400 percent in 1910, 2,500 percent in 1911, and 3,800 percent in 1912.[18] For each thousand-mark share investors in this company owned, they received 3,800 extra marks in 1912.

This process explained how a former frontier railroad worker like Stauch became a multimillionaire. Buoyed by dividends, Stauch and his Bergbaugesellschaft's major stakeholders diversified into other assets around Lüderitz Bay: a new, gas-engine-powered electric service and a colonial stock brokerage. In addition, this same company's directors undertook expensive improvement projects: first, to build private railroads connecting mining fields and delivering mail to workers; second, to connect their diamond fields via a network of private telegraph lines eventually spanning the entire Forbidden Zone. So spectacular was Stauch's rise that in 1913, when his company paid out 2,500 percent in dividends rather than 3,800 percent, the *Wall Street Journal* called it "the greatest cut in dividends ever known."[19]

The salient point here was that diamond company dividends were a singular phenomenon in Imperial German financial history. They dwarfed not just those offered by typical colonial companies, but also those offered by Germany's more established and profitable businesses. A bonus was that the German state did not tax stock dividends, even as it heavily taxed basic consumer good purchases made by workers.[20]

Extravagant colonial dividends won attention from more than a dozen German banks, which moved to develop "colonial" trading desks in response to surging retail interest. The ranks included luminaries such as the Cologne-based A. Schaaffhausen, Elberfeld's Bergisch-Märkische Bank, Mannheim's Rheinische Creditbank, and Wuppertal's staid Bankhaus von der Heydt-Kersten und Söhne. With these institutions eager to supply people, trading in German diamond shares remained so heavy through 1909 that it crowded out other potential market transactions. For a time, colonial shares became the most significant force on the domestic stock market.[21]

To explain the frenzy was difficult. When it began, Social Democrats predicted an imminent "cold shower." A "swarm of speculators," they warned, was "exploiting new finds" by filling public fora with "happy noise," showing investors modest returns, and getting marks to buy in just before pros cashed out. While specialists raced to attend new university courses on "colonial shares," the left-liberal *Frankfurter Zeitung* and conservative *Berliner Lokal-Anzeiger* both urged restraint.[22] After all, Germany's speculators did not yet have a firm sense of Southwest's diamond business.

All the objections were sound, but the diamond stock bubble grew further, by a factor of four, easily outstretching levels that skeptics found dubious. With the advantage of hindsight, two factors stand out as explanations. Partly, share prices in German diamond companies soared on the expectation of windfall profits and dividends. Partly, too, the rise was a product of marketing. Dernburg did his part with favorably curated statistics, giving lectures that touted stock gains and encouraging favorable newspaper coverage. Inside Germany, financial papers created supplements and editorial desks devoted solely to colonial shares, and they ran stories uncritically peddling German colonial stock opportunities. Mutualistic relationships developed between some papers' low-paid journalists and stock professionals who functioned as their sources, often leading to what one would now deem insider trading. Less venally, German papers stoked national pride, noting that the German diamond industry, though in infancy, claimed a significant role in the world.[23]

A herd mentality was clearly at work in share prices' upward movement, evoking classic bubbles: John Law's Mississippi Scheme, Britain's South Sea Company, and the foundation era attending German unification. When reports of colonial diamond discoveries hit in mid-1908,

German stock exchanges were awash in money. Bankers enjoyed relatively low interest rates and near-record access to the German Central Bank's discount window. And investor confidence was spiking because of favorable crop reports from Germany and the United States, along with a reduced fear of war in the Balkans.[24]

The German federal government eased buying requirements on stock in the summer of 1908, re-legalizing the long-closed futures market and making it easier for average people to speculate. Precisely as the government relaxed its rules, and precisely as coal and potash companies signaled disappointing earnings prospects, the nascent colonial diamond sector appeared as an attractive alternative. Heavy buying of colonial shares subsequently occurred on the strength of speculators who were agnostic about diamonds but happy to ride market momentum. A diamond company's financials did not necessarily induce people to buy in; likewise, supply-and-demand theory explained spikes in share prices less than did greed or a fear of missing out.[25]

In December 1908, an individual speculator scraped together some money to buy a share of a newly formed diamond company. Weeks later, he received an offer of 40,000 marks for his share. A source in Berlin invested 50,000 marks and walked away with 500,000 in three months' time. These success stories enticed habitual risk-takers from elite circles. But they worked on traditionally risk-averse individuals, too. Among the latter were Junkers, such as the owner of a large estate in Mecklenburg. Other buyers swapped their humdrum holdings in Rhineland mining firms for shares of suddenly glamorous diamond companies. Even civil service officials and military officers figured prominently among the crowd.[26]

The geographical scope of this activity was wide, with undersized towns in the Vogtland, for example, seeing local brokers push shares with ease. Consequently, the diamond share bubble grew so big in 1909 that observers joked about schoolchildren being the only members of German society uninvolved. Widows, teachers, and diverse members of society's lower strata joined up—often in no position to sustain a loss on high-risk bets, but nonetheless chasing higher returns on their capital at a time when rises in living costs were outpacing wage growth and interest payments on (struggling) state bonds.[27]

Settlers in Southwest also entered the arena, hoping for quick gains that they could reinvest into farming or equipment to mine. Fueling their hope was the Deutsche Afrika-Bank—the only retail bank branch in Lüderitz Bay and the sole bank licensed to take diamond deposits before their transfer out of town. The Deutsche Afrika-Bank sponsored a column of telegraphic stock updates in each edition of the local paper. In the colonies, unlike in Germany proper, no law prohibited the direct listing of colonial share prices by news outlets. As a result, stocks featured in Lüderitz Bay's paper consisted overwhelmingly, and usually in itemized form, of German colonial companies with diamond interests.[28]

As the greater German public developed an appetite for colonial shares, promoters sought to capitalize. Whereas 1907 witnessed the founding of just thirty-three German companies in the colonies, 1908 would see sixty-five companies founded, and 1909 would feature 100 new companies in the diamond sector alone. It took so much less effort to start a company than to establish a mining claim in Southwest Africa that a visitor joked: "If three men were standing on a corner, they were founding a company." A prominent newspaper added that "nearly every day witnesses the launch of a new speculative diamond venture." By this measure Germany had arrived as a colonial power, for a similar "founding fever" was detectable in the French and Belgian Congo throughout the 1890s.[29]

. . .

This bubble proved rife with predation. Not long into the boom, German bankers abruptly called in loans to Southwest Africa's farmers with an eye toward seizing the farmers' shares in local diamond companies.[30] But the most numerous victimizations took place in and around stock transactions themselves.

In 1908, an average German investor, let alone a colonial one, did not understand what a futures contract was or what determined its price. Many did not even understand how basic stock share movements worked. Inexperienced buyers often failed to grasp the mechanics of their speculation or its possible outcomes. A confusing regulatory landscape for colonial speculation only exacerbated their ignorance.[31]

Insiders knew colonial shares did not face the same legal scrutiny appertaining to book-keeping, taxes, oversight, and financial reporting as applied to traditional firms. The latter complex of legal standards was known as the *Reichsstempelgesetz*—a new edition of which took effect in the summer of 1909, at the height of colonial share madness. The

Reichsstempelgesetz appeared at a juncture when many educated Germans saw financial markets as casinos rigged against outsiders. In this context, the German state had at times weighed measures outlawing futures trading and pushed through legislation to this effect.[32]

The *Reichsstempelgesetz* promised to help would-be investors distinguish between investment-grade securities and riskier objects of betting. But the new edition of this law only appeared widely in print a few years *after* 1909, and it had little to say about colonial shares because they had not been relevant *before* 1909. That caveat was a pity, because precisely as droves of speculators remained ignorant about the legal nuances and risks surrounding colonial shares, they were inundated with unregulated colonial financial products, unscrupulous pitchmen, and confidence tricks that included the use of mass mail marketing to transmit bogus information.[33]

An especially notorious case occurred in August 1909, when shares of the South African Territories Ltd. swelled for seventeen days on reports that the company had found diamonds outside the Forbidden Zone. These reports were a scam devised by veterans of the German colonial army, along with a stock promoter from Hamburg, convicts from Kiel, the mayor of Lüderitz Bay, and a prominent director of German diamond companies. Under cover of darkness, three impoverished agents working for the conspirators toted burlap bags of sand filled with diamonds stolen from other fields, then "salted" the empty fields belonging to the Territories Ltd. by pouring out the contents of the bags. Their way smoothed by the mayor, these agents later claimed that they found the fields laden with diamonds—a story that received a stamp of approval from official inspectors.[34]

Having already purchased shares before this "news," schemers watched a buying sensation erupt on exchanges, with over a third of the company's stock changing hands. After share prices swiftly doubled, so much money moved into the shares that authorities in Southwest Africa complained about a shortage of cash on hand for other economic activity—a frenzy that separately inspired businessmen in London to found a similarly named predatory venture that also lied about its holdings. Behind the scenes, the shares' ascent created a nice arbitrage trade for insiders of the South African Territories Ltd. The moment gave them a chance to flip ownership rights to their worthless fields to another company. To cap off the gluttony, the company's directors exercised options to buy stock at previously set (low) prices at precisely the moment of the price spike in shares on the open market—allowing insiders another ostensibly miraculous selling opportunity.[35]

Such frauds were hardly new to this company, which, just a month earlier, had guaranteed as "entirely true" secondhand reports of diamond strikes that turned out to concern planted rubies.[36] One may therefore ask why Germans proved so gullible. An answer is that, because Southwest's diamonds already strained credulity by sitting in sand, people struggled to discern which new reports were legitimate—irrespective of whether newspapers glossed them as "credible." Secrecy around mining rights such as those controlled by the Colonial Corporation further complicated attempts to clarify boasts in prospectuses while also incentivizing promoters to mislead or lie. After Dernburg decreed the Forbidden Zone, it became legally impossible for civilians or unaffiliated journalists to do any research by visiting a mining site and inspecting its operations. Prior esteem of a business team did not necessarily matter, either: August Stauch harvested hundreds of thousands of carats as an amateur, whereas more impressive names backing some companies accompanied no other activity than stockjobbing.[37]

It was chimerical to expect German company directors to scrutinize financial reporting and management; at least one was a known fraudster who serially misrepresented the size of his deliveries. Better reputed directors had incentives to misinform, too. Overreporting earnings and finds was an easy way to boost a company's shares, or to ensure their successful flotation. It could also prove profitable not to report anything conclusive at all, amid wildly favorable public speculation. In some cases, even underreporting the number of stones found in a given company's field could bring benefits, for doing so would allow company executives to buy up undervalued or distressed shares of their own stock. Executives could then strategically leak information to entice investors, and thereby optimally drive up the share price.[38]

Dernburg privately worried about broad public speculation in mining stocks. Other promoters of colonial stock investment, however, encouraged citizens to rely on board members and state officials watching the shop. Men like Dernburg supposedly knew how to foil confidence men and "to distinguish between illusory and real values." One splashy column dismissing worries was written by Karl von der Heydt, a financial backer of the Pan-German League. Heydt, who doubled as a board member of the Regie and a partner in a banking firm that promoted colonial shares in Germany and Southwest, championed stock-market mechanisms as more reliable kinds of regulation than parliamentary legislation.[39]

Such reassurances were empty. In 1910, of about thirty colonial companies headquartered in Berlin, few complied with government guidance for financial filings or board protocols. The naughty list included the German Colonial Corporation, which deliberately kept shareholders in the dark about important developments and endeavored to hide appendages' accounts from official inspection. Another offender was Edmund Davis, a member of several diamond miners' boards who split his time between three continents and no fewer than seventy-two distinct companies. Thirty-seven of Davis's companies folded between 1909 and 1913; of the rest, he functioned as president for twenty-one.[40]

The logistical lunacy surrounding Davis substantiated rumors in Germany about "founding factories" set up to exploit eager investors through the rapid issuance of shares for new, and largely bogus, colonial companies. In prospectuses for such ventures, people like Davis touted their other board memberships in order to imply, falsely, broader backing for fledgling companies. Another shameless promotion claimed "concessions" it did not have and mentioned prominent people's names as "backers" without their knowledge or consent. In any event, many companies' real purpose was to funnel investor money into surreptitious purchases of a new diamond company's shares at inflated prices. After seeing a desired spike in share prices for the second company, directors who sat on both companies' boards stealthily dumped their shares at a profit.[41]

To a cynic's eye, Dernburg looked unlikely to check such excess in view of his personal friendship with Davis. Prior to taking office, Dernburg himself sat on a ludicrous number of boards. Not to be outdone in its regulatory capture was the Imperial German state, whose own interest in revenue provided an institutional logic for inaction. Diamond mania meant more transactions in domestic stock markets. More transactions meant more state duties collected on stock trades, or nearly 1.5 times the prebubble tax revenue. It is likely that this fiscal enhancement motivated public stock regulators who normally stepped in during volatile periods to absent themselves from the scene.[42] In 1909, after all, Germans witnessed both the colonial stock bubble and a bitter domestic struggle on how to fix Germany's federal fiscal deficits.

Nationalism also militated against intervention. In order to satiate a perceived "internal" need for capital, the German state took pains to bar from German exchanges certain "foreign" securities offering high returns. Official toleration of colonial shares' wild ascent, by contrast, kept speculative money "inside" Germany that might have otherwise been lost to, for example, American railroad stocks. This rationale explained why, in the case of Southwest, a sizeable group of bureaucrats condoned the diamond bubble and even participated in it.[43]

In late 1909, loose oversight heavily impacted the fortunes of shareholders in the South African Territories Ltd. After the company's shares spiked and before the related deception became public, the stock brought insiders major profits. After exposure, shares promptly lost 60 percent of their value. The dip cost the company's largest shareholder—an aristocratic naïf who had bought in near the top—seventeen million marks. In a final indignity, the shares declined a further 3 percent in a single day upon news of his suicide.[44]

Fraud was not confined to diamond stock shares. In Southwest, European engineers often took jobs with diamond companies on handshake deals, only to see their employers subsequently renege in order to lower labor costs. Likewise, settlers who offered to work as guards in exchange for stock options, or who marked out fields with the promise of an ownership stake, frequently relied on promises made in bad faith. These sleights further depleted victims by forcing them to face steep court costs and health problems resulting from legal battles whose proceedings lasted years.[45]

For their part, colonists in Southwest had to cope with false reports of remote diamond strikes circulating to alarming credulity. Con men pushed opportunities to buy low and sell high to any who journeyed to Lüderitz Bay: maps describing the location of buried treasure that actually led to random desert terrain; ostensibly discounted diamonds that were just aquamarine; and, of course, stock shares linked to imaginary companies. Sales pitches ranged from the relaxed to the aggressive. One lodger, sitting in a hotel room in Lüderitz Bay, heard a knock on his door from a porter to inform him that a stranger desired to see him "on business of the utmost importance," whereupon the stranger appeared, swore his mark to secrecy, and drew the window shades before soliciting participation in fifty-one diamond claims. Weeks later, the claims proved valueless.[46]

In the end, fraud around the diamond bubble, while egregious, was no worse than that in and around the diamond industry itself. Once a rough diamond left the ground, fraud coincided with virtually each stage of value creation. De Beers and the German producers cheated workers and skirted fiscal obligations to home countries. The states overseeing diamond supply lied about export totals. The syndicates in London and Antwerp sorting diamonds misled people about which stones were available and what wholesalers were willing to pay for them. Diamond importers in America deceived about their commitment to paying for deliveries, misrepresented cut stones as roughs to customs officials, and falsely denied their complicity in smuggling schemes. Finally, American retailers often defrauded customers by advertising prices they did not intend to honor, by lying about stones on sale from competitors, and by switching stones undergoing evaluation with less desirable ones whose defects would prove undetectable to an inexpert eye.[47]

•   •   •

In theory, the German state had taken a step to guard against bubbles like the one in colonial shares. By law, the face-value price for an individual share in a traditional publicly traded German company ran no lower than 1,000 marks. The purpose of such paternalism, which curbed market access for small- and medium-sized capitalists, was to avoid such painful stock crashes as Germany had experienced in the 1870s. As the colonial bubble formed in 1908 and 1909, though, fringe investors easily circumvented the thousand-mark limit. People who might have bet on horse races instead wagered on diamond companies. Brokers offered margin buying power that allowed individuals to speculate in thousand-mark shares for as little as 200 marks down—albeit at five times the risk. In a related development, bucket shops popped up to finance eager gamblers, always at usurious interest rates.[48]

Because colonial fraud touched multiple classes, political consequences followed. The more investors from the ranks of big business cashed in on the bubble, the more people suspected Colonial Secretary Bernhard Dernburg, a former banker, of corruption. The socialist leader August Bebel, describing Dernburg's relationship with financial traders, said he was "flesh of their flesh." True or not, that reputation stuck. Any detail of his personal life, such as the anger generated when Dernburg's wife Emma wore extravagant diamond jewelry in public, only enhanced this opinion. "There must be an end," an exasperated Dernburg complained in vain, "of my being treated by people [. . .] as if I were a company promoter."[49] There was not.

The speculation associated with Dernburg had either excluded settlers in Southwest or wrecked their livelihoods. Already offended by what they saw as Dernburg's unilateral decisions, made without consultation of the colony's white population, settlers in Southwest often lacked access to brokers and the funds necessary to buy shares in large diamond companies. By the early months of the boom, the best blocks of stock shares were also owned by the financially strongest among the metropolitan population. One high-flying stock saw four-fifths of its shares in the hands of the German Colonial Corporation.[50]

In response, merchants in Lüderitz Bay founded their own informal stock exchange, which they built on the ballroom floor of a hotel near the local train station. This exchange allowed locals to invest in smaller diamond companies whose shares traded around town and among members of desert expeditions. But such smaller companies legally could not issue shares in denominations of less than 1,000 marks, whereas the big colonial companies registered in Germany had all the capital they needed. That difference made Lüderitz Bay–based shares harder to move during downturns. Besides, the smaller companies to which they attached found it difficult to attract capital from Germany, a far richer market.[51]

In Lüderitz Bay, fallout from small-stock frauds proved sobering. In late 1909, the town's unlicensed stock exchange, built up in direct proportion to the trading boom, virtually shut down on account of inactivity after shares in the discredited South African Territories Ltd. became unsellable. This company in particular had seduced droves of settlers with a swindle whose mechanics they still did not comprehend. In the bargain, the company had attracted the interest of a broad swathe of buyers within Germany who could not afford to buy in to the German Colonial Corporation but who wanted to cash in on the boom.[52]

When the dust settled, Southwest Africa was left with a severe cash shortage. Some once-precious share certificates had turned into worthless paper, and the confidence of investors flagged. Confidentially, officials lamented the "particularly difficult [. . .] struggle for daily bread" facing marginal Europeans in the colony. Throughout this time, Dernburg's Forbidden Zone decree not only heightened the feeling of exclusion among settlers, but idled their ancillary businesses ranging from equipment sales to food vending. The big diamond miners, who were really the only ones allowed in the Zone, did not need local businesses. They got their supplies from large merchants based in Germany, the same place where the bulk of extravagant colonial dividend payments wound up.[53]

So, colonists lost another potential avenue by which to recover money lost in the stock bubble.

Certain stock shares continued to thrive: into 1910, trading volume in Corporation shares remained as low as twenty shares a day—thus driving up prices further. Volatility ran correspondingly high—resulting in daily swings in some cases that could wreck a small investor's account if he or she succeeded in buying in, or, worse still, did so on margin. Trading in such stocks ought not, cautioned a spokesperson for the Corporation, "be everybody's thing."[54]

This was to say nothing of groups legally or socially restricted from participation. For European women, buying into the stock madness was possible but carried social risks; men might perceive a lady haggling over shares around an exchange as having corroded or compromised her femininity. In Southwest, Ovambos whose labor harvested diamonds had no access at all to the market. Nor did the town of Bethanie's Nama. Amid drought, livestock loss, malnutrition, and rampant scurvy, the Nama heard stories about excessive stock wealth and protested—correctly, if ineffectively—that the ground containing diamonds had been stolen from them via fraudulent contracts.[55] Fraud being visited upon German speculators must have seemed delicious justice to the Nama, who for years had been systematically robbed by unscrupulous German traders, often operating with police assistance and the weight of law.

Even in Germany, where nearly everyone anticipated an explosion in future earnings of diamond companies, few civilians got rich. On trading days, general members of the public could pay thirty cents to tour the stock exchange in Berlin. But the roughly four thousand traders walking its magnificent floors worked for elites, whereas the common person lacked real access within the exchange's walls to the roughly 1,500 stocks that traded there. When stock analysts spoke about sellers of large colonial share blocks being "the only ones to have profited from the diamond blessing," they had a point. The sellers of large blocks were Germany's biggest banks, which essentially shared intelligence about timing. Without the aid of such intelligence or coordination, small investors lost gigantic sums. Indeed, they often bought in precisely when insiders like the Deutsche Bank, blessed with inside information, privately advised their own clients to sell.[56]

* * *

The stock bubble had deep social repercussions. Not everyone agreed with an aristocrat who enthused about "well-priced colonial shares" being "the best advertising" for colonialism. Disaffected Germans complained about an "unhealthy" spirit unleashed by betting on diamonds. The governor of Southwest Africa—finding his 40,000-mark annual salary dwarfed by the riches of newly minted millionaires—chided mining companies for hyping "illusory" riches and criticized investors for putting too much faith in finance.[57]

Perhaps the most widespread concern was that German stock madness was causing inebriation to pervade Southwest and in particular Lüderitz Bay, where even well-paid engineers showed up to work drunk. For decades, alcohol had coursed through the veins of Germany's colonial project. Colonial laws incentivized suppliers through low import taxes, which endowed alcoholic beverage sales with high profit margins. Steady demand existed among migrant African workers, to whom some Europeans sold rotgut spirits at a cut rate. As for European settlers, beer formed a staple in many diets otherwise heavy in preserved meats, jam, bread, and coffee.[58]

Notwithstanding this larger context, visitors to Lüderitz Bay expressed shock at the copious consumption of alcoholic beverages in town after 1908, with the diamond stock bubble underway. Precisely as Germans abroad spoke of a need to cure Indigenous Africans' alcoholism, the breadth of local Europeans' addiction astonished. One banker arriving by train at Lüderitz Bay noticed "rivers" of beer bottles lining the tracks; other guests blamed "capital" for alcoholic "mountains" strewn across dirty town streets.[59]

No shortage of explanations existed: dry climate; reckless frontier personalities; sheer boredom; and, finally, stock failures. Lüderitz Bay admittedly offered no leisure activities beyond gambling or swimming in choppy, cold, shark-infested seas. Accessibility, too, was a factor. Locally, beer proved cheaper—and tastier—than did the area's stale water. The population had outstripped the town's ability to provide clean water for drinking.[60]

Lüderitz Bay's municipal government had been waging a battle with alcohol since the town's early days, when a ship from the Cape known as the "flask post" made deliveries consisting of little else. Immediately prior to the diamond boom, officials sought not only to curtail the issuance of permits to sell alcohol, but to revise tax policy so as to discourage alcohol consumption. The Brussels Antislavery Acts of 1890 and 1899 had imposed taxes on alcohol sales, but only for extreme northern areas of Southwest Africa most densely populated by Africans; Lüderitz Bay, as well as Swakopmund and Windhoek, remained outside the regulatory framework. Once introduced in 1908, alcohol taxes became the colony's second-largest net source of government revenue, trailing only diamonds. Efforts to address alcoholism heated up in 1909, when the colonial governor fought to cap sale permits at one for every eighty residents in a given town, to impose an additional tax on consumption, and to cease issuance of permits outside towns.[61]

In a tough housing and rental market, bars offered bargain lodging with the expectation of recouping the difference through lodgers' spending on drinks with ludicrous profit margins. A .4-liter glass of "Munich" beer in Lüderitz Bay cost one mark, or about as much as 3.785 liters of beer in Munich. And yet, notwithstanding markups, locals largely viewed alcohol as a commodity for which no price could run too high, and in deference to whose consumption they would shrink other spending. Hence, the problem of excess did not abate much in the years after 1908. While Dernburg preached temperance and talked about raising taxes on spirits, attempts to import alcohol-free wine from Germany floundered. Soon recruitment propaganda for prospective European migrants requested that not only "habit drinkers" stay away but "social drinkers," too.[62]

Fallout from the speculation produced alcoholic washouts in the colony, but it was not confined to them. As money within Southwest Africa poured into diamond stocks and activities, many of the colony's farmers struggled to get credit and faced insolvency. Back in Germany, the working class encountered articles on how diamond excess distorted the domestic stock market. Around Hamburg, a Social Democratic stronghold, reports of quick riches spread in grimy alleyways and sleepy boroughs.[63]

The stock bubble peaked in 1909, just as parliament in Berlin debated tax reform. Addressing budget deficits seemed like a necessity for the German Empire, whose increased social spending and enormous military outlays were pushing it into a predicament in which the passage of federal budgets proved enormously difficult. According to the German Empire's constitutional structure, the federal state did not control direct tax revenues; that prerogative resided with the empire's twenty-five member states, each paying some annual monetary contributions to the federal level but otherwise guarding against interference. The federal state had substantial power to raise revenues only through issuing new debt or through imposing indirect duties. But the federal debt had grown alarmingly high. And more indirect duties would disproportionately burden the working class and so seemed politically unpalatable to progressives, Social Democrats, and the Catholic Center. That left the government one substantial option: to tax the inheritance of large estates. An inheritance tax targeted about 55 million marks in additional annual revenue for the federal coffers.[64]

Into this situation entered the contemporaneous bubble in colonial diamond shares: a "singular" event, according to the Disconto Bank's board of directors, and one than minted some millionaires overnight. While the bubble took hold, politicians could foster illusions of an alternative whereby the state could successfully tax tremendous volumes of stock trades. The Catholic Center deputy Richard Müller made this case in parliamentary debates by special reference to colonial shares. Stocks looked like a target for fresh taxes that did not augur social uproar, and stocks had long been scapegoated by German conservatives, who derided any inheritance tax as a blow to widows and orphans.[65]

The euphoria of 1909 did not last, of course, and by 1910 the stock bubble began to burst. That said, in the months leading up July 1909, at the moment when the federal parliament finalized changes to tax law, the potential for greater indirect revenues from the stock boom looked real. Conservative deputies could seize on this circumstance to avoid what seemed like more painful decisions. They could help to divert the reform campaign by zeroing in on "capitalism" as it related to financial markets and consumption, rather than to inherited wealth. Diamond mania, then, was another reason why conservatives broke forcefully with the German government's proposals for an expansion of federal taxes to include inheritances.[66]

Instead, conservatives joined with Catholics to push for major tax hikes on real-estate and stock-market speculation, as well as on liquor. The success of this new alliance in 1909 was illustrated in a contemporary publication explaining Germany's new federal tax code. Of 607 pages in total, 186 dealt with financial instruments, 156 with alcoholic beverages, and just 50 with inheritance. Notably, a fresh provision hiked the federal duty on colonial stock trades: a duty that, before 1908, was 0 percent. Shortly into the boom, parliament had debated a proposed duty of 1 percent. In the final version of the bill, passed months later, the duty rose to 3 percent.[67]

A vast majority of Germans could never afford to buy into diamond stocks. Nonetheless, they either did so or were made to feel conscious of missing out. In early 1909, news broke that a single share of the Corporation would fetch more than 20,000 marks. A laborer at a brush factory outside Hamburg earned perhaps a tenth of that amount annually. The boom in diamonds and diamond shares manifestly made fortunes for some parties who moved in, or exploited, financial markets. But that was only one fate in a year that otherwise disappointed the working class. Evidence of the gulf appeared in Lower Franconia, where one resident, reading about diamond wealth but legally obligated to take care of a girl whose beer-brewer father had decamped to Lüderitz Bay, demanded that the Colonial Office garnish the absentee father's wages.[68]

Selective benefits from the stock boom outraged millions of taxpayers and prompted international headlines about a "German diamond scandal." Quickly, the debate on diamond wealth grew so outsized as to dwarf debates about relatively more consequential features of German life. Instead of talking about, say, concentration in the domestic coal industry—where the stakes outran those seen in Southwest Africa—German public opinion focused to a disproportionate extent on colonial treaties and the Corporation's flashy diamonds.[69]

Against this backdrop, a Reichstag committee tasked with examining a preliminary treaty draft for the renewal of Dernburg's Forbidden Zone pushed to void the arrangement. Germany's "small men" had paid a heavy price for the "protection" of German Southwest, as well as the railroads assisting access to the diamond fields. In the interim, workers gained little amid the diamond boom. But bankers seemed to benefit from having their fingers all over the empire's diamond laws.[70] And the empire, for its part, appeared to deliver corporate welfare and to enable insider trading.

In Southwest, the German Colonial Corporation's favored miner paid less in royalty fees to the Corporation than did its competitors. Likewise, the banks behind the Corporation received promises from Dernburg that he would waive several months of their export tariffs. Adding insult to injury, the Corporation correspondingly raised the royalty fees it charged to Southwest miners from 2 percent (the pre-diamond standard) to 3.5 percent—absent any new services or added exertion. With the German government's approval, the Corporation further required that Southwest's diamonds be transported through a particular bank in Lüderitz Bay with ownership in Hamburg—hardly a friendly face, or a forgiving trek, for small-time frontiersmen. The Corporation and the state even stipulated that miners could not pay their fees in diamonds. They had rather to make good with cash—thus necessitating frequent conversion transactions that allowed an additional arbitrage opportunity for banks and for rich individual buyers, who collectively formed the greatest fountain of capital around Lüderitz Bay.[71]

Certain circles back in Germany seethed at these perceived affronts. The hypernationalist poet Max Bewer gushed about a Nibelung Treasure buried in Southwest Africa's sand. But, as Bewer put it in a verse, the earth holding this treasure "glowed with diamonds" because German soldiers had sacrificed themselves. While German soldiers in Southwest "died for the Fatherland" or became invalids, the Corporation dawdled. Anti-Semites joined Bewer in pointing out the contrast. They also demonized colonial stockjobbers, to whom Dernburg appeared linked by virtue of his time as a banker, and a tone that a prominent Catholic member of parliament derided as that of a "counting-house."[72]

Amid the stock boom, hypernationalists, conservatives, and anti-Semites defined the stones flowing through the offices of the Regie as blood diamonds—but not owing to violence against Africans or the exploitation thereof. Instead, these notional blood diamonds glistened with the "tears" afflicting wretched German soldiers in their dying moment. Soldiers' blood was "being used," editorialized the *Mecklenburger Warte,* for "impersonal great companies, whose stockholders, without actual work, want to feast on the colonies," and who were not even German but rather "more or less" representatives of "international great capital." The disgraced General von Trotha agreed, publicly complaining about the "omnipotence of money" in Southwest.[73]

Social Democrats saw the matter not entirely differently. In the aftermath of the Second Anglo-Boer War, many on the German left agreed with Norman Angell's analysis that the British public spent millions in cash and lives to conquer South Africa, only to "not get a solitary diamond." German diamond debates also coincided with an abiding international concern surrounding the popular writings of J. A. Hobson, who sought to convince readers that colonial powers fought wars to the benefit, not of average workers and entrepreneurs, but of bond-holders and speculators. In this era, left-wing German economists should have been interrogating the thesis of Hobson in public fora and considering its applicability to analyses of the economy as a whole. But Hobson's work seems to have made remarkably little impact on Germany's Social

Democrats. Instead, their furor over the costs and benefits of empire centered on diamonds, with the official Social Democratic convention bemoaning the diamond system's "plundering of the German Empire and its taxpayers." Like their counterparts on the right, Social Democrats frequently dismissed diamond wealth as an illusory, passing phenomenon that would leave in its wake only moral and physical damage.[74]

CHAPTER 8

UNDERWORLD

◈   Mere months into the German diamond rush, state prosecutors in the Cape Colony charged Harry Langa, a black African, with criminal possession of unlicensed diamonds. This charge was fairly common. In a surprise, however, Langa beat it by referencing the disorder Germans had unleashed on the world market.

Langa testified that he had acquired his diamonds during a pre-1908 stint as a locomotive driver in Southwest Africa. Biased as judges at the Cape were, they found Langa's account credible. The judges also did not know how to enforce the Cape's domestic illicit diamond-buying (IDB) laws in reference to diamonds coming from German Southwest. For their part, the Germans could not argue that Langa had violated their laws, either. He had accumulated his stones in an era when the Germans did not yet know where diamonds existed in large quantities in their colony. Furthermore, while Germans had since passed legislation concerning diamonds' handling, that legislation did not require Langa, if abroad, to register what he called a "gift received from his father in heaven."[1]

With the Cape Colony conceding these points, Langa won his case. His success was part of a larger phenomenon in which South Africa and the Germans were struggling to police an inherently international diamond trade by 1909. In Europe, buyers of rough stones in major markets—Amsterdam, Antwerp, and London—noticed a flood of illicit parcels from Southwest Africa, delivered via sellers operating outside the Regie network. Official German estimates confirmed that as much as 50 percent of Southwest African stones hitting the world market did so through smuggling. Rumors put the figure even higher. Though concern about leakage was hardly new to the diamond business, the German statistics looked alarmingly high. In 1910 alone, Southwest Africa's licit diamond exports amounted to something on the order of 1,000,000 carats. One million illicit carats would have fetched more than twenty-six million marks at market if sold via the Regie to bidders in Antwerp at the previous year's prices. Once cut and marketed, the diamonds' retail value would have nearly quintupled.[2]

Illicit diamond buying posed a multitude of threats to the government. First, smuggling deprived German authorities of revenue. At the time, a licit exporter had to pay the government a duty of 33.3 percent *ad valorem*: that is, relative to the assessed value of each rough diamond. Second, smuggling compromised Dernburg's construction of a national cartel by swamping the market with too many, and too often discounted, German diamonds. Third, smuggling was of grave consequence for Southwest Africa, whose colonial economy was increasingly counting on diamond revenues to make budgetary ends meet.[3]

The proliferation of illicit stones from Southwest Africa also affected the way the German metropole viewed the colony. Lüderitz Bay's newspaper implored Germans not to brand Southwest's population as criminal on the basis of reports about illicit diamond activity. Dernburg's underlings issued like-minded statements. "No one would deny," one press release read, "that across the world, now as ever, some smuggling cases may pop up." Bureaucrats in Southwest also assured a visiting journalist that local diamond mines witnessed fewer theft and smuggling cases than did others in the world.[4] But to so assure was to protest too much.

Within and without Southwest Africa, German smuggling had long been booming. Diamonds fit nicely into the colony's black market, as well as into a larger, global black market stretching to the United States. In New York City, by far the leading site for American diamond imports, trade experts estimated half of the diamonds already in circulation were either illicitly sourced, or illicitly imported, or both.[5]

When American customs authorities calculated that perhaps three million dollars' worth of illicit diamonds entered the United States annually after 1908, it turned out that most of these were the small stones in which the Germans specialized. Nor did this activity necessarily culminate in shady alleys. In 1910, 25 percent more illicit diamonds than licit arrived with major American importers, who in many cases distributed illicit stones to retailers in respected jewelry shops, which sold them on to couples for engagements. Even reputable importers participated in smuggling.[6]

On the strength of America's strong demand, and given the many outlets for smuggled diamonds, international criminal elements in Southwest Africa thrived. In Lüderitz Bay, an increasingly visible underworld formed a counterpoint to rosy accounts that deemed the town a real-life "Cockaigne." Medieval Europeans had imagined "Cockaigne" as a land of unending wealth and ease, but such a place could never successfully regulate human behavior. At the Cape, where Langa withstood his diamond prosecution, Lüderitz Bay and Southwest Africa both developed a reputation as "the land of sun, sand, and sin."[7]

As major money slipped away from the German state, officials looked for fixes. Because illicit stones from the Namib were tiny and thus easily concealed, investigators had to scan numerous problem sites. In Europe, ship travel from Southwest Africa to Hamburg often involved a layover in Antwerp and a chance to stroll around that city. Sellers uninterested in German diamond laws could arrange a casual swap at one of Antwerp's cafés. Alternatively, sellers could strike such a deal in nearby Amsterdam, whose absence of a connection to the Regie left it ravenous for small stones. German state investigators even had to scrutinize the mail, through which packages from Southwest Africa bearing uninspected diamonds routinely made their way to the continent.[8]

The fledgling bureaucracy in Southwest Africa proved simultaneously corrupt and lax. In 1910, a director of the post office serving Kolmanskop, a prominent diamond mine, committed mail tampering and embezzlement. At Lüderitz Bay's customs house, residents could enter the grounds to greet arriving boats without passing a security check; once inside, just a few spectators would outnumber the staff on hand. No surprise, then, that packages awaiting inspection frequently went missing. The Colonial Office considered a redesign of the facility but shelved it due to funding shortfalls. Elsewhere the office had to deal with distractions posed by the closures of customs facilities throughout the colony's interior, such that it was difficult to identify, and easy to contest, where and when customs inspections took place.[9]

As for the colonial police force, it proved outmatched when it came to diamonds. Lüderitz Bay was barely a few years old as a distinct jurisdiction. Entering 1909 its police were few, comprising only ten diamond specialists, in addition to thirty-two other personnel—and this, during a year in which twenty-nine of these employees were underpaid new hires. Arguably more than the rest of colonial bureaucracy, the heavily overworked diamond police specialists looked amateurish. They clumsily blew undercover officers' identities during raids on jewelry shops trafficking in stolen goods. They also allowed prisoners in the cells of the jail in

Lüderitz Bay to escape by climbing out through a faulty roof. The rest of the colony's police provided little help. Instead of devoting more resources to tackle diamond criminals, Southwest's colonial governor obsessed about alleged theft of cattle and destruction of telegraph lines by Indigenous people. Making matters worse, the extraordinary volume of crimes and lawsuits involving Southwest's settlers clogged the court system.[10]

Already, the Namib Desert was so vast, and its territory so sparsely populated, as to render systematic enforcement of diamond laws impossible. "Day and night, unmolested and unobserved," reported a local source, people moved back and forth between Lüderitz Bay and the Forbidden Zone. It was easy to understand how they did so when looking at Prinzenbucht, a diamond field deep in the Zone. Prinzenbucht's police station, hastily constructed in 1909 to curb smuggling, amounted to a wooden shed housing a single officer. The officer, living with a dog, struggling to keep healthy, and tending a pitiful succulent garden, shouldered responsibility for inspecting enormous swathes of territory.[11]

Mining foremen complained about dropping off accused smugglers at such remote outposts, only to learn from a sign that the officer on duty was "out on patrol" indefinitely. This phenomenon's recurrence shook confidence in law enforcement, even as remote stations added an extra body or two. Through April 1909, Southwest's police arrested just eight people on smuggling charges. As if to provide the perfect metaphor, one contemporary account spoke of a wandering dune enveloping a police station inside the Zone during a windstorm.[12]

Southwest Africa's skeleton force hardly looked exceptional when compared to South Africa. Before De Beers built its own private security network, diamond theft was rampant around Kimberley, and even relatively industrialized Johannesburg lacked a professional, organized police.[13] That said, South African investigators had the advantage of monitoring true mines, around which nature had established sealed perimeters. By contrast, German authorities in Southwest traversed shifting terrain where typical markers of property boundaries—during a frenzy—were piles of rocks with a wooden post on top stating the owner's name.

While signs in the Zone carried fine print in English and German, property lines made little sense. In Lüderitz Bay, it was not uncommon for someone to wake up and find a diamond on their doorstep after a morning sandstorm. Visitors to the Zone reported being hit in the face by windswept diamonds, and recognized owners of fields credibly found sand lots without diamonds one day and restocked by capricious weather the next. Insofar as nature's furtive, fifty-meter-high dunes did not respect artificial rectangles supposedly corresponding with legal boundaries, time could easily conceal markers of theft.[14]

Police tried to keep down difficult plots of sand by hammering large poles to the ground, over which a large canvas tent sat to block any movement.[15] When such environmental management proved futile, investigators sought instead to replicate the system De Beers had created in South Africa: a force of diamond detectives and secret agents, as well as strict control over employee movement through the issuance of identity cards to personnel authorized to enter mining compounds. The cards recorded workers' full names and physical traits.

Dernburg's office, consulting with De Beers through back channels, proposed not only these measures, but also new ones: the creation of an international registry with fingerprint samples of known offenders; the installation of surveillance departments within companies to keep tabs on contract laborers migrating back and forth between Southern African locations; and the maintenance of a list of suspicious persons.[16] Germany might work hand in hand with South Africa. But first they had to identify the criminals.

·　　·　　·

European "foreigners" figured as scapegoats in most Germans' explanation of colonial problems. But no one quite agreed which Europeans were foreigners. In some instances, the waiting period to shed one's legal status as such a foreigner was about two years' residency in Southwest. Magnifying the uncertainty were mixed marriages between different European ethnicities—themselves symptomatic of the colony's shortage of eligible women. In any case, so-called European foreigners fielded blame for problems with colonial food supply, land speculation, profiteering, and stock scams.[17]

As diamond smuggling impacted Lüderitz Bay, police focused on "international" criminality—for example, by charging multiple merchants visiting from Cape Town on meager evidence. Anti-Semitism was a key prong in such efforts. Lüderitz Bay's police took it as axiomatic that smuggling culprits were "partly Jewish, partly English fencers and swindling vermin." German residents, using the diamond boom as a setting for adventure stories, portrayed Jewish characters as villains with non-German names. A German consul in Cape Town insisted on hiring Jewish private detectives to penetrate smuggling networks, because only such a person would "know how to get around well in the circles where he would chiefly need to direct his attention." Less delicately, Southwest's governor ranted about "international trash, frequently of Russian- or Galician-Jewish extraction." If "the inclination to diamonds," as a contemporary anti-Semitic organ alleged, was "a particular attribute of the Jewish race," then it followed that illicit diamond activity was, too.[18]

Smuggling reinforced a discourse among colonists about what was supposedly inordinate Jewish influence in the diamond business. This stereotype was not entirely false. Diamonds were no different from the contemporary world's other luxury goods, in whose markets Jews had participated disproportionately since the Middle Ages, owing to their exclusion from most guilds and to their functions as brokers for European royal courts. The ranks of Belgian middlemen whom Germany engaged to cut and market its diamonds thus noticeably included Jews. Likewise, the man who put Dernburg's Regie in touch with Antwerp's buyers carried the surname Abraham, while a contemporary estimate held that 90 percent of diamond personnel in Antwerp were Jewish. Antwerp was the home to the largest Jewish population in Belgium by far.[19]

Many of the "Anglicized Germans" dominating the diamond business in 1908 also remained Jewish, including those comprising the London syndicate that controlled De Beers's output. Although the London diamond syndicate underwent periodic modifications, its membership consistently looked like a German-Jewish emigration roll, beginning with the predominant Wernher, Beit & Co. This group consisted of Alfred Beit, Rhodes's Hamburg-born partner, along with the Prague-born Jules Porgès and Julius Wernher, originally of Bernhard Dernburg's hometown, Darmstadt. Anton Dunkelsbuhler, from Fürth, appeared alongside the German-born A. Mosenthal and Sons. Finally, yet more "Randlords" of German-Jewish heritage played major roles in the orbit of De Beers: George Albu, Gustav Imroth, and Carl Meyer.[20]

When German diamond smuggling materialized, Antwerp and the "Randlords" figured in the popular appraisal of culpability. So did Bernhard Dernburg, who was of Jewish heritage and engaged in regular correspondence with the suspected parties. To Dernburg's dismay, a nascent discourse about "Jewish" smuggling intersected with anti-Semites' appraisal of colonialism over a long duration. For anti-Semites, smuggling was the fault of Jews, and so was the Colonial Corporation, the choice of Antwerp over Hanau, and everything else that went awry during the country's thirty-odd colonizing years. In this upside-down narrative, Christian Germans legally tied to colonial fraud were good people—patriots falsely accused of theft and corruption. By contrast, Dernburg, Paul Kayser (Germany's first head of colonial affairs), and anyone with Jewish ancestry engineered fraud. That Dernburg and Kayser underwent baptisms made no difference. While in their rare mentions as heroes their Jewish heritage vanished, it otherwise figured prominently. From the moment Dernburg took office, he remained tied to it, as when the headline for an article announcing his appointment in a prominent Munich-based newspaper carried a Star of David. Perhaps more surprising, though, was how, in the German colonial imaginary, many of the diamond business's non-Jews *became* Jewish.[21]

Smuggling expanded a perceived battle over the definition of "Jewishness" in the German diamond business, beginning with the man at the top. Dernburg sometimes cooperated with anti-Semites in parliament; more often, he derided them as a fringe group while they in turn undermined and tarred him as "Sternburg"—another allusion to the Star of David. In his earlier years, Dernburg had managed to avoid mounting any public defense of Jews in Germany; a journalist visiting Dernburg's office for comment on domestic anti-Semitic attacks once heard he had arrived "at the wrong address." Later, after Southwest Africa's diamond riches surfaced, Dernburg not only became the victim of such attacks but saw his identity reshaped in the public eye to one in which the things most "important" to him were allegedly "banks, stocks, Jews" and the crass, often criminal behavior around the German diamond industry.[22]

Nor was Dernburg's stigmatization entirely the handiwork of the Deutschsoziale Partei, Germany's explicitly anti-Semitic political party. It was typical even for left-leaning moderates like Heinrich Köhler, a member of Germany's Catholic Center Party, to define Dernburg brusquely as "a Jew." A related phenomenon was that some Germans who were not affiliated politically with the anti-Semites came to associate the enjoyment of diamonds with Jewishness. One contemporary article in the influential weekly *Die Zukunft* felt compelled to state that, although it was "true that the women of Jewish high finance love an ostentatious display of diamonds," so, too, did lots of other women. This conflation by Germans of diamonds with Jewishness occurred in a country where domestic consumption of diamonds historically lagged behind that of other industrialized nations.[23] By extension, therefore, when people posited that there *was* a peculiar Jewish affinity for diamonds, "German" and "Jewish" behaviors stood opposed, and German-Jewish assimilation seemed less feasible.

Jewish residents of Southwest soon found their noticeably expanded presence around Lüderitz Bay being attributed, even by pro-Jewish organs, to predatory impulses about diamond wealth. A majority of Jewish newcomers in Southwest Africa consisted of single males working jobs connected to, or dependent on, diamonds—people like Wilhelm Wasserstein, a tailor. By 1910, Lüderitz Bay's Jewish population rose to 7 percent of the town's European total. This figure represented a level more than double the colony's average and seven times that seen in mainland Germany.[24] Anti-Semites pounced on such statistics, attesting to a paradox familiar to Indigenous people who had served alongside the German army in recent campaigns. Jews might collaborate with Germans but remained outsiders in the eyes of many Germans, not least the soldiers and settlers who dominated colonial politics.

As smuggling thrived, Jewish residents of Southwest Africa could neither win admission to the ranks of the civil service nor settle into a life beyond suspicion. Established Jews conceded that "bad elements" among their coreligionists had been "enticed" by diamond riches. Separately, Jewish immigrants feared an "especially strong national sentiment." From 1909, the municipal government in Lüderitz Bay refused to extend the franchise to non-German Europeans.[25] Elections and electability accordingly became infeasible for most of the local Jewish population, reinforcing their outsider status.

◆　　　◆　　　◆

While Jews never escaped popular association with Southwest's illicit diamond trade, authorities assigned an equal share of blame to another group seen by Southwest's residents as foreigners: Africans. A common conjecture had it that "Jewish" crooks thrived at Lüderitz Bay because ignorant African workers sold them stolen diamonds at cut-rate prices. In part to avoid scrutiny of deficient company security, the Lüderitz Bay mining chamber touted such complaints and scrutinized African migration routes through the Namib under the mistaken impression that these must have emerged for smuggling. To be sure, South African counterparts did confirm that some migratory paths were used to move illicit stones: first, across the (haphazardly demarcated) southern border of Southwest along the Orange River; second, via the docks of Cape Town, where many migrants returned by ship from stints in German fields.[26] Nonetheless, the focus on these routes largely proved fruitless for police and destructive to Africans.

In 1911, Timothy Stephen, a well-dressed Basotho, tried to board a steamship departing Lüderitz Bay for the Cape. Stephen's modest signs of prosperity, including a portmanteau, led German customs officials to accuse him of diamond smuggling. In fact, Stephen had merely spent some of his earnings as a servant in the colony. Nonetheless, police roughed him up and arrested him for hitting back—a charge that ultimately brought him nine months' imprisonment. A similar mistrust befell scores of migrant workers whenever they exited or entered Southwest. Authorities suspected nearly every African who touched German railroad construction sites of diamond theft, jailing many without evidence. German miners also employed an inspector whose sole purpose was to stalk Ovambos on their return home and to ferret out illicit diamonds.[27]

A corresponding climate of surveillance took hold in the diamond fields. German foremen complained of "clever Cape Boys who must be watched down to the finger." "They are capable of anything," said a boss, "and it is difficult to follow how they hide it." One visitor witnessed a company's sorter accusing a Cape migrant of smuggling a matchbox full of stones in his pocket. The sorter had an incentive to misreport or fabricate because a reward of 1,000 marks awaited any European who informed on a proven smuggler. As it turned out, the sorter had planted diamonds in the pocket of the accused Cape migrant in the hope of claiming this reward. Such European foreman, surrounded as they were by subordinate laborers who were denied the ability to witness, were unlikely to be identified as offenders.[28]

A gradual decline in the use of Cape migrant labor hardly dispelled German fantasies about African lawlessness. Some Germans thought Ovambos less likely to smuggle because they were "not so advanced culturally" as "to know the value of a diamond." But this reasoning proved self-contradictory. On the one hand, Germans dismissed Nama and Herero culture as nonexistent in relation to that of Europeans.[29] On the other hand, in portraying Nama and Herero as habitual smugglers, Germans attributed to Nama and Herero culture a mark of putative sophistication ordinarily reserved to Europeans: the valorization of diamonds.

Diamond smuggling hardly abated after a shift to Ovambo labor. Ovambos, like all Southern Africans, did know the value of certain jewelry.

They happened not to prize diamonds, but, to cite one example, they cut off wire from German telegraph lines with an eye toward circulating it at home for adornment. This is not to say that no Ovambos smuggled. In view of the comparative experience of African colonized peoples, it would be absurd to deny that Ovambos, along with Nama, San, and Cape migrants, sometimes took advantage of a lucrative trade Europeans attempted to control. Still, when it came to tackling smuggling, Germans' focus on perceived foreignness was so informed and misled by racism as to prove counterproductive.[30]

The first measure that officials in Southwest weighed to counter illicit trade was the criminalization of diamond sales by Africans. Contemporary public education about illicit sourcing typically centered on "natives" and "the different ways they have of smuggling stones." As for future measures, when one editorialist in Southwest talked about intensifying antismuggling efforts to include body searches of Africans, he analogized it to "the necessary evil" of "mass murder" in wars. (The writer actually deployed the German word *Massenmord,* despite doing so in the shadow of the genocidal violence against Herero and Nama.[31])

Because German authorities widely presupposed African guilt, they missed many of the real culprits, including European women working either on their own or as mules for larger networks. To cite one example: A group of German ladies departing Southwest with two million marks' worth of illicit diamonds feigned helplessness with their diamond-laden baggage, counting on an unwitting but friendly ship's steward to transport that baggage without giving it a close look. Should this plan falter, the ladies could successfully blame the steward by relying on gender stereotypes about passivity. Similarly, a girl taking a walk around Lüderitz Bay might swipe a few diamonds by veering off the established path. If caught, she could reliably plead ignorance, claiming to have found these stones in her boots upon returning home.[32]

Perhaps the greatest desideratum in German antismuggling efforts was that, according to the gender norms of the time, female police largely needed to inspect women. Again owing to gender norms, however, virtually no women held police positions, giving many would-be women smugglers a free pass. Other legal loopholes existed on this basis. German soldiers stationed in Southwest could send their wives "care packages"—sealed containers of chocolate or tobacco—with the understanding that such packages would be exempted from import tariffs in Germany, and that they would undergo at most cursory customs inspection. Provided a soldier carefully removed and replaced a few seals, his sweetheart might receive tins that featured two dozen diamonds embedded within mounds of South African tobacco.[33]

Less socially acceptable ladies also exercised agency, with at least three brothels in Lüderitz Bay turning their clandestine rooms into smuggling nodes. Prostitutes maneuvered among pimps, bookmakers, and forgers eager to exploit the vulnerabilities of the diamond sector and its growing cadre of workers. The number of active members in this underworld had grown since 1906, when authorities started releasing convicted prisoners on the condition that they fight against Nama and Herero. Now, amid the diamond boom, strong demand for consorts in Lüderitz Bay multiplied the means and opportunities for activity.[34]

Inconveniently for investigators, itinerant criminals moving through brothel corridors launched some ventures with respected members of the settler community, including army officers. New recruits at Lüderitz Bay could tackle cases touching the latter group only with great difficulty. For many, a mere social association with a prostitute, or with any other "problem" category, sufficed to warrant official investigation. Still, scrutiny generally fell on men who were unemployed, unsatisfactorily employed, itinerant, Jewish, or some combination thereof. As for criminal women, whether prostitutes or not, their path to lawbreaking owed in part to a deficit of decent-paying traditional jobs for unmarried ladies in Southwest Africa.[35]

Racism and obsession with social status further induced German inspectors to overlook the demand side of smuggling: chiefly, the United States. It was thither, in the world's foremost market for diamonds, that smugglers sent illicit diamonds and exploited a customs system incentivizing them. Provided that illicit shipments out of Southwest Africa made it to New York City and were reported to local customs authorities as roughs, the recipients would benefit from an American system that, until 1913, levied no duty at all on uncut stones. Skirting levies guaranteed fat profit margins for merchants. It also guaranteed the persistence of an illicit supply chain that started in the fields of Southwest Africa. Between 1912 and 1914, New York customs officials seized two million marks' worth of illicit stones shipped by just one crime syndicate from Antwerp, via Montreal.[36]

A contemporary Sears catalogue spoke to the ease of illicit transfers. The catalog stated that returns of a diamond ring purchased from Sears were possible, but only with an original receipt and an accompanying certificate recording the diamond's cut, clarity, and weight. Here as else-where, licit dealers evidently found it difficult to distinguish one stone from another, absent documentation. A one- or two-carat diamond, once broken down into smaller parts and cut into brilliant forms, became yet more untraceable.[37]

Smuggled diamonds could arrive in the United States and easily land with dealers, some of whom were deceived about stones' provenance, and some of whom looked the other way, knowing they could make dirty stones look clean with quick alterations. A smuggled stone could be set into a pre-existing ring or pendant—the kind of jewelry for which virtu-ally no contemporary carrier had proof of provenance. An astute dealer could launder diamond wares in retail shops for a mark-up of somewhere between 25 percent and 50 percent relative to the wholesale price. Last, someone bearing a smuggled stone in a market like New York was in a position not uncommonly experienced by legitimate owners who had pur-chased diamonds in the past and later showed up, their jewelry setting missing, willing to sell at steep discounts.[38]

Owing to disproportionate incentives and to a democratizing market for diamonds, smuggling of Southwest African diamonds to the United States continued apace. It hardly dissipated after 1913, when the US Con-gress's new Underwood Tariff Act placed an import toll on rough dia-monds (10 percent) for the first time and also doubled the import toll on cut diamonds (from 10 to 20 percent). On the contrary: Some American dealers complained that these new tariffs forced them to buy diamonds from smugglers, lest their profit margins vanish. In New York City, so many stones were discovered hiding in coffins, vegetable cans, hunting rifles, teeth, furs, boot heels, necklaces, and business suits as to substan-tiate ongoing rumors about millions in lost customs revenue.[39]

Because German fields mainly pumped out diamonds of small caratage, even more methods of illicit concealment existed than for usual black-market items. Consider the 700,000 carats confiscated by German au-thorities during the two years following 1908. Grand as this portion sounded in newspapers, it looked minuscule in person. Extrapolating from the formula that 5 carats equaled one gram, the combined mass of smuggled German diamonds in this period came to 140 kilograms.[40] Two strong men could lift such a weight by themselves—thereby encouraging minor, and even amateur, smugglers to think their work a modest enterprise.

At a given field in the Forbidden Zone, repurposed soup pots held chunks of licit diamonds in rinsing solution designed to enhance their clarity. The containers could fit diamonds extracted from about twenty-five days of work, at a rate of about 1,000 carats daily. That same amount represented 750,000 marks in exchange value, should a thief or smuggler get the product past German controls and fence it to potential buyers in Europe. This enormous profit potential explained why a handful of women concealed the equivalent of $400,000 in illicit stones inside their dresses. The odds of detection at the origin of the smuggling proved so long as to disproportionately incentivize theft from the fields—already "an entirely simple thing," according to a civil servant surveying the Forbidden Zone on horseback.[41]

There was another, hidden incentive to steal diamonds in Southwest and circulate them throughout the world. Criminals liked acquiring and moving diamonds because diamonds were difficult to trace—as were gold, platinum, and silver. But, when compared with those other untraceable stores of wealth, diamonds carried more value in terms of density. In 1909, one gram in cut diamonds could fetch 5,000 marks in cash on the open market, whereas one gram of platinum would bring 5 marks, one gram of gold 3.4 marks, and one gram of silver just .06 marks.[42]

·   ·   ·

Germany sought to stem the tide of smuggling by coordinating extradition arrangements with crucial foreign customs authorities: Portuguese in Mozambique, Americans in New York. Yet, possession of diamonds without a license was legal outside German or South African territory. So some foreign governments requested that German authorities extradite, in return, people accused of similar-level offenses abroad. In one instance, Portuguese authorities in Lourenço Marques (today's Maputo) simply released a suspect they had arrested on an international warrant from German Southwest when it became clear that the Germans would not reciprocate. With regard to the British Empire, there is evidence that German officials cooperated somewhat more successfully—notifying the British consulate at Lüderitz Bay, for example, about which Cape workers suspected of smuggling would be denied reentry to German ports. On Dernburg's orders, the German consul in Cape Town hired clerks to arrange enhanced monitoring of ships arriving there. In turn, Cape police alerted their German counterparts to outstanding warrants and aliases for veteran diamond criminals.[43]

In 1909, Dernburg pledged directly to crush smuggling and theft through collaboration across borders. Several of the German Empire's twenty-five member states, notably Hamburg, opened up files on how to stop the illicit trade. German jewelers started sharing intelligence internationally and worked with police to track and report jewelry crimes. In Southwest, colonial officials took measures to stigmatize "vagabonds" among Herero, San, and Nama who, consciously or not, found themselves in the Forbidden Zone.[44]

Another step was the unveiling of a supplementary police force, the Diamanten-Polizei, consisting initially of perhaps thirty men stationed at eleven points throughout the Zone who would enforce rules for diamond circulation. One such rule was that anyone exiting the Zone must submit their diamonds within twenty-four hours to a single location in Lüderitz Bay—a bank branch cofounded by the powerful Disconto Bank—or else face a lengthy jail sentence. Local support for such efforts proved elusive, however, with local courts releasing some prominent offenders on the grounds that they thought Dernburg's system unfair.[45]

One might assume that European owners of fields victimized by thieves would prove willing to assist in the recovery of their stolen property. Through 1913, though, such individuals lacked an incentive to do so. Stolen stones, if located by the police, would be transferred to the custody of the Regie, rather than returned to private companies or individuals. "Every stolen item is returned to its owner," merchants complained in a colonial council overseen by the governor, "except in the case of diamonds."[46]

In Berlin, parliament proved only moderately helpful in funding Dernburg's enforcement initiatives. In 1909, deputies weighed an emergency addition to the colonial budget asking for 800,000 marks to protect diamond fields and prevent smuggling. Jails were supposedly overflowing with Africans accused of illicit trade, and a new cutter ship was requested to intercept suspicious boats sailing the waters around Lüderitz Bay. After parliament granted this emergency funding, colonial officials requested around 19 percent more money annually, citing salaries for newly hired customs employees in Lüderitz Bay, as well as the increased difficulty in provisioning the patrol stations sprouting up across the Namib Desert. Because colonial bureaucrats showed a preference for hiring married or soon-to-be-married men—the better, it was thought, to minimize vulnerability to criminal elements—they needed to make sure families could live alongside policemen in the Forbidden Zone. Construction of new police homes thus became a necessary supplement to funding requests, which had initially called for little more than shacks.[47]

By 1911, the German government's annual budget to combat illicit diamond dealing rose to 1.5 million marks, while customs revenues on the licit diamond trade came to 5–6 million marks. More money for special police efforts theoretically meant higher revenues; still, the total police budget for Southwest Africa reached, at its apex circa 1913, just 3.75 million marks. From the perspective of public finance, Germany should have spent twice as much. Instead, by 1912, the fiscally strapped German parliament reduced funding for tackling diamond smuggling, in order to show that the colonies could do more with less through conspicuous belt-tightening. The diamond staff received inadequate relief and assistance, not least because an underappreciated consequence of ramping up diamond production was to increase diamond theft. More diamonds from the ground meant more sifting at fields, and that meant more opportunities for, and temptation to, pilfering.[48]

Notwithstanding the state's penny-wise, pound-foolish approach, official investigators compiled dozens of human leads. They learned, above all, that smuggling thrived on German ships. On small vessels, entire crews sometimes participated in schemes to take illicit stones aboard in Southwest Africa and ferry them back to Europe. Smugglers also utilized large commercial ships, with routes from Lüderitz Bay to Cape Town, and Cape Town to Antwerp, proving especially fruitful.[49]

Official vessels could figure as illicit channels, too. In a trial held on October 21, 1909, a defendant confessed to delivering a stolen diamond parcel to a deck officer on board the *SMS Sperber,* a navy cruiser, shortly before its departure from Lüderitz Bay. With such personnel in mind, Chancellor Bethmann Hollweg received reports concerning a police sergeant traveling on official business via an imperial postal steamer. The consulate in Antwerp correctly suspected the sergeant of engaging in diamond smuggling.[50]

Here as elsewhere, water and diamonds went together. In Lüderitz Bay, if smugglers managed to sneak illicit stones past guards and dump the merchandise into the harbor, those same smugglers or a company linked to them could launder the stones by claiming they had been picked up from nearby guano islands—that is, in areas not falling within the Forbidden Zone. Similarly, when fishing boats arranged for stops along the coast at spots police deemed too risky to visit, a smuggler might swim ashore to swipe some diamonds, then return to Lüderitz Bay to claim "accidental" finds made while trawling the ocean floor.[51]

Dernburg hoped shows of force would deter potential criminals. As early as 1909, agents of the colonial state shut down criminal wildcat operations inside the Forbidden Zone. Dernburg even stationed artillery- and machine-gun units outside the Zone to intimidate would-be smugglers. "I must and will," he later told parliament, "preserve the dignity of the Empire." Added to this mix were SMS *Sperber* and SMS *Panther,* cruisers that anchored in the harbor of Lüderitz Bay at months-long intervals to serve as a psychological deterrent for potential diamond thieves.[52]

Heavy-handedness posed its own problems. Big guns around the harbor could not stop highway robberies in a vast desert, where bandits shot company couriers and stripped them of diamonds. "Theft is easy and supervision difficult," reported an analyst, for no other reason than that the diamonds "are found in an extensive territory." The governor in Southwest, while issuing antismuggling decrees, struggled to explain where exactly the boundaries lay for them. Augmentation of police personnel also had the effect of worsening relations with Southwest's European civilians, who complained about a "perpetual" enlargement of law enforcement and "monstrous" associated costs.[53]

The inconvenient truth was that illicit diamond trade in the colony was enabled by average Germans, not just by European foreigners or Africans. An intellectual affinity between pro–illicit trade sentiment on the one hand, and opposition to Dernburg and his rules on the other, manifested itself by 1909, when the first notable cases of smuggling popped up. While the European contingent around Lüderitz Bay was unlikely to demonstrate against the bow of a naval cruiser, a railroad construction contractor might abscond with several hundred stolen carats. So, too, might a licensed diamond miner upset with the Regie or high rates of taxation.[54]

Everyday resistance added up. By July 1910, police at the edge of the Forbidden Zone had detained dozens of ordinary citizens' wives attempting to smuggle out roughs. The 700,000 carats confiscated from these basic patrols represented the equivalent of nearly 70 percent of licit German exports in the following year. Customs inspectors and police clearly needed to expand their criminal imaginary. To this end, they performed more creative physical inspections of canteens and clothing. Inspectors even tore open animals, aware that a pelican's beak could harbor the equivalent of thousands of pounds sterling in diamonds, and that smugglers could feed their terriers some meals with diamonds sprinkled in. Finally, diamond companies intensified their own examinations, culminating in humiliating body searches of Africans that probed every orifice, hair, finger, toe, and wound.[55]

Even after apprehension, prosecutions of illicit diamond trade consumed immense time and manpower. The process was not so simple as depicted in *The Black Diamond,* a popular 1913 film in which a detective trekked between Hamburg and Africa in under forty-five minutes. In real life, a widow spent four years appealing the German government's conviction of her deceased husband—ultimately winning the attention of the Supreme Court in Leipzig in an embarrassing blow to state attorneys. A second, similar case dragged on for several years and required state's evidence amassed through elusive witness interviews and deal-making with convicts. Because the interstate nature of diamond trading necessitated interstate investigative coordination, consulates complained about a corresponding drain on resources: paperwork, telegrams, and private detectives contracted at the last minute because of a hot tip from the Colonial Office in Berlin or the South African police.[56]

Should an investigation require extraditions, German authorities reckoned with more large bills and complications. Consider the case of Reinhold Krapp, a Berlin-based merchant charged with diamond smuggling. In October 1909, the German Foreign Office requested Krapp's arrest while he was traveling in Suez. Egyptian police placed Krapp on a ship to Lüderitz Bay. Five months later, though, Krapp sued the German government for negligence: the Egyptian ship in question harbored mosquitoes that gave him malaria, which exacerbated his preexisting heart condition and venereal diseases. Krapp won compensation of 10,000 marks, as well as reimbursement for two months' recovery in a Bavarian sanitorium.[57]

Another representative case was that of Hermann Freyberg. German prosecutors hounded Freyberg from Lüderitz Bay, to Berlin, to London, in the process amassing piles of paperwork and unopened letters. Upon declaring Freyberg guilty of illegal diamond possession in March 1911, a court at Lüderitz Bay fined him 1,000 marks plus court costs of 150 marks—a theoretically light sentence for a merchant who claimed to control Southwest stock shares worth 20 million pounds. Instead of settling his fine outright, Freyberg arranged a monthly payment plan of twenty fifty-mark installments. Then he relocated to Berlin, defaulted on his payments, and surreptitiously decamped to London.[58]

Freyberg's wife, Erna, officially remaining in Berlin, petitioned to overturn the fine. An appeals court denied her request and issued her husband a sentence of two months' imprisonment, a notice of which arrived at his "new" London address. Alas, the notice returned unopened to Berlin and Erna Freyberg launched another appeal, this time requesting reversal of the sentence on account of her husband's health problems and suggesting a restoration of the payment plan. After yet more appeals and the passage of three years since his initial conviction, Hermann Freyberg remained on the run, periodically taunting authorities with letters about his "spa cures" along the Côte d'Azur. Hermann's total fines—never paid—rose to 6,520 marks. Two decades later, as if to seal the humiliation of colonial prosecutors, he published popular "fiction" about diamond smuggling.[59]

·   ·   ·

In Southwest Africa, the colonial state failed to convict the overwhelming majority of people it accused of violating diamond laws. Even in rare cases of success, convicted lawbreakers enjoyed widespread sympathy. Given a wish to protect police sources and methods, authorities widely declined to publish trial transcripts and, when they did, tended not to use full names.[60] Besides, the illicit diamond trade easily found willing participants among the local European population.

Consider Emil Popelle, an ex-train engineer who served in Southwest's army until 1907. Popelle claimed to have loaned 1,600 marks of his discharge pay to a diamond miner in late 1908. According to Popelle's later court testimony, he accepted $58,000 worth of rough diamonds as his share of the profits from the diamond venture. Then—or so Popelle claimed—he left Southwest for Europe, his bag of uncut stones in tow.

Popelle lied. He left Southwest *years* after Dernburg criminalized the possession of unregistered Southwest African diamonds, along with any roughs not submitted to the Regie. As if determined to arouse further suspicion, Popelle next concealed "his" diamonds in a pint aboard the RMS Mauretania from Liverpool to New York—where there was a new 10 percent import duty on the importation of rough stones. Without declaring his cargo, the freshly arrived Popelle got past customs inspectors, who on average stopped one passenger in 100. Popelle's cover story was that he traveled in a third-class berth in order to seek work in Ohio as a bricklayer. But his first move was to seek out jewelers in New York City's financial district, where he tried to sell roughs at a discount. One jeweler tipped off a licit supplier: the syndicate in Antwerp with which Dernburg had forged a connection. Antwerp forwarded the news to Berlin, where Dernburg's office determined that Popelle had stolen the stones over four years while working as a sorter for Stauch. American customs authorities made an arrest and initiated criminal prosecution in a federal district court. Popelle retained a high-priced defense attorney and was acquitted by a jury.[61]

Southwest also saw smugglers emerge from the ranks of Europeans in positions of authority. Among the most prolific were German guards stationed at diamond fields for the purpose of monitoring Africans. Over a period of several months in 1909, one guard stole 300,000 marks' worth of stones—an amount of money that represented 1.5 times the tax revenues of Lüderitz Bay's municipal government. Also playing a part were European sorters, who ran deposits of sediment through sieves. The local diamond recovery rate per digging load oscillated between one extreme (70 percent diamonds) and another (0 percent), making the fields ripe for embezzlement. Police typically ignored European sorters because the government believed them well paid. Management also worked to mitigate embezzlement by replacing hand-sorting with machines, which employed closed compartments humans would struggle to manipulate. Unhappily for the owners, though, high up-front costs of such technology rendered it slow in taking hold. In an added complication, a company's internal efforts to uncover smugglers might ensnare managers or directors—thereby threatening to harm the company's reputation and share price.[62]

In view of statistics on stolen stones, perhaps 1,000 Germans would need to have contributed over a calendar year to provide the manpower necessary for just one stage of illicit diamond activity in Southwest Africa. Beyond soldiers and sorters, therefore, a stream of collaborators evidently materialized. Already disgruntled by Dernburg's tactics, some settlers refused to obey police summons. Others sheltered fugitives or bristled at the high export toll levied on diamonds—a toll that further sapped profit margins small producers already deemed too thin.[63]

Amateur producers operating in the Forbidden Zone did more than protest court decisions that denied them claims to fields they believed were rightfully theirs. In one case, a trio of residents sat watch over a field for two years, investing considerable sums in legal fees and equipment, only to see their claim dismissed in favor of the large German banks' preferred company, which controlled some 4,000 other fields in the Zone. The aggrieved trio then arranged with smugglers to transport sacks filled with rough diamonds in the amount of 1.5 million marks.[64]

With highly uneven economic gains attending the boom, smugglers found recruits easy to tempt. Ship passengers in second-class berths, for instance, agreed to wear gold necklaces with illicit Namibian roughs hidden in plain sight. In the meantime, although customs inspectors scrutinized passengers boarding a ship, they did not apply the same standard to officers. Naval vessels sent by Dernburg as deterrents thus provided ideal venues for illicit activity. The more numerous the navy grew around Lüderitz Bay, the more chances smugglers had to pounce on an underpaid deck officer. Civilians also noted a mismatch between smuggling's risk and reward. The possibility of a three-month prison sentence and fines from 5,000 to 100,000 marks for illicit diamond possession sounded draconian, but such measures might not dissuade people who had scant money or reputation to lose.[65]

The colonial state adjusted by deporting offenders, not just after proven participation, but on mere suspicion. To this end, the state heightened restrictions on identity cards used to track those entering and exiting the Forbidden Zone—a policy enforced without exception. In 1911, the governor of Southwest expanded this system by stipulating that workers must surrender their pass upon exiting the Zone or risk jail time. The idea was to ensure no passes were sold to or shared with unauthorized persons, making smugglers stand out. Alas, such measures mainly broadened the state's reach into African lives without yielding improved results.[66]

Closer to the Namib, enhanced police presence faltered on account of environmental obstacles. Pursuits of suspects through the desert risked the lives of personnel, and dunes nearly two hundred feet high and powerful winds made attempts to track footprints nigh impossible. Most of the diamond police branch traveled on imported camels. While riding camelback perhaps made sense to a quartermaster, it was hardly a winning formula when chasing a suspect amid the twists and turns of shifting sands.[67]

To track the everyday actors fueling smuggling, human intelligence-gathering needed to play a larger role in the government's campaign. The center of the web emerged in Berlin, where a police captain began running a team of undercover agents masquerading as authors looking to research the industry. The undercovers set up meetings with people who knew what was happening in Southwest, then reported back about a covert process by which smugglers used codes in newspapers to communicate with each other. Perhaps the most visible fruit of this campaign was a series of arrests made in Lüderitz Bay, where authorities prominently charged several prospectors for selling "outside" Dernburg's system.[68]

Dragnets depended on confidential informants as well as undercover agents, so Germany began contracting with veterans from South Africa. The agents, targeting workers from the diamond fields, impersonated buyers from a reputable German trading house, then informed local police about parties who expressed readiness to make illicit deals. Before long, one credible source speculated that two of every three people trying to buy diamonds were undercovers. Eventually, the network of agents grew to include detectives in continental European countries. One of these was a commissar dispatched from Berlin to monitor Hamburg's jewelers and ascertain who was supplying them with the illicit roughs that they were then selling to Hanau—the site, it will be recalled, of the aggrieved German diamond cutting industry. Another undercover posed as a waiter in an Antwerp hotel frequented by diamond traders. He would catch word of dodgy dealings, then tip off the local German consulate to authorize a buy/bust operation as he played the role of buyer.[69]

Several logistical challenges confronted the undercover network. A planned deployment took six months to get up and running; detectives needed this time to establish an alias (for example, as an insurance agent) and to outfit a rented apartment with peepholes and transparent mirrors in order to implement a "trap system." Assuming the gambit succeeded, an undercover was wise to wait a while before working again. Many undercovers thus received a paid leave of absence abroad after any bust. That was no easy, or inexpensive, process—especially when it came to remote Lüderitz Bay. From a recruiting standpoint, it also hurt that the Germans paid detectives poorly in comparison to De Beers.[70]

Along with officials' acceptance of bribes from smugglers, legal uncertainty abroad frustrated antismuggling efforts. When American customs officers arrested suspected diamond smugglers, German officials could cooperate, supply relevant materials, and seek prosecution. But the Germans had to struggle with limits of their own law when recovering such illicit diamonds, which were generally not German government property but rather that of the German companies whose diamonds had been stolen. In order to get back cash for what it was owed as customs revenue on the diamonds, the government was bound first to evaluate the stones in question through the Regie—an act which was done only in Berlin, and only in relative secrecy.[71] From the perspective of international law, moreover, the German government further needed to prove that it or the companies delegating it owned the illicit diamonds. This surprisingly difficult task would prolong an already slow-moving case, such that the trial of a suspected smuggler might not even start for nine months after arrest.

Besides, the United States also wanted to be paid, and most smugglers, lacking cash necessary to make amends for missed customs duties, could only offer the diamonds themselves as wealth—leading the United States to claim the diamonds for itself before Germany could get a word in otherwise. That dynamic obviously meant trouble for the spirit of international cooperation. Even if haggling could allow Germany to recoup some proceeds—25 percent of the gross sale price, in one large case—the settlement would need to be agreed upon by both the German government and the affected producer in yet another tortuous delay. The German government would also have to pay a lawyer in the United States to make its case in civil proceedings—for which, crucially, the costs would run high enough to discourage claims relating to all but the largest cases.[72]

* * *

An archived trial record furnishes clues about "everyday" smugglers in Southwest.[73] Over the course of a single day in late 1909, four suspects came before a judge in Lüderitz Bay on charges of entering the Forbidden Zone without a license, retrieving diamonds from someone else's field, and attempting to sell them on the black market. The source of evidence against each defendant was the same person, a watchmaker named Pragan.

Of the four defendants, three were brothers—a pair of sibling bakers and their older brother, a confectioner losing his shop. Among the accused, however, was also an engineer who had spent time in Amsterdam and who evidently knew a swindle when he saw one. As it turned out, Pragan went to police to inform only after the engineer pulled a gun on him for refusing to pay. Here the spectrum of savvy-naïve behavior proved hard to read, complicating public efforts to assess guilt. One defendant credibly claimed that he was a victim of circumstance, and that Pragan preyed on "human weakness" to entrap him. Another testified that because the defendants found their stones in the Namib before it legally became the Forbidden Zone, the defendants thought the stones were licit. Many people around Lüderitz Bay *were* confused by, or unaware of, the rules.[74] Diamond legislation was nascent and in a state of near-continual flux. Smugglers could fall victim to the fluidity and the lack of clear criminal precedents, even as they could also exploit them.

Unconvinced, Dernburg denounced the complicity and active participation of settlers in Southwest, whose discontentment greased the wheels of illicit diamond activity. Early in 1910, his penchant for speaking carelessly again on display, Dernburg declared to German parliament that Southwest's European residents would, if left alone, steal 85 percent of annual diamond output. Dernburg had a point. The historic smuggling in the colony did not happen without lots of civilians looking the other way or committing crimes. Moreover, statistics compiled on illicit diamond trade in Southwest looked worse than those published by South Africa in its campaign against a relatively more developed domestic smuggling network.[75]

But the German public discourse about smuggling was never entirely rational—something Dernburg, in the face of unremitting anti-Semitism, came to learn. The colonial state's apparent coziness with big business prejudiced settlers in favor of illicit activity. Leading figures in Lüderitz Bay painted Dernburg's antismuggling measures as underhanded ways to protect the Corporation, the Forbidden Zone, the Regie, and the "Jewish" connection to Antwerp. Admittedly, Southwest Africa's inaugural antismuggling legislation came from decrees issued by the German Colonial Corporation, which remained deeply unpopular. The customs house that kept middling enterprisers from "illegal" shares of diamond wealth also sat adjacent to the Corporation's offices, which locals saw as benefiting from ruinous tax policies.[76] Unfortunately for Dernburg, the colony's embittered white population came to believe that while they may have been guilty of illicit behavior, the capitalism their government protected was immoral.

Residents of Southwest soon found a champion. In Berlin, the enterprising politician Matthias Erzberger channeled colonial anger and debates about diamonds into a broader opposition campaign against the German government's economic policies. In the process, he toppled Dernburg.

CHAPTER 9

POLITICS

◆ When the diamond boom hit, Matthias Erzberger was an unlikely rising star in the Reichstag. "A big fellow with a smart and vulgar face," recalled one colleague, the thirty-three-year-old Erzberger was "in every way rotund," and at first sight "nobody would guess that this mass of unhealthy looking fat" possessed a superior political mind. Despite Erzberger's unphotogenic quality—a perceived flaw compounded by his being a pince-nez-wearing Swabian of low birth—he distinguished himself upon taking his seat in 1903. Germany's youngest parliamentary deputy proved skilled in the art of presenting statistics. His voice shrill but steady, he arrived at work each morning around 8:30 to prepare speeches. Those speeches had four knacks: catchy aphorisms, political contortionism, self-aggrandizement, and a tendency to run on for hours.[1]

Erzberger's famed witticisms, accompanied by a coarse laugh, belied serious aspirations. Erzberger raised his profile from 1905 to 1906, when his exposés ushered in the largest round of criticism yet faced by the colonial administration. One of Erzberger's favorite targets was Bernhard Dernburg's predecessor, Prince Ernst von Hohenlohe-Langenburg. Hohenlohe had awarded colonial government contracts to monopoly companies, without competitive bidding. That decision brought big profits to the companies' largest shareholders, which included the wife of the Prussian minister for agriculture, Victor von Podbielski. Mrs. Podbielski, Erzberger revealed, collected enormous dividends on her company stock during the Southwest African military campaign, the largest armed German engagement since the Franco-Prussian War. Erzberger's further investigation into this connection eventually took down Hohenlohe, Podbielski, and other officials charged with accepting bribes and maintaining secret bank accounts. Erzberger looked like a giant slayer.[2]

Scandals of this kind called into question not just the amount of funding for colonial projects—a subject parliament discussed regularly—but whether parliament could control the directions of such funding. Following the money often led to big banks, whose apparatuses collected fees for processing a swollen volume of colonial transactions. From 1905, at Erzberger's instigation, parliament engaged in unprecedented scrutiny of these transactions.[3] Deputies examined civilian and military files on negotiations ranging from the monopoly company supplying soldiers with boots, to the monopoly company running the harbor at Lüderitz Bay.

To protect Germans in Southwest Africa cost an estimated 173 times more per capita than it did to protect residents of mainland Germany. With Erzberger in the lead, the Reichstag moved to address that disparity by trimming prospective colonial budgets where possible: reducing Southwest's subsidies by nearly a fifth, refusing an aid package for colonial settlers impacted by the war, and suggesting that Southwest pay the costs of its continued military occupation. This austerity course contrasted with the behavior of other great powers, who generally charged expenditures for colonial troops to the accounts of the metropole.[4]

Erzberger's crusade against petty corruption started to frighten the German government when it delved into knottier issues: for example, whether to permit a Reichstag deputy chairing a committee on colonial funding to serve simultaneously as the president of a colonial concession company receiving government subsidies. In the domestic political arena, Erzberger's parliamentary muscle-flexing also threatened the so-called personal rule of Emperor Wilhelm II, who vouched for officials later exposed as corrupt.[5] Just as the emperor's standing was waning, anyway, thanks to public-relations gaffes, Erzberger's agenda promised to leverage parliamentary control of colonial budgets into active control of German military and social policies. Such spillover represented a bugbear to Germany's conservative, and overwhelmingly Prussian, elites.

Over the course of 1906, Erzberger induced his Catholic Center Party to block the passage of colonial budgetary bills in parliament. At Bernhard Dernburg's urging, rival parties retaliated. Along with the million-odd members of Germany's Navy League, they fostered one of the country's strongest outbreaks of anti-Catholicism since the *Kulturkampf*. Then, again at Dernburg's behest, the government used a legislative deadlock about Lüderitz Bay's railroad funding as a pretext to dissolve parliament and call snap elections.[6]

The election results in 1907 favored the government, as they had in previous parliamentary dissolutions in 1887 and 1893. German voters, their sense of honor stoked by cross-country speeches from Dernburg, turned out in record numbers. Conservatives, liberals, and progressives, having formed a preelection alliance, won just enough votes to form a fresh Reichstag coalition excluding ostensibly less patriotic parties: Social Democrats, but also Erzberger's Catholic Center. As a corollary, this sidelined party struggled to overcome a perception that Catholics contributed less to colonial efforts than did Protestants. True, the Catholic Center remained, from 1907 to 1912, Germany's largest party. But it was riven by internecine disagreement. Thanks to Dernburg, the party also had to rebut the charge—which Adolf Hitler continued to make decades later—that it "systematically sabotaged" Germany's colonial project.[7]

The election "bloc" formed after 1907's elections crumbled in July 1909. Divided over Prussia's three-class franchise and unable to pass substantial reforms to the German tax system, the coalition succumbed to its contradictions. Dernburg hoped that Germany's newfound diamonds might distract from domestic tax disputes. Instead, Dernburg's diamonds made the German state look overly friendly to the wealthy just as the government was scrounging for cash and preaching austerity. In mid-1909, when the government's last-minute tax overture to the Center Party faltered, in the process further alienating conservatives and some liberals, the government's standing with parliament grew tenuous.[8] There followed the exit of Bernhard von Bülow, the chancellor who had appointed Dernburg.

Entering 1910, Dernburg had to work under a less amenable replacement chancellor, Theobald von Bethmann Hollweg. Bethmann saw Dernburg as a leftover; Dernburg saw Bethmann as regressive. In this context, Bethmann condemned colonial companies operating with extensive privileges and sought to distance himself from Dernburg's feud with settlers in Southwest. Meanwhile, Erzberger moved to assert leadership over an older, less dynamic fraction within the Center Party. Remembering the humiliation Dernburg had visited on his party, Erzberger likened 1907's snap elections to a "con." Haughty as ever, Dernburg chirped that Erzberger was "only" a former schoolteacher whose economic analysis one should not take seriously. Dernburg sought to punish officials for leaking embarrassing information to Erzberger, who had no scruples about publishing stolen documents. The Colonial Office prosecuted Catholic missionaries issuing negative reports about the colonies. And Dernburg made a show in parliament of pointing out Erzberger's recurrent mathematical errors.[9]

In fact, Erzberger and Dernburg were remarkably alike. Both men were bad-mannered, self-promoting egotists who presumed to understand everything and never hesitated to air their views. Both were indefatigable careerists. Both massaged statistics when it suited their purposes. And both displayed genuine religious devotion.[10]

Arguably the most significant trait the men shared, though, was that they saw themselves as reformers. Consistent with the Catholic Center Party, whose members were broadly growing more supportive of nationalistic campaigns and increased military spending, Erzberger proved no inveterate colonial critic. To be sure, he had once entertained "giving up" Southwest Africa, and he sometimes mocked Germany's overseas troops, joking that their purpose was to spread syphilis. But Erzberger also championed missionary work in colonies and fumed when Germany was shut out of Morocco. He even condoned General Lothar von Trotha's monstrous extermination order against the Herero in Southwest Africa.[11]

Committed to avoiding future calamitous violence, Erzberger worked with Dernburg on several policies to restructure German colonialism. The men agreed to revise contracts that had allowed egregious profiteering during the military campaign in Southwest Africa. They supported prosecution of habitual offenders. And they periodically aroused the ire of Germany's most virulent racists by speaking about Africans as human beings.[12]

But Erzberger was a professional politician. His oratory conveyed studied elegance, whereas Dernburg spoke carelessly and without preparation, laying out points with blunt force. Erzberger proved an abler political chameleon, too, with one colleague complaining that he had "no convictions, only appetites." These differences became more apparent after 1908, as Erzberger started to disagree with Dernburg over how to channel and apportion diamond wealth. At the time, Erzberger served on a commission examining colonial land and mining rights. The commission's remit was not just to request colonial reform, but to decide among multiple species of reform. In reality, the commission provided Erzberger a vehicle to do two things: first, to stage a kind of referendum on monopoly capitalism; and second, to take revenge on Dernburg by investigating the German Colonial Corporation in Southwest Africa, a widely despised company apparently being coddled by the colonial secretary.[13]

•   •   •

In 1905, with violence raging in multiple German colonies, Erzberger couched his criticisms of colonial economics in a prediction that Southwest Africa would never produce significant mineral wealth. After 1908's major diamond strikes, his outlook shifted. Erzberger at first flattered Dernburg by suggesting that the state ennoble the colonial secretary. Erzberger also supported Dernburg by agreeing that the Forbidden Zone was a necessary measure to help the diamond industry compete with De Beers.[14]

Neither stance lasted long. By 1909, with rumors circulating that Erzberger wanted Dernburg's job, he took greater interest in the diamonds seizing the public's attention. Erzberger agreed with Dernburg that settler dreams of prosperity would falter without strong state management. In that spirit, Erzberger claimed to find the legal claims of autonomy by the Colonial Corporation distasteful. He particularly objected to the Corporation's light treatment from Dernburg, whose appointment he said he had opposed. Erzberger alleged that Dernburg's diamond rules had become "a complete fiasco."[15]

As stock speculation created and erased fortunes overnight, Erzberger rightly argued that the Forbidden Zone inordinately profited large German banks, whose majority stakeholders controlled the Corporation, the Regie, the best mining stocks, and Southwest's leading diamond companies. This ruthless, state-ordained diamond cartel, according to Erzberger, explained if it did not justify rampant smuggling by colonial residents. As important, the disparity in colonial wealth aroused constituencies in Germany whom Erzberger's Center Party targeted: voters from villages and mid-sized towns, many anxious about the effects of modernity and pessimistic about cultural changes.[16]

Conveniently for Erzberger, the Center Party's ideal voters in Germany held a status to which many settlers in Southwest Africa equated their own. Each constituency supported tighter regulation of cartels in an era when such oversight was lacking, and when cartel masters were thought to make fortunes on the back of lax or venal regulators. As well, each constituency saw itself facing tax squeezes and could credibly accuse

German liberals—prominently represented by Dernburg—of caring too little about farmers and agricultural questions fundamental to life.[17]

"In the budget," wrote contemporary Austrian sociologist Rudolf Goldscheid, "lies the skeleton of the state with all deceptive ideologies stripped away." Erzberger presumed to identify the skeleton in Southwest's diamond fields. In Germany, enterprising small and medium-sized businessmen of the *Mittelstand* fought against legislation that discriminated in favor of large liquor, beer, and match industries. Erzberger cast the diamond debates as an overseas extension of that conflict—with colonial capitalism reflecting the domestic variety. In so doing, he gave new definition and purpose to his political party in Germany. A refreshed Center looked to poach voters from other moderate parties by showing how the Corporation and the stock market—playgrounds for German colonization's glaring winners—stood in league with the National Liberals and Left Liberals tied to Dernburg.[18]

In 1910, for the first time, colonial settlers in Southwest were asked to pay property- and value-added taxes. Southwest's largely agrarian way of life—like that of some parts of Germany—appeared to be under threat. Many of the colony's settlers resented the move, considering themselves systematically disadvantaged. These were people who were "creating" with their hands, in Erzberger's terminology. They seemed to form a stark contrast to stock speculators and rich investors, who, like Dernburg, performed no physical labor save shuffling paper deeds.[19]

Gossip circulated in Germany about insider trading in relation to the Forbidden Zone, with heavy purchasing by banks having begun just a few days before the Zone's creation. Erzberger recognized the signs, having profited from similarly questionable financial speculation since arriving in parliament. He added grist to the rumor mill by alleging that Dernburg created the Zone as a corrupt quid pro quo with high finance. Evidently fearful of such accusations, multiple bureaucrats working under Dernburg took leave.[20]

Erzberger's claims of venality gained traction with the public when Dernburg spearheaded a crackdown on colonial share excesses. In the wake of fraud scandals surrounding the South African Territories Ltd, a court in Southwest sentenced some offenders to four years in jail. Dernburg followed up by taking some strong regulatory steps. Despite his image as a friend of finance who openly admired "the boys from the stock exchange," he limited publication of prices for shares in unlisted companies, which had provided fodder for manipulative promoters and insider traders. Dernburg also moved to prohibit trading outside the auspices of official exchanges in Berlin and other major German cities. Finally, he proposed to place a supertax on stock dividends that exceeded 20 percent annually.[21]

Dernburg's steps did not satisfy Erzberger, who charged that the entire colonial diamond business needed sweeping reform. Bankers behind the German Colonial Corporation knew what was going to happen in diamond stocks before the general public did. Accordingly, they could alert friends or powerful clients ahead of news releases that would move share prices one way or another. Such maneuvering reflected information asymmetry around the mining, sale, and marketing of diamonds—all enabled by Dernburg's secretive Regie. Another twist lay in the treaties on which the Corporation based its claims to rule the Forbidden Zone. These paper documents, Erzberger noted, had emerged through deceitful representations made by Adolf Lüderitz to Southwest Africa's Indigenous population. Ethically, no impediment existed to overriding such bogus treaties in the interest of adjusting the distribution of diamond wealth. "When it is a question of millions," Erzberger declared, "only justice should speak."[22]

What was the purpose of developing a colony, Erzberger asked, when all the profits went to private investors, rather than to the taxpayers who funded the infrastructure and military protection? And why were private investors parking their colonial profits in metropolitan banking centers, rather than circulating capital to productive effect in Southwest? Erzberger spotlighted these cracks in the colonial edifice. Unrefined as ever, Dernburg could only admit to parliament that he did not care to break the legal shackles placed on him by the mistakes of Bismarck and other predecessors.[23]

In 1909, conservatives, Erzberger, and the Catholic Center Party succeeded in killing a parliamentary proposal to raise inheritance taxes on the rich. The German federal government, groaning under the weight of a naval arms race and colonial expenditures, desperately needed more tax money. But the government was not going to get this money from new direct taxes (for which parliament lacked constitutional authority) or from expanded inheritance taxes (which conservatives and the Center opposed). Instead, the additional money would come from indirect taxes on imports and consumption, the brunt of which fell on lower-income consumers. Erzberger appealed precisely to these taxpayers, including

voters for the Center who disapproved of their party's abetting of conservatives against tax reform. Erzberger suggested that Germans, having
already shouldered major colonial losses and facing rising living costs,
ought to demand a fair share of diamond money. Alternatively, the
German public should demand state ownership and control of the diamond business, as the government had contemplated arranging (mostly
unsuccessfully) in the domestic potash and coal markets.[24]

Erzberger estimated that, as it stood, the arrangement with the Colonial Corporation would bring the German state millions of marks per
annum less than it deserved. This loss would sting all the more because
Germany had shelled out hundreds of millions of marks to build railroads in Southwest between 1904 and 1906, only to follow that up
with additional subsidies, bailouts, and buy-ins. The diamond boom
starting in 1908, he claimed, became possible only because of such state
investment.[25]

Erzberger joined Dernburg in predicting more than a billion marks'
worth of wealth generation from the diamond fields—a dramatic underestimate, as it turned out. Erzberger surmised that, of this wealth, hundreds of millions would drop into the laps of the Corporation and the
large German banks behind it. True, the government took a large rent
from every diamond-related transaction, including extraction, cutting,
and marketing. Added together, those rents amounted to the majority
of all reported diamond revenue.[26] But such rewards did not make up
for opportunity cost. Were surplus funds to flow to another group in
Germany—like the small-business taxpayers whom Erzberger's Catholic
Center Party coveted—secondary and tertiary gains could be realized.

Dernburg pleaded to parliament that the banks' apparently inordinate
degree of diamond control owed to little-understood treaties dating to
the start of German colonial history, when Bismarck had called on private enterprises to rule colonial protectorates. Dernburg did not view
these old treaties as "one-way" grants of privileges from the German state
to private powers—to be voided at the state's pleasure, more or less in
the way Dernburg had cancelled the contracts of the worst war profiteers.
Dernburg asserted that the treaties were reciprocal, binding agreements
between equal members of an international community that could only
be dissolved by mutual consent. In 1910, the Imperial Justice Office, Germany's highest legal authority, agreed with Dernburg's interpretation.[27]

The Imperial Justice Office's decision attested to an underlying weakness of the German government's negotiating position. Tugging hard on

the Corporation's rights, as Erzberger demanded, could shake apart the whole colonial apparatus of treaties providing a veneer of legality to the German colonial presence in Southwest. It could also pop the stock bubble on which a socially diverse population was attempting to capitalize.[28]

Into 1910, Dernburg declared that for the state unilaterally to revise the status of the Corporation, however just in theory, would amount in practice to expropriation of property holders. Such radicalism could cost Dernburg the support of big banks behind the Corporation—banks necessary to build infrastructure in Southwest and other German colonies. A still larger worry for Dernburg and liberals sympathetic to him was how governmental confiscations of diamond rights might create a precedent for future socialist governments to nationalize private property. Social Democrats in Imperial Germany figured as a bugaboo party whom liberals accused of wanting to rob farmers and businessmen. Even without a shiny precedent such as the diamonds could afford, Social Democratic messaging was proving effective enough domestically that, in the four years preceding the diamond discoveries, German union membership doubled, and the country saw an explosion in the number of workers' strikes. At the height of the diamond boom, the notion of the German state experimenting with collectivism and large-scale abolition of private property sounded like Social Democracy in action. That potential affinity was significant, because conservatives accused Dernburg and German liberals of being too friendly to Social Democratic ideas for economic planning. After all, conservatives rejecting federal plans to tax inheritance and income cited a slippery slope to the elimination of private property.[29]

•   •   •

In the early months of 1910, Dernburg sought to reach a financial settlement with the Colonial Corporation whereby the Corporation would at last relinquish its claims to autonomy and governance inside the Forbidden Zone, in exchange for yet more money. Dernburg's task was rendered somewhat easier by a revolving door existing between government bureaucrats, the Corporation, and certain businessmen poised to benefit from the Regie. Ferdinand Bugge, a Corporation director, was an army veteran who became a prominent politician in Berlin and who, on the side, managed colonial trading businesses and served on the board of the Regie. Not to be outdone was Curt Pasel, who directed Stauch's fields while conducting high-level mining assessments in the employ of the government. Last but not least, there was Heinrich Ernst Göring, a former governor of German Southwest Africa as well as a shareholder and director of the Corporation.[30]

Partly because of this incestuousness, the Forbidden Zone itself had originally been proposed by the Corporation to Dernburg—and not, as the public might assume, vice versa. That discomfiting history, which Erzberger exposed, embarrassed Dernburg. In one surviving memo, Dernburg enumerated points challenging the Corporation, only to then cross them out. In other moments, he sought to assure the Corporation in secret meetings that his policies were flexible in accordance with their wishes.[31]

As he negotiated for the Corporation's buyout in 1910, Dernburg—who put great effort into image maintenance—made a show of being seen to wrest some concessions. In late January 1910, with Erzberger continuing in his investigations, the Reichstag passed a resolution demanding that Dernburg revise a draft agreement with the Corporation that paid the Corporation too much money. In response, Dernburg started withholding the payment of royalties owed to the Corporation on state-owned blocks of mines—a "considerable" sum for which the Corporation immediately demanded restitution.[32]

To Erzberger, notwithstanding Dernburg's withholding of royalties, the colonial secretary's use of kid gloves on the Corporation appeared unwarranted. In 1906, colonial officials had introduced the concept of a "Forbidden Zone" in Southwest Africa in order to distinguish between an area fully under their control and surrounding areas in which polities like Ovamboland retained governing powers. Erzberger recalled that only Africans with passes from the government could enter or leave the defended Forbidden Zone of 1906, in which German settlers overwhelmingly resided.[33] Now, in 1910, Erzberger charged the government in Berlin with giving legal force to a curious, and extra-legal, inversion of its earlier formula. In Southwest Africa, a new Forbidden Zone took hold as a piece of territory in which the Corporation, not the state or military, licensed and administered people moving within boundaries. The Corporation effectively exercised the control for which Germany, elsewhere, had killed.

What galled Erzberger was that not just laymen but agents of the state figured among the new Forbidden Zone's excluded parties. State personnel walking into the Zone without the Corporation's approval to investigate worker abuses could fall into the category of smuggler and thus find themselves in criminal breach. Hardly surprising, then, that

Erzberger soon declared the diamond trade "the worst in the history of the world."[34]

Rather than concede the power of such imagery, the Corporation responded by trying to blackmail the German parliament in multiple newspaper editorials. Should Erzberger continue to push for expropriation of the Corporation, the Corporation threatened to air Bismarck's dirty colonial laundry before the public in a series of embarrassing lawsuits.[35] Erzberger did not wait to see. He published widely about the Corporation's malfeasance and transformed "Dernburg" into a metonym for corporate welfare precisely as the German Colonial Corporation stood locked in negotiations with Dernburg for a buyout.

The latter parties had agreed to preserve the status quo until 1911, when Germany's initial endorsement of the Forbidden Zone would expire. As the date drew closer, Erzberger raised the stakes. Attempting to tax the Corporation out of existence rather than to expropriate it, he demanded the imposition of a one-time levy on the wealthy in Southwest Africa: specifically, every person or business in the colony whose net worth surpassed 300,000 marks. Erzberger's revenue target was 81 million marks, or about 10 percent of the value he estimated as existing inside the Forbidden Zone. Crucially, while suggesting that this tax could be paid to the government via the transfer of land and mining rights, Erzberger challenged Dernburg to publish his negotiations concerning the Corporation's claims to sovereignty. Separately, Erzberger turned a second Reichstag commission—this one on the budget—into a debate forum on the Corporation's willingness to shoulder costs from recent colonial wars.[36]

Erzberger knew that Dernburg's domestic enemies were legion. Among them were the Catholics, whose Center Party Dernburg had once derided as an "abscess on the German body politic" but which, after 1909, formed a key part of the German government's parliamentary coalition. Then there were conservatives, the Center's new ally. Conservatives welcomed Erzberger's charge, resenting Dernburg for his coarseness, his refusal to grant meetings, and his cosmopolitanism. To conservatives, as well as political anti-Semites, Dernburg's rise to power stemmed from an original sin. Not only was Dernburg a bourgeois banker—"His Excellency the money-maker," to quote a contemporary slur among Junkers—he had also replaced Hohenlohe, an aristocrat. Even worse, the new colonial secretary, although a baptized Christian, had Jewish heritage and thus functioned as a prominent example of Jewish assimilation into a secularizing German society.[37]

Next on the enemies list came agrarians, who stressed how 1910 proved a particularly bad year for colonial residents. A drought-induced bad harvest and heavy consumption of foodstuffs by railroad workers had driven up the price of Southwest's wheat, forcing the colony to increase its imports of rice and maize in order to feed itself. With food prices and other costs rising for settlers, German agrarians joined conservative and anti-Semitic politicians to blame Dernburg.[38]

In step with that sentiment, settlers painted a picture of endless condescension by the colonial secretary. "For days and years," they complained, Dernburg "has not ceased in his presentations and in the press to discredit us before the public." They continued: "We are supposedly drunks and swindlers, have no family values, and are addicted to lawsuits." Colonial mining interests expressed gripes about their treatment, too. Dernburg had told the Reichstag that no one in Southwest cared what Lüderitz Bay miners thought, and he belittled the miners' grievances by saying they wanted the German Empire to "work for the benefit of 250 people." As for the notables leading the colonial mining contingent, Dernburg called August Stauch "Staub" (dust), mocked him as the "Desert-King," and insisted his wealth was less than the millions he claimed. Separately, Dernburg talked about colonial fraud when dismissing proposals made by Lüderitz Bay's mayor.[39]

Also rallying to Erzberger's side were employees in Germany's colonial service. Prior to Dernburg's tenure, many of these bureaucrats had been used to arriving at work just before lunch. They had experienced scant judicial or office review. And they had benefited from graft, which Dernburg sought to contain. For years, these enemies anonymously boasted to reporters that they intended to witness Dernburg's downfall, and they eventually found their opening in his failures to vanquish the Colonial Corporation and regulate the colonial stock market.[40]

As Dernburg's diverse enemies coalesced, they dropped Erzberger's tax ideas but supported his push for fundamental reforms of the German diamond industry Dernburg had created. Disgruntled producers in Southwest proposed a syndicate that would take over all rights to the Forbidden Zone in exchange for paying 80 percent of future profits to the German colonial state. That unrealistic scheme failed, but it accompanied a new demand by Erzberger for "little Bernhard" Dernburg's sacking. "The man," the parties allied to Erzberger agreed, "must go."[41]

*　　　*　　　*

While never popular with colonial settlers, Dernburg remained widely admired by economic experts. The financial editor of the *Berliner Tageblatt* celebrated Dernburg's Regie as a cartel that profited private and public parties alike. Regarding Dernburg's favoring of Antwerp, the *Frankfurter Zeitung* deemed it "the lesser evil" when compared to the alternative of De Beers. Leaders from the South African mining industry also respected Dernburg's achievements, though few said so publicly.[42]

The diamond system set up by Dernburg even won over some socialist "revisionists," who broke with Karl Liebknecht's doctrinaire rejection of imperialism in the wake of the Social Democratic Party's 1907 election defeat. "Because of Dernburg's powerful initiative," wrote one revisionist, "the German colonies will in the not too distant future become a true goldmine." Gustav Noske, an outspoken moderate Social Democratic deputy in the Reichstag, challenged Dernburg's diamond system because he wanted it tweaked, not abrogated, and because he believed diamond wealth could facilitate colonial prosperity. Noske's pragmatists ultimately joined revisionists in calling for a reformed overseas empire, with the idea that these groups could leverage their support for the government's colonial policy into concessions on domestic taxation.[43]

When assessing Dernburg's political fortunes, however, one cannot avoid acknowledging that an estimated three-quarters of the Reichstag stood against him by early 1910, when Erzberger mounted his charge for Dernburg's dismissal as colonial secretary. Not everyone believed Erzberger's allegation that Dernburg jeopardized diamonds' claim to a "first-rate position" in the colonial economy. But Dernburg had alienated enough Catholics, conservatives, agrarians, anti-Semites, and colonial bureaucrats that he was a marked man in the wake of Chancellor Bülow's resignation. Dernburg had, besides, lost some progressives and liberals on account of his autocratic behavior toward Southwest African settlers— whose wish for greater autonomy liberals inclined to support.[44]

With regard to the general populace, Dernburg's reputation suffered from his portrayal as a protector of the Corporation. After its attempts to blackmail the government in early 1910, the Corporation enjoyed the distinction of being uniformly censured by a Reichstag that rarely agreed on anything. When negotiations with Dernburg to renew the Forbidden Zone dragged on for several months longer than expected, shareholders worried that the Corporation would either lose its "rights" to the Zone or see its operations so curtailed as to endanger its exorbitant profits. The entire Reichstag, unable to compromise on numerous fiscal issues, was in fact eyeing the reviled Corporation's riches. Heavy selling of Corporation stock started to occur on a more or less daily basis as 1910 went on, sometimes with downward swings surpassing 10 percent. In just one month, the share price retreated from around 20,000 marks per share to 13,000.[45] Given that the foundation for runaway gains in diamond stocks had never been sound, panic selling set in for mining companies whose rights were dependent on the status quo in Southwest—and thus on the Corporation.

With Erzberger's calls to nationalize the diamond industry gaining traction in the Reichstag, the Corporation's meteoric share rise ended and the colonial stock bubble started to pop. As the "sad list of colonial disappointments" grew, to quote one journalist, average people investing in diamond mining shares lost much of their money. Erzberger blamed Dernburg. Others pointed a finger at the financial press, which had directly hyped diamond stocks and indirectly facilitated interactions between readers, bucket shops, and other predatory swindles. Two companies, Zillertal and German Southwest Diamond Company, dropped to 29 percent and 13 percent of their peaks, and even stronger firms, such as Kolmanskop, lost a third of their value. Such precipitous drops quickly turned into a rout.[46]

Angry shareholders demanded answers. One had bought a huge block of shares at 1,860 percent of face value only to see their course drop by half in a short time. Brokers scrambled for talking points to mollify distressed clients. As the price of the Corporation's stock ebbed to a quarter of peak levels, a prominent economist in Berlin advised investors to avoid colonial shares entirely. "The people," assessed another academic, "had sacrificed their gold to a mirage." In fairness, Dernburg had not encouraged average individuals to invest in colonial stocks. That role fell to Erzberger, who indirectly enticed by speaking ad nauseum about phenomenal shareholder profits.[47]

Diamond stock dividends that proved outrageous in 1909 did not remain so. In 1911, the Deutsche Diamanten-Gesellschaft, the one-time darling of the Corporation, delivered virtually nothing to its shareholders. The Corporation saw its dividends decline from 64 percent in 1909 to 35 percent in 1911 and 25 percent in 1913—hardly a lethal blow, considering its laughably low overhead costs. Clearly, though, the golden hills for dividends Erzberger painted when accusing Dernburg shone less brightly when the state began aggressively focusing on laws in the Forbidden Zone.[48]

While share prices later recovered somewhat, colonial shares broadly lost their allure throughout 1910. Fewer transactions became the order of the day, and the largest volume of trading in colonial shares afterward belonged not to any diamond company but to Southwest Africa's Otavi copper company. Consequently, bankers' attitudes turned. They inclined to accept tighter regulation of stocks—and this, not just relative to diamond companies, but to all colonial ventures. Keen to avoid a recurrence of fraud, German authorities moved to create a central office to distribute more reliable colonial business information. Less visibly, they sought advice on how to prevent the establishment of fake mining firms without real business.[49]

In Lüderitz Bay, joy turned to anger as once-prized stock certificates became largely worthless. An "excessive quantity of paper" had emerged from unregulated stock exchanges, ran one complaint. Nor was the maelstrom of loss confined to the colony. Back in Germany, anecdotes circulated about families who had invested their savings into now-distressed diamond shares. An arresting consequence was noticeable in the Reichstag. Between 1910 and 1913, the body at several points debated "agiotage": the practice of manipulating a stock to make quick money off share price movements. In two-thirds of these moments, the discussion referenced doomed colonial shares.[50]

•   •   •

The reversal of stock gains was, like Dernburg's unpopularity, a major factor in Erzberger's duel with the colonial secretary. In January 1910, amid the first major attacks and during negotiations with the Corporation, Dernburg told parliament that his office was "too high and his assignment too serious" to respond to criticism. Five months later, with the stock bubble bursting, he resigned. The German government gave no reason for Dernburg's exit. But clearly the diamond debates and stock swings had eroded his parliamentary standing, decreased his public credibility, and further rendered him a liability to a shaky government. The chancellor, Bethmann, hoped to stave off a threat from the left, which was set to advance resoundingly in the 1912 elections. Bethmann was cobbling together a coalition of Catholics and conservatives—the former opposed to Dernburg's diamond policy, the latter opposed to Dernburg. Bethmann thus had strong motives to sack Dernburg, lest the chancellor himself fall.[51]

Through a press campaign, Erzberger tarred Dernburg with the stock collapse, with the inequality occasioned by diamond wealth, and with the dubious colonial treaties that had long favored the Corporation. Unquestionably, Dernburg had also damaged Germany's relationship with colonists who were increasingly articulating grievances, requesting oversight of diamond affairs, and gesturing toward autonomy. Some commentators referred to the trend as a *los von Berlin* movement; others surmised that Southwest could be kept in the imperial fold only if Dernburg exited the stage.[52]

At the same time, Dernburg had lost support among some top German bankers by taking a relatively aggressive negotiating stance toward the Corporation. Under pressure, Dernburg stuck to his conviction about compensating the Corporation generously to relinquish its governing prerogatives in the Forbidden Zone. A treaty was concluded to this effect in May 1910. In the treaty, though, Dernburg forced a bargain in which the Corporation transferred its vast land holdings to the government. Having so toughened his stance, Dernburg angered leading businessmen, even as he continued to woo them.[53]

Dernburg considered himself "assailed at every turn by arrogant ignorance." Despite the uproar, the German state's takings were not as bad as many assumed. The takings looked even better when viewed alongside those of South Africa, where a mild export tax yielded significantly less government revenue. But the German state did not give this loot to its people; instead, the state steered colonial diamond revenues towards the completion of colonial railroads. Consequently, anger against Dernburg grew large enough to threaten a German government that saw cultivating the public sphere as an emergent political necessity. While Dernburg won over financial experts, Erzberger persuaded the masses and tied diamonds into larger uncertainty about capitalism. Whereas Erzberger had no qualms about diamond debates stretching out across several committees and years, Dernburg perceived the "endless" nature of this process as undercutting his mission—which, incidentally, he had largely completed by rallying interest in the colonies and finishing the railroads. Once Dernburg concluded negotiations with the Corporation in late May, therefore, he capitulated and left office in June 1910.[54]

In Germany, conservatives, the Catholic Center, the radical Socialists, the Agrarian League, and the Anti-Semites all celebrated the colonial secretary's downfall, even as Erzberger cynically extended his sympathies. A contemporary satirical cartoon in *Simplicissimus* depicted a melancholic Dernburg, head down, vainly trying to make an African elephant perform enough tricks for a German circus and so taking a bow. Ever the promoter, Dernburg apprised the press of his future plans— including his vacations. Ever the pugilist, he also defended his tenure in various fora, attempting to correct the record about points minor and major. In one instance, he boasted that his time in office had witnessed no scandals. Elsewhere he spoke of overcoming obstacles. "The world," he complained, "forgets fast how the situation in which I found myself on the occasion of my start as state secretary was deplorable." Unsurprisingly, Dernburg attempted to shape the narrative of his resignation by sending letters about it to the editors of prominent newspapers.[55]

When Dernburg lost his job, the German *Reichsregierung* lost its sole member of the German Peace Society and arguably its most capable international economic representative. Dernburg, who advocated détente with Britain and worked toward the avoidance of inter-European armed conflict through early 1910, became more distanced from the circle of power as 1914 approached. As Germany's irresponsible leaders steered the country into war, he was no longer in position to exert any influence on an incorrigible emperor. Nor was Dernburg able effectively to counsel against pushing for new colonial acquisitions, as he tried to do in 1912. Few people listened when Dernburg deemed the pursuit of more colonies a questionable proposition for the nation—even with diamond wealth and millions of marks figured into the equation.[56]

Beneath the bluster, the next years gave glimpses of a vainglorious man being humbled. A prominent Catholic paper suggested that Dernburg—a Lutheran whom no one allowed to forget his Jewish ancestry—consult Proverbs 23. "Labor not to be rich," the passage warned. Keen to avoid further attention, Dernburg's wife Emma swapped out her diamond jewelry for cheaper amber. But fate was not to spare the family. Between late 1910 and 1913, Dernburg saw his daughter and father die, and his son take seriously ill. While visiting London, Dernburg nearly perished in a hotel fire, only to find his enemies gloating over the loss of his property. Shortly thereafter, he faced charges from a state's attorney in Berlin for having distributed posters lamenting the plight of housing-insecure residents in the city. Though Dernburg later had the charges dismissed, he sweated over the prospect of three years' imprisonment for "inciting class hatred."[57]

Long accustomed to driving his automobile to work every day at nine in the morning, Dernburg started riding the streetcar. His once-plump figure grew gaunt; his pitch-black beard turned white-gray. He still signed his letters "Dr. Dernburg," and the University of Berlin endowed him with further honors. But his legendary energy ebbed, his nerves faltered, and top businessmen dismissed him as "watered down." Anti-Semites, calling Dernburg "the man who served up the colonies to big capital," experienced little pushback when urging Germans to keep this "cold-blooded, cosmopolitan rat" away from power. Enemies lambasted his charity drives for Berlin's homeless and for environmental conservation. Prussian nobles joined in to mock his hard-negotiated title of "Excellency." Hanseatic merchants rued what they perceived as his betrayal of the Corporation.[58]

In a matter of a few years, Dernburg had become yesterday's fashion. For this change, one had to credit Erzberger, who, from 1911, won greater acclaim. In Upper Swabia, a pasta manufacturer started selling noodle packets named after Erzberger and bearing his image—with his seal of approval. These were the kind of purchase, so the label read, that a "smart" businessman made. More significantly, Erzberger took private meetings with state secretaries, entered the inner sanctum of foreign-policy deliberations, and acted as a high-profile mediator between Silesian miners and the Thyssen firm, whose board of directors he joined. In 1913, the German chancellor nominated Erzberger for state honors.[59]

Erzberger's exhortation of the German public notwithstanding, Dernburg's defeat would have proven unthinkable absent a concurrent surge of popular resentment among settlers. Not without justification, this smaller group claimed it was their "political and moral victory."[60] With Dernburg gone, the settlers would acquire greater control over Southwest Africa's minerals. Germans convinced themselves that such a concession to colonial opinion would undo the inequity of capitalism exposed in and around Erzberger's campaign. They were mistaken.

CHAPTER 10

TAKEOVER

◆ Between 1911 and 1914, Southwest Africa's trade grew rapidly. In a sign of improvement through infrastructure, the cost of drinking water dropped in Lüderitz Bay and the nearby diamond fields. Pundits, hopeful that more water would spur more farming, expected the colony to prosper. In turn, the colonial state grew more confident about keeping Indigenous peoples from rising up. Theater director Carl Hagemann, visiting Southwest, spoke for many when he declared the colony's future bright. One could detect similar optimism in German fashion articles, such as a column about Wilhelm II giving Empress Augusta Victoria a brooch bearing diamonds from Southwest.[1]

Erzberger believed that Bernhard Dernburg's departure in June 1910 represented the key step to fixing Germany's diamond problems, along with a related determination by the German Colonial Corporation to keep out of the public eye. Regarding Dernburg's controversial treaties, finalized with the Corporation in May 1910, a prominent former governor of Southwest Africa, Friedrich von Lindequist, did not declare them a boon. But he did not think them a burden, either, and he affirmed their propriety. One of Germany's foremost law professors weighed in with the same verdict.[2]

The Corporation did retreat after Dernburg's exit, even going so far as to transfer most of its controversial assets to another company it controlled. Still, the Forbidden Zone remained intact, and disagreement lingered about popular control of diamond wealth. Nowhere did the second dynamic hold more than in discussions of the Regie, which big banks continued to own and run. In 1911, Erzberger and his allies supported a parliamentary commission calling for dramatic reform of the Regie's management. The commission's eventual proposal, implemented in 1912, gave Southwest African settlers more control over the Regie's decision-making apparatus. These settlers proceeded to democratize the extraction of loot from Southwest Africa's soil, if not that extracted from its Indigenous people.[3]

The redesigned Regie failed to reward the broader colonial economy, let alone the metropolitan German. The problem became less Dernburg's autocratic or oligarchic capitalism than the introduction of heightened transparency into a business that depended on secrecy and illusions. After 1911, the new masters of German diamonds did not respect the artificial mechanisms by which the diamond market thrived. In time, therefore, their populism undermined the viability of Germany's most lucrative colonial asset. It also created an opening for De Beers, a British company, to encircle and penetrate the German diamond industry.

Talk of economic inequality persisted among Southwest Africa's settlers through 1914.[4] The difference was that now politics compromised the long-term viability of German diamonds, the primary means to resolve colonial distributive conflict.

.   .   .

Ethnically German but born in the Baltic, theologian-turned-journalist Paul Rohrbach functioned as a champion of *Weltpolitik* in the early 1900s, before becoming the official in charge of settlement policy in Southwest Africa from 1903 to 1906. At the peak of violence in the colony, Rohrbach dismissed Nama and Herero as "incapable in all economic matters." But he argued for retaining Indigenous people as the workforce in a revamped colonial economy—an argument that looked sound to Germans after 1908, when the colonial state in Southwest struggled to draw out laborers to its diamond fields.[5]

Starting in 1909, Rohrbach accepted payments from settlers in Southwest Africa to write newspaper articles attacking Bernhard Dernburg's policies.[6] Rohrbach believed in the long-term viability of Southwest's extractive industries. His real dream, though, was that the colony transform into a "New Germany": an idyllic home to virtuous German ranchers and farmers that would provide a counterpart to the modernizing German metropole. In the press, Rohrbach proposed to fuse his envisioned settlement community with Dernburg's diamond economy in a way that, while vague, made him popular in a German Empire struggling to decide which sort of colonial reforms to undertake.

To this end, Rohrbach insisted that global demand could accommodate an expanded supply of diamonds from Southwest Africa. Germany needed to export as much as 2 million carats a year, rather than the 1–1.5 million carats that Dernburg saw as an upper limit. Exporting more diamonds from Southwest each year would theoretically mean earning more in tax revenues to support Southwest's agriculture. In turn, more diamond mining and more agriculture would force more of the colony's Indigenous people into subservient positions, thus relieving pressure on labor markets and realizing a social engineering goal inherent in Rohrbach's dream of settler colonialism.[7]

Through 1911, the Regie's head and Dernburg's ally, the banker Carl Fürstenberg, resisted Rohrbach's arguments. In major German newspapers, the public read headlines about a fight over how many diamonds to produce. Gradually, however, the Reichstag embraced Rohrbach's call for expanded output, owing not least to a tightening of the credit market for farmers in Southwest Africa, where bankers had to write off lots of bad debts in down years. Erzberger's muckraking contributed to this shift, with his Center Party supporting Rohrbach's proposals. Important, too, was an ongoing propaganda campaign consisting of speeches given throughout the German Empire and countless anonymous press notices.[8]

Rohrbach's push to relax restrictions on diamond output won parliamentary endorsement in April 1912. After two months of debate, the Reichstag passed a resolution calling for Germans in Southwest to win a more active role in the Regie. Settlers in Southwest had insisted that local knowledge should be wed to distant, scientific rule by experts—a kind of rule the Regie epitomized. A majority in the Reichstag now recommended that this marriage occur in the form of a modified Regie, which obliged by expanding and diversifying its management to represent some settler interests. The Regie carved out a new board seat for Rohrbach. The Regie also welcomed people like August Stauch, the frontier tycoon, and Carl Bödiker, a Lüderitz Bay–based merchant who supplied groceries, clothes, and Ovambo workers to the diamond fields.[9]

Rohrbach and his associates, Germany's designated representatives of "local knowledge," took the position that the diamond was not scarce; that the diamond's value was inherent, rather than cleverly manufactured and maintained; that people could extract diamonds profitably without concern for sustainability; and, finally, that tightly controlling output was improper. To reshape the Regie in accordance with these conceptions would reflect democratization of economic governance—a moral good, in the eyes of many Germans, and one symbolically supported by a Colonial Office looking to move on after Dernburg's departure. But the reshaped Regie also reflected ignorance and short-term thinking. Over time, changes under Rohrbach and decisions about diamond production actually cost Germany control of a precious resource. The fallout even caused tension with Erzberger, whom some colonists started to accuse of taking too much credit for too little engagement, and of having elitist tendencies in the bargain.[10]

Once seated in the Regie, Rohrbach built on a longstanding impression that the German diamond cartel took an unnecessarily high commission and treated Germans worse than it did Antwerp. Digging in as a populist reformer, Rohrbach reduced the influence of large German banks in decisions about diamond production and sales. He cut into Antwerp's power by insisting that Antwerp allow the Regie to buy a share in its cutting businesses. Next, he channeled a larger portion of the Regie's roughs through cutters in Germany—a policy that name-checked Hanau, and that accompanied third-party audits of Antwerp's books. Finally, Rohrbach's Regie relaxed stringent payment arrangements that had disproportionately burdened the few small producers in Southwest that were unaffiliated with German banks.[11]

Under Rohrbach, Southwest's diamond miners and settlers successfully cultivated German public opinion. Whereas the original board of the Regie had consisted of renowned bankers (Max Warburg, Paul von Schwabach) and financial experts (Karl Helfferich), the expanded board started to look full of nonelites. Multiple Stauch associates joined in and voted, with the result that the board reported consistently rosy projections to people reading about diamonds in newspapers. Proceedings of the Regie's meetings, once shrouded in secrecy and accompanied by cursory bookkeeping, became more open and friendly. Thus, reporting on the meetings became popular. Notices about the opening of bidding rounds, complete with terms, even appeared in the press for everyone to read.[12]

Rohrbach's push for reform soon spilled over into the realm of taxation. In January 1913, Chancellor Bethmann Hollweg decreed that, henceforth, the colonial state would tax Southwest Africa's diamond companies relative to net, as opposed to gross, revenues. A handful of small diamond producers in the colony had been paying their taxes but complained either that the burden made "poorer" fields unviable, or that it turned settlers into willing smugglers and criminal collaborators. On

Rohrbach's watch, Germany modified the colonial tax structure partly in order to appease the settlers, and partly to curb illicit diamond trade.[13]

To be fair, such high export taxes as Germany had enforced in Southwest were not unheard of in the context of Southern African minerals. Prior to the Second Anglo-Boer War, the Orange Free State and Transvaal levied massive taxes on mines, maintaining rates of 40 percent and 60 percent on grosses in certain cases. Here settler populism around Rohrbach offered another solution, however. As a corollary to the reduction in some diamond companies' taxation, the German colonial state increased taxation of large miners based in Germany—that is, miners controlled by the big German banks. Lüderitz Bay's town council, in this vein, asserted its prerogative to tax the income of "foreign" persons and corporations doing business in the colony's diamond sector.[14]

Reforms to the Regie and the German tax regime did initially relieve pressure on the small business community in Southwest. But, in a short time, these reforms also resulted in a 15 percent reduction in revenue collected by the colonial state. Some producers took advantage of the new "net" taxation rules by inflating their accounting of operating costs in order to underreport profits and minimize tax payments. Dodgy accounting, once it became known, occasioned a sustained drop in share prices for German diamond miners, many of which were interlocked via shares held in each other's operations. Even the Regie's finances took a hit when it lowered its own fee—essentially a tax—for evaluating the stones of Southwest producers. According to a confidential accounting made by South African tax experts, the Regie was previously appropriating the "equivalent to from ten to twelve per cent" of the profits in the entire German diamond business.[15] Now those numbers dropped.

While not necessarily good business, Rohrbach's diamond reform agenda proved simultaneously progressive, aggressive, nationalistic, and opposed to big banks and elites. This populist mix fit well with two contemporary strains in German public opinion. In 1911, negotiations over the fate of colonial Morocco dominated the news and threatened to embroil Germany in a war as part of the Agadir Crisis. Afterward, there was a rising sentiment on the German left against high colonial politics and the large banks associated with it. From the right, a strain of ultranationalist chauvinism charged that the government ought not to have backed down in Morocco, and that the government should accept only lopsided colonial concessions from other European powers if those powers wished to avoid war.[16] Rohrbach's Regie held appeal for both the left and right.

Between 1911 and 1914, the German state overhauled the Regie as a concession to German public opinion. Carl Fürstenberg, a cosmopolitan banker whose enormous resources and friendship with the emperor allowed him to make wry jokes about shadiness on the stock exchange, had served as the Regie's inaugural spokesman. Now, the German parliament and Colonial Office entrusted that task to Rohrbach and Stauch. Stauch emerged as a hero and won the formal chairmanship of the Regie. His was a more genial image of patriotism. It was associated, not with Dernburg or any banker in Berlin, but with what the German public broadly perceived as unobjectionable settlers making good in the world and pushing for Germany to adapt to challenges. Along with Rohrbach, Stauch came to wield effective veto authority over the German diamond business, forcing brokers like the colonial secretary, and even Erzberger, to woo him.[17]

The fruit of Rohrbach's reforms was evidenced in the Southwest African colonial state's spending. In the years after 1911, the budget called for lavish tributes to the German victory over the Nama and Herero, chiefly Windhoek's new Equestrian Monument. The budget also guaranteed the completion of administrative buildings and spending sprees on further railway work. Most important, colonial officials developed plans to leverage diamond money on behalf of the settler causes of agricultural lending and water provisioning. Multiple dam projects—ranging from the Fish River in the center of the colony to the vicinity of Lüderitz Bay—topped the agenda.[18]

However, in direct proportion to the growth of diamond exports in the Rohrbach era, the colonial state's expenditure increased precipitously. So pronounced was the rise that metropolitan German constituencies took note. In the Reichstag, deputies on the left called to protect the German taxpayer. Social Democrats maintained that the new, and enhanced, revenues coming out of Southwest should be applied first toward extinguishing colonial debts. Some liberals agreed. A majority in parliament did not.[19]

Social Democratic deputy Gustav Noske warned his colleagues about a resource curse in which Southwest Africa produced and depended on "too many diamonds." Yes, the going was good for now. But what if annual diamond production peaked or dried up in a decade, as internal government documents thought possible? And what if the price of diamonds nosedived, as it likely would during a war? In these scenarios, German Southwest Africa would remain debt-ridden and need to roll back accelerated social spending for a population increasingly accustomed to it.[20] The German taxpayer would be no better off, either.

By 1912, diamond takings supplied 75 percent of Southwest's budget, with the export tax on diamonds functioning as the backbone of the colonial state's revenue. So many diamonds were flowing out of the colony that minerals represented 95 percent of its total exports—an even higher number than the 80 percent figure recorded by neighboring South Africa. Absent continued, and probably enlarged, mineral revenues, Southwest Africa likely would experience trouble in extinguishing its official debts, for only 2,000 of its roughly 10,000 European residents paid taxes on property.[21]

Uncertain about the future of Southwest in the wake of reforms and budget risks, executives of German diamond mining companies began to encourage a practice of incomplete mining known as *Raubbau,* or cherry-picking. In 1908, Dernburg had warned against cherry-picking. In his opinion, miners needed to dig up diamond deposits with modest amounts and sizes of stones at the same time as they attacked those of a high grade (full of many carats and large stones). Only in this way could Germans get the most out of the ground over the long term, with steady output and revenues. In the years of Rohrbach's ascent, though, miners in the colony started disregarding such rules. Miners ignored deposits except those of a high grade—thus rendering unattended but viable deposits less economical to mine in future.[22] The justification for such behavior was that it helped to keep output totals high, which in turn benefited colonial revenues, the Regie, and companies' share prices.

But another result was the rapid exhaustion of some rich fields, whose loss caused worry about the German diamond industry's survival. To be sure, by 1914 most of the richest fields being worked were still robust and generating enormous profit margins. In Pomona, where average diamond caratage ran highest, some miners laid out a little over 2 German marks in working cost per carat, with their carats fetching more than 51 marks at sales to the Regie. Yet, while working costs remained quite viable at such fields, "poorer outlying claims" told a different story. There, some miners were seeing working costs balloon to an average of 35 marks to extract a single carat.[23]

The best analysis of German overmining came in reports compiled by Ernest Oppenheimer, the man who, more than any other, determined the fate of world diamond mining in decades to come. In early 1914, De Beers hired Oppenheimer, then the mayor of Kimberley but also a fluent speaker of German, to survey the fields of Southwest Africa and make a thorough estimate of the area's economic potential. So tasked, Oppenheimer managed to enter the Forbidden Zone and inspect operations. His trip ran from Schmidtfeld, fifteen kilometers north of the Forbidden Zone entrance, down to Bogenfels, in the heart of the Zone. Oppenheimer's findings—recorded for De Beers's board in such secrecy that Oppenheimer himself retained no copies—emphasized that Southwest's fields contained far more diamonds than contemporary German officials estimated. The only real problems facing the Germans were cherry-picking and overproduction.[24]

In his final report to the De Beers board, Oppenheimer concluded that, if managed professionally, the fields of Southwest Africa could prove productive for decades. The key to harnessing that potential was still more consolidation: the amalgamation and regulation of every inch of production on the order of Rhodes's earlier experiment in South Africa.[25] German deposits needed to be worked by an experienced monopoly company that possessed such overwhelming financial might as to allow for economies of scale and scope. De Beers, in other words, should do its utmost to buy up Germany's production—or, more accurately, to buy out Germany's production, as a syndicate arrangement made in 1914 would propose to do.

In 1908, De Beers had attempted without success to cajole Germany into forging a new, worldwide cartel. When competition instead heated up and Germany became a true rival, De Beers spent the next few years focused on keeping South Africa's share of diamond production as high as possible. From 1911, in the wake of German reforms to the Regie, conditions ripened for a rapprochement.[26]

◆   ◆   ◆

In 1912, an impending rollout of tariffs on diamond imports in the United States induced American jewelers to overspend—and so pile up exceptionally large stocks. At the same time, worries over a possible American war with Mexico frightened off consumers and kept inventory from moving. To get a sense of the problem, consider that in 1913 Germany officially produced 1,500,000 carats. That year, the United States—75 percent of the world market—imported just 1,140,000 carats.[27] By itself, then, Germany reported the export of more diamonds than American consumers could handle.

In 1913, the global diamond market entered into a full-fledged slump. Aware of the market pinch, De Beers blamed German overproduction. Owing to a populist shift under Rohrbach, the Germans in 1913 extracted twice as many diamonds annually as they had before; thus, the Germans flooded the world with small stones increasingly favored by America's unwashed. De Beers, its profits sinking, weighed dividend cuts and witnessed prospective equity investors back off. For the first time in memory, the London syndicate saw retail jewelers refusing to buy their allotted "sights." This disturbance was reflected in the stock market, as a result of whose declines in mining shares German capitalists were estimated to suffer losses of one billion marks in 1913—to say nothing of their British counterparts.[28]

De Beers, constrained in its ability to sell stones at a profit, had to resort to massive stockpiling. In 1913, total world diamond output came to over 6.1 million carats, but world demand encompassed just 1.52 million carats. With the Germans pushing to sell 1.5 million carats, data suggest that De Beers and the London syndicate purchased millions of other carats that year with the purpose of secretly withdrawing them from the market. Such extraordinary shadow buying, combined with a loss of faith from sight-holders, placed the core of the diamond business in jeopardy.[29]

In Europe, the Antwerp syndicate buying German production separately weakened. Antwerp's contracts were contested by a revamped Regie under Rohrbach, with German rivals urging the government to ditch the Belgians. Antwerp functioned as an object of hate for hypernationalists who charged that because it was "not in the German Reich," Germans should avoid supplying it. As well, Antwerp found its status eroded by rumors that "certain members of the Regie" friendly with Dernburg had surreptitiously invested in Belgian cutting factories. Although Lüderitz Bay's Chamber of Mines eventually lost a libel trial for spreading this gossip, the Reichstag cited it in 1912 when initiating investigations that forced the Regie to open up its bidding process to public scrutiny.[30]

Despite the Regie's willingness to dump Antwerp, domestic German consortia did not provide a credible alternative in 1913, so Antwerp succeeded in keeping its prize that year. The real effect was to frighten Antwerp into issuing too high a bid. As Antwerp made new offers—to the tune of 58 percent over 1912's average tender—colonial settlers and staunch nationalists welcomed the apparent windfall. Simultaneously, State Secretary for Colonies Wilhelm Solf drafted expansionist plans to acquire a portion of the Belgian Congo that had started to prove diamond-rich and was just making its first delivery to Antwerp.[31] Perhaps in the future, Germany's share in world output would grow yet greater, thus leading to a strengthening of its negotiating power vis-à-vis London.

The bidding victory of Antwerp proved pyrrhic. Having spent too much amid a lull in American consumer demand, Antwerp soon sat on as much as 30 million marks' worth of unsold, mostly German, diamonds. Throughout 1913, the city's inventory remained alarmingly high. Marketing splashes such as awards, fashion shows, and free public Christmas parties failed to reverse the damage. "Away with banal diamonds," advised a ladies' style correspondent for the season. Throughout it all, more diamonds than ever were coming out of the ground in Southwest, as the reformed Regie wanted.[32]

Playing defense, Antwerp dumped large blocks of shares in De Beers's stock, with the aim of reducing confidence in their rival. Antwerp's merchants also lobbied officials in Berlin for relief. In one instance, they sent Wilhelm II ivory statues carved in the image of Lodewyk van Bercken, a fifteenth-century Flemish diamond cutter who pioneered polishing methods. The statues, their senders told the emperor, contained the first diamonds ever evaluated by "his" Regie. When the emperor did not intercede, the Antwerp group asked to excuse itself from future bidding rounds lest it risk insolvency. The Regie, demonstrating little sympathy, told the public that it was "not going to help by delivering smaller quantities."[33]

Private transcripts of Regie meetings around this time show that working arrangements with De Beers were no longer considered impolitic—even if, to quote one source, such a shift meant ending the "diamond war" with De Beers that had once flattered German national pride.[34] In the summer of 1913, as Antwerp begged for mercy, De Beers stepped in to make the Germans a very high offer. The price De Beers offered represented a rise from the usual 29 marks per carat to 45 marks—more than Antwerp thought it reasonable to pay, especially when Antwerp held excess inventory.

While De Beers dazzled the Regie, fledgling German consortia mounted insufficient bids. Amsterdam, starved of stones, lay in crisis. Dernburg loyalists, under populist pressure, had already consented to ending the secrecy surrounding the Regie's bidding process in the hope that Germans would see Antwerp as the best long-term business partner. Hence, heightened transparency increased wishes for immediate gratification through De Beers's offer. The Dernburg loyalists recommended reduced deliveries to Antwerp, along with the construction of a stockpile until market conditions stabilized and Antwerp's finances improved. The populists around Rohrbach prevailed, accepting De Beers's offer and continuing to recommend the biggest sales on the best possible terms for Southwest.[35]

Dernburg's remaining disciples resigned from the Regie. Chaos set in by late 1913, as one resigning banker accused a fellow board member of character assassination, then made allegations about Stauch's motives "being the least clean imaginable." Experts complained about the Germans driving the diamond industry to death. Still, a majority of the Regie's board refused to agree to output cuts, even as American demand slumped. In Paris, the city's foremost diamond merchant filed for bankruptcy in early 1914, leading French investors to dump their shares in diamond equities. A panicking Regie responded only with further housecleaning, this time in the form of isolating its remaining Jewish board members.[36]

Chancellor Bethmann Hollweg's government, dissatisfied with the tumult and fearful of De Beers's incursion, began quietly buying shares in the Regie with the intention of nationalizing it. This nationalization scheme was to be overseen by Walther Rathenau, the prominent Jewish industrialist responsible for creating aspects of Dernburg's diamond system in 1908. Rathenau's prospective nationalization would comprise two parts: first, having the state buy up Regie shares sold by bankers exiting the group; second, imposing a production cut of 30 percent on diamonds from Southwest to sustain the illusion of diamonds' scarcity.[37]

Southwest African settlers dismissed Bethmann's move to nationalize diamond production as a slap to small German colonists; one assumes they also resented further participation by Rathenau, in view of his Jewish heritage. For their part, Social Democrats mainly focused on blowing up the Antwerp deal because Antwerp's workers seemed less in need of relief than Germany's. In the Reichstag, progressive deputies—normally economically liberal—suggested an alternative course whereby the German government would not just sell to De Beers but join up with it to form a bigger cartel. Remarkably, as Woodrow Wilson made contemporaneous calls for stronger antitrust laws in the United States, prominent Germans were cozying up to the idea of a different, more powerful cartel featuring new partners and considerable state participation.[38]

A diverse array of political camps decided that the best tactic to thwart nationalization was to increase the association between Germany and De Beers. Aware of this perception, De Beers's proxies made further buys from the Regie at inflated prices so as to mollify critics of an Anglo-German deal. De Beers also bragged to bankers about the benefits of growing collaboration with the Germans.[39]

As 1913 ended, De Beers reached out to the German government and proposed joining forces permanently, and on a larger basis. Both parties could form an international, public-private cartel controlling some 98 percent of the world diamond supply. This radical proposal was the antithesis of the system Dernburg had set up, and the antithesis of what powerful German banks wanted.[40] Colonial settlers and German politicians, not German oligarchs, decided to say yes.

Like the Regie, German statesmen had begun to think of the diamond industry's "national" interest in terms of maximized short-term gain, rather than as a long-term industry suited for development. Discarding the nationalization scheme, Bethmann and the German Colonial Office warmed to the Regie's request to form "a new diamond trust" that would secure everyone the largest possible profits—whether or not that meant keeping free from De Beers or keeping the German diamond industry sustainable in the long term.[41]

The idea of a new trust or cartel was increasingly welcome, too, within the South African government. Its champion was General Jan Smuts, best known to posterity as an intellectual founder of the League of Nations and the United Nations. Smuts knew that the public finances of the Union of South Africa looked shaky in 1913. That year's Union government bond issue failed spectacularly. A wave of white miners' unrest on goldfields in the Rand was also disrupting the South African economy. In some urban areas, such as Johannesburg, strikes temporarily displaced local governments, and the turmoil spread to state-owned railways.[42]

Against this backdrop, Smuts invited the German government to attend a conference of diamond producers in Cape Town in early 1914. He was, reported one insider, "bent on German cooperation," despite objections from South Africans who feared that "the Germans will certainly agree to a conference, make a lot of fuss, gain all the information possible, benefit in their next contract for the sale of their diamonds [to Antwerp . . .], but otherwise do nothing." Such scruples made sense, not least because legal uncertainty surrounded the German government's potential participation in a cartel that mixed public and private offices. South African diamond producers had no guarantee that the German government would honor production quotas. Nor was there a mechanism for enforcement or penalties.[43]

Nonetheless, De Beers and the Germans dived in. Smuts's inclination to conciliate the Germans through favorable terms, and to create an absolute worldwide monopoly, overpowered all objections. In June 1914, he realized his wish. The German chancellor, the German Colonial Office, the Regie, and the German diamond miners in the Forbidden Zone agreed to a quota system with De Beers in which Southwest Africa would contribute roughly 21 percent of global production.[44]

Such collaboration among rival colonial powers was hardly unprecedented. In the Namib, a bustling flow of migrant labor already connected the British and German imperial regimes. Increased interdependence had followed from the contemporary injection of German money into the Cape Colony—money that bought not just water and labor, but enormous quantities of guns and pack animals. Weapons in turn impinged on the biggest collaboration of all: a united front against the expansion of rights for Africans living under European colonialism. Many affected Africans resided in borderlands under German and South African control; many did not recognize or obey the regulations the colonizers sought to impose upon them; and many led uprisings that fell to combined British and German military expeditions. German and South African colonial leadership, in this context, exchanged source materials on matters of law.[45]

In June 1914, as Smuts and the Germans sealed their diamond deal, a squadron of the British navy spent a week on a friendly visit with the German navy. That was a minor moment in comparison to the colonial sphere, where, starting in 1912, both powers had negotiated major accords concerning the future partition—in Germany's favor—of Portuguese Mozambique, and perhaps of Angola and of the Belgian Congo as well.[46]

The Anglo-German deal for diamonds played a role in the trend of improving relations between German and British colonial authorities in the aftermath of the Second Moroccan Crisis. Indeed, the world diamond cartel agreed upon in June 1914 appears to have been a pillar in a broader plan to form a kind of Anglo-German "commercial entente" in colonial theaters. The German chancellor Bethmann evidently offered diamonds to the British Empire as a sweetener, in exchange for this miniature entente. Bethmann hoped the mini-entente would buy time to strengthen the German military.[47]

The cartel's formation had a second, entirely different significance for Europe, coming as it did in the month preceding an Anglo-German world war. Here as elsewhere, colonial grounds functioned as a kind of laboratory, only this time with the formation of a public-private cartel that featured states and companies on a level plane as members in a price- and output-fixing conspiracy. The newness and uniqueness of this phenomenon was reflected in contemporary coverage. Germans did not know whether to call the agreed cartel a "great combine," an "international diamond trust," or an "English-German league," and this new incarnation of the diamond "trust" was seen as unprecedented by virtue of lending multiple sovereigns' force to compulsory international output quotas and cuts. All of this reform was occurring at the behest of *states*, rather than primarily through the private companies. That dynamic represented a major deviation from the usual syndical arrangements controlling, say, coal mining or steel pipe–making. "Were it only a question," reported Natty Rothschild, "of private rival enterprises under various directors who may be inimical to each other and probably not over friendly, this would be of less importance." Instead, the Union of South Africa and German government were committed participants with much at stake.[48]

While Germany's taking a little more than a fifth of world diamond production may not seem significant today, the agreement made waves across the Atlantic. Diamond brokers in New York's Fifth Avenue shops took notice. They recognized Germany's *volte-face* as a crucial move, because many German financial journalists had only recently expressed misgivings about trusting the British. From 1908, after all, De Beers had tried to undertake corporate espionage against their German rival.[49]

To be fair, not all was forgotten. The cartel contract Germany signed ominously included a self-destruct clause in the event of an Anglo-German war—a feature approved by the German government, which quietly became the majority shareholder in the Regie but left the visible leadership to the likes of August Stauch and Paul Rohrbach. Prominent German outlets also indicated wariness. "Now we are strong enough," mused the *Vossische Zeitung*, "to sell our stones to the De Beers syndicate for a time." "Without harm," the newspaper continued, "we can, as necessary, separate ourselves again."[50]

Assuming that Germany was otherwise going to have to slash output from Southwest Africa in order to prop up prices—and it was, by all accounts—then the deal with De Beers would allow Germany to freeze output levels where they were, on favorable terms. That said, in colluding with De Beers, the Germans who championed German-first policies in regard to cutting and sales had undermined their own vision of a "German diamond empire." With the sidelining of Antwerp, a city loathed by nationalists, De Beers became a necessary partner. That partnership in turn destroyed Germans' hope of vertical integration with regard to potential cutting in German locations and (long-term) control of German production in Southwest Africa.[51]

A pact with the British, the *Frankfurter Zeitung* recognized, was thus "the act of delivering the fate of German diamond production, for all time, into foreign hands." In effect, De Beers would now exercise a veto power in regard to German extraction. In so doing, they could leverage indirect control of prices to ensure that the Belgian syndicate was further weakened, and that licit exports to America predominantly ran through London, thereby buoying the English dominance of the secondary and tertiary stages of the diamond business.[52]

Germany was still going to collect plenty of revenues from diamonds—perhaps even more than it had before. But the German diamond business was going to turn into an annex of an international money cartel—essentially the same body that Erzberger and the populist settler lobby had vilified during the tenure of Dernburg. To this extent, Germany's thinking proved remarkably short-sighted.[53]

The First World War would have something to say about that approach.

CHAPTER 11

GUNS

When war broke out across Europe in August 1914, it also came to German colonial Africa: first to Togo and Cameroon, then to East Africa, and finally to Southwest. In Berlin, officials displayed a somewhat indifferent attitude toward defending these overseas possessions. Entering 1914, Germany retained fewer colonial troops than its British and French rivals, and that after nearly a decade and a half of a German "surge" to suppress Indigenous resistance. The prevailing logic among German war planners was that whichever fleet won in the North Sea would later triumph in the colonies. And so it was that, with the exception of East Africa, major combat operations in Africa came to an end relatively quickly.[1]

Quickly did not mean quietly. In September 1914, South African forces mounted an armed assault on Lüderitz Bay. German troops welcomed them by poisoning water sources and imprisoning the British consul. Notwithstanding such violations of international law, however, the German government's response generally proved haphazard. After Britain severed cable and wireless connections between Germany and its colonies, officials in Berlin proved unable to contact Southwest Africa until mid-October 1914, in the process missing payments to bureaucrats responsible for monitoring the Forbidden Zone. A German gunboat, cut off from naval command, comically departed the harbor at Lüderitz Bay just before South African invaders arrived.[2]

Officials proved more attentive when it came to Southwest's diamonds. Along with the Regie, the German Finance Office had strategized about protecting precious colonial minerals in wartime because they could fetch hard currency and prove as easily liquidated in some areas of the world as gold. As a result, Germany's military took certain steps to keep production going in the diamond fields outside Lüderitz Bay.[3]

Because the diamond fields sat inside an inhospitable desert, German officers reckoned that they could guard them with a handful of troops; early on in the war, some Germans even sent telegrams to South African forces daring the latter to attack. The key, theoretically, was to endure the harsh desert until hostilities ended in Europe, which, as the emperor infamously declared, would be over by the time the autumn leaves fell in 1914.[4]

But German forces held onto the Zone for only a brief time, their failure owing mainly to inferior manpower. No amount of German colonial maneuvering could have compensated for South Africa's superiority in numbers and supplies. When a convoy of two cruisers, four torpedo boats, and twelve transport ships dropped anchor off Lüderitz Bay on September 18, 1914, it carried 750,000 gallons of bottled water, along with an extra locomotive, spare railway tracks, and thousands of pack animals. Two thousand of the 8,000 troops South Africa deployed to Southwest landed at Lüderitz Bay. As they did, they brought maps of diamond deposits and spies with intimate knowledge of the industry.[5]

When the colony and its diamond reserves were lost, the Regie developed plans for a smuggling network. For years the German colonial state had policed against this practice; now, the state encouraged it. Via a steamer to Salvador, Brazil, government agents received instructions to send packages marked "mineral samples," sometimes containing tens of thousands of carats apiece, away from potential confiscation and toward neutral territory. The agents could dump the goods in Brazil in return for coveted foreign exchange.[6]

Just prior to invasion, the German colonial state seized the rest of August 1914's diamond take—normally sent to Berlin—and allowed it to "disappear" into secret desert locations. One ditch, dug hastily next to a desert anthill on the way to the Okavango Delta, held a massive tin box containing roughly 75,000 carats. Another site housed a flawless seventy-carat specimen.[7]

Insurance complicated efforts to smuggle these stones out of the South African occupation area. The Regie had long paid two firms, Allianz of Munich and Lloyds of London, a high premium to cover licit diamond shipments by land and sea. But illicit diamonds were not really insurable, and with German ships consistently failing to make it past British patrols upon leaving Lüderitz Bay, transport without insurance became too risky. Besides, a shipment of stones smuggled from Southwest could get to Europe only via a handful of friendly shipping companies, and these were in short supply. Holland America, for example, was a neutral shipper that arguably offered the best cloak for the German Foreign Office. But Holland America did not make stops at Lüderitz Bay and quietly partnered with the British government to inspect for any diamond parcels falling outside licit British channels.[8]

As if insurance and logistics were not challenging enough, German officials in Southwest faced a shortage of hard money to pay diamond personnel early in the war. Prior to the South African invasion, settlers raided grocery stores, made runs on banks, and hoarded cash. An internal report estimated the supply of marks on hand as half of what was needed to mobilize soldiers and arrange for payment of wages to thousands of migrant African workers, whom the government summarily stiffed and deported.[9] Steamships normally brought cash and food to the colony on a regular basis, departing thereafter with diamond exports. When regular shipping runs were suspended by war, such exchange became impossible.

The ability of the German colonial state to cover its balance of payments correspondingly eroded. Diamond export revenues had come to pay for most of the colonial state budget, and now there were no such revenues. When the Governor of Southwest, Seitz, implored the Regie for a loan, even the week he was told to wait proved too long. Incredibly, Seitz also heard from the Colonial Office in Berlin that he could not legally issue replacement marks in Southwest lest he upset the balance of the imperial paper mark, which nominally remained tied to gold and silver. Going rogue, Seitz ordered price controls and issued four million marks in scrip in an attempt to calm thousands of German settlers who could not conduct their farming, cattle-raising, or other basic business. To back his scrip, Seitz then confiscated diamonds in circulation locally. The governor designated these stones to serve as a backstop for his fledgling currency. He positioned them as a commodity Southwest could exchange with neighbors—be they Portuguese Angola to the north, or, illicitly, British Botswana and South Africa to the east.[10]

Not long after South African troops stormed into Lüderitz Bay in September 1914, they seized the nearby diamond fields and what amounted to several hundred thousand carats of upcoming production. "There were diamonds, and we wanted to get them," recalled a South African soldier. Extant sources attest as much. Southwest had exported roughly 1.5 million carats in 1913. South Africa now presided over the discontinuation of that production, in a subtler kind of plunder. Taking Southwest out of the global equation promised to help De Beers, especially with a decline in American luxury spending on the horizon as a result of global uncertainty.[11]

•   •   •

The American market, initially shaken by the outbreak of war in August 1914, recovered by 1915, with particularly strong buying of stones ranging from one-quarter to one-half in caratage. Resilient demand owed to engagement ring culture but also to inflation hawks' efforts to preserve wealth. Paper currency was thought likely to lose purchasing power during wartime, and gold was growing less accessible as an alternative. In the event, American imports of uncut, rough diamonds increased five-fold during the war's first two years, while the country's imports of cut diamonds surged by thirty times.[12]

Global violence did make it more difficult to satisfy American consumers. Faced with a lack of diamonds from London, where most of 1914's South African output sat locked in the syndicate's vaults, American merchants appealed to Berlin to obtain diamonds. The Regie greeted such requests with delight. German officials knew their supplies could not last long, even if they dipped into stocks legally reserved for London-based syndicate members. In addition, the German government had pledged some of its diamonds as collateral for war loans.[13] Still, insofar as German diamonds were sitting in warehouses, it seemed to make sense to sell stones at then-high prices. The war, after all, surely would *not* last, and sales would assist the Imperial German balance sheet.

Early in 1915, German war planners dispatched August Stauch to Antwerp. His task was to size up Antwerp's ability to assist Germany in exporting the Regie's diamonds out of Europe. Forgetting his clash with Dernburg, Stauch recommended restarting the old Antwerp connection. With German forces occupying the city, they could strong-arm Belgian merchants to reopen and to run cutting factories at cheap labor costs.[14] In turn, Germany could channel its diamonds to experienced cutters in Antwerp, rather than to less-skilled spots without Antwerp's links to the United States.

Germany's diamonds represented around a quarter of world supply on the eve of war. As of early 1915, though, normal mining in Southern Africa had ceased, so the world's diamond "supply" consisted of a few stockpiles—of which the *Reich* owned one. With the London syndicate disinclined to make regular sales, Germany temporarily became the world's main seller of roughs, and cash registers in Berlin began to ring so loudly that the chancellor, Bethmann Hollweg, received daily updates. This positive news stood out amid a climate in which the Central Powers, throttled by the Entente's naval blockade, struggled to export wares to overseas foreign markets and thereby to earn the foreign exchange they needed to import food and raw materials. Freed from international legal worries because of war, the Regie banked on regular sales through Antwerp, even as it sometimes sold to merchants in other cities at heavy markups, accepting, in its own words, "every selling opportunity." Swiss watchmakers and jewelers to Eastern European royalty paid fortunes for parcels of decorative stones. Even an officer of the Dutch navy sought to arrange secret delivery.[15]

By mid-1915, heavy demand was depleting the Regie's supplies. In Germany, jewelry for social occasions increasingly featured inexpensive and less glaring stones, such as onyx. Still, the colonial secretary saw no reason to decline further diamond sales, provided they occurred "for a very good price." Economists noted brisk business in bijouterie shops in Paris and Birmingham, away from the trenches. One could find plenty of conspicuous consumption abroad in Bucharest, too, where the German publicist Willy Frerk complained about a proliferation in war profiteers' diamonds, and where the like-minded Austrian author Karl Rosner wrote of well-to-do women entering trendy cafes with "nut-sized diamonds" adorning their necks. Dutch cutters paid a premium for rough stones, and Russian elites drove a robust stream of purchases via Scandinavian intermediaries.[16]

•   •   •

British officials watched the wartime diamond trade carefully. As 1914 gave way to other years of fighting, diamond sales came to represent more than wealth demonstration or preservation for American citizens.[17] In fact, diamonds turned into a matter of life and death insofar as they funded the German war cause.

British officials suspected that certain diamond brokers in New York City held pro-German sympathies, and that these same brokers assisted the Germans in distributing their stones via Antwerp to American markets. A leading importer, Ludwig Nissen, was a German émigré, and one of the city's prominent diamond merchants had ties to the Freundschaft

Society, a German cultural club. Another major player was Stern Bros. & Co., owned by a family of German immigrants who ran the largest diamond-cutting operation in America and who operated a retail store at 68 Nassau Street, in the heart of Manhattan's financial district.[18]

In early 1915, Britain decided to choke the flow of diamonds to such figures by establishing a monopoly on licit diamond traffic across the Atlantic. So far as Britain was concerned, the only legal exports of cut diamonds to America now had to come from the British Empire or France—not Germany or Belgium. And yet, as each month of the war went by, more diamonds reached the United States than were distributed by the syndicate in London. So who was smuggling the goods past the British blockade of Europe, and by what methods were they evading detection? As Britain sought to solve these twin riddles, it took steps to fix leaky controls. First, Britain turned to allow importation of diamonds into its own jurisdictions only via the Netherlands—as opposed to other neutral European countries. Second, Britain instantiated a system whereby rough stones exported to the European continent from London always needed to go to Amsterdam, not Antwerp, for cutting. Third, Britain pushed the Dutch government to require a license for every diamond circulating in the Netherlands. If a diamond showed up in Amsterdam for cutting, polishing, or export, then that diamond now required a certificate showing its origin, shipping history, and ownership, all the way from extraction to its present status.[19]

The cumulative effect of these moves was that the world's dealers and cutters had to comply with Britain or else land on the "Diamond Black List." Placement on the black list meant one's ostracism from legitimate participation in diamond commerce; it also brought scrutiny for associates of people blacklisted in places where British power had not legally been inscribed. British authorities followed up by creating an "approved list," such that would-be participants in diamond deals had not only to prove they were not blacklisted, but to undergo vetting by contemporaries from various review boards. As a result, parties who had dealt with the German government or expressed pro-German sympathies largely fell out of the licit diamond trade.[20]

In relation to the United States, Britain added a "polished diamond guarantee" and a "rough diamond guarantee." These guarantees brought the implementation of redundant checks in order to ensure compliance by Americans. American manufacturers seeking diamonds from Britain's syndicate needed to fill out applications with the British consul, along with references from the relevant committees, before winning approval to receive a parcel. That same parcel would arrive only after the presentation of requested certificates. Moreover, should the parcel have at any point entered France—where French authorities retained autonomy in diamond exports—the parcel would not enter New York City without first clearing British controls.[21]

Newspapers around the world informed readers of the lengths to which British and US customs officials went in pursuit of illicit wartime "diamond runners." Reports sometimes sounded silly, as when a consignment of diamonds turned up in a pot of soup in the kitchen of a trans-Atlantic liner. Accounts were more sobering about Southwest Africa, however, where, despite the shutdown of production by South African occupying forces, the immense openness of Southwest African fields remained an invitation to smuggling.[22]

In the United States, diamonds smuggled into the country by German agents were indeed laundered by pro-German parties, with importers often mixing licit with illicit material in order to circumvent British controls. In one important case, a police raid on a diamond-cutters' warehouse in New York turned up 5,100 carats of illicit diamonds, along with evidence that another 3,000 carats had made their way to market from this site. From Britain's perspective, it was not enough to confiscate illicit diamonds and transfer them to the custody of well-vetted merchants. Rather, Britain had to broaden their anti-smuggling campaign by targeting middlemen in Europe.[23]

Working off tips from De Beers, Britain continually expanded its black list of dealers and associates—widening the net of suspicion across the European continent to include people with Teutonic names, or people with family immigration histories that tied them to German-speaking lands. As part of this effort, Britain performed covert inspections of packages suspected of bearing minerals to Europe. Britain also denied the American consul at Amsterdam the privilege of approving and sealing packages for export. People receiving diamonds without proof of lawful provenance would have their diamonds confiscated. Nor was this rule confined to the Atlantic, for, as far away as East Africa, proclamations published by the British colonial governor made clear that unlicensed diamonds would be treated as contraband.[24]

British escalations, even in tandem with a blockade, did not suffice. Blacklisted figures skirted regulations by paying "clean" associates as the lead-men in deals. Meanwhile, neutral countries in Europe continued to leak. Frustrated British authorities resolved to scrutinize these sites, including Switzerland, the home to a major jewelry industry and to relatively porous borders. Switzerland was a venue through which, rumor had it, German spies passed parcels of illicit diamonds along with encoded messages. Another problem spot was Copenhagen, where enterprising jewelers shipped goods from Germany to America without notifying Danish authorities.[25] But the greatest leak came in the vicinity of the Hague, in the Dutch coastal resort town of Scheveningen.

* * *

In the run-up to Germany's occupation of Antwerp in October 1914, hundreds of diamond businessmen fled the city. Many of them headed to Scheveningen, a coastal town in the Netherlands that functioned as a haven for rich and aristocratic Europeans. Scheveningen had sufficient money to trade in diamonds and was a relatively short journey from Antwerp. Scheveningen also afforded Antwerpians an opportunity to trade while not helping Amsterdam, their chief rival. Within months, so many Belgian diamond personnel flooded into Scheveningen that it earned the moniker "Antwerpia."[26] Refugees typically arrived with little property to their name, save for large parcels of cut and rough diamonds with which they set up a rudimentary trading floor in a local café.

October 1914 saw the start of big diamond shipments from Scheveningen to the United States—a licit operation, briefly, and a business that would continue to grow well after the British rendered it illicit. Cut stones shipped out of Scheveningen in 1914 amounted to $237,000; the following year, the total came to $1,558,199.[27] By 1916, a single café in town had come to operate as Europe's gateway to illicit diamonds—a veritable "diamond exchange." A visiting agent dispatched by American firms to this café could simply walk in and proceed to make a deal.

Trade at the café depended partly on unregistered stones smuggled out of Africa by venal South Africans stationed in and around Lüderitz Bay. A more vexing flow of goods in the context of war was the one in which German agents smuggled stones from Antwerp through Scheveningen (in the neutral Netherlands), and thence to New York. Such transfers usually occurred at the behest of the German Colonial Office, where bureaucrats specializing in diamonds received coded requests from Dutch diamond brokers to supply a "veterinarian" with "professional magazines" at a particular address in Scheveningen.[28]

As Britain investigated Scheveningen for its ties to the German government, sympathetic leaders of the Amsterdam diamond lobby offered assistance, in order to suppress Antwerp and its refugees. Even before the United States' entry into the war, US customs officials also cooperated by slapping fines on captains of ships known to have transported illicit goods from Scheveningen.[29] The town remained a problem, however, because of smugglers' adaptability.

Suppose that an illicit parcel made its way to Scheveningen, where such strict British controls as existed in Amsterdam were absent. The parcel in question could be divided up and sold to several local buyers. Upon making purchases, these buyers could each transport their illicit stones to Amsterdam. In Amsterdam, the Jeweling Union would declare—or agree to declare, in exchange for a bribe—that a particular package of diamonds had been obtained, cut, and polished licitly, by local "Dutch" workers. British intelligence explained this laundering of stones by citing pro-German sympathies among Austrian-Jewish members of the Jeweling Union. King George V called on the Dutch government to denounce the practice.[30]

Aggravating British antismuggling efforts was US legislation that lagged behind maneuvers on the European black market. Once the United States entered the war in 1917 as an Associated Power to the Entente, Washington banned wire transfers involving German marks. Yet, so long as diamond smugglers shifted their dealings in Scheveningen into the currencies of powers technically not at war with the United States, the smugglers could limit their legal liability on American soil. This loophole fed an appetite for risk, spurred by the argument that Americans dealing in illicit stones were not trading with the enemy if they transacted in nonbelligerent currency with nonbelligerent powers and citizens.[31]

American customs officers faced their own obstacles when it came to confiscated shipments. Prior to America's formal entry into war, the customs officers "privately and confidentially assured" the British consul-general that they would make it difficult for diamond smugglers in the United States to reclaim illicit property after seizure. Because officers could only delay so long, though, seized shipments eventually went up for public auction to the highest bidder. And auctions proved a perfect opportunity for German sympathizers to snatch up material.[32]

There remained the matter of getting illicit packages through United States customs and British consular controls, of course. And here Britain had arguably its greatest advantage in its ability to spy on mail traffic between the United States and Europe. Intercepting letters from suspect merchants and associates on the Diamond Black List, the British Directorate of Special Intelligence zeroed in on coded language in alleged family correspondence between New York and Scheveningen. One example, sent from the Manhattan diamond district, asked for "mother" to send diamonds in exchange for a large cash transfer to a particular Dutch bank. Another message, dispatched from Scheveningen to New York as a "New Year's greeting," spoke of "sister" having received 25,000 guilder but waiting for "the remainder" of payment before she could send "brother"—a black-listed dealer of no real relation—his "little packet" from "mother." Virtually every conceivable type of familial bond featured in such elaborate conceits. "Fathers," "brothers," "cousins," and "in-laws" negotiated shipments of diamonds to New York City while discussing the health of putative family members. Interested parties went by nicknames and aliases, instead of proper names tied to black-listed dealers.[33]

Prior to America's entering the war in 1917, Britain could not easily extend its system of controls to the United States, whose strong demand for diamonds drove the world market. Because of this circumstance, there would always be demand for leaks from neutral countries, whatever the potency of Britain's blockade. After 1917, Britain convinced the American government to adopt much of its system, principally its black list, its authentication measures, and its restriction of countries that could participate in the diamond trade.[34]

The new regime promptly spanned the Atlantic. Owing largely to an idea supported by Lord Robert Cecil, Britain began from April 1917 to sanction a series of "diamond committees" in important markets from the United States to Europe. In France, Britain worked with the Parisian Commission du Diamant, which became the sole entity overseeing the importation of rough and cut diamonds into France. The commission also presided over exportation, with the proviso that exportation of a stone would only occur if it had already been cut and polished. Violators risked serious prosecution under acts regulating trading with the enemy. In the United States, Britain similarly collaborated with the American Diamond Committee, a New-York-based chamber staffed with merchants vetted by the British consul.[35]

Zeroing in, Britain placed the American Diamond Committee in charge of all sales in the vicinity of New York City—effectively making the committee the approved vehicle for large-scale importation into America. In turn, when the committee's members took possession of rough stones and cut and polished gems—storing them in safes until final sales—they agreed to sign guarantees pledging not to sell their wares "indirectly or directly" to countries at war with Britain.[36]

Signing such a guarantee involved other, attendant commitments. One was to refuse diamond imports, for the war's duration, from continental European countries other than Holland and France. Another commitment was to abjure transactions not involving firms on the approved list. Neutral states such as Switzerland and Sweden no longer received exemptions on the condition that their British or American consuls produce "certificates of non-enemy origin" to prove the provenance of stones.[37]

Perhaps the most successful measures undertaken by Britain in its diamond war related to ship inspection. After consultation with the Dutch government, Britain secured the right to board ships docked in the Netherlands, including those entering and leaving Amsterdam.[38] Dutch shippers even had to carry British inspectors tasked with examining luggage and travelers' jewelry for stones. Under this regime, any cut stone found on a ship not destined for Britain theoretically fell into the category of contraband.

In hindsight, one can grasp how complicated it was to identify an illicit "cut stone" in wartime. Smuggling techniques were constantly evolving. And while it may have been a consistent wartime policy to demand that every traveling grandmother produce documentation for her brooch or submit to an enema, it was impractical. Still, Germany felt the cumulative effect of British security measures on Dutch ships and struggled to move its diamonds. Separately, in Scheveningen, the outlook eventually turned grim on account of Britain's seizing mail and placing undercover operatives in the café "diamond exchange." Owing to detective work, Britain came into possession of reports on illicit deliveries in other locations like Amsterdam, where Britain could also count on access to letters sent to the local Diamond Trade Exchange (*Diamantbeurs*) in the Weesperplein.[39]

*   *   *

In 1915, British authorities founded the War Trade Advisory Committee, a body tasked with denying raw materials to the enemy. The Committee's definition of raw materials included industrial diamonds, sometimes labeled *boort, carbonados,* or *ballas.* Industrial diamonds, because small and of inferior quality, had long been confined to abrasive purposes: cutting other diamonds, polishing stones, calibrating grinding wheels. But experiments by Krupp and others had shown from the 1890s that industrial diamonds could serve as an essential element in cutting drills, the manufacturing of steel or electrical wire, or even for rifle making. In the years preceding 1914, this potential became a reality, rendering diamonds only partial luxury items. Factories in Bavarian towns, for example, depended on these stones to craft elements of the German war machine.[40]

"German" stones thus fit into another strategic picture—the "diamond war," as European jewelers called it. Before 1914, African workers in German Southwest extracted some inferior stones for industrial purposes, but the workers mostly targeted gems. The Regie in turn sold industrial diamonds at perhaps a tenth or less of the price achieved for higher-quality roughs.[41] Later, though, as war squeezed the world's industrial diamond supply, cut and rough diamonds in German hands functioned as a substitute, with some plants crushing up gemstones to keep production going.

In the German metropole, the official task of securing industrial diamonds for war manufacturing fell to Kriegsmetall AG, one of the raw materials corporations set up by Dernburg's erstwhile confidant, Walther Rathenau, to monopolize procurement and production of essential items. Although Kriegsmetall specialized in nonferrous metals, the corporate files indicate its central role in the domestic industrial diamond trade. They also reflect the immense difficulty of obtaining material.[42]

From the onset of war in 1914, Krupp and other German manufacturers drew on a stockpile of industrial diamonds held by the Regie itself. By 1916, however, the Regie had sold off the rest of its stockpile to capitalize on the high prices being offered on the market. Germany thus no longer had the industrial diamonds it needed, and government-assisted smuggling could not fill the deficit, with the consequence that losses of diamond revenue *for* Germany started to coincide with a lack of stones available to war manufacturers *in* Germany. Critics conceded that, because the war had lasted longer than expected, the Regie's stockpile had dwindled.[43] Nonetheless, it was tough to excuse the Regie's having chosen immediate, large cash returns over a strategically superior, long-term, and national priority.

By 1917, with the Regie in the peculiar position of being cash-rich and diamond-poor, officials had no clear path to get the military its diamonds. Unless Germany suddenly proved "successful in keeping Southwest Africa for the *Reich*" via a victory or negotiated peace, mused a trade journal, there were no "favorable prospects." Adding to this pressure was the temporary decline of Antwerp as a viable diamond center. The German military had occupied Antwerp starting in early October 1914, but by 1917 the city was left without access to German-supplied stones and saw its work grow precarious.[44]

Yet another factor hurting Germany was manufacturing orders placed by American firms. The United States had no strategic diamond stock-piles of its own with which to make munitions and so began to scour Europe for buying opportunities. Britain, for its part, needed to supply the United States with industrial diamonds in order to ensure American production of vital goods such as ammunition. But, with the British some-times refusing to assist the United States with expediting deliveries—the British ambassador cited the risk of stones falling into German hands upon crossing the Atlantic—the buying environment became even more challenging. Between 1916 and 1917 alone, as use of natural abrasives such as diamonds increased by 33 percent, the artificial abrasive market's 177 percent rise only heightened the frenzied atmosphere. Even with a favorable relationship to Britain, American manufacturers complained in trade journals about "the scarcity, expense and unreliability of diamonds at this time."[45]

Faced with a zero-sum game, Germany experienced still greater scar-city. The country's largest jeweler, Karl Ginsberg, sought to secure in-dustrial stones from his contacts in Eastern Europe, where turmoil in Russia eventually induced many nobles to arrive, diamonds in hand, at pawn shops and jewelry stores. German officials even turned their eyes further afield, first to the Belgian Congo and then to Borneo, where stones of "good quality" could be had from a largely Arabian network of traders exporting through East Africa to Indigenous Malay cutters. Such wide-ranging schemes gave British officials endless cause to worry. But the sit-uation grew so desperate for Germany that, by mid-1917, Kriegsmetall AG celebrated the acquisition of a few thousand carats, or a parcel about 1/300th of the size of the Regie's stockpile upon the outbreak of war.[46]

●   ●   ●

Just as Germany's war planners sought in vain to obtain diamonds from a limited pool late in the war, so did a number of civilians across Ger-many, Europe, and the United States. Foremost among the causes was money laundering. Many people earned an undocumented income in cash and wished to avoid paying (rising) taxes on it by converting it into cut brilliants or roughs. After 1916, when domestic supplies dried up, these same actors targeted foreign diamond markets.[47]

Not every civilian dalliance with diamonds was so unethical. With wartime devaluations occurring in virtually every country, savers in Germany looked to diamonds to combat the erosion of their savings—and an overall decline, from 1916, in their living standards. Some Germans even hoped to stock up abroad on what they thought was momentarily undervalued diamond jewelry. The savers' urge, along with buoyant retail demand, meant that civilians competed with the German government to drive up the asking price of diamonds; in the process, civilians indirectly undermined the war effort by means of their shrewd asset diversification. Commentators identified diamonds as an effective shadow currency that sometimes outpaced gold. As buyers in Germany swooped in to test the theory, Hungary, the Balkans, and Russia saw similar activity.[48]

Diamond prices rose consistently in Germany throughout 1917. Aggregate German buying of diamonds become so pronounced that, according to the French War Ministry's internal analysis, diamonds became a major vulnerability for Imperial German finances. "The big German capitalists," ran one report, "unwilling to subscribe to the domestic war loan, have [. . .] bought jewels, diamonds and silks, and deposited them in Switzerland, to await peace there and avoid the loss on exchange, the enormous German import tolls, and the risk of bankruptcy in Germany."[49]

A German civilian's acquisition of diamonds had two sides: a buy and a sell. Germans looking to obtain diamonds at inflated wartime prices typically paid in marks—with the chain of transactions involved in this payment ultimately leading to merchants in foreign countries. In practice, such a chain meant giving Germany's neighbors paper marks in exchange for hard assets which, had they landed in the German government's hands instead of civilians', could have been used to purchase on better terms when securing desperately needed raw materials abroad.

Notwithstanding this vulnerability of the state, all kinds of Germans looking out for their own interests hoarded diamonds where they could—from the markets of Amsterdam, to the winding roads of Prague, to the German-controlled streets of Antwerp. It was easier for a German civilian to obtain an illicitly sourced diamond and use it as a store of wealth than it was for her to invest in shares on the Dutch stock exchange. Doing the latter would entail too much distance: stuffing bank notes into an envelope, sticking the envelope in the mailbox, and waiting for receipt from Dutch banks. Already risky, such propositions became still less appetizing after 1917, when German authorities outlawed civilian attempts to send monetary values exceeding three silver marks across the border.[50]

Black market grocery suppliers also found it convenient to take payment in diamonds, and in many cases they transacted so heavily via makeshift diamond clearing-houses that the latter functioned as banks. In step with this process, undesirable German marks came onto important foreign markets in yet greater quantities than the Reichsbank intended to allow. A British report estimated that during the war, the jewelry market of Geneva saw eight hundred million German marks fill its coffers in exchange for diamonds and other "safer" assets.[51]

This kind of outflow became "a grave danger" for the currency, in the words of a Reichsbank director. Diamonds thus carried large-scale economic significance, belying their popular image as baubles.[52] If merchants in foreign cities like Amsterdam already disliked marks, they were outright inclined to dump them when marks kept pouring in on account of local diamond sales. Amsterdam's merchants would resell the marks as quickly as possible, often at a severe discount, in order to exit an unfavorable trade. Given the downward pressures on the mark that already existed, this exit threatened to tip Berlin's tenuous monetary situation into oblivion.

The Reichsbank cracked down on German civilian transactions starting in 1917. Strict controls in the vicinity of the Netherlands stipulated that diamonds could not enter Germany without passing through government channels. A spokesman acknowledged that the new decree was addressing "extraordinarily strong demand," but criticized the unlawful importation of diamonds as veritable treason damaging "to our currency and to our war finance, insofar as it is tax evasion."[53] The German state had decided to curb the illicit sales it had encouraged in the earlier years of the war—sales it was still encouraging when they assisted German industrial manufacturers. Here was a circle that could not be squared.

Germany's campaign formed an interesting contrast with domestic propaganda encouraging German citizens to liquidate their jewelry as a public good. Berlin famously sponsored mass donation drives for gold and jewelry, conceiving these campaigns to assist war veterans through the revitalization of an old Prussian trope, "Gold gab ich für Eisen." In order to help pay off war loans, the government also announced a sale in Copenhagen of the German Empress's diamond necklace, composed of 375 brilliant-cut stones.[54]

Prominent political figures and economists encouraged Germans to donate their jewelry to the state. Anyone retaining their jewelry, General Ludendorff added early in 1918, "failed to appreciate the gravity of the hour." Appeals like this one flooded newspapers, even touching the pages of the Social-Democratic daily *Vorwärts*. Over time, the message grew more frantic and widespread. To defend the mark, the state started to amass diamonds, as it did gold, to bolster its creditworthiness for foreign loans. The state also sought to sell diamonds in neutral countries on its own account, in exchange for hard currency from Holland, Scandinavia, and Switzerland.[55]

The key to this second design was an old fixture, the Regie, left without any real access to Southwest African stones by 1917 and 1918. Rather than have civilians simply donate their diamonds to the government, Rudolf Havenstein announced during a national "jewel-sale week" in June 1918 that citizens should sell diamonds to the Regie. The Regie pledged to resell the stones abroad within the span of six months, or else return them. Civilians could even stipulate a minimum price that they would accept at market.[56]

Predictably, the span of six months seldom elapsed before a sale took place; the average duration was less than a month's time, allowing for a bit of back-and-forth in negotiation between the Regie and foreign buyers. Predictably, too, the Regie insisted that the foreign buyers pay up front, with no credit offered, and that the payment occur in foreign currency.[57] Thereafter, the Regie compensated civilian sellers in (rapidly weakening) German paper marks according to exchange rates set by the German government. This rule left an opening for multiple arbitrage trades on the part of government insiders. Not only could the Regie deny fair compensation to the civilian by selectively citing rapidly changing exchange prices; the Regie could also misreport the sale price to German civilian sellers, provided the price met or exceeded the civilians' floor, then simply pocket the difference.

*   *   *

From the outbreak of war, Germany and Britain both planned to renege on the tentative diamond cartel agreement they had signed in mid-1914. British insiders spoke of the war as having made the agreement "inoperative." The prospect of total victory likewise stiffened the resolve of resisters around occupied Lüderitz Bay. It was no accident when Germans staffing management positions at the diamond mines, having had modest production quotas forced upon them by the South African army, proudly failed to meet them. As late as 1917, some Germans believed that the more diamonds they kept in Southwest's sand, the better positioned they would be to fight against De Beers once the war ended. Whatever diamonds came onto the wartime market would surely wind up with De Beers, and thus in the De Beers stockpile—which De Beers could deploy against the Germans after the war.[58]

Mining companies headquartered in Prussia but with assets in Southwest Africa queried an uncertain German government about what would become of their rights in various wartime scenarios. By 1918, disillusionment set in as businessmen behind the Regie and several of Southwest's larger producers began to fear German military defeat, bevies of lawsuits, and outright expropriation. A few officials within the South African government saw that this fear was cresting—as well they should have, since confidential German queries also landed on their desks. The Entente's propaganda fueled the angst by blaming German colonialism for having helped to start the war. Also causing unease was the disastrous state of record-keeping in Southwest, where August Stauch's Koloniale Bergbaugesellschaft, among others, had clerks scrambling to sort through balance sheets literally blown to pieces by explosions.[59]

One well-connected official in the South African government, Henry Hull, sensed a business opportunity. Hull, just a few years removed from serving as an agricultural specialist and treasury secretary in Louis Botha's cabinet, did not know what would happen to Southwest in a postwar settlement. No one else did, either. But Hull could see how much the confusion meant to rank-and-file German soldiers. Their estates comprised colonial stock shares of whose value no one could be certain by 1917 and 1918, but about which one read articles touting the potential of a "bull market" despite the parlous overall finances of the lost German colonies. This uncertainty became still more pregnant to Hull in 1918, when workers around one diamond field, Bogenfels, mounted an armed confrontation with local company officials over resuming mining.[60] As Hull saw it, panicked German investors would believe whatever someone close to the government told them.

Louis Botha and Jan Smuts—the only authorities that mattered, so long as they oversaw an occupation of Southwest under martial law—refused to provide decisive answers about the fate of German diamond mines in Southwest Africa. The significance of this murkiness was apparent in view of the maneuvers of the German Colonial Corporation. As it sought to resume significant dividend payments put in abeyance by war, the Corporation experimented with different ideas about how to protect its interests and payments via a legal relocation of its headquarters.[61]

Starting in late 1917, Henry Hull corresponded with Ernest Oppenheimer about a proposal to buy out the Germans in Southwest Africa. One might guess that Hull went to Oppenheimer because the two were business associates in the Anglo-American Corporation of South Africa, then a growing force in the gold mining industry.[62] Beyond personal intimacy, though, Hull believed the best chance he had of winning the German government's approval lay in the shy Oppenheimer, a German-Jewish emigrant born to a Hessian cigar merchant.

Owing to the war, De Beers's major backer in London, the Rothschilds, faced major losses. As a result, De Beers was not in a position to lend the millions of pounds Hull thought necessary for his plan. Oppenheimer, by contrast, had come to access an abundance of capital between 1914 and 1917. For years, he had dreamt of emulating Cecil Rhodes and becoming chairman of De Beers.[63] Oppenheimer also believed the key to becoming chairman was acquiring control over enough diamond production to extort an appointment from De Beers.

"I am always on the lookout," Oppenheimer confided, "with regard to diamonds." Oppenheimer aimed to "create the biggest Corporation in South Africa, not only in gold, but also in diamonds." That quest meant tapping into global demand showing renewed vitality across Europe, Britain, and the United States. But arguably a more important aspect came in securing American funds from certain parties largely immune to the wartime crunch: William Boyce Thompson's Newmont Mining Corporation, J. P. Morgan, and Herbert Hoover. From late 1918, these figures ironed out agreements to back a diamond venture through Oppenheimer's Anglo-American Corporation.[64]

In November 1918, Matthias Erzberger, whose rising political star had recently made him a state secretary, journeyed to the outskirts of Paris and signed the armistice unconditionally surrendering on behalf of Germany. Months later, Oppenheimer attended the Paris Peace Conference as an observer and signed off on Henry Hull's proposal for buying out the Germans. Versed in the intricacies of Southwest African fields and endowed with connections to the various German producers, Oppenheimer conferred with Sir David Graaff, a former South African minister of finance, one of the richest men in South Africa, and at one time a stakeholder in one of Southwest's prominent diamond miners. In the wake of these discussions, Oppenheimer discreetly approached Erich Lübbert, a board member of the Pomona Gesellschaft, lawyer to the Vereinigte Diamant-Minen A. G., and co-founder, with August Stauch, of the large Koloniale Bergbaugesellschaft. Lübbert then contacted Stauch in Berlin. Somewhere in the middle of 1919, and in early August at the latest, Stauch approved the idea of a consolidation at the hands of the "important people from South Africa," while also agreeing to serve as a proxy for the other German producers in negotiations.[65]

Insider trading followed, with share prices of the German diamond companies experiencing major rises. Stock in Pomona, a prominent company tied to Stauch, doubled in less than a month and would rise sevenfold by year's end. The course of trading for the German Colonial Corporation likewise improved, with an immediate jump of more than 50 percent in September and a subsequent climb by a factor of eight. Partly, this rise kept pace with inflation relative to prewar levels. Partly, the rise also owed to speculators hoping to store wealth in non-German denominations tied to the "foreign property" ex-German colonial companies were certain to become. In either case, rising share prices amounted to a remarkable feat, given that the shares were for companies over which Germany exercised infinitely less control in 1919 than it did in 1914. Indeed, German economists encouraged investors to treat colonial shares as a dangerous asset class because, in the now-unlikely event that Germany retained colonies, Germans would forego investing funds in colonies until deficits were repaired at home.[66]

In late 1919, as the Germans debated the consequences of the Versailles Treaty, the diamond claims in Southwest Africa became another contentious subject—albeit a since-overlooked one.[67] In October 1919, with German colonial shares strangely on the uptick, Oppenheimer, Hull, Graaff, Stauch, and Lübbert met at the Hague to discuss their own sort of peace settlement. This informal German delegation enlisted a savvy voice in Walter Bredow, who came both as the director of the German

Colonial Corporation and as a representative of his other employer, the Deutsche Bank.

Merely by virtue of existing, the diamond delegation substantiated the German government's complaints, made separately at Versailles, about economic damage done through loss of colonies. Some German officials argued that Wilson's Fourteen Points, the fifth of which vaguely called for colonies to be distributed "impartially" among interested powers, should restore German Africa. But the new republican government under Scheidemann focused its limited colonial agitation on seeing German New Guinea returned from Japan, in the belief that this path was more realistic and—given phosphates available for fertilizer on the South-Sea island—most expedient for a rebuilding metropole. Once that hope proved false, the Scheidemann cabinet, its grip on power tenuous, resolved to leverage colonial claims to extract better terms from the Allies—particularly in relation to reparations payments. This effort, too, failed abysmally in the months running up to Oppenheimer's big meetings. So German officials' leveraging of territory for reparations relief eventually turned away from colonies to coal-rich Upper Silesia.[68]

At the Hague, Oppenheimer used his conversations with the German investors to play up fears about a last-minute confiscation of German property—and a corresponding loss of the share-price gains investors had begun to see. Despite private assurances by Smuts and Botha that no such actions would be taken, Oppenheimer indicated to the German negotiators that Germans could well walk away with nothing to show for their holdings. As for the German businessmen's internal deliberations, they were streamlined by virtue of indebtedness. The large Diamanten-Pacht Gesellschaft (DPG), for example, owed Stauch's Koloniale Bergbaugesellschaft (KBG) 383,000 marks at the end of 1917. Accordingly, by mid-1919 the DPG signed over its negotiating powers in all diamond matters to the KBG.[69]

Colonial mining shares, trading at fractions of their prewar value until rumors of foreign buyers emerged, looked sure to lose further ground absent any intervention, given the exchange-rate upheavals facing the mark. Directors of the board for the diamond miners no longer wanted even to receive their advisory fees in marks. The situation hardly looked different for the German Colonial Corporation—in which August Stauch had become the largest shareholder outside of big German banks, and the most powerful individual in terms of voting rights. Stauch in particular faced major exposure: Though his prewar fortune came to around

100 million pounds in today's terms, this wealth consisted overwhelmingly on paper—in diamond shares. Real vulnerability lay buried under the surface of his riches, despite the grand facades of his villa in Berlin and his three farming estates in Southwest Africa.[70]

Whatever the veracity of Oppenheimer's statements, his German counterparts proved credulous. Feeling pressure from the Regie board members to agree on a price, the Germans decided to cash in on the transaction by earning tens of thousands of pounds each in foreign-, that is, not the depreciating German-, denominated stocks and currency. A few board meetings in the halls of the Deutsche Bank sufficed to seal a deal. In exchange for 3.5 million pounds (1.85 million in sterling and 1.65 million in shares)—a better offer than had initially been made by Oppenheimer—the German diamond producers sold all their interests and rights in Southwest Africa's Forbidden Zone to a new company, Consolidated Diamond Mines of Southwest Africa.[71]

A similar agreement was signed with the German Colonial Corporation, which agreed to accept shares of Consolidated Diamond Mines in return for whatever its own, residual rights and interests in the Forbidden Zone were. These rights went unspecified even at the time of sale, in November 1919, since disagreement still obtained in Germany about what those rights entailed. In fact, many claims about the rights were still pending German litigation begun before the outbreak of war in 1914, including issues related to an old favorite: the so-called "mining sovereignty."[72]

Still, on the strength of his dealmaking at the Hague, announced piecemeal between September 1919 and early 1920, Oppenheimer succeeded in bringing the entire production of Southwest under his control. Reporting on the process, the *New York Times* and a German trade journal told readers that "the exit of the Germans from the row of powers bringing diamonds onto the market" meant "that the domination of the English monopoly regulating supply had been sealed anew." Historians have since followed this same, simplistic interpretation.[73] But while the consolidation meant that the world's entire diamond production was now in British imperial hands, those hands were not exclusively those of De Beers.

Oppenheimer's coup incensed De Beers, fresh from licking the wounds it had received from the failure of its own, hasty bid to control the German mines in 1914. In 1920, acting as the true power behind Consolidated Diamond Mines, Oppenheimer struck an agreement with a reluctant De

Beers to take the 21 percent of world production formerly allotted to the Germans by the cartel agreement of June 1914. This gain proved insufficient for Oppenheimer, who earned a knighthood in 1921. Already influential within the Diamond Syndicate in London, he soon leveraged his influence over an ever-expanding supply of global sources outside the Union. He came to dominate not only the production of Southwest Africa, but also that of the Forminière mines in the Belgian Congo and Angola—a significant feat because Congolese production tripled between 1914 and 1928.[74] His commanding position established, Oppenheimer steadily took control of the London-based syndicate. Then, gradually and in increments, he took over De Beers.

Working or idling the deposits near Lüderitz Bay remained a powerful trade weapon in the 1920s. Therefore, Oppenheimer threatened at sensitive junctures to dump his Namibian diamonds on the market, should he not receive what he deemed "a share of the trade commensurate with" the Namib's "potential." Diamond prices, which soared through most of 1919 on concerns about inflation, did not stay high indefinitely. As early as 1921, Southwest Africa's official diamond revenues plummeted, in a larger reflection of a muffled, fearful year for producers. The year 1922 began with high hopes and several reopened mines; reports had Lüderitz Bay's "shops [. . .] crammed with goods" and eagerly awaiting "prosperous times."[75] But the effects of reopening proved minimal.

With his threats, Oppenheimer saw his share of global diamond production capacity steadily raised to 25 percent. He began essentially to exchange his diamonds—which, once purchased, would promptly be taken off the market by De Beers—for ever larger shareholdings in De Beers. The latter company's vulnerability was growing acute, for the prestige of the diamond was threatened by a growing public perception that diamonds were no longer rare. Diamond transactions had come to constitute 90 percent of all the world's trade in precious stones. In a contemporary trend reported only to advertising insiders, when people in the American Northeast read repeatedly about diamond production spiking from multiple sources in Africa, the result was that sales in New England, New York, and New Jersey declined 35 percent relative to the previous year's level.[76]

CONCLUSION

◆ Widely cited, if flawed, statistics have misled historians into thinking that the economic reach of German colonialism was brief and minimal. This book has proven otherwise by tracing flows of labor, violence, capital, politics, and commodity chains related to German diamonds in Southwest Africa. In each respect, German colonialism became entangled in ways that made a deep impact not only at home, but on the relationship between the German Empire and the world.

Let us now turn to situating the book's other findings within larger, ongoing debates. To start, the German pursuit of diamond wealth in Southwest Africa reveals an economic pattern in which Germany resembled rival colonial powers more often than not. Like Britain and Belgium, Germany deputized private enterprises to act in place of the colonial state in Africa over significant stretches of time and land, with unforeseen complications. In Germany as elsewhere, these semi-sovereign private enterprises booked monopoly profits but complained about unremunerative colonial governing responsibilities. Later, when significant mineral deposits materialized and the enterprises' legal claims hampered colonial development, Germany (again like its rivals) carefully negotiated to buy out the enterprises, instead of expropriating them.

Between 1908 and 1911, Germans experienced a diamond stock bubble that citizens misjudged and regulators tolerated in ways familiar to observers of Belgian and French colonialism. During and after the stock bubble, the German state let colonial budgets grow overly dependent on mineral exports and taxed those exports heavily—just like contemporary South Africa. A final similarity lay in the realm of labor economics. German colonial authorities borrowed methods to expropriate Nama and Herero, and to combat mineral smuggling on the diamond fields, from South African counterparts. Similarly, the German public, in displaying apathy to the widespread suffering of Indigenous people in the diamond sector, did not fundamentally differ from the French with their (later) Congo-Océan Railway, or the British and Boers with their gold and diamonds.

The history of Germany's diamonds helps us to understand not only how Germany resembled other colonial powers, but how it acted singularly among them. First, amid a mineral rush, the German state created a public-private cartel—in marked contrast to the United States' contemporary progressivism. Second, Germany tried to fight De Beers by imitating the company's monopolistic practices through a series of laws that, while more ambitious than those in South Africa, also proved more hurried. Third, when Germany showed itself willing to tinker with colonial laws in an effort to capitalize on mineral wealth, this legal creativity emerged partly as a response to Germany's lacking the resources and capital investment available to the British Empire. Fourth, Germany's repeated reforms to its colonial mining regulations, along with its unsustainable mining practices, fit into a larger German pattern of short-term planning in state affairs.

Beyond revealing new areas of similarity and difference in varieties of European practice, Germany's history with diamonds offers a new insight about possible continuities between German colonial violence and the Holocaust. In the wake of a genocide that left few Nama and Herero alive, Germany's officials and settlers pushed to draw in more African labor to diamond mines. However, when in close proximity with such workers, Germans overseeing diamond extraction fostered vicious conditions that led to extremely high death rates. Such irrational behavior, steeped in racism, occurred between 1908 and 1914, after the end of the military campaign led by General Lothar von Trotha but with the participation of many army veterans. Moreover, this behavior paralleled conditions in later wartime forced labor camps under the Third Reich, whose ideologies also generally overpowered its economic interests. Diamond labor dynamics thus constitute a new kind of link "from Windhoek to Auschwitz."

As a result of the diamond boom traced in this book, German thinking about colonial "values" underwent its own unique transition. After 1908, because of the mineral wealth flowing out of Southwest Africa, many Germans again started seeing colonies as a good bet—with peculiar ramifications for the country's culture. Consider Paul Rohrbach, Dernburg's erstwhile antagonist and one of his successors in managing diamond affairs. In his 1912 book, *Der Deutsche Gedanke in der Welt,* Rohrbach opined that, should Germany fail to fulfill its "world ambitions" peacefully, "the language of guns" would "decide." Among the "world ambitions" Rohrbach named was the diamond trade, which, with the "merchant Dernburg" gone, was "up and running." Rohrbach cited diamonds as a reason for Germans to be "convinced" of "future value" in an era of "great colonial politics ahead." Readers evidently agreed. Within two years of its release Rohrbach's tome sold 75,000 copies and, according to his translator in the United States, "probably inspired more Germans than any other book published since 1871."[1]

Like Rohrbach, we should recognize diamonds as a factor in Germany's relations with the prewar European world. Germany's government pursued colonial expansion with renewed vigor starting toward the end of 1909, at the height of a domestic diamond stock bubble. German hypernationalists pushed hard in Morocco in 1911, to the point that their zeal prompted an international diplomatic crisis the German government struggled to control.[2] Lastly, Britain spent the years between 1911 and 1914 negotiating with the Germans to trade off naval concessions against Belgian and Portuguese colonies. Given the deep pessimism attending German colonial affairs prior to the diamond rush in 1908, it is reasonable to posit (a) that Southwest Africa's diamonds heightened the intensity of such interactions, and (b) that diamonds resuscitated German leadership's hopes to acquire, or to use the theme of, colonial riches the reality of which had seemed debunked only a handful of years earlier.

How much the perception of colonial wealth affected German foreign policy again became apparent in 1914. When war broke out that year, leadership in Berlin under Chancellor Bethmann Hollweg considered what demands to place on vanquished European powers. Bethmann's infamous memorandum in early September recorded ideas, including a section on colonial acquisitions with an eye toward the French Congo, Belgian Congo, and Portuguese Angola, all of which had just tested positive for diamonds. By no means did Bethmann's memorandum represent a clear, or definite, program, and the colonial gains he mentioned figured as less important than the fate of European territories like Antwerp. But the memorandum indicated that a sizeable portion of Germany's population and leadership still thought enhanced colonial control in Africa would enrich them. One firm believer was Matthias Erzberger, a diamond expert who insisted on the insertion of African annexations into Bethmann's list of demands.[3]

Of course, colonial wealth did not accrue to Germans as a result of war between 1914 and 1918. The prospect of such riches proved illusory, like the case for war. But illusions remained potent, and Dernburg's successors in office, along with many in the wartime German government, remained convinced of broader colonial payoffs. They were in good company, for, writing in 1915, W. E. B. Du Bois explained European imperialism in Africa by saying that European nations spent "a few hundreds of millions in steel and gunpowder" in order to make "a thousand millions in diamonds and cocoa." Throughout the war, diamonds did indeed prove important, not least by retaining the power to bolster and drain the German currency. Hence, following the war, right-wing nationalists found some credulity when complaining about Germany's losing "its" colonial diamonds to "robbers." So did Adolf Hitler, who privately derided African "escapades" under Emperor Wilhelm II while appealing to the public to "reclaim" Germany's "lost" colonies. Even postwar liberals who doubted the economic benefits of colonialism identified diamonds as an exception that had created national wealth.[4]

The custody of German diamond "value" continued to matter well into the interwar period. Adolph Hoffmann, one of Prussia's foremost socialist politicians, joined many of his party colleagues in dismissing colonies and "Dernburg's diamonds" as irrelevant. By contrast, Kurt Tucholsky, the brilliant journalist who counseled against Germany's resuming overseas colonialism, astutely identified diamond wealth as an effective theme in renewed pro-colonial agitation by right-wing parties. Hans Grimm's novel, *Volk ohne Raum,* sold 315,000 copies between 1926 and 1935 largely because it valorized an open, diamond-laden colonial space in Southwest Africa as a means to combat social and urban decay in Germany. The German Right, digesting their Grimm and seeing his fiction promoted by Joseph Goebbels, insisted that colonial value accrued to a colonizing power over time. Yes, such raw materials as diamonds would have to compete with concerns for living space and settlement. But Germany could easily push for both—as the Nazis cynically did.[5]

*   *   *

At the conclusion of the First World War, Matthias Erzberger and Bernhard Dernburg, their prominence enhanced and diminished respectively by diamonds, became key figures working on the question of the Versailles settlement. Dernburg, mindful of his past, noted that he could never trust Erzberger. Still, as Dernburg struggled with shot nerves, crying fits, insomnia, pan-German doubts about his patriotism, and being passed over for another tenure managing Germany's colonial claims, Erzberger triumphed. In 1919 and in the collective German memory to come, Erzberger easily surpassed his foe.[6]

In January 1919, in a move credited with securing the fledgling Weimar Republic, Erzberger induced his Center Party colleagues to form a coalition government with left liberals and Social Democrats. This brave act was worthy of a great statesman. But it soon found itself diminished by allegations that, while he served as the Republic's finance minister, Erzberger had engaged in corrupt stock market deals and tax evasion. Tragically, his enemies pursued their allegations with a zeal he had reserved for Dernburg.[7] Erzberger resigned from office in 1920. In 1921, amid torrents of conservative and nationalist invective that somehow painted this devout Catholic patriot as a Jewish traitor, he was assassinated while vacationing in the Black Forest.

The 1920s also proved unkind to the other German diamond titans. August Stauch, the self-educated millionaire credited with diamond discoveries, flourished for a time. His business taking place via one of Germany's largest banks, where he claimed a board seat, Stauch won membership in a new colonial assembly, launched a splashy record-player company in Berlin, and funded a program to attract German settlers to Namibian farms, complete with prebuilt homes, complimentary livestock, and—appropriately—assistance with irrigation. But Stauch eventually squandered his fortune through overextension, failed stock market bets, and theft at the hands of crooks he naively thought his friends. He even lost his title of "Diamond King"—a moniker increasingly attached by German papers to Ernest Oppenheimer.[8] Broke and isolated, his mansions sold off, Stauch lived out his days in a Germany that hardly knew him, rather than in Southwest Africa, whose remaining Germans venerated him.

Still more ignominious was the fate of Emil Kreplin, mayor of Lüderitz Bay throughout the diamond boom and sometime fraudster. Not long after Kreplin's wealth vanished in the hyperinflation of the early 1920s, he walked into the cold waters of the Atlantic and shot himself.[9] His power gone, his history tainted with questionable stock dealings, Kreplin's only positive legacy lay in the desert, where the progeny of racing horses he had imported roamed without care for human rules.

Then there were the German workers in Kreplin's home and South-west Africa's diamond mining center, Lüderitz Bay. In 1923, the South African prime minister, Jan Smuts, spoke out against excessive reparations demands and decried the French occupation of the Ruhr. Not long thereafter, Smuts's successor agreed that ethnic Germans living under the new South African mandate should have the option to retain their German citizenship, and that the children of these Germans must enjoy the same privilege. Accordingly, Lüderitz Bay retained much of its pre-1914 colonial culture in the first decades of the South African mandate. Shops in town continued to import their goods from Germany. Street names stayed German, along with mayors, food, customs, and masonic lodges. The German flag flew.[10]

Gradually, though, Lüderitz Bay turned impoverished. The sunbathing beach closed down, residents traveled through sand in mule carts, and the mood became one of "sadness." Water costs returned to oppressive levels. The town's remaining German diamond companies, as well as the German Colonial Corporation for Southwest Africa, folded. Colonists who had accepted loans from German banks during the halcyon prewar days were forced by courts in Germany to repay creditors, not in depreciated German marks, but in scarce hard currency. German foremen and sifters commuting to the Forbidden Zone even had to reckon with wages that ran far lower than before the war—unadjusted for rampant local inflation.[11]

Some residents around Lüderitz Bay maintained a trade in zombie German "colonial shares," their holders hoping to catch a kind of reparation for pennies on the dollar. German banks added to the pain by dropping colonial stocks from their lists of offerings. The Regie lingered, clinging to residual privileges regarding the domestic marketing of diamonds and paying some handsome dividends to insiders. But the German supply chain connecting Lüderitz Bay to the world became a distant memory, with Antwerp, the crucial node, instead finding an easy, quasi-domestic supply in the form of incipient diamond extraction in the Belgian Congo.[12]

The lone success story around Lüderitz Bay was that of Ernest Oppenheimer, who became chairman of De Beers and successor in practice to his idol, Cecil Rhodes. In 1929, De Beers, its existence threatened by the stock market crash, merged with Oppenheimer's Consolidated Diamond Mines. This merger represented the British imperial takeover of Southwest African diamonds that Bernhard Dernburg had feared in late

1908, and against which he had designed the Forbidden Zone. The merger also sealed the decline of Lüderitz Bay, for, after Oppenheimer seized control of De Beers, his combined company began shutting down production in the fields abutting the town. These fields were still loaded with stones, and the community "lived on diamonds," in the words of local labor organizers.[13] Unfazed, Oppenheimer chose periodically to choke off Southwest's supply in the interest of the larger diamond industry.

"Once so important," recorded a German settler in her diary, Lüderitz Bay "lost much of its significance" in the interwar period. The town's luminaries moved on to investment ventures farther afield, their pockets lined by cash and shares earned at the time of their buyout from Oppenheimer. Capital flight provided another inducement for colonial propagandists to belabor what Germany had "lost." Paul Leutwein, son of one of Southwest Africa's former governors, blamed a handful of German businessmen for having wasted the country's diamond wealth. Leutwein alleged that select Germans, just like the negotiators at the Paris Peace Conference, had sold out their countrymen: as with the Allies, so with Oppenheimer. A sale of German assets to Oppenheimer had perhaps seemed more palatable because he was born near Frankfurt. But this genealogy was, so the thinking went, a mere fig leaf for a sale made out of equal parts self-interest and desperation—a sale that turned De Beers from a near monopoly into what Germans soon complained was "one of the most perfect monopolies" ever known. In an added insult, insiders reported that a majority of the stockholders profiting from Oppenheimer's operations resided in the United States.[14]

Wounds from the "loss" of German colonies smarted anew after 1929 and the ensuing economic depression, with the trope of diamonds remaining salient. Oppenheimer, being of Jewish heritage, became a target of acrimony in an increasingly anti-Semitic climate for remaining German settlers at Lüderitz Bay, many of whom dreamt of reunion with Germany and of renewed competition against what they perceived as an Anglo-South-African-Jewish diamond cartel. In 1930, Lüderitz Bay's German residents, numbering around 900, cheered the prospect of a visit by a German warship. Contemporary media in the former metropole did their part, too. A political cartoon featured South Africans rushing to diamond wealth while hungry Germans—shut out of their colonies—settled for a "feeding trough" at home. Albrecht Wirth, a pan-Germanist pseudoscientist whose writings on race influenced key Nazis, reminded his readers of the potential latent in Southwest's diamonds.[15]

After 1933, Lüderitz Bay's right-leaning population turned to embrace Hitler, with complaints about exclusion from the Forbidden Zone still circulating among them. As agents from the Reich Finance Ministry ran around Southwest Africa conducting clandestine surveys of mineral deposits, visitors reported that the area around the diamond fields became a "hotbed of Nazism." Paul Rohrbach—not officially a Nazi but sympathetic to the party's racism—railed against the South African takeover of Southwest's diamond wealth as a "dark chapter" in the books of law. In another echo of German colonial history, Rohrbach lamented that the South African state did not play a firmer role in protecting the livelihood of European residents in Lüderitz Bay.[16]

A closer look at the 1930s reveals how pro-Nazi activity in Southwest Africa mixed with the German diamond legacy. Gymnasts participating in a tournament in Lüderitz Bay waved a flag featuring the swastika above the birth and death dates of Kolmanskop, a once-prosperous mine. Managers for Oppenheimer's Consolidated Diamond Mines refused to hire Jewish workers and agitated for the adoption of Nazi programs; Oppenheimer, in a move reminiscent of Bernhard Dernburg, confined himself to discreet inquiries, lest he lose local white support. Local Jewish businesspeople who had arrived long ago, during the diamond boom between 1908 and 1914, now had to deal with mailed death threats and forced removal of their children from school. A journalist reported Jewish people, "not tolerated," were leaving town.[17]

In interwar Germany, fallout from colonial diamonds merged with rising anti-Semitism. From 1919, as German officials continually attempted to renegotiate reparations, Dernburg came under sustained attack by diverse precursors to the Nazi movement. In contemporary propaganda widely distributed by pan-Germanists and the German Nationalist Protection and Defiance Federation, Dernburg's name appeared on lists scurrilously naming Jewish advisors who had "betrayed" the emperor and the German war cause. Likewise, Dernburg's short-lived role in the Weimar Republic's inaugural cabinet supposedly represented a sign that "Wall Street" and "Jewish circles" controlled the country. The left-leaning German Democratic Party, a key constituency in the Republic's early years, stood discredited in right-wing screeds because Dernburg's membership rendered the party the vessel of the "Jewish stockjobber." As late as 1926, Gottfried Feder, author of one of Hitler's formative intellectual experiences and an early Nazi deputy in the Reichstag, denounced the old colonial secretary's alleged role in a Jewish banking conspiracy.[18]

Germany's moment as a diamond power had the effect of confirming many German anti-Semites' worldview, and of propagating a part of that worldview for the masses. Like Oppenheimer and the diamond business, Jews allegedly figured as mysterious, secretive, scheming, cosmopolitan, and prone to corrupting labor with luxury. Dernburg, universally cast as a biological Jew while he acted as Germany's chief diamond promoter, stood accused of having mismanaged colonial wealth to the detriment of hard-working, "real" Germans, and to the benefit of Jews and elite bankers.

After Dernburg fell from power in 1910, his personality still found outsized press coverage and merited him considerable attention in Rudolf Martin's best-selling tome *German Power-Wielders*. In 1911, Germany's most popular and widely read economist, Werner Sombart, published *The Jews and Modern Capitalism*, in whose pages Dernburg went unmentioned but where Sombart argued that Jews, in addition to being prime movers in modern European economic life, "played the decisive role" in European colonial expansion. Full of contradictions and widely criticized though Sombart's book was, it mainstreamed in Germany some anti-Semitic notions analogous to those J. A. Hobson had separately presented to readers in Britain: that Europe faced a "Jewish problem," and that Jews, based on the alleged colonial example, manipulated governments to their own ends.[19]

The world, Sombart would go on to elaborate in a book promoting German warfare, seemingly stood divided between heroes and traders. German heroes valued chivalry and shed blood for their country, whereas English traders lacked a sufficiently martial spirit and sought peace at the expense of honor. True, Sombart's analysis was not always welcomed by rabid anti-Semites. But it was easy for his many readers to imagine how Jews and the German colonial experience fit into his picture. In an addendum, Sombart named Dernburg a statesman through whose work "Jews" achieved success. As for America, to which Germany had sent its diamonds—well, it was a "Jewish land."[20]

In the wake of a financial crash in 1929, when the republican government surprisingly recalled Dernburg to help clean up the wreckage, anti-Semites again mobilized the legacy of colonial diamonds. Arthur Schumann, head of the Nazi Party's intelligence bureau and a supplier of curated news reports for Hitler, portrayed Dernburg as being in thrall to "big capitalists." Another prominent nationalist with ties to the Nazis discredited Dernburg's new public service because of the latter's putative responsibility for an earlier stock bubble burst: the one around companies in Southwest Africa.[21]

By the early years of the Third Reich, Dernburg, still alive in a society that was criminalizing his Jewish ancestry, had become so socially isolated as to have no chance of contesting his unfair portrayal. In 1937, in a widely printed brochure accompanying the notorious art exhibition *The Eternal Jew,* his photo topped a list of "Jewish politicians," along with a caption mocking his attempts at "mimicking" probity while in office. Dernburg died two weeks before the exhibition opened. Well into the era of the Final Solution, further Nazi propaganda spotlighted his alleged "representation of Jewish interests" while colonial secretary.[22]

Whereas Nazi state organs lamented the loss of diamonds, "the greatest wealth" Southwest Africa had to offer, they hypocritically excoriated Britain for fighting wars over "control of diamond mines." So, too, did German ephemera, from cigarette cards to popular literature. A poem published in a popular magazine elaborated on the theme. On September 24, 1939, as German planes damaged Warsaw and Britain formally stood at war with Germany, the author opined that Lüderitz Bay went lost to a covetous British Empire because Imperial German politicians proved too weak to defend it. Only one part of the old diamond apparatus survived by this time: the domestic cutting sites Dernburg had long ago shunned. Chillingly, they found new purpose in removing from their settings and reshaping the diamonds in the jewelry of expropriated European Jews.[23]

The revisionist history of Lüderitz Bay's "loss" was nonsensical myth-building typical of Nazi propaganda. But its effect was that, perhaps more than other former colonial sites, Lüderitz Bay occupied a place in the social construction of "Greater Germany," and vice versa. The town was once, a German-language Romanian newspaper noted days after the Austrian *Anschluss,* "a rich colonial land." And it was because of this place, or so a Nazi textbook misled secondary-school students, that the German overseas colonies had profited the German people broadly.[24]

As part of the thesis known as "From Windhoek to Auschwitz," a number of historians have argued for viewing German colonialism not just as an antecedent but as a precursor to the Holocaust. The experience of Bernhard Dernburg supports such an approach by presenting a continuity between the fallout from German colonial diamonds, on the one hand, and the rise of National Socialism, on the other. Anti-Semitism and colonialism clearly interacted in Imperial Germany.[25] Following the path of diamonds and Dernburg, however, shows that colonialism fueled German anti-Semitism both during and after the imperial era, in ways that supported a popular embrace of certain National Socialist tenets.

●　　　●　　　●

Hardly any diamonds would have departed Southwest Africa in the twentieth century were it not for the labor of Ovambos, Nama, and Herero. Well after the end of German colonial rule, these people toiled in the Forbidden Zone under a new, South African mandate government. In the meantime, the Zone largely remained unchanged. "Patrols and restrictions," remarked Ernest Oppenheimer, "were never relaxed." Employers also continued to act as a government in all but name. In 1923, an astonished magistrate complained to superiors that, in order to enter the Zone on official business, he had to obtain a permit from Oppenheimer's company, in addition to the colonial administration of Southwest.[26] *Plus ça change.*

Smuggling remained common throughout the Zone and Southwest. Tales spread about diamonds baked into bread loaves or plastered into canteens. A black market in uncut diamonds flourished. There were fresh, futile attempts at crackdowns, including keeping ships from shore, dismantling automobiles, and flushing workers' orifices with castor oil. Smugglers always adapted. As a response, Oppenheimer's company placed X-ray machines at entrance and exit points of the Zone to scan every single person in every instance. The new practices disproportionately harmed African workers, many of whom fell sick from repeated radiation exposure.[27]

Reporting on labor abuses remained highly difficult. Oppenheimer heightened surveillance by installing a private radio network across the territory, with an eye toward ending unauthorized access and tracking people's movements. Still more important, a bond of white supremacy emerged between Boers and German colonial settlers. A Boer magistrate at Lüderitz Bay, for example, would trust testimony by Germans, who predominated in sorting jobs, over the word of any African diamond worker alleging mistreatment. Perhaps this continuity explained why

German propagandists counted the postwar growth in Southwest's white population as a sign of the "upswing of *our* colonies."[28]

To a significant degree, South Africa preserved the migrant labor system as it was imposed under German rule. From 1924, the mandate government even awarded the diamond mines preferential treatment over all other businesses in their efforts to recruit Ovambos. Calls for investigation of ongoing excessive mortality rates in the diamond fields surfaced at the Geneva-based International Labor Organization. A charge circulated among members of the League of Nations' Permanent Mandates Commission that Southwest Africa's people were being treated ruthlessly, "solely for the sake of the diamonds." Nothing came of it. At a banquet in Antwerp, European guests did not question Oppenheimer when he said the diamond was "the civilizer of Africa."[29]

In another echo of the German era, migrant diamond workers had to seek change through resistance. In the spring of 1925 alone, 167 Africans escaped from the fields into the desert at high risk of starvation and dehydration in order to leave their nominally elective "jobs." Fewer than half of the escapees survived, and police arrested those who did. Less grimly, some Ovambo families began to plant roots around Lüderitz Bay, such that by the end of the 1920s the permanent population of the area amounted to 1,200 Europeans and 2,000 Africans. Lüderitz Bay's environs also proved a successful target for Marcus Garvey's Universal Negro Improvement Association, whose acolytes spread a message of pan-Africanism throughout the diamond fields via smuggled newspapers and astute, transnational organizers.[30]

From 1915, South Africa promised that its brand of colonialism would catapult ahead of the Germans'. To this end, South Africa pledged to do away with the powerful colonial corporations that, in the view of one official inspector, had proven the "most sinister and crooked" elements in the "sordid" German colonial era. Yet, on this score South Africa's mandate again achieved remarkable continuity with its German predecessors in a series of agreements signed with Oppenheimer between 1920 and 1923. The old German Colonial Corporation had ended. But it was replaced by a more powerful monolith with the enthusiastic support— even "advocacy," to quote one insider—of Jan Smuts.[31] South Africa legally enforced the Forbidden Zone, but it effectively lay in Oppenheimer's hands. Similarly, the old German laws restricting diamond traffic were changed only cursorily through the replacement of German agencies like the Regie with De Beers, in London.

South African colonial administrators, again like their German predecessors, cautioned that Southwest's diamond economy would not last, and that ranching and farming would be needed to sustain the colony over the long term. The South African state, in a story familiar to Berlin, also tried to encourage settlement in Southwest by whites who could not afford or access land at home. But, when those plans faltered, diamond revenues and African workers continued to prop up the colony's finances and to foster its dreams of state-subsidized agricultural expansion. "Viewed from an economic standpoint," wrote a visiting reporter, minerals and mineral workers "*were* Southwest."[32]

Clashes over the shape of the economy did little to detract from South Africa's absolute grip on power. For seventy years, Southwest Africa remained a South African colony whose officials were committed to the oppression of the Indigenous people. Operating largely under German rules laid down by Dernburg, South Africa worked symbiotically with De Beers, a private company, to make immense profits from the Forbidden Zone. In 1958, the pot of colonial wealth actually grew larger when a group of miners licensed by De Beers succeeded in dredging the first significant pile of diamonds from the seafloor near Lüderitz Bay. Billions of dollars in further earnings awaited the company and the colonial state. Rather than mine sustainably, however, diamond companies honored their German predecessors by engaging in overmining throughout the 1980s, as Namibian independence grew more likely.[33]

•   •   •

It is not entirely fair to accuse today's Germans of amnesia about their country's brush with global diamond power, let alone colonialism. German newspaper articles sporadically remind readers about the wild lives of Southwest African pioneers, such as August Stauch. Buses even funnel German tourists to the outskirts of the Forbidden Zone, where they can visit a former mining camp renowned for its faded, sand-filled colonial architecture in an exotic desert locale.

Inside a museum accompanying the tour, run jointly by the Namibian state and De Beers, German guests will find various exhibits with information in their language about the colorful personalities of early prospectors and the carats they extracted. What Germans will not see, though, is any record of the terrible conditions and rampant death that characterized diamond extraction between 1908 and 1914. The museum

Inside the café of a tourist museum at Kolmanskop, Namibia, July 2017. In the background, in the top left photo among four, sits a portrait of an Ovambo worker, c. 1914. The text explaining the photo to guests says only: "Contract Worker—two years."

exhibits say nothing on the subject of Africans at all, unless one counts a single photo, in the café, of an Ovambo "contract worker" holding a shovel.

This asymmetry is glaring. It is also curious, because Namibia, the sovereign state in which the Forbidden Zone sits since 1990, otherwise goes to considerable lengths to remember and honor the victims of the German genocide. Namibia appears keen to encourage tourism, but reluctant to confront German tourists or to besmirch the glitter of the diamonds on which the Namibian economy depends. While such a strategy is not unreasonable, it produces lamentable effects: keeping the labor history behind diamonds taboo, distorting Germans' memory of the Zone, and whitewashing the economic violence of the German colonial era.

In Namibia, where blood and diamonds have intersected amid profound devastation for more than 112 years, the Forbidden Zone remains sealed to the public in a way that allows for little independent oversight of profits, environmental conditions, or worker health. As for people living in Lüderitz Bay (now called Lüderitz), many are struggling with abject poverty and dangerous conditions in a shantytown hidden beyond the hills. Within a 200-mile radius of this site and the sands that still yield diamonds for foreign consumers' pleasure, multiple communities drink from a water supply that, according to twenty-first-century reports, is as "unfit for human consumption" as the brackish liquid forced on Ovambo workers in the diamond fields under German rule.[34]

One Namibian town, Bethanie, illustrates the plight powerfully. In the early 1880s, Bethanie was the site where agents of the German trader Adolf Lüderitz lied about "purchasing" rights to own and govern much of the Namib Desert. Today Bethanie's water-sickened inhabitants, left without any real share in their country's mineral wealth as a result of Lüderitz's shenanigans, reside in an environment that does not meet basic standards for health. Luxuries exported from their country have failed to pay for necessities at home. They have mainly enriched people who live far away, and whose predilection for ostentation contrasts starkly with the life of the average Namibian.

One possible takeaway from this circumstance is that we should revise our thinking about twenty-first-century relations between Africa and the Anglo-European world when it comes to so-called conflict diamonds. In 2000, the United Nations stated: "Conflict diamonds are diamonds that originate from areas controlled by forces or factions opposed to legitimate and internationally recognized governments, and are used to fund military action in opposition to those governments."[35] While the German and South African colonial states functioning in Southwest Africa enjoyed international recognition from 1884 to 1990, one could credibly deem them illegitimate regimes and argue that they sold minerals to fund "military action," or occupation, in opposition to legitimate Indigenous governments such as that of the Herero and Nama.

In recent decades, public discourse about "conflict diamonds" has focused exclusively on a few sites of postcolonial civil war in Africa: Sierra Leone, Liberia, the Democratic Republic of the Congo. Leaders in the struggle against "conflict diamonds" include De Beers and Antwerp, through whose venues an estimated 84 percent of the world's rough diamonds passed at some point in 2018. Yet, insofar as diamonds mined violently under German or South African colonial rule fit the criteria we observe for conflict diamonds, the concept should be backdated to include millions of engagement rings acquired during the European colonial period and channeled through De Beers and Antwerp. Once redefined chronologically, the concept of conflict diamonds should then be extended geographically to include sites like Namibia and South Africa, from which nearly all the world's diamonds flowed in the years of high imperialism preceding 1914.

By extension, an enlarged definition of "conflict diamonds" should bring further reflection on history's relationship with the subject of conflict minerals. Well-intentioned legislation in the United States and Europe seems to operate with a very limited time horizon in which people only recently began to purchase commodities fueling violence in Africa. But, however inconvenient it may prove, the passage of a century has not rendered clean most diamonds or gold acquired long ago from places like Kimberley, Lüderitz Bay, and the Rand.

In turn, the history of diamonds ought to find a place in twenty-first-century debates about how Germany should make amends for its colonial military campaign against the Herero and Nama. In recent years, state negotiations have accelerated and focused mainly on two issues: first, a German apology for genocide; second, the return to Namibia of certain human remains that pseudoscientists in Imperial Germany acquired for discredited research on racial hierarchies. Notwithstanding the importance of such gestures, colonial economics deserves attention, too.

Highly lucrative diamond deposits existed on Southwest African land stolen through treaty deceit by Germans in the 1880s, during the inaugural period of colonial rule. In the decades that followed, as Germans slaughtered Nama and Herero, they did so partly with an eye toward finding and monetizing diamonds. After 1908, the Namib Desert and Indigenous people generated enormous wealth, but only for select Germans and South Africans operating on German rules. As Germans continue to discuss reconciliation with Namibia, they would do well to make reparations that account for this economic injustice, and not solely the genocide between 1904 and 1907. In the history of German colonialism, blood and diamonds belong together.

NOTES

•

ACKNOWLEDGMENTS

•

CREDITS

•

INDEX

NOTES

ABBREVIATIONS

AVEM   Archive of the United Evangelical Mission, Wuppertal, Germany

BAB   German Federal Archive, Berlin, Germany

BAK   German Federal Archive, Koblenz, Germany

BL   Brenthurst Library, Johannesburg, South Africa

BW   Barloworld Limited Archives, Johannesburg, South Africa

CCL   Claremont Colleges Library Special Collections, Claremont, CA, United States

HID   Historical Institute of Deutsche Bank, Frankfurt, Germany

HStAD   Hessian State Archive, Darmstadt, Germany

NAN   National Archives of Namibia, Windhoek, Namibia

PAAA   Political Archive of the German Foreign Ministry, Berlin, Germany

RAL   Rothschild Archives, London, United Kingdom

RL   David M. Rubenstein Rare Book and Manuscript Library, Duke University, Durham, NC, United States

UCSB   Special Research Collections, University of California, Santa Barbara, CA, United States

UKNA   The National Archives, Kew, United Kingdom

Introduction

1. Cf. Peter Tarr, *The Potential Role of Environmental Assessment in Promoting Sustainable Development in Namibia* (PhD diss., University of Aberdeen, 1999), 140.

2. "Lüderitzbucht," *The Times,* April 8, 1947.

3. Leo Weinthal to Dernburg, December 14, 1908, Bundesarchiv Berlin (hereafter BAB) R1001/1341. Percy Wagner, *Die Diamantführenden Gesteine* (Berlin: Borntraeger,

1909), 206. Max Ewald Baericke, *Lüderitzbucht: Historische Erinnerungen eines alten Diamantensuchers* (Windhoek: Namibia Wissenschaftliche Gesellschaft, 2001), 107. Jean Georges Escard, *Pierres Précieuses* (Paris: Pinat, 1914), 154.

4. "Diamantenfieber," *Die Zukunft* 66 (Berlin: Bernstein, 1909), 80. "Dernburg," *The Spectator,* January 23, 1909.

5. Winfried Baumgart, "Imperialism," in *Germans in the Tropics,* eds. Arthur J. Knoll and Lewis H. Gann (New York: Greenwood, 1987), 158. See Karl Helfferich, *Deutschlands Volkswohlstand 1888–1913* (Berlin: Stilke, 1914), 82.

6. Cf. Erik Grimmer-Solem, "The Professors' Africa," *German History* 25, no. 3 (2007): 313. Also cf. Imperial Statistical Office, *Statistisches Jahrbuch für das deutsche Reich,* vol. 35 (Berlin: Puttkammer, 1914), 181; Max Warnack, *Unsere Kolonialwirtschaft* (Berlin: Kolonialgesellschaft, 1914), 10.

7. Norman Angell, *This Have and Have-Not Business* (London: Hamilton, 1936), 84. See, e.g., George Steinmetz, *The Devil's Handwriting* (Chicago: University of Chicago Press, 2007), 136. See Jeremy Sarkin-Hughes, *Germany's Genocide of the Herero* (Cape Town: UCT Press, 2010), 5; Helmuth Stoecker, "Die wirtschaftliche Bedeutung des deutschen Kolonialreiches," in *Drang nach Afrika,* ed. Helmuth Stoecker (Berlin: Akademie, 1991), 164; Francesca Schinzinger, *Die Kolonien und das Deutsche Reich* (Stuttgart: Steiner, 1984), 30. August Bebel's speech to Reichstag, December 1, 1906, in *August Bebel: Ausgewählte Reden und Schriften,* vol. 8, eds. Anneliese Beske and Eckhard Müller (München: Saur, 1997), 124. Cf. Hans Poeschel, *Kolonialfrage* (Berlin: Mittler, 1920), 22. See Boris Barth, *Die deutsche Hochfinanz und die Imperialismen* (Stuttgart: Steiner, 1995).

8. "Rechtsverhältnisse der Deutschen Kolonialgesellschaft für Südwestafrika," *Berliner Börsen-Courier,* February 15, 1910. Cf. "Widersprüche über Diamanten-Aussichten," *Berliner Börsen-Courier,* October 26, 1909.

9. In this spirit, compare Elise Huillery, "The Black Man's Burden: The Cost of Colonization of French West Africa," *Journal of Economic History* 74, no. 1 (2014): 1–38; Ewout Frankema and Marlous van Waijenburg, "Metropolitan Blueprints of Colonial Taxation? Lessons from Fiscal Capacity Building in British and French Africa, c. 1880-1940," *Journal of African History* 55, no. 3 (2014): 371–400.

10. On the concept of "colonial effect," see Geoff Eley, "Empire by Land or Sea? Germany's Imperial Imaginary, 1840–1945," in *German Colonialism in a Global Age,* eds. Geoff Eley and Bradley Naranch (Durham, NC: Duke University Press, 2014), 19–45.

11. D. E. Moggridge, *Keynes* (London: Routledge, 1992), 422. Norman Angell, *Great Illusion* (New York: Putnam's, 1910), 105–129. Cf. James Ritchie, *Imperialism* (London: Clarke, 1881), 47. A. J. P. Taylor, *From Boer War to Cold War* (New York: Penguin, 1995), 31. But see Fritz Stern, *Gold and Iron* (New York: Knopf, 1977), 395. Cf. Wolfgang Reinhard, "Öffentliche und andere Hände: Privatisierung und Deregulierung im Lichte historischer Erfahrung," in *Markt und Macht in der Geschichte,* eds. Helga Breuninger and Rolf Peter Sieferle (Stuttgart: Verlags-Anstalt, 1995), 281.

12. On rationality in British Empire, see Avner Offer, "British Empire," *Economic History Review* 46, no. 2 (1993): 215.

13. See Robert N. Proctor, "Anti-Agate: The Great Diamond Hoax and the Semiprecious Stone Scam," *Configurations* 9, no. 3 (2001): 381–412.

14. Jean Demuth, *Der Diamantenmarkt* (Karlsruhe: Braun, 1912), 14. "Diamonds and Prosperity," *Washington Post,* July 11, 1909. "Union Loses Fight," *New-York Daily Tribune,* January 23, 1909.

15. See Niels Petersson, "Kaiserreich in Prozessen ökonomischer Globalisierung," in *Kaiserreich transnational,* eds. Jürgen Osterhammel and Sebastian Conrad (Göttingen: V&R, 2004), 55.

16. See above all Isabel Hull, *Absolute Destruction: Military Culture and the Practices of War in Imperial Germany* (Ithaca: Cornell University Press, 2005). See Jürgen Zimmerer, *Deutsche Herrschaft über Afrikaner: staatlicher Machtanspruch und Wirklichkeit im kolonialen Namibia* (Münster: LIT, 2004). On camps, see Casper Erichsen, 'The Angel of Death Has Descended Violently Among Them': Concentration Camps and Prisoners-of-War in Namibia, 1904–1908* (Leiden: African Studies Centre, 2005); Jonas Kreienbaum, *Concentration Camps in Southern Africa, 1900–1908* (New York: Berghahn, 2019).

17. Fred Cornell, *Glamour of Prospecting* (London: Unwin, 1920), 42. Kreienbaum, *Sad Fiasco*, 91. Cf. Walther Rathenau, "Notizen zur Afrikareise 1908," in *Schriften der Wilhelminischen Zeit 1885–1914*, ed. Alexander Jaser (Düsseldorf: Droste, 2015), 680; Casper Erichsen, "Zwangsarbeit," in *Völkermord in Deutsch-Südwestafrika*, ed. Jürgen Zimmerer and Joachim Zeller (Berlin: Links, 2003), 80.

18. Pathbreaking works include Horst Drechsler, *'Let Us Die Fighting': The Struggle of the Herero and Nama Against German Imperialism, 1884–1915* (London: Zed, 1980); Helmut Bley, *Kolonialherrschaft und Sozialstruktur in Deutsch-Südwestafrika, 1894–1914* (Hamburg: Leibniz, 1968). For cultural history, see most recently Birthe Kundrus, ed., *Phantasiereiche: Zur Kulturgeschichte des deutschen Kolonialismus* (Frankfurt: Campus, 2003); David Ciarlo, *Advertising Empire* (Cambridge, MA: Harvard University Press, 2011); John Short, *Magic Lantern Empire* (Ithaca: Cornell University Press, 2012). Other seminal work includes Lora Wildenthal, *German Women for Empire* (Durham: Duke University Press, 2001); Gesine Krüger, *Kriegsbewältigung und Geschichtsbewußtsein* (Göttingen: Vandenhoeck & Ruprecht, 1999); Steinmetz, *The Devil's Handwriting*; Andrew Zimmerman, *Alabama in Africa* (Princeton: Princeton University Press, 2010).

Hannah Arendt and Helmut Bley are key figures in the discussion of the ongoing legacy of colonialism. See Matthew Fitzpatrick, "The Pre-History of the Holocaust?" *Central European History* 41, no. 3 (2008): 477–503; Birthe Kundrus, "Continuities," *Journal of Namibian Studies* 1, no. 4 (2008): 25–46; Robert Gerwarth and Stephan Malinowski, "Hannah Arendt's Ghosts," *Central European History* 42, no. 2 (2009): 279–300.

On genocide, see Jürgen Zimmerer, *Von Windhuk nach Auschwitz?* (Münster: LIT, 2011). On German military culture, see most recently Susanne Kuss, *German Colonial Wars* (Cambridge, MA: Harvard University Press, 2017); Shelley Baranowski, *Nazi Empire* (Cambridge: Cambridge University Press, 2010).

19. J. M. Keynes, *Economic Consequences of the Peace* (New York: Harcourt, 1920), 81. Eckart Kehr, "Englandhaß und Weltpolitik," in *Der Primat der Innenpolitik*, ed. Hans-Ulrich Wehler (Berlin: de Gruyter, 1970), 149–175. Niall Ferguson, *Paper and Iron* (Cambridge: Cambridge University Press, 1995).

20. One exception: Barth, *Hochfinanz*, 328–342.

21. See Sean Wempe, *Revenants of the German Empire* (Oxford: Oxford University Press, 2019); Wolfe Schmokel, *Dream of Empire* (New Haven: Yale University Press, 1964).

1. Rulers

1. See Steven Press, *Rogue Empires: Contracts and Conmen in Europe's Scramble for Africa* (Cambridge, MA: Harvard University Press, 2017), chapters 4 and 5.

2. See Hans-Ulrich Wehler, *Bismarck und der Imperialismus* (Berlin: Kiepenheuer & Witsch, 1969). See Horst Gründer, *Geschichte der deutschen Kolonien* (Paderborn: Schöningh, 2004), 58. See Hartmut Pogge von Strandmann, *Imperialismus vom grünen Tisch* (Berlin: Links, 2009), 50.

3. Friedrich Krauel's memorandum, May 2, 1890, BAB R1001/1523.

4. See Rudolf von Albertini and Albert Wirz, *Europäische Kolonialherrschaft, 1880–1940* (München: Heyne, 1982), 448.

5. Marion Wallace and John Kinahan, *A History of Namibia* (New York: Columbia University Press, 2011), 59–112.

6. Wehler, *Bismarck und der Imperialismus*, 264. Horst Drechsler, *'Let Us Die Fighting': The Struggle of the Herero and Nama Against German Imperialism, 1884–1915* (London: Zed, 1980), 22. Adolf Lüderitz to Richard Lesser, December 1, 1884, *Die Erschliessung von Deutsch-Südwest-Afrika*, ed. C. A. Lüderitz (Oldenburg: Stallings, 1945), 105. Herbert Jäckel, *Die Landgesellschaften in den deutschen Schutzgebieten* (Jena: Fischer, 1909), 29.

7. Hans Merensky to Bernhard Dernburg, September 6, 1909, BAB R1001/1529.

8. Gerhard Rohlfs, *Angra Pequeña* (Bielefeld: Velhagen, 1885), 10.

9. Deutsche Kolonialgesellschaft für SWA to Bismarck, October 16, 1885, BAB R1001/1537. See "Geschäftsjahr," *Deutsche Kolonialzeitung* 3, no. 23 (1886): 792. "King of the Nama," cf. "Wie die Kolonie entstand," *Swakopmunder Zeitung*, July 19, 1905.

10. Oberbürgermeister Weber's memorandum, March 6, 1885, printed in Ludwig Sander, *Geschichte der deutschen Kolonial-Gesellschaft für Südwest-Afrika*, vol. 1 (Berlin: Reimer, 1912), 20. Cf. Friedrich Ratzel, *Wider die Reichsnörgler* (München: Oldenbourg, 1884), 22.

11. "Sovereign," see Bleichröder and Hugo zu Hohenlohe-Öhringen to Bismarck, March 30, 1885, BAB R1001/1532. Heavy hitters, see transcription of contract dated April 19, 1885, BAB R1001/1537; cf. "Börse und Kolonien," *Vorwärts,* February 4, 1909. "Identical," see Karl Helfferich's memorandum, December 22, 1908, Historical Institute of Deutsche Bank (hereafter HID), Archives of Deutsche Bank Zentrale Berlin, Sekretariat (Frankfurt), S096.

12. Verzeichniß der Einlagen zum Kapitalvermögen der Deutschen Kolonialgesellschaft für SWA, April 9, 1885, BAB R1001/1532.

13. Hans Merensky to Bernhard Dernburg, September 6, 1909, BAB R1001/1529. Woodruff Smith, *German Colonial Empire* (Chapel Hill: University of North Carolina Press, 1978), 55. Deutsche Kolonialgesellschaft für SWA to Bismarck, March 21, 1887, BAB R1001/1322. "Geschäftsjahr," *Deutsche Kolonialzeitung* 3, no. 23 (1886): 792; Deutsche Kolonialgesellschaft für SWA to Bundesrat, July 6, 1885, BAB R1001/1524.

14. Staatskommissar bei der Deutschen Kolonialgesellschaft für SWA to Bismarck, March 30, 1886, BAB R1001/1534a. "Army," see Deutsche Kolonialgesellschaft für SWA to Oswald von Richthofen, February 5, 1897, BAB R1001/1523. Curt von François to Reichstag, December 15, 1907, BAB R1001/1323. "Mineral treasures"; "of importance," see Colonial Corporation to Wilhelm I, April 12, 1885, BAB R1001/1532.

15. W. O. Henderson, *Studies in German Colonial History* (Chicago: Quadrangle, 1962), 30; Wehler, *Bismarck und der Imperialismus*, 289. Sander, *Geschichte*, vol. 1, 58–62, 112; cf. Eckart Schremmer, *Steuern und Staatsfinanzen während der Industrialisierung Europas* (Berlin: Springer, 2013), 205. See "Die deutsche Kolonial-Gesellschaft für Südwest-Afrika," *Neue Preußische Zeitung*, September 22, 1892; Curt von François, *Deutsch-Südwestafrika* (Berlin: Reimer, 1899), 56. Cf. James Beethom Whitehead to Paul Kayser, January 4, 1894, BAB R1001/1523.

16. But see Gustav Stresemann, "Brauchen wir Kolonien?" *Gustav Stresemann*, ed. Hartmuth Becker (Berlin: Duncker & Humblot, 2008), 77.

17. See Roger Chickering, *We Men Who Feel Most German: A Cultural Study of the Pan-German League, 1886–1914* (Boston: Allen & Unwin, 1984); cf. Hans Fenske, ed., *Unter Wilhelm II* (Darmstadt: WBG, 1982), 92. See Jan Rüger, *The Great Naval Game* (Cambridge: Cambridge University Press, 2007); Jonathan Steinberg, *Yesterday's Deterrent*

(London: Macdonald, 1965), 36–46. Richard J. Evans, *Proletarians and Politics* (New York: St. Martin's, 1990), 175. Matthew Fitzpatrick, "Wilhelm II," *Crowns and Colonies*, eds. Robert Aldrich et al. (Manchester: Manchester University Press, 2016), 81.

18. Friedrich Engels to August Bebel, October 11, 1884, *Bebels Briefwechsel mit Engels*, ed. Werner Blumenberg (The Hague: Mouton, 1965), 190; Friedrich Engels to Eduard Bernstein, September 13, 1884, *Bernsteins Briefwechsel mit Engels*, ed. Helmut Hirsch (Assen: Van Gorcum, 1970), 296. Michael Stürmer, *Das Ruhelose Reich: Deutschland 1860–1918* (Berlin: Severin und Siedler, 1983), 233. "Aggrandizement of millionaires," see August Bebel to Reichtag, March 13, 1906, *Stenographische Berichte*, 1982; Wehler, *Bismarck und der Imperialismus*, 408–410.

19. Horst Gründer, *Geschichte der deutschen Kolonien* (Paderborn: Schöningh, 2004), 30.

20. Alfred Kirchhoff, "Kolonisation," *Deutsche Revue* 12, no. 2 (Breslau: Trewendt, 1887), 56; Ludwig Stacke, *Erzählungen*, vol. 3 (Oldenburg: Stalling, 1894), 605; Franz Giesebrecht, "Spekulationen," *Neue Deutsche Rundschau* 6 (Berlin: Fischer, 1895), 1085; Kurt Hassert, *Kolonien* (Leipzig: Seele, 1899), 3. Georg von Siemens to Henry Villard, July 29, 1887, in Karl Helfferich, *Georg von Siemens,* vol. 2 (Berlin: Springer, 1923), 338; Eduard Bernstein, *Die englische Gefahr und das deutsche Volk* (Berlin: Vorwärts, 1911), 22. Cf. August Bebel's speech to Reichstag, January 26, 1889, *Stenographische Berichte,* 627–628.

21. On diversity, see Ann Stoler, "Rethinking," *Comparative Studies of Society and History* 31 (1989): 134–161.

22. Friedrich Naumann, *National-Sozialer Katechismus* (Berlin: Kundt, 1897), 13. Cf. Woodruff Smith, *Ideological Origins of Nazi Imperialism* (Oxford: Oxford University Press, 1989), 40. Oberstabsarzt Mankiewitz, *Kohlstocks Ratgeber für die Tropen* (Stettin: Hermann Peters, 1910), 1. "Painful colony," see "Neue Kämpfe," *Neue Hamburger Zeitung*, March 20, 1908; "Kolonien," *Allgemeine Zeitung* (Munich), April 18, 1899. Fritz von Unruh, *Offiziere* (Berlin: Reiss, 1911), 59. "Foresee," see Theodor Leutwein, *Elf Jahre Gouverneur* (Berlin, 1906), 548. "Good but poor," see Protocol of Dernburg's meeting, August 12, 1908, BAB R1001/1465. Cf. "Twixt Sand and Sun," *Rhodesia Herald*, October 29, 1920.

23. See Marc Grohmann, *Exotische Verfassung* (Tübingen: Mohr, 2001), 281–282. Leutwein, *Elf Jahre Gouverneur,* 13. "Lüderitz Bay," see Report of Commander of SMS Habicht, April 9, 1891, BAB R1001/1523. See Daniel Joseph Walther, *Creating Germans Abroad* (Athens: Ohio University Press, 2002), 9. See Adam Blackler, "From Boondoggle to Settlement Colony," *Central European History* 50 (2017): 449–470. Sander, *Geschichte,* vol. 1, 79, 84. Hans Rafalski, *Niemandsland* (Berlin: Wernitz, 1930), 318.

24. Jakob Zollmann, "Becoming a Good Farmer—Becoming a Good Farm Worker: On Colonial Educational Policies in Germany and German South-West Africa, Circa 1890 to 1918," *Education and Development in Colonial and Postcolonial Africa* (London: Palgrave Macmillan, 2020), 114.

25. "Deutsche Kolonialgesellschaft für Südwestafrika," *Berliner Börsen-Courier,* April 14, 1909.

26. "Südwest unter Dernburg," *Windhuker Nachrichten*, March 3, 1909. "Stepchildren," see "Der 'stiefmütterlich' behandelte Süden," *Windhuker Nachrichten*, August 8, 1908. Three percent, statistics extrapolated from data in "Konzessionsgesellschaften," *Sozialdemokratische Partei-Korrespondenz*, August 9, 1906; for 38 percent, see Hans Oelhafen von Schöllenbach, *Die Besiedelung Deutsch-Südwestafrikas* (Berlin: Reimer, 1926), 72. See Klaus Epstein, *Matthias Erzberger and the Dilemma of German Democracy* (Princeton: Princeton University Press, 1959), 644–645; Wilhelm Külz,

Deutsch-Südafrika im 25. Jahre (Berlin: Süsserott, 1909), 287; Birthe Kundrus, *Moderne Imperialisten* (Köln: Böhlau, 2003), 47; Helmut Bley, *Kolonialherrschaft* (Hamburg: Leibniz, 1968), 174.

27. Quoted in Jon M. Bridgman, *Revolt of the Hereros* (Berkeley: University of California Press, 1981), 43.

28. See Mack Walker, *Germany and the Emigration* (Cambridge, MA: Harvard University Press, 1964). Cf. Emil Reich, *Germany's Swelled Head* (Walsall: Walsall Press, 1907), 151; Wehler, *Bismarck und der Imperialismus.*

29. See Kundrus, *Moderne Imperialisten,* 108. Walther, *Creating Germans,* 15. Artur Nap, "Diamanten," *Das Freie Wort,* vol. 11 (Frankfurt am Main: Neuer Frankfurter Verlag, 1912), 869. Bernhard Dernburg, "Weltwirtschaft," *Berliner Tageblatt,* April 11, 1911. Oelhafen von Schöllenbach, *Besiedelung Deutsch-Südwestafrika,* 83. See Robbie Aitken, "Looking for Die Besten Boeren," *Journal of Southern African Studies* 33, no. 2 (2007): 343–360.

30. Schuckmann to the DKSSWA, May 27, 1909, BAB R1001/1528. Franz Giesebrecht, "Koloniale Spekulationen," *Neue Deutsche Rundschau* 6 (Berlin: Fischer, 1895): 1086. Anton Meyer-Gerhard's report, April 13, 1912, BAB R1001/2087; Schuckmann to RKA, October 12, 1909, BAB R1001/1324.

31. See Karl von Stengel, *Rechtsverhältnisse der deutschen Schutzgebiete* (Tübingen: Mohr, 1901), 184–186.

32. Hermann Hesse, *Die Landfrage,* vol. 1 (Jena: Costenoble, 1906), 63. "Konzessionsgesellschaften," *Sozialdemokratische Partei-Korrespondenz,* August 9, 1906; Oelhafen von Schöllenbach, *Besiedelung Deutsch-Südwestafrika,* 72, but see Epstein, *Matthias Erzberger,* 644–645; Külz, *Deutsch-Südafrika,* 287.

33. See Charles van Onselen, "Reactions," *Journal of African History* 13, no. 3 (1972): 473. Philipp N. Lehmann, "Between Waterberg and Sandveld," *German History* 32, no. 4 (2014): 541; Wilhelm Rickmann, *Tierzucht* (Berlin: Schoetz, 1908), 156; cf. G. Miescher, *Namibia's Red Line* (New York: Palgrave Macmillan, 2012), 59.

34. German General Staff, *Die Kämpfe der deutschen Truppen in Südwestafrika,* vol. 1 (Berlin: Mittler, 1906), 9. Anonymous, "Wassererschließung," *Deutsches Kolonialblatt* 23 (Berlin, 1912), 406. G. Goldberg, "Diamantenabbau," *Dinglers Polytechnisches Journal* 329, no. 34/35 (Berlin: Dietze, 1914): 531.

35. See "Trinkwasser," *Deutsches Kolonialblatt* 8 (Berlin, 1897): 275. "Wasserversorgung," *Gesundheits-Ingenieur* 29, no. 14 (München: Oldenbourg, 1906): 254; Ludwig von Estorff, *Wanderungen,* ed. Christoph-Friedrich Kutscher (Wiesbaden, 1968), 140.

36. See Theodor Rehbock, *Deutsch-Südwest* (Berlin: Reimer, 1898), 51. Hans Reiter, ed., *Grundriss der Hygiene* (Berlin: Springer, 1940), 202. Captain Behntsch of SMS Panther to Wilhelm II, March 10, 1911, BAB R1001/1909.

37. Friedrich von Dincklage-Campe, *Deutsche Reiter in Südwest* (Berlin: Bong, 1908), 356; Albert Herrlich, *Schwarze Reise* (Berlin: Oestergaard, 1937), 199. Rudolf Böhmer's Decree, May 7, 1906, printed in *Die deutsche Kolonial-Gesetzgebung,* vol. 10 (Berlin: Mittler, 1907), 191. Hertha Brodersen-Manns, *Wie alles anders kam* (Windhoek: Kuiseb, 1991), 7, 10. See Kurt Dinter, "Sarcocaulon," *Monatsschrift der Deutschen Kakteen-Gesellschaft,* vol. 1 (Berlin, 1929), 145; Fred Cornell, *Glamour of Prospecting* (London: Unwin, 1920), 10.

38. Jakob Zollmann, "Becoming a Good Farmer," 117. G. Goldberg, "Technische Fortschritte unserer Kolonien," *Zeitschrift für Kolonialpolitik, Kolonialrecht und Kolonialwirtschaft* 14 (Berlin: Süsserott, 1912): 532. See "Wasserverordnung," *Deutsche Kolonialzeitung* 31 (1914): 269; "Trinkwasser," *Deutsche Kolonialzeitung* 31 (1914): 513. Cf. Rolf Hobson, *Imperialism at Sea* (Boston: Brill, 2002), 89.

39. One percent arable, see W. du Plessis, "In Situ Conservation in Namibia," *Dinteria* 23 (1992): 132; Ernst Hermann, *Viehzucht und Bodenkultur in Südwestafrika* (Berlin: Meinecke, 1900), 66. Rudolf Schmick, "Wichtigkeit der Bewässerung," *Jahrbuch über die deutschen Kolonien,* vol. 4 (1911), 147. Jakob Zollmann, *Koloniale Herrschaft und Ihre Grenzen* (Göttingen: Vandenhoeck and Ruprecht, 2010), 281. Cf. John Short, *Magic Lantern Empire* (Ithaca: Cornell University Press, 2012), 71.

40. Lindequist to Reichstag, February 3, 1910, *Stenographische Berichte,* 1004. Theodor Rehbock, *Deutschlands Pflichten* (Berlin: Reimer, 1904), 21. Christian Storz to Reichstag, February 3, 1910, *Stenographische Berichte,* 1006. Cf. Erwin Rupp, *Soll und Haben* (Berlin: Reimer, 1904), 31. Hans Berthold, "Die Besiedlung Deutsch-Südwestafrikas," *Jahrbuch über die deutschen Kolonien,* vol. 4 (Essen: Baedeker, 1911), 202.

41. Cf. Paul Rohrbach, *Kolonialwesen* (Leipzig: Gloeckner, 1911), 27. Cf. Carl Uhlig, "Der südafrikanische Bundesstaat und Deutsch-Südwestafrika," *Geographische Zeitschrift* 21, no. 4 (1915): 221. "Deutscher Kolonialkongreß," *Berliner Volkszeitung,* October 9, 1910. Dernburg to Stresemann, February 17, 1911, Political Archive of the German Foreign Ministry (hereafter PAAA) NL Stresemann 120; "Zur Lage in Deutsch-Südwest," *Vossische Zeitung,* July 12, 1912. J. Kuntz, "Diamanten," *Der Tropenpflanzer* 18 (Berlin, 1915): 482.

42. Cf. Hans Merensky to Bernhard Dernburg, September 6, 1909, BAB R1001/1529; Kurd von Strantz, "Die Neue Kolonialzeit," *Der Türmer: Monatsschrift für Gemüt und Geist* 10, no. 2 (1908): 364.

43. See Isabel Hull, *Absolute Destruction* (Ithaca: Cornell University Press, 2005), 54.

44. "Sand Profiteering Society," see Erzberger's speech to Reichstag, *Stenographische Berichte,* November 30, 1906, 4037. "Deutsche Kolonialgesellschaft für Südwestafrika," *Frankfurter Zeitung,* May 22, 1909.

45. See Dörte Lerp, "Prairie," *Journal of Modern European History* 14, no. 2 (2016): 225–244. See Protocol of Dernburg's meeting, August 12, 1908, BAB R1001/1465; anonymous, "Südwestafrikaner," *Zeitschrift für Kolonialpolitik, Kolonialrecht und Kolonialwirtschaft* 12 (Berlin, 1910): 386; see Henriette Arendt, *Erlebnisse* (München: Süddeutsche Monatshefte, 1910), 96. "Justice," see Walther Rathenau, "Denkschrift über den Stand des Südwestafrikanischen Schutzgebietes," *Schriften der Wilhelminischen Zeit 1885–1914,* ed. Alexander Jaser (Düsseldorf: Droste, 2015), 658. Erzberger to Reichstag, March 2, 1909, *Stenographische Berichte,* 7277.

46. Wilhelm Hübbe-Schleiden, *Warum Weltmacht?* (Hamburg: Friederichsen, 1906), 17; Gustav Noske, *Kolonialpolitik* (Stuttgart, 1914), 67. Commitment of 750,000,000 marks, see Dernburg to Bruno von Schuckmann, November 27, 1909, BAB R1001/1324. See Hans Spellmeyer, *Kolonialpolitik* (Stuttgart, 1931). Artur Nap, "Diamanten," 869.

47. Hartmut Pogge von Strandmann, *Imperialismus vom Grünen Tisch* (Berlin: Christoph Links Verlag, 2009), 58; Boris Barth, *Die deutsche Hochfinanz und die Imperialismen* (Stuttgart: Steiner, 1995), 43. Norman Angell, *This Have and Have-not Business* (London: Hamilton, 1936), 204, 115. Andreas Eckert and Michael Pesek, "Bürokratische Ordnung," *Das Kaiserreich transnational* (Göttingen, 2004), 102; see Lora Wildenthal, *German Women for Empire* (Durham: Duke University Press, 2001), 84; see Frank Bösch, "Grenzen des 'Obrigkeitsstaates,'" in *Kaiserreich,* eds. Sven Müller and Cornelius Torp (Göttingen, 2009), 143. "Model Colony," see Rebekka Habermas, "Lost in Translation," *Journal of Modern History* 86 (March 2014): 47–80. Nationalliberale Partei, *Kolonialpolitik, nicht Kolonialskandale und Nebenregierung* (Berlin: Buchhandlung der Nationalliberalen Partei, 1907), 4.

48. See Smith, *Ideological Origins,* 124. Katharine Lerman, *Chancellor as Courtier* (New York: Cambridge University Press, 1990), 164. Cf. "Unter den Auserwählten,"

Berliner Tageblatt, August 10, 1913. Werner Schiefel, *Dernburg 1865–1937* (Zürich: Atlantis, 1974), 41, 156. Cf. "Dernburg und Meyer-Gerhardt über Frauenstimmrecht," *Lehre und Wehre: Theologisches und kirchlich-zeitgeschichtliches Monatsblatt,* vol. 61 (St. Louis: Concordia, 1915), 413. Alfred Fried, *Die moderne Friedensbewegung* (Leipzig: Teubner, 1907), 120. "Exzellenz Bernhard Dernburg," *Neues Wiener Journal,* April 20, 1913. Schiefel, *Dernburg,* 19–27. M. J. Bonn, *Wandering Scholar* (New York: John Day Company, 1948), 147. Ernst Friedegg, *Millionen und Millionäre* (Berlin: Vita, 1914), 298. Schiefel, *Dernburg,* 218, n150.

49. Gustav Radbruch to his parents, October 27, 1906, printed in Gustav Radbruch, *Gesamtausgabe,* ed. Arthur Kaufmann, vol. 17 (Heidelberg, 1991), 106.

50. Friedrich Wilhelm von Loebell, *Erinnerungen,* ed. Peter Winzen (Düsseldorf: Droste, 2016), 129. "Wien, 6. Juni," *Neue Freie Presse,* June 7, 1910. Rudolf Martin, *Unter dem Scheinwerfer* (Berlin: Schuster, 1910), 123. "Dernburg," *New York Times,* September 9, 1906. Adolf Zimmermann, *Mit Dernburg nach Ostafrika* (Berlin: Schwetschke, 1908), 3. "Dernburg in Kapstadt," *Windhuker Nachrichten,* June 20, 1908.

51. "Ministeralter," *Neue Hamburger Zeitung,* July 18, 1914. "Maßgebliches," *Die Grenzboten* 65 (1906): 591. See August Stein, *Irenaeus* (Frankfurt: Societätsdruckerei, 1921), 65.

52. Karl Kraus, "Aus dem Sautrog," *Die Fackel* 9, no. 249 (Wien: Fackel, 1908): 13. Edgar Vincent D'Abernon, *Ambassador,* vol. 1 (London: Hodder & Stoughton, 1929), 149. "Dr. Dernburg knows everything," see Francis Welch, "Germany's Chief Aid," *Vanity Fair,* March 1915, 35. "Captain of industry"; "the Morgan of Germany," see Felix Pinner, "Bernhard Dernburg," *Die Weltbühne* 18, no. 2 (Charlottenburg: Weltbühne, 1922): 466; Lerman, *Chancellor as Courtier,* 164. Astonishing memory, see Estorff, *Wanderungen,* 142; George Viereck, *Roosevelt* (New York: Jackson, 1920), 105.

53. Epstein, *Matthias Erzberger,* 55; Theodor Bohner, *Die Woermanns* (Berlin: Brücke, 1935), 218. Erich Eyck, *Das Persönliche Regiment Wilhelms II* (Zürich: Rentsch, 1948), 455. Dernburg's speech to Reichstag, May 4, 1907, *Stenographische Berichte,* 1407.

54. Heinrich Schnee, *Als letzter Gouverneur* (Quelle & Meyer, 1964), 83; Resolutions of the Colonial Office, October 1, 1907, *Landesgesetzgebung des Schutzgebietes Togo,* ed. Imperial Government of Togo (Berlin: Mittler, 1910), 367; Bettina Zurstrassen, *"Ein Stück deutscher Erde schaffen"* (Frankfurt: Campus, 2008), 107. René Puaux, *German Colonies* (London: Wightman, 1918), 10. Woodruff Smith, *Politics and the Sciences of Culture* (Oxford: Oxford University Press, 1991), 171; Smith, *Ideological Origins,* 126. L. H. Gann and Peter Duignan, *Rulers of German Africa* (Stanford: Stanford University Press, 1977), 54.

55. "Jannasch," *Koloniale Rundschau 1910,* no. 7 (1910): 434.

56. Rudolf Morsey, "Die Erfüllung von Aufgaben," *Deutsche Verwaltungsgeschichte,* ed. Kurt Jeserich et al., vol. 3 (Stuttgart: Deutsche, 1984), 162.

57. Bley, *Kolonialherrschaft,* 266. Dernburg to Colonial Government in Daressalam, March 7, 1908, BAB R1001/6938; protocol of Dernburg's meeting, August 12, 1908, BAB R1001/1465; "Dernburgs Kolonialprogramm," *Vorwärts,* February 22, 1908. "Place in the sun," see Smith, *Ideological Origins,* 60. Bradley D. Naranch, "'Colonized Body,' 'Oriental Machine,'" *Central European History* 33, no. 3 (2000): 305, 321. "Higher civilization," see Bernhard Dernburg, *Zielpunkte* (Berlin: Mittler und Sohn, 1907), 5.

58. "Encumbrances on the state" quoted in Ben Kiernan, *Blood and Soil* (New Haven: Yale University Press, 2007), 388. "His Excellency," see "England Traitor," *New York Times,* January 2, 1916. Robert von Friedeburg, "Konservatismus," *Historische Zeitschrift* 263, no. 1 (1996): 381; Arnold Wahnschaffe to Friedrich von Loebell, December 24, 1908, BAB R43/927. Jürgen Zimmerer, "Colonialism and Genocide," *Ashgate Research Companion to Imperial Germany,* ed. Matthew Jefferies (New York: Routledge, 2016), 447.

59. See John Iliffe, *Tanganyika under German Rule, 1905–1912* (Cambridge: Cambridge University Press, 1969), 27. Robert Gerwarth und Stephan Malinowski, "Holocaust," *Geschichte und Gesellschaft* 33, no. 3 (2007): 456. See Klaus Bade, "Kolonialexpansion," *Afrika im Geschichtsunterricht*, ed. Walter Fürnohr (München, Minerva, 1982), 13–49. See Matthias Erzberger, *Die Wahrheit über die Kolonien* (Berlin: Germania, 1908). "Solidarity," see Bernhard Dernburg, *Von beiden Ufern* (Berlin: Kronen, 1916), 57; see Bonn, *Wandering Scholar*, 147. "Favored one-sidedly the natives," see Estorff, *Wanderungen*, 142; quoted in Sarah Gertrude Millin, *General Smuts* (New York: Faber, 1936), 296.

60. Richard Lewinsohn, *Das Geld in der Politik* (Berlin: S. Fischer, 1930), 39. Cf. Horst Drechsler, *Südwestafrika unter deutscher Kolonialherrschaft: Die großen Land- und Minengesellschaften* (Stuttgart: Steiner, 1996); John Williamson, *Karl Helfferich* (Princeton: Princeton University Press, 1971), 68; "Dernburg in Kapstadt," *Windhuker Nachrichten*, June 20, 1908.

61. Bernhard von König, "Eisenbahnpolitik," *Das neue Deutschland*, vol. 2, March 8, 1913; see Franz Baltzer, *Kolonialbahnen* (Berlin, 1916), 82; Oelhafen von Schöllenbach, *Die Besiedelung Deutsch-Südwestafrikas*, 110; Alfred Zimmermann, *Kolonialreiche* (Berlin: Ullstein, 1916), 221. See "Maßgebliches," *Die Grenzboten* 67 (1908): 396. "Diamond Fields," *The Sun* (New York), August 22, 1909. John Lowry, "African Resistance," *Central European History* 39, no. 2 (2006): 262. Otto Wiemer, *Volkspartei* (Berlin: Deutsche Presse, 1907), 8.

2. Riches

1. Joseph Conrad, *Victory: An Island Tale* (New York: Doubleday, 1915), 3.

2. Joan Dickinson, *Book of Diamonds* (New York: Crown, 1965), 1–2; see Robert N. Proctor, "Anti-Agate: The Great Diamond Hoax and the Semiprecious Stone Scam," *Configurations* 9, no. 3 (2001): 385. Ernst Steiner, *Der internationale Diamantenmarkt* (Wien: Richards, 1933), 7.

3. "Of no use but as ornaments," see Adam Smith, *Wealth of Nations*, ed. Edwin Cannan, vol. 1 (London: Methuen & Co., 1904), 84, 48. "Valley of diamonds," see James Remington McCarthy, *Fire in the Earth* (New York: Harper, 1942), 218.

4. George Frederick Kunz, *The Magic of Jewels and Charms* (Philadelphia: J. B. Lippincott, 1915), 395. "Roughs," see Charles P. Kindleberger, *A Financial History of Western Europe* (London: Allen & Unwin, 1984), 236–237; Proctor, "Anti-Agate," 387. "Kaiserin's Jewels," *New York Times*, July 21, 1917; see Dan Atkinson, "Rocks and Rackets," *The Guardian*, October 2, 1996. Ronald Findlay and Kevin H. O'Rourke, *Power and Plenty* (Princeton: Princeton University Press, 2007), 273.

5. Robert Vicat Turrell, *Capital and Labour on the Kimberley Diamond Fields, 1871–1890* (New York: Cambridge University Press, 1987), 4. Eric Hobsbawm, *The Age of Empire, 1875–1914* (New York: Pantheon, 1987; rpt., New York: Vintage, 1989), 5. "An important factor," see "Diamonds in Demand," *Rhodesia Herald*, November 11, 1910; cf. Richard von Kühlmann, *Erinnerungen* (Heidelberg: Schneider, 1948), 160–161.

6. But see Proctor, "Anti-Agate," 398. "Diamanten," *Deutsch-Südwestafrikanische Zeitung*, November 1, 1905; "Vol de 150,000 fr. de diamants," *Le Petit Parisien*, May 1, 1912. Ludwig Bamberger, *Ausgewählte Reden und Aufsätze über Geld- und Bankwesen* (Berlin: Guttentag, 1900), 229. Proctor, "Anti-Agate," 383. Natty Rothschild (1st Lord Rothschild) to Édouard de Rothschild, Paris, July 7, 1908, Rothschild Archives, London (hereafter RAL) XI/130A/2/127.

7. See C. R. Boxer, *Golden Age* (Berkeley, 1962), 204–225. Wallis Cattelle, *Diamond* (New York: Lane, 1911), 46; Edwin Streeter, *Precious Stones* (London: Bell, 1898), 43; Frank

Dawson, *Debt Crisis* (New Haven: Yale University Press, 1990), 182. Paul Baer, "Diamantenpolitik," *Zeitschrift für Kolonialpolitik, Kolonialrecht und Kolonialwirtschaft*, vol. 14 (1912): 784. Hjalmar Schacht, "Diamant-Industrie," *Preußische Jahrbücher*, ed. Hans Delbrück, vol. 114 (Berlin, 1903), 309; Jean Georges Escard, *Les pierres précieuses* (Paris: Pinat, 1914), 142.

8. Arno Jollast, "Diamantenfieber," *Die Zukunft*, vol. 66 (Berlin: Zukunft, 1909), 80. Cf. Stefan Kanfer, *The Last Empire* (New York: FSG, 1993), 24–25; Frank G. Carpenter, *How the World Is Clothed* (Chicago: American, 1908), 281.

9. Turrell, *Capital and Labour*, 9.

10. Emile Denekamp, *Die Amsterdamer Diamantindustrie* (Heidelberg: Hörning, 1895), 35. Dernburg to Wilhelm II, January 7, 1909, BAB R1001/1341. Jürgen Osterhammel, *Die Verwandlung der Welt* (Munich: C.H. Beck, 2010), 327; Cattelle, *Diamond*, 46. "Diamantengeschichte," *Rumburger Zeitung*, April 5, 1873, 179.

11. J. H. Esterhuyse, *South West Africa, 1880–1894* (Cape Town: Struick, 1968), 11. Friedrich Fabri, *Deutsche Kolonialbestrebungen* (Elberfeld: Friderichs, 1884), 18; Johannes Olpp, *Angra Pequeña* (Elberfeld: Friderichs, 1884), 10. G. Gürich, "Über die Diamantlagerstätten von Deutsch-Südwestafrika," *Verhandlungen des Naturwissenschaftlichen Vereins in Hamburg 1912*, vol. 3, no. 20 (Hamburg: Friederichsen, 1913), lv; William Eveleigh, *South-West Africa* (London: Unwin, 1915), 203; "Kolonien," *Allgemeine Zeitung* (Munich), April 18, 1899; Gustav Meinecke, *Die deutschen Kolonien in Wort und Bild* (Leipzig: Weber, 1899), 40; Emil Zimmermann, *Unsere Kolonien* (Berlin: Ullstein, 1912), 231; "A la recherche de cinq milliards," *Paris-soir*, January 24, 1939. "Diamond Mountain," see H. Pohle, "Bericht über die von Herrn Lüderitz ausgerüstete Expedition nach Südwestafrika, 1884–85," *Petermann's Mitteilungen*, vol. 32 (Gotha: Perthes, 1886), 236. See "Studienreise," *Deutsche Kolonialzeitung*, 25, no. 35 (1908): 629; Hans Rafalski, *Niemandsland* (Berlin: Wernitz, 1930), 323. Cf. Carl Schmidt, *Geographie der Europäersiedelungen* (Jena: Fischer, 1922), 96.

12. W. P. de Kock, *Report of Assistant Mines Inspector to Board of Consolidated Diamond Mines of South West Africa* (Windhoek: Meinert, 1936), 7, accessed via National Archives of Namibia (hereafter NAN), Source A.809. Wilhelm R. Schmidt, *Als Telegrafenbauer in Deutsch-Südwest* (Erfurt: Sutton, 2006), 114. "Damaraland Diamonds," *Rand Daily Mail*, September 26, 1908. "Colossal mine," see Adolf Lüderitz to Richard Lesser, December 1, 1884, *Die Erschliessung von Deutsch-Südwest-Afrika*, 105. See Harry Johnston, "German Colonies," *Edinburgh Review*, vol. 19 (1914): 301.

13. Cf. Protocol of Board Meeting for Deutsche Kolonialgesellschaft für SWA, September 30, 1886, BAB R1001/1534a. Walter Moritz, *Hermann Heinrich Kreft, der Diamantenmissionar aus Wallenbrück* (Bielefeld: Afrika-Verlag der Kreis, 1976), 25–27. Fred Cornell, *Glamour of Prospecting* (London: Unwin, 1920), 3. Emily Hahn, *Diamond* (New York: Doubleday, 1956), 272. G. Gürich, "Diamantfunden," *Die Umschau: Übersicht über die Fortschritte und Bewegungen auf dem Gesamtgebiet der Wissenshaft und Technik*, ed. J. H. Bechhold, vol. 12 (Frankfurt: 1908), 891. NAN ZBU, 1619, R.XIV.i.3, Golinelli to the Reich, June 4, 1898. NAN ZBU, 1484, R.II.e.3, vol. 1, Bl. 1–33; Margarethe von Eckenbrecher, *Im dichten Pori* (Berlin: Mittler, 1912), 13, 139.

14. Heinz Gustafsson, *Namibia* (Delmenhorst: Aschenbeck & Holstein, 2003), 152–153. Omitted the incident, see, for example, in Maximilian von Spee to Maria von Spee, November 18, 1884, *Spee*, ed. Hermann Kirchhoff (Berlin: Marinedank, 1915), 253.

15. See Proctor, "Anti-Agate," 399. Ewald Banse, *Afrikaner* (Berlin, 1942), 223–224. Cf. Anthony Hocking, *Oppenheimer & Son* (New York: McGraw-Hill, 1973), 32. "Deutsche Schutzgebiete," *Frankfurter Zeitung*, September 5, 1909.

16. "Hundreds of wagons," see "Lüderitzbucht," *Diamond Fields Advertiser,* January 4, 1909. Ernest Oppenheimer to William Honnold, August 26, 1908, Claremont Colleges Library Special Collections (hereafter CCL) Honnold Papers, Box 3, Folder 15. Maximilian von Spee to Fernanda von Spee, November 18, 1884, *Graf Spee,* ed. Hermann Kirchhoff (Berlin: Marinedank, 1915), 253. Paul Rohrbach, "In den Diamantfeldern," *Deutsche Zeitung,* July 23, 1910.

17. Twenty-five days, see Jon M. Bridgman, *Revolt of the Hereros* (Berkeley: University of California Press, 1981), 140. Eighty miles, see Lawrence Green, *At Daybreak* (Cape Town: Timmins, 1950), 154. "Was der Tag bringt," *Vorwärts,* August 17, 1928.

18. "British Soldiers Seek," *The Spokesman-Review,* July 18, 1916. See Niall Ferguson, *House of Rothschild: The World's Banker 1849–1999* (New York: Viking, 1999), 171. Georg Simmel, "Psychologie des Schmuckes," *Morgen* 2, no. 15 (Berlin, 1908): 455. "No one," see J. M. Keynes, "Control," in *Collected Writings,* ed. Donald Moggridge, vol. 19, part 2 (Cambridge: Cambridge University Press, 1981), 547–548.

19. Hugo Blumhagen, *Südafrika* (Hamburg: Friederichsen, 1921), 44; see Sarah Stein, *Plumes* (New Haven: Yale University Press, 2008). "Cost of Diamonds," *New York Times,* April 3, 1910. "Price of Diamonds," *Wall Street Journal,* November 16, 1912.

20. David Cannadine, *History in Our Time* (New Haven: Yale University Press, 1998), 209. Quoted in Robert Rotberg, *The Founder* (Oxford: Oxford University Press, 1988), 492; see also 199; Rob Turrell, "Rhodes, De Beers, and Monopoly," *Journal of Imperial and Commonwealth History* 10, no. 3 (1982): 329.

21. Stanley Chapman, *Merchant Enterprise in Britain* (New York: Cambridge University Press, 1992), 276. See Charles Sydney Goldman, *South African Mines,* vol. 2 (Johannesburg: Argus, 1896), 194. "The richest, the greatest," see F. Y. Verschoyle, *Cecil Rhodes: His Political Life and Speeches 1881–1900* (London: Chapman and Hall, 1900), 779. Dernburg to Wilhelm II, July 1, 1909, BAB R1001/1341.

22. Figures for known diamond deposits cited in Bishop J. C. Hartzell to "Friend," April 25, 1907, Methodist Episcopal Church Missionary Correspondence, 1846–1912: Africa, General Commission on Archives & History, United Methodist Church (Gale Microform Series Call #1:3–6), 5. See Hobsbawm, *Age of Empire,* 318. Siegfried Passarge, "Durch die Karroo," *Globus* 77, no. 5 (1900): 80. Turrell, *Capital and Labour,* 146; on South African diamond labor, see also William Worger, *City of Diamonds* (New Haven: Yale University Press, 1987).

23. See Edward Jay Epstein, *Rise and Fall of Diamonds* (New York: Simon & Schuster, 1982), 66–87; Colin Newbury, *The Diamond Ring* (Oxford: Oxford University Press, 1989). Leopold de Rothschild to Rothschild Cousins, Paris, January 31, 1908, RAL XI/130A/2/28. S. D. Chapman, "Rhodes and London," *Historical Journal* 28, no. 3 (1985): 656. Ronald Hyam, *Failure* (London: Macmillan, 1972), 24. Richard Voeltz, "Penetration," *International Journal of African Historical Studies* 17, no. 4 (1984): 630.

24. Edward Jessup, *Ernest Oppenheimer: A Study in Power* (London: Rex Collings, 1979), 43. Cf. A. Goerz & Co. to Dernburg, February 12, 1909, BAB R1001/1342. "Umschau," *Plutus: Kritische Wochenschrift für Volkswirtschaft und Finanzwesen,* October 26, 1912, 846. See Osterhammel, *Verwandlung,* 327. "Superabundance of money," see "World Scarcity of Diamonds," *American Jeweler,* vol. 39, no. 11 (1919): 430. "Sheriff Says Maid Not Suspected," *San Francisco Chronicle,* March 3, 1905.

25. World diamond consumption, see Jean Demuth, *Der Diamantenmarkt* (Karlsruhe: Braun, 1912), 14; "Diamonds and Prosperity," *Washington Post,* July 11, 1909; "Union Loses Fight," *New-York Daily Tribune,* January 23, 1909. "£400/M of Diamonds [. . .] I think is the quantity the English jewel trade consumes every year"; Rothschilds in London

to Édouard Rothschild, Paris, April 11, 1913, RAL XI/130A/7/73; Rothschilds in London to James de Rothschild, May 12, 1914, RAL XI/130A/8/94. "Les importations de diamants aux États-Unis," *Journal de Genève,* December 2, 1908; "Diamond Profit $25 per minute," *Chicago Daily Tribune,* September 27, 1908. Humboldt-Dachroeden to Bethmann Hollweg, June 23, 1913, BAB R901/789. German consulate at Johannesburg to Bethmann Hollweg, February 27, 1912, BAB R901/787.

26. "No fashion in them," see "Buying Wedding Rings," *Washington Post,* November 25, 1883; "Price of Engagement Rings," *Chicago Daily Tribune,* November 27, 1904. Ninety percent, see "Künstliche Edelsteine," *Berliner Börsenzeitung,* September 18, 1909.

27. "Fairer sex," see "Deutscher Reichstag," *Berliner Börsenzeitung,* January 26, 1910. "Woman's vanity," see Lewis Atkinson, "The Forthcoming Exhibition at Kimberley," *Journal of the Society of Arts,* vol. 40 (London, 1892): 312. "Weakness," see "Geology of South Africa," *The Spectator,* vol. 95 (London, 1905): 198. "Woman is consumed with a passion," see Loftis Bros. & Co., *How Easily You Can Own and Wear a Diamond* (Chicago, 1908), 15, Special Research Collections, University of California, Santa Barbara (hereafter UCSB), Lawrence B. Romaine Trade Catalogue Collection (Mss 107), Series 1, Subseries A, Box 8; cf. Jan de Vries, *The Industrious Revolution* (Cambridge: Cambridge University Press, 2008), 47.

28. "Customary," see Proctor, "Anti-Agate," 394. "Custom decreed," see "The Month of Engagements," *The State* (South Carolina), April 30, 1910. "Substitution," see "War Increases Cost of Becoming Engaged," *St. Louis Post-Dispatch,* March 15, 1915. "Traditional," see "Etiquette of Jewels," *New York Times,* March 10, 1912; Burton Kingsland, *The Book of Good Manners: Etiquette For All Occasions* (New York: Doubleday, 1904), 207; on invented tradition, see Eric Hobsbawm and Terence Ranger, eds., *Invention of Tradition* (Cambridge: Cambridge University Press, 1983). "Purposes," see "Engagement Rings Going Out," *Washington Post,* October 10, 1909; "Stringency in Diamonds," *Wall Street Journal,* June 25, 1904; "Buying Wedding Rings," *Washington Post,* November 25, 1883; "World of Women," *The Penny Illustrated Paper,* September 29, 1906. Cf. "Rubies Superseded," *San Francisco Chronicle,* August 8, 1909.

29. "Breach of promise," see Rebecca Tushnet, "Rules of Engagement," *Yale Law Journal,* vol. 107, no. 8 (1998): 2586. "Insurance," see "The Law and the Lady," *St. Louis Post-Dispatch,* April 12, 1908. See Proctor, "Anti-Agate," 396. "Of No Concern to the Assessor," *Kansas City Star,* April 19, 1913. William Jennings Bryan, *Speeches of William Jennings Bryan,* vol. 1 (London: Funk, 1913), 170.

30. Cf. Demuth, *Diamantenmarkt,* 52.

31. For figures, see Oberstleutnant Gallus, "Die Diamantvorkommen (Schluss)," *Zeitschrift für Kolonialpolitik, Kolonialrecht und Kolonialwirtschaft* 12 (1910), 38. "Secret reserve," quoted in Rotberg, *The Founder,* 495. Natty Rothschild (1st Lord Rothschild) to Robert Philippe Gustave de Rothschild in Paris, April 29, 1909, RAL XI/130A/3/74.

32. "Adding value," see appendix 1 in Steiner, *Diamantenmarkt.* Cf. "Cost of Diamonds," *New York Times,* April 3, 1910.

33. Twenty percent markup, see "Raising the Price," *Wall Street Journal,* November 16, 1912. German consulate at Johannesburg to Bethmann Hollweg, April 7, 1913, BAB R901/789.

34. "Die deutschen Diamanten," *Frankfurter Zeitung,* August 11, 1909. "You buy on their terms," see "No Slump," *New York Times,* June 10, 1900.

35. Steiner, *Diamantenmarkt,* 15; Paul Samassa, "Zanzibar-Phantasien," *Kolonialpolitische Abhandlungen,* no. 1 (Leipzig: Zukunft, 1909), 5. "Diamantenhandel," *Berliner Tageblatt,* December 27, 1910. "A Billionaire Bachelor," *San Francisco Chronicle,* April 1,

1906. "Steadily increase in value," see "Diamonds," *The Parisian* (Tennessee), November 26, 1920.

36. A. Harou, "Diamant," *Société Royale Belge de Géographie: Bulletin* (Bruxelles, 1885), 479–480. "Diamond Stocks Low," *New York Times*, January 15, 1915.

37. BAB N2181/86, Karl von Lumm's report, May 22, 1918, 3. Adrienne Munich and Maura Spiegel, "Heart of the Ocean," in *Titanic*, eds. Kevin Sandler and Gaylyn Studlar (London: Rutgers University Press, 1999), 158. Black, Starr and Frost, *At the Sign of the Golden Eagle 1810–1912* (New York: Black, Starr and Frost, 1912).

38. See Loftis Bros. & Co., *How Easily You Can Own and Wear a Diamond* (Chicago, 1908), 6, UCSB, Lawrence B. Romaine Trade Catalogue Collection (Mss 107), Series 1, Subseries A, Box 8. "Commonest household necessity," see Sears, Roebuck and Co. Chicago, *Catalog No. 120, Spring 1910* (Philadelphia: Sears, Roebuck and Company, 1910), 464.

39. Cf. Wehler, *Bismarck und der Imperialismus*, 286, 293. See R. Scheibe, *Blue Ground* (Berlin, 1906). "Rundschau über die deutschen Schutzgebiete," *Globus* 53 (1888): 112; Bley, *Kolonialherrschaft*, 143. See Boris Barth, "Banken und Konzessionsgesellschaften," *Annali dell'Istituto storico italo-germanico in Trento*, vol. 24 (Bologna, 1998), 198.

40. Horst Drechsler, *Südwestafrika unter deutscher Kolonialherrschaft: Die großen Land- und Minengesellschaften* (Stuttgart: Steiner, 1996), 193–221. Frank Woodcock to German Embassy in London, BAB R1001/1341, April 25, 1904. "Reisen der Fischflußexpedition," *Allgemeine Zeitung* (Munich), April 25, 1904. "Goldfunde in Südwestafrika," *Berliner Börsenzeitung*, March 1, 1888; Johann von Bernstorff to Bülow, April 26, 1904, BAB R1001/1341; Albrecht Macco, "Bodenschätze," *Zeitschrift für praktische Geologie* 11 (Berlin, 1903): 193; "Die nutzbaren Bodenschätze," *Windhuker Nachrichten*, December 23, 1908; Rafalski, *Niemandsland*, 323. Kolonialabteilung to Bernstorff, April 30, 1904, BAB R1001/1341; Woodcock to Metternich (in London), December 29, 1909, BAB R901/786; "Die nutzbaren Bodenschätze," *Schlesische Zeitung*, July 23, 1908.

41. "Not rule out the possibility," see Georg Kollm, "Geographentag," *Verhandlungen der Gesellschaft für Erdkunde zu Berlin*, vol. 28, no. 6 (Berlin, 1901), 309. "Berichte," *Zeitschrift der Gesellschaft für Erdkunde zu Berlin*, 1902 (Berlin, 1903), 745. Director of Königlichen geologischen Landesanstalt und Bergakademie zu Berlin to Foreign Office, November 29, 1901, BAB R1001/6451. "High probability," see Bergassessor Mentzel, "Kommen in Deutsch-Südwestafrika Diamanten vor?" *Glückauf* 39, no. 24 (Essen, 1903): 554; "Südafrikanische Diamanten," *Altonaer Nachrichten*, February 25, 1903.

42. "Blue ground," see "Politische Nachrichten," *Berliner Börsenzeitung*, June 26, 1901. Fifteen spots of "blue ground," see "Wirtschaftliche Möglichkeiten," map no. 6 of *Wirtschafts-Atlas der deutschen Kolonien*, ed. Kolonial-Wirtschaftliches Komitee (Berlin: Deutsche Kolonialgesellschaft, 1907); "Blaugrund," *Tägliche Rundschau*, January 29, 1906; "Kleine Nachrichten," *Globus* 92 (1907): 196, see attached list in Leutwein to Foreign Office, June 27, 1902, BAB R1001/6451; Ernst Friedrich, *Wirtschaftsgeographie* (Leipzig: List, 1908), 101. August Seidel, *Unsere Kolonien* (Leipzig: Dietrich, 1905), 45. See I. Goldblatt, *History of South West Africa* (Cape Town: Juta, 1971), 159, 164; Drechsler, *Kolonialherrschaft*, 102. Wernher to Hirschhorn, August 6, 1909, Barloworld Limited Archives (hereafter BW) Wernher, Beit vol. 143. Con Weinberg, *Fragments of a Desert Land* (Cape Town: Timmins, 1975), 81. Cf. Arthur von Gwinner's memo, March 30, 1900, HID, Archives of Deutsche Bank Zentrale Berlin, Sekretariat (Frankfurt), S1370. Gibeon Schürf und Handelsgesellshaft to German Foreign Office, March 1, 1905, BAB R1001/1679.

43. "Diamantfelder von Lüderitzbucht," *Deutsche Nachrichten Kapstadt*, November 14, 1908; "Diamantenvorkommen in Südwestafrika," *Frankfurter Zeitung*,

February 17, 1909. "Deutsche Kolonialgesellschaft," *Frankfurter Zeitung,* August 22, 1911; "Südwestafrikanische Diamanten," *Berliner Börsen-Courier,* March 23, 1911; Paul Rohrbach, "Diamanten," *Frankfurter Zeitung,* July 29, 1910; "Bergbau," *Glückauf* 49, no. 10 (Essen, 1913): 367; "Diamanten," *Plutus: Kritische Wochenschrift,* October 26, 1912, 846; Diamanten-Regie to Solf, May 22, 1913, BAB R1001/1346. "Incoherent and without rules," see "Deutsche Diamanten," *Vorwärts,* November 30, 1913; Paul Rohrbach, "Diamantlager," *Velhagen & Klasings Monatshefte, Jahrgang 1910/1911,* vol. 1 (Berlin: Verlhagen & Klasing, 1911), 464; cf. "Deutsches Reich," *Frankfurter Zeitung,* February 4, 1909. "Small white stones," see Natty Rothschild to Rothschild cousins, Paris, December 9, 1909, RAL XI/130A/2/228.

44. "Nothing in common," see Jollast, "Diamantenfieber," 80; "Diamantfunde," *Globus* 96 (1909): 507; see Bruno Simmersbach, "Bergbau," *Zeitschrift für die gesamte Staatswissenschaft* 72 (1916): 421; Blumhagen, *Südafrika,* 103. "Zu den Goldfünden," *Berliner Börsen-Courier,* August 2, 1911. Paul Rohrbach, "Diamanten," *Frankfurter Zeitung,* July 17, 1910; Wilhelm von Humboldt-Dachroeden, *Diamantenpolitik* (Jena: Fischer, 1915), 17. Cf. Clara Brockmann, *Briefe eines deutschen Mädchen* (Berlin: Mittler, 1912), 182. Peter Rainier, *African Hazard* (London: Murray, 1940), 33.

45. "Almost certain," see Henning von Burgsdorff to Leutwein, November 1, 1896, BAB R1001/1207. Credit for source to Horst Drechsler, *'Let Us Die Fighting': The Struggle of the Herero and Nama Against German Imperialism, 1884–1915* (London: Zed, 1980), 130. Report of S. M. S. Wolf to Admiralty, September 14, 1898, BAB R1001/1652. "Vom Tage," *Allgemeine Zeitung* (Munich), December 2, 1898. "Fond of Diamonds," *Washington Post,* December 10, 1899. "Kaiser's Diamond Mines," *Washington Post,* April 10, 1900. See also BAB R1001/1276, Gürich, "Diamantfunden," 889, "Zu dem angeblichen neuen Diamantenfunde," *Berliner Börsen-Courier,* March 1, 1911, and Drechsler, *Kolonialherrschaft,* 256. Burgsdorff to Leutwein, November 1, 1896, BAB R1001/1207.

46. "Blue ground," see attached list in Leutwein to Foreign Office, June 27, 1902, BAB R1001/6451. Cf. Ludwig von Estorff, *Wanderungen,* ed. Christoph-Friedrich Kutscher (Wiesbaden, 1968), 101. "Hauptversammlung der Deutschen Kolonialgesellschaft," *Allgemeine Zeitung* (Munich), June 6, 1900. "Legal measures," see file BAB R1001/1354; Cf. "Ueber die Notwendigkeit und die Rentabilität des Baues einer Eisenbahn," *Windhuker Nachrichten,* October 5, 1905; "South Africa's Diamond Fields," *The Daily Morning Journal and Courier* (New Haven), January 21, 1903.

47. Bülow to Wilhelm II, September 16, 1904; Wilhelm II to Bülow, September 18, 1904, BAB R1001/1679.

48. Isabel Hull, *Absolute Destruction* (Ithaca: Cornell University Press, 2005), 29–30; John C. G. Röhl, *Wilhelm II: Into the Abyss* (Cambridge: Cambridge University Press, 2014), 298, but see Sarkin-Hughes, *Germany's Genocide,* 156. "With all possible haste," see Georg Hartmann to German Foreign Office, October 18, 1904; see also attachment in Hartmann to German Foreign Office, March 12, 1906, BAB R1001/1679.

49. Georg Hartmann, "Wiederaufbau," *Verhandlungen des Deutschen Kolonialkongresses 1905* (Berlin: Reimer, 1906), 657; Kurd Schwabe, "Ueber die Diamantgewinnung," *Deutsche Kolonialzeitung* 24, no. 39 (Berlin, 1907): 392. "Responsibility," see "Diamantmuttergestein," *Deutsches Kolonialblatt,* vol. 17 (Berlin, 1906), 312–313.

50. "Worth" fighting for, see "Südwest-Afrika," *Berliner Börsenzeitung,* March 29, 1904. "Die geheimnisvolle Insel," *Windhuker Nachrichten,* October 25, 1906. "Confidence," see "Welche Aussichten eröffnet die neuere Entwicklung des Diamantbergbaues im britischen Südafrika?" *Deutsche Kolonialzeitung* 24, no. 28 (1907): 281.

51. "Eisenbahnbau," *Windhuker Nachrichten,* May 30, 1907. Cf. Hull, *Absolute Destruction,* 67. Gibeon Schürf- und Handelsgesellschaft to German Foreign Office,

June 2, 1905, BAB R1001/1679. "Problem," "extinction," see Drechsler, 'Let us Die Fighting,' 210, and Helgine Ritter-Peterson, The Herrenvolk Mentality in German South West Africa (Pretoria: Unisa, 1992), 232.

52. Walter Nuhn, Feind überall (Bonn: Bernard, 2000), 176. Cf. Erzberger to Reichstag, December 11, 1908, Stenographische Berichte, 6169. Deutsche Kolonialgesellschaft Tagung Stuttgart, Gegenwartsfragen der Deutschen Kolonialpolitik (Berlin: Deutsche Kolonialgesellschaft, 1928), 85. Hence the dimensions of Nama oral history, which periodizes the war as 1903–1908; see Memory Biwa, 'Toa Tama!Khams Ge': Remembering the War in Namakhoeland, 1903–1908 (Master's Thesis, University of Cape Town, 2006), 111. "Südwestafrika in der Kommission," Berliner Tageblatt, March 11, 1908. Marion Wallace, History of Namibia (New York: Columbia University Press, 2011), 178.

53. Cf. Biwa, 'Toa Tama!Khams Ge', 111.

54. The soldier was Wilhelm Freiherr von Humboldt-Dachroeden. "Lüderitzbucht," Diamond Fields Advertiser, January 4, 1909 and September 3, 1909. Margarethe von Eckenbrecher, Was Afrika mir gab und nahm (Berlin: Mittler, 1940), 46. Schwabe, "Ueber die Diamantgewinnung," 392. "Streams of blood and money" quoted in Drechsler, 'Let us Die Fighting', 154; cf. Sebastian Conrad, Deutsche Kolonialgeschichte (Nördlingen: Beck, 2012), 10.

55. Cf. Hans Grimm, Afrikafahrt West (Frankfurt: Hendschel, 1913), 84; Kenyon-Collis to Dernburg, January 1, 1907, BAB R1001/1351; "Die Kolonialbahn," Berliner Tageblatt, December 12, 1906; "Etat für Südwestafrika," Freiburger Zeitung, December 14, 1906. Speech of Johannes Semler to Reichstag, March 6, 1907, Stenographische Berichte, 274.

56. "Hot-air artist," see Alfred von Tirpitz, Erinnerungen (Leipzig: Koehler, 1920), 432. "Big bluffs," see Edward Goschen to Edward Grey, August 25, 1911, The National Archives, Kew (hereafter UKNA) FO 413/55; Eduard Goldbeck, Deutschlands Zukunft (Leipzig: Rothbarth, 1907), 64.

57. "Bernhard der Kleine," Die Tribüne (Erfurt), August 14, 1907. "Die homogene Regierung," Berliner Tageblatt, June 7, 1910; "Dernburg," Tägliche Rundschau, October 3, 1912; Jacques Willequet, Le Congo belge (Bruxelles: Presses Universitaires, 1962), 233. "Endless advertisement," see Hedwig Pringsheim to Maximilian Harden, June 27, 1915, Meine Manns, eds. Helga and Manfred Neumann (Berlin: Aufbau, 2006), 158. See Walter Moszkowski, Persönlichkeiten, vol. 1 (Charlottenburg: Virgil, 1908), 3. Cyrus Adler, Jacob Schiff, vol. 2 (New York: Doubleday, 1928), 119. "Wilhelm II," Berliner Tageblatt, April 24, 1912. "Accidentally," see Martin Schröder, Prügelstrafe (Münster: LIT, 1997), 90; cf. Harden to Rathenau, September 15, 1908, Rathenau/Harden Briefwechsel, 561; Oron James Hale, Publicity (New York: University of Virginia Press, 1940), 298; see Francis Walker, Monopolistic Combinations (New York: Macmillan, 1904), iv. "Half-truths," see "Dernburg," The Times, September 6, 1915.

58. Ernst Friedegg, Millionen und Millionäre (Berlin: Vita, 1914), 298; Paul Braeunlich, Zentrum und Regierung (Leipzig: Braun, 1907), 18. Cf. Leo Weinthal to Dernburg, November 3, 1909, German Federal Archive, Koblenz, Germany (hereafter BAK) N1130/35.

59. "Sitting giant," see "Dernburg," Die Zukunft, vol. 58 (Berlin: Zukunft, 1907), 374. M. J. Bonn, Wandering Scholar (New York: John Day Company, 1948), 144; Estorff, Wanderungen, 142; Frederic Wile, Men around the Kaiser (Indianapolis: Bobbs-Merrill, 1914), 179; "Walfisch Bay and Germany," The Standard, December 7, 1908. Bernhard von Bülow, Denkwürdigkeiten, vol. 2 (Berlin: Ullstein, 1930), 267. Robert Zedlitz-Trützschler, Zwölf Jahre (Berlin: Verlagsanstalt, 1925), 234; Adolf Stein, "Dernburg Africanus," Der Deutsche 7, no. 3 (Berlin: Verlag des Deutschen, 1907): 65. "Chingachgook," see entry for

March 20, 1922, Harry Graf Kessler, *Diaries of Count Harry Kessler,* ed. Charles Kessler (New York: Grove, 1999), 155; Harden to Rathenau, August 15, 1911, *Walther Rathenau/Maximilian Harden Briefwechsel,* 636; "Grobianus triumphans," *Germania,* December 30, 1906; Burton Hendrick, *Life and Letters of Walter H. Page,* vol. 1 (New York: Doubleday, 1923), 436. "Ill-mannered brute," see Max Hoffmann, *War Diaries,* vol. 1 (London: Secker, 1929), 90.

60. Entry of January 27, 1911, Kurt Riezler, *Tagebücher, Aufsätze, Dokumente* (Göttingen: V&R, 1972), 169. Dernburg to Francis Oats, July 8, 1909, BAB R1001/1343. George Viereck, *Roosevelt* (New York: Jackson, 1920), 107; Pinner, *Wirtschaftsführer,* 166. Henry Villard to Deutsche Bank, March 3, 1893, in Alfred Vagts, *Deutschland und die Vereinigten Staaten,* vol. 1 (New York: Macmillan, 1935), 446. "Think as hard as he likes," see Cyrus Adler, *Jacob H. Schiff,* vol. 2 (Garden City, NY: Doubleday, 1928), 190.

61. Jollast, "Diamantenfieber," 80. Natty Rothschild to Édouard de Rothschild, December 15, 1908, RAL XI/130A/2/232. "Deutsch-Südwest-Afrika," *Deutsche Nachrichten (Kapstadt),* November 21, 1908. Cf. "Deutschen Diamanten-G.m.b.H. Berlin," *Frankfurter Zeitung,* August 2, 1909; "Diamantenfunde," *Berliner Lokal-Anzeiger,* December 11, 1908; "Robert Scheibe," *Glückauf* 59, no. 29 (1923): 716; Captain Menger to Wilhelm II, January 16, 1909, BAB R1001/1909.

3. Rush

1. Arno Jollast, "Diamantenfieber," *Die Zukunft,* vol. 66 (Berlin: Zukunft, 1909), 80. "Diamantenfunden," *Journal der Goldschmiedekunst* 29, no. 52 (Leipzig 1908): 33; cf. entry for January 8, 1906, Johannes Spiecker, *Mein Tagebuch: Erfahrungen eines deutschen Missionars in Deutsch-Südwestafrika 1905–1907,* eds. Lisa Kopelmann et al. (Berlin: Simon, 2013), 143.

2. Hans Cloos, *Gespräch mit der Erde* (München: Piper, 1949), 67. Hartmut Pogge von Strandmann, ed., *Walther Rathenau: Industrialist, Banker, Intellectual, and Politician: Notes and Diaries 1907–1922* (Oxford: Clarendon, 1985), 69; "Diamond Profit $25 per minute," *Chicago Daily Tribune,* September 27, 1908.

3. For an official report on the discovery, made in April 1908: NAN BBL, 5, II.A.5.a, letter from Bezirksamtmann Brill, July 6, 1908. Also: NAN ZBU, vol. 156, A vi, a 3, Bd. 18, Bl. 92. Stauch did not notify authorities of his finds until June, months after the fact. NAN ZBU, vol. 1618, R X iv, h, Bd. 1, Bl. 18. See, e.g., "Diamantenproduktion," *Mittheilungen der kaiserlich-königlichen Geographischen Gesellschaft in Wien,* vol. 61 (Wien: Lechner, 1918), 478. Oberstleutnant Gallus, "Diamantvorkommen," *Zeitschrift für Kolonialpolitik* 11 (1910): 945. On size: Theodore Gregory, *Oppenheimer* (London: Oxford University Press, 1962), 64. See Paul Rohrbach, "Diamanten," *Frankfurter Zeitung,* July 17, 1910.

4. "Robert Scheibe," *Glückauf* 59, no. 29 (1923): 716. Gallus, "Diamantvorkommen," 944–945. On children, see oral interview with Marianne Stauch, cited in Shelagh Nation, "The background, architectural philosophy and work of Hellmut Wilhelm Ernst Stauch" (M.Arch. thesis, University of Pretoria, 1985), 3. Oskar Bongard, *Staatssekretär Dernburg in Britisch- und Deutsch-Süd-Afrika* (Berlin: Süsserott, 1909), 72. Hans Berger-Peyer, *Schweizer in Namibia* (Effingerhof: Merker, 2018), 68.

5. G. Gürich, "Diamantfunden," *Die Umschau: Übersicht über die Fortschritte und Bewegungen auf dem Gesamtgebiet der Wissenshaft und Technik,* ed. J. H. Bechhold, vol. 12 (Frankfurt, 1908), 891. "Diamantenfund," *Deutsch-Südwestafrikanische Zeitung,* June 24, 1908; Christian Barth, *Schutzgebiete* (Leipzig: Teubner, 1910), 72. Gallus, "Diamantvorkommen," 950. Bongard, *Staatssekretär,* 74.

6. "Diamond-King" nickname mentioned in Else Frobenius, *Erinnerungen einer Journalistin*, ed. Lora Wildenthal (Köln: Böhlau, 2005), 141. "Studienreise," *Deutsche Kolonialzeitung* 25, no. 39 (1908): 699; Ludwig von Estorff, *Wanderungen*, ed. Christoph-Friedrich Kutscher (Wiesbaden, 1968), 142; "Deutsche Schutzgebiete," *Kölnische Zeitung*, November 5, 1907; Karl Tanzer, "Diamanten," *Neues Wiener Tagblatt*, December 28, 1935. Cf. Otto Wiemer to Reichstag, December 7, 1908, *Stenographische Berichte*, 6043.

7. "Wild and indiscriminate pegging," see Fred Cornell, *Glamour of Prospecting* (London: Unwin, 1920), 44. "Like apples," see Breitmeyer to Hirschhorn, April 16, 1909, BW Wernher, Beit vol. 143; Hans Rafalski, *Niemandsland* (Berlin: Wernitz, 1930), 330. "In hand," see "Studienreise," *Deutsche Kolonialzeitung* 25, no. 37 (1908): 648. Egon Freiherr von Dalwigk zu Lichtenfels, *Dernburgs amtliche Tätigkeit* (Berlin: Reimer, 1911), 15; Heinrich Schnee, *Als letzter Gouverneur* (Heidelberg: Quelle & Meyer, 1964), 97. See Felix Pinner, *Wirtschaftsführer* (Charlottenburg: Weltbühne, 1925), 166; "Zeitungsstimmen zum Rücktritt Dernburgs," *Windhuker Nachrichten*, July 13, 1910. "Türmers Tagebuch," *Der Türmer: Monatsschrift für Gemüt und Geist*, ed. Jeannot Emil Freiherr von Grotthuß, vol. 10, part 2 (Stuttgart: Greiner, 1908), 409; Holstein's memo, April 29, 1908, *Holstein Papers*, eds. Norman Rich and M. H. Fisher, vol. 4 (Cambridge: Cambridge University Press, 1963), 527; Hans Dieter Hellige, *Rathenau/Harden Briefwechsel* (München: Müller, 1983), 538. "Important," see Franz Schädler's speech to Reichstag, *Stenographische Berichte*, November 28, 1906, 3972. Adolf Stein, "Dernburg Africanus," *Der Deutsche* 7, no. 3 (Berlin: Verlag des Deutschen, 1907): 65. Schnee, *Als letzter Gouverneur*, 83. "Self-respect," see "Von Papen Carried Letters," *New York Times*, January 25, 1916.

8. "Lump of sugar" quoted in translation in I. Goldblatt, *History of South West Africa* (Cape Town: Juta, 1971), 179. See "Diamantfelder," *Deutsche Zeitung für die Ostmark der Kap-Provinz*, November 14, 1908, BAB R1001/1341. See Olga Levinson, *Diamonds in the Desert* (Cape Town: Tafelberg, 1983), 47; Olga Lehmann, *Merensky* (Göttingen: Schütz, 1965), 47; See Oskar Hintrager, *Südwestafrika in der deutschen Zeit* (München: Oldenbourg, 1955), 117. Wilhelm von Humboldt-Dachroeden, *Diamantenpolitik* (Jena: Fischer, 1915), 42.

9. "Diamantengewinnung," *Windhuker Nachrichten*, October 7, 1908; "Diamanten," *Plutus: Kritische Wochenschrift*, October 26, 1912, 846. Breitmeyer to Hirschhorn, April 16, 1909, BW Wernher, Beit vol. 143; "Steinkunde," *Journal der Goldschmiedekunst* 29, no. 46/47 (Leipzig, November 7, 1908): unpaginated; Hedley A. Chilvers, The Story of De Beers (London: Cassell, 1939), 199. "Studienreise," *Deutsche Kolonialzeitung* 25, no. 37 (1908): 649. See BAB R1001/1394, attachment to E. Lübbert to Gouverneur in Windhuk, March 16, 1911; cf. "New Fields," *Transvaal Leader*, November 25, 1908.

10. See Estorff, *Wanderungen*, 142.

11. "Sektflaschen," *Banater Deutsche Zeitung*, March 20, 1938. Figure in Berger-Peyer, *Schweizer in Namibia*, 69. Cf. Johanna Niedbalski, *Die ganze Welt des Vergnügens* (Berlin: be.bra, 2018), 232. Oral interview with Marianne Stauch, cited in Nation, "Hellmut Wilhelm Ernst Stauch," 3. See Max Ewald Baericke, *Lüderitzbucht: Historische Erinnerungen eines alten Diamantensuchers* (Windhoek: Namibia Wissenschaftliche Gesellschaft, 2001), 33–35; 131–136.

12. Estimate was Dernburg's own. "Dernburg," *Otago Daily Times*, July 4, 1908; for 1913 figure: Hans von Schoellenbach, *Die Besiedlung Deutsch-Südwestafrikas bis zum Weltkriege* (Berlin: Reimer, 1926), 111; cf. R. Hermann-Weilheim, "Statistik der farbigen Bevölkerung," *Koloniale Monatsblätter* 15, no. 12 (Berlin: Kolonialgesellschaft, 1913): 517. "Dernburg," *Current Opinion*, ed. Edward Wheeler, vol. 58 (New York,

1915), 401; Bernhard Dernburg, *Die Vorbedingungen für erfolgreiche koloniale und über-seeische Betätigung* (Berlin: Borngräber, 1912), 15. See Gregory, *Oppenheimer*, 65.

13. Gallus, "Diamantvorkommen (Schluss)," 41.

14. Clara Brockmann, *Briefe eines deutschen Mädchens* (Berlin: Mittler, 1912), 199–200. Dr. Hummel's report, undated, *Arbeiten aus dem Kaiserlichen Gesundheitsamte*, vol. 21 (Berlin: Springer, 1904), 97; see Zimmerer, "Musterstaat," in *Völkermord in Deutsch-Südwestafrika*, ed. Jürgen Zimmerer and Joachim Zeller (Berlin: Links, 2003), 36; Baer-icke, *Lüderitzbucht*, 166.

15. Brockmann, *Briefe*, 199–200.

16. "Forlorn collection," see Cornell, *Glamour*, 9. Bongard, *Staatssekretär*, 78. "Reise," *Deutsch-Südwestafrikanische Zeitung*, June 20, 1908. Cloos, *Gespräch*, 66. See Bonn, *Wandering Scholar*, 144.

17. "Lüderitzbucht," *Diamond Fields Advertiser*, September 23, 1908. Population figures, see Walter Moritz, *Die 'Sandwüste' hat eine Zukunft: Tagebuch und Zeichnungen des Malers Ernst Vollbehr 1910* (Windhoek: Meinert, 1994), 8. "Lüderitzbucht," *Diamond Fields Advertiser*, September 23, 1908 and July 26, 1909; construction inventory in Edda Schoedder's register, National Archives and Records Service of South Africa, SWA001 #_#_A380_#; Compare Hubert Henoch, "Schutzgebiete," *Weltwirtschaft: Jahr- und Lesebuch*, ed. Ernst von Halle, vol. 3, no. 2 (Berlin: Teubner, 1908), 187. Peter Conze's report, October 12, 1909, BAB R1001/1500. U.S. Navy Department, *Index to Notices to Mariners 1911* (Washington, DC: Government Printing Office, 1912), 10; "Sektflaschen," *Banater Deutsche Zeitung*, March 20, 1938.

18. See Ulrike Lindner, "Encounters," *Hybrid Cultures*, eds. Ulrike Lindner et al. (Amsterdam: Rodopi, 2010), 14; "Appoint Agent," *Christian Science Monitor*, October 19, 1909. "Les diamants," *Journal de Genève*, December 7, 1908; "Diamond Fields," *San Francisco Chronicle*, November 6, 1908. Peter Rainier, *African Hazard* (London: Murray, 1940), 28; G. Goldberg, "Diamantenabbau," *Dinglers Polytechnisches Journal* 329, no. 34/35 (Berlin: Dietze, 1914): 531. Franz Rusch, *Himmelsbeobachtung* (Leipzig: Teubner, 1911), 47. Brockmann quoted in Lora Wildenthal, "She Is the Victor," *Social Analysis* 33 (1993): 70; "Aus Lüderitzbucht," *Lüderitzbuchter Zeitung*, August 20, 1910.

19. For ships arriving, see incidental mention by Sebastian Mantei, *Entwicklungsge-schichte* (Halle: Universität Halle-Wittenberg, 2004), 105. "Hauptversammlung," *Bauzei-tung für Württemberg, Baden, Hessen, Elsass-Lothringen* 9, no. 24 (Stuttgart, 1912): 188. "Kriegsschiff," *Lüderitzbuchter Zeitung*, October 23, 1909. See "Vorwort" to Humboldt-Dachroeden, *Diamantenpolitik*; Paul Leutwein, *Leistungen der Regierung* (Berlin, 1911), foreword.

20. "Increasing trade and traffic," see "Einleitung," *Lüderitzbuchter Zeitung*, February 13, 1909; Bley, *Kolonialherrschaft*, 226. Mantei, *Entwicklungsgeschichte*, 144. On streetcar and slaughterhouse: "Aus Lüderitzbucht," *Lüderitzbuchter Zeitung*, August 20, 1910; "Stadtgemeinde," *Lüderitzbuchter Zeitung*, October 29, 1910; see Reichskolonialamt, *Schutzgebiete in Afrika und der Südsee 1910/1911: Amtliche Jahresberichte* (Berlin: Mittler, 1912), 129. On desalination plant: Paul Rohrbach, "Diamantlager," *Velhagen & Klas-ings Monatshefte, Jahrgang 1910/1911*, vol. 1 (Berlin: Verlhagen & Klasing, 1911), 457.

21. Kolonial-Wirtschaftliches Komitee, *Unsere Kolonialwirtschaft* (Berlin: Deutsche Kolonialgesellschaft, 1909), 76, BAB R1001/7803. Cf. Stefan Kanfer, *The Last Empire* (New York: FSG, 1993), 15–16, 23. See Ulrike Lindner, *Koloniale Begegnungen* (Frankfurt: Campus, 2011), 282. Christopher Clark, *Wilhelm II* (New York: Longman, 2000), 132. Veit Valentin, *Kolonialgeschichte* (Tübingen: Mohr, 1915), 206.

22. See "Diamond Fields," *The Sun* (New York), August 22, 1909. See Albert Calvert, *German African Empire* (London: Laurie, 1916), 19. Oskar Hintrager to RKA, January 18,

1909, BAB R1001/1815; "Bäckereien in Deutsch-Südwestafrika," "Schlächtereien in Deutsch-Südwestafrika," "Mechaniker in Deutsch-Südwestafrika," undated, BAB R1505/10. Reichsstelle für das Auswanderungswesen, "Schneiderinnen in Deutsch-Südwestafrika" and "Schneidermeister in Deutsch-Südwestafrika," undated, BAB R1505/10.

23. "Infused a new life, see "Ça et La," *L'Univers* (Paris), October 18, 1908. "Overwhelming," see Baericke, *Lüderitzbucht, 167. Die deutschen Diamanten und ihre Gewinnung* (Berlin: Reimer, 1914), 15; on overall number: Dernburg to Wilhelm II, December 22, 1908, BAB R1001/1341; Rafalski, *Niemandsland, 328*; but see "Maßgebliches und Unmaßgebliches," *Die Grenzboten*, vol. 67 (1908), 396. Harald Nestroy, *Duwisib* (Windhoek: Meinert, 2002), 70. "Sektflaschen," *Banater Deutsche Zeitung*, March 20, 1938.

24. Bezirksamtsmann Brill to Colonial Governor at Windhoek, July 6, 1908, NAN ZBU 1618, R.XIV.H, Band 1. Rafalski, *Niemandsland, 324–325*. "Diamantenfieber," *Volksstimme: Sozialdemokratisches Organ für den Regierungsbezirk Magdeburg*, January 10, 1909. "Official," see Judgement of Prussian Oberverwaltungsgericht against Emil Schneider, March 27, 1912, BAB R1001/5591. See Albert Ganz, *Imperial German Navy* (Columbus, OH: Ohio State University, 1972), 58.

25. I borrow here from the concept of William Sewell, "Strange Career," *History and Theory* 49 (2010): 146–166. "Colorful population," see Apostolische Präfektur Groß-Namaland, "Neugründungen in Lüderitzbucht," *Die katholischen Missionen: Illustrierte Monatsschrift*, vol. 39, no. 7 (Freiburg: Herder, 1911), 176; Lehmann, *Merensky, 47–48*; H. R. Hahlo, "Diamond Case," *South African Law Journal* 76 (1959): 156–157. "Kleine Briefe," *Der Deutsche* 8, no. 17 (Berlin: Verlag des Deutschen, 1908): 528. Clara Brockmann, *Frau in Südwestafrika* (Berlin: Mittler, 1910), 64; "Deutsches Geld gegen das Deutschtum," *Alldeutsche Blätter* 19, no. 4 (1909):, 64. One can confirm the variety of origins and occupations through inspections of the passenger manifests from the German East-Africa-Line's *Gertrud Woermann*—for example, on March 10, 1912. Population figures, see "Volkszählung," *Lüderitzbuchter Zeitung*, February 26, 1910.

26. "Lüderitzbucht," *Diamond Fields Advertiser*, September 23, 1908. "Really German," quoted in Birthe Kundrus, *Moderne Imperialisten* (Köln: Böhlau, 2003), 101. Will Sellick, ed., *Autobiography of Eugen Mansfeld* (London: Jeppestown Press, 2017), 78–79. "Stream of suspicious elements," see "Diamantenfund," *Deutsch-Südwestafrikanische Zeitung*, June 24, 1908.

27. "Diamantbergbau," *Journal der Goldschmiedekunst* 29 (1908): 36. "Living like dogs," see "Deutsches Geld gegen das Deutschtum," *Alldeutsche Blätter* 19, no. 4 (1909): 64. "Volk ohne Raum," *Berliner Börsenzeitung*, August 27, 1926.

28. "Thrill," see "Diamond Way," *Louisville Courier-Journal*, April 2, 1911. "Epidemic," "lose respect," "corrupt character," see Brockmann, *Briefe, 176*. "Degenerated," see Ewald Banse, *Unsere großen Afrikaner* (Berlin: Haude und Spener, 1942), 224. "Spurious prospects," see ""Neugründungen in Lüderitzbucht," *Die katholischen Missionen: Illustrierte Monatsschrift*, vol. 39 (Freiburg, 1911), 176.

29. Brockmann, *Briefe, 206*. Hans-Otto Meissner, *Traumland* (Stuttgart, 1968), 372. See Rainier, *African Hazard, 37*; see Jana Moser, *Kartographiegeschichte* (Dresden: Universität Dresden, 2007), 97; see ads for "Familien-Auskünfte," *Lüderitzbuchter Zeitung*, December 18, 1909; and "Karte der Diamantenfelder," *Windhuker Nachrichten*, June 11, 1910. Cf. Lene Haase, *Raggys Fahrt* (Berlin: Fleischel, 1910), 391. See Erich Lübbert to RKA, April 13, 1910, BAB R1001/5404. "Appear objective," see C. Reinshagen to Dernburg, September 13, 1909, BAB R1001/5398. "Rennen zu Lüderitzbucht," May 31, 1909, BAB R1001/1343. "Belegung von Diamantfeldern," *Berliner Börsen-Courier*, April 9, 1909.

30. "Secularizing European mind," see Owen Chadwick, *Secularization* (Cambridge: Cambridge University Press, 1975). Compare J. P. Daughton, *Empire Divided*

(Oxford: Oxford University Press, 2006). ""Neugründungen in Lüderitzbucht," *Die katholischen Missionen,* 176. See Mantei, *Entwicklungsgeschichte,* 93, note 260.

31. Archiv der Vereinten Evangelischen Mission, Wuppertal (hereafter AVEM), Rheinische Missionsgesellschaft, 2.628, Emil Karl Laaf, "Besetzung der Diamantfelder," 1912; 1.648 d, Christian Wilhelm Friedrich Spellmeyer, "Besuch auf den Diamantfeldern"; see Pomona station reports in AVEM, Rheinische Missionsgesellschaft, 2.525. Nils Ole Oermann, *Mission, Church and State Relations in South West Africa Under German Rule (1884–1915)* (Stuttgart: Steiner, 1999), 232. Wilhelm Heumbo to Karl Sckär, 1908; "Jahresbericht d. Ovambo-Gemeinde Lüderitzbucht-Diamantfelder," 1919, AVEM, Rheinische Missionsgesellschaft, 1.658 a-b.

32. "Diamantenfunden," *Journal der Goldschmiedekunst* 29, no. 36, August 29, 1908 (Leipzig): unpaginated; Hans Grimm, *Afrikafahrt West* (Frankfurt: Hendschel, 1913), 92; Hertha Brodersen-Manns, *Wie alles anders kam* (Windhoek: Kuiseb, 1991), 7. "Diamond Way," *Louisville Courier-Journal,* April 2, 1911. "Gold-digging," see Rüdiger Weck, *Deutsch-Südwestafrika* (Berlin: Siegismund, 1919), 112. "Grave danger," see Nestroy, *Duwisib,* 70; Brockmann, *Die deutsche Frau,* 63.

33. "Lüderitzbucht," *Diamond Fields Advertiser,* June 11, 1909. See Lawrence Green, *At Daybreak* (Cape Town: Timmins, 1950), 154; Hermann Thomsen, *Deutsches Land* (München: Alpenzeitung, 1911), 105; Eugen Hobein, *Ungeschminktes Afrika* (Essen: Verlagsanstalt, 1938), 145. Charles Dawbarn, *My South African Year* (London: Mills & Boon, 1921), 147. Ewald Niemann, July 30, 1909, R1505/4. Prices for pack animals, see Goldberg, "Diamantenabbau," 533; see the oral history of August Stauch's widow, Ida, relayed by Hans-Otto Meissner in *Traumland,* 370. Ludwig Roland-Lücke's speech to Reichstag, May 2, 1912, *Stenographische Berichte,* 1646; Lindequist to Reichstag, March 24, 1911, *Stenographische Berichte,* 5862.

34. Thomsen, *Deutsches Land,* 105; cf. A. P. J. Beris, *Making the Desert Bloom,* vol. 1 (Windhoek: Diocese of Keetmanshoop, 2001), 156. Südwestafrikanische Bodenkredit-Gesellschaft to Rechnungsrat Hintze, March 2, 1914, BAB R1001/6427. Moritz, *Sandwüste,* 8. Alwin Wünsche, *Kolonien* (Leipzig: Voigtländer, 1912), 145–146. Speech by Ludwig Quessel to Reichstag, March 8, 1913, *Stenographische Berichte,* 4417.

35. "Outsider," see Kundrus, *Moderne Imperialisten,* 113. "German," see Carl Schlettwein, *Deutsch-Südwestafrika* (Wismar: Michael, 1907), 63; see Karl Dove, *Wirtschaftsgeographie* (Jena: Fischer, 1917), 231; see Dernburg, *Vorbedingungen,* 14.

36. Rohrbach, "Diamantlager," 456; Paul Rohrbach, *Um des Teufels Handschrift* (Bamberg: Dulk, 1953), 110; Rafalski, *Niemandsland,* 317; Emil Zimmermann, *Unsere Kolonien* (Berlin: Ullstein, 1912), 236. Philipp N. Lehmann, "Between Waterberg and Sandveld," *German History* 32, no. 4 (2014): 538–541. "Die nutzbaren Bodenschätze," *Schlesische Zeitung,* July 23, 1908. "Auf dem Wege zum Polizeistaat," *Kolonialpolitische Korrespondenz,* July 17, 1908.

37. Wilhelm Külz, *Deutsch-Südafrika im 25. Jahre* (Berlin: Süsserott, 1909), 363; Hintrager's decree, January 13, 1909, BAB R1001/2040; cf. Decree of September 1, 1902, in *Taschenbuch für Südwestafrika,* ed. Kurd Schwabe (Leipzig: Weicher, 1908), 320. Decree of March 19, 1909, *Deutsches Kolonialblatt* 20 (Berlin, 1909): 479; "Steuern," *Windhuker Nachrichten,* December 19, 1908. Walther Rathenau, "Notizen zur Afrikareise 1908," in *Schriften der Wilhelminischen Zeit 1885–1914,* ed. Alexander Jaser (Düsseldorf: Droste, 2015), 683; see Harold James, *Globalization* (Cambridge, MA: Harvard University Press, 2001), 19. "News and Notables," *Daily Picayune* (New Orleans), October 15, 1909. "Berliner und Afrikaner," *Berliner Tageblatt,* January 21, 1910.

38. "Turn our diamonds into water," see Hintrager, *Südwestafrika,* 140. Background on Pomona in: NAN BBL II.B.4.A. "Über die Diamantenfunde," *Berliner Lokal-Anzeiger,*

December 11, 1908; cf. "Die südwestafrikanischen Diamantfunde," *Frankfurter Zeitung,* December 31, 1908; "Die südwestafrikanischen Diamanten," *Frankfurter Zeitung,* July 8, 1909.

39. Cf. Jöhlinger, "Rundschau," *Koloniale Rundschau, Jahrgang 1914* (Berlin, 1914), 316. Cornell, *Glamour,* 9. Moritz, *Sandwüste,* 16.

40. See Susanne Kuss, *German Colonial Wars and the Context of Military Violence,* trans. Andrew Smith (Cambridge, MA: Harvard University Press, 2017), 44. Paul Range, "Gross-Namaland," December 14, 1908, *Zeitschrift der Gesellschaft für Erdkunde zu Berlin 1908* (Berlin: Mittler, 1909), 665. U.S. Hydrographic Office, *Africa Pilot* 1 (Washington, DC: Government Printing Office, 1916), 486. "Gathered 8000 carats," see "Diamond Way," *Louisville Courier-Journal,* April 2, 1911.

41. See Grimm, *Afrikafahrt West,* 91. Alexander Kuhn, *Fischfluss-Expedition* (Berlin: Mittler, 1904), 219. Cited in Dernburg's speech to Reichstag, *Stenographische Berichte,* March 6, 1907, 270; "Eisenbahnen," *Militär-Wochenblatt* 97, no. 2, ed. Generalmajor von Frobel (Berlin: Mittler, 1912): 2482; Rainier, *Vanished Africa* (New Haven: Yale University Press, 1940), 32. "Trinkwasser," *Deutsches Kolonialblatt* 9, no. 9 (Berlin, 1898): 275; Christian Schäder, *Brauindustrie* (Marburg: Tectum, 1999), 177. Cf. "Deutsche Schutzgebiete," *Frankfurter Zeitung,* September 5, 1909. Zimmermann, *Unsere Kolonien,* 238.

42. Kaiserlicher Gouverneur to RKA, March 21, 1910, Attachment 10, BAB R1001 / 2064; see Rudolf Fitzner, *Deutsches Kolonial-Handbuch,* vol. 1 (Berlin: Paetel, 1901), 187–188; cf. Deutsche Colonial-Gesellschaft, *Kurze Übersicht über die Tätigkeit* (Berlin, 1907), 10. "Erzbergers Niederlage," *Berliner Volkszeitung,* April 26, 1910.

43. "Sovereign," see DKSSWA to Auswärtiges Amt, February 16, 1887, BAB R1001/1522. "Create an army," see Curt von François, *Deutsch-Südwestafrika* (Berlin, 1899), 20. "Die Goldfunde," *Deutsche Kolonialzeitung* 4 (Berlin: Deutsche Kolonialverein, 1887): 746. "Studienreise," *Deutsche Kolonialzeitung* 25, no. 35 (Berlin: Deutsche Kolonialgesellschaft, 1908): 629.

44. Reinhard Reinecke, *Finanzrecht* (Hildesheim: Borgmeyer, 1912), 30. Georg Wunderlich, "Wertzuwachssteuern," *Zeitschrift für Kolonialrecht* 16, no. 1 (Berlin: Deutsche Kolonialgesellschaft, 1914), 2. "Deutsche Kolonialgesellschaft für Südwestafrika," *Berliner Börsen-Courier,* January 14, 1910. Deutsche Colonial-Gesellschaft, *Übersicht,* 25. "Stadtgemeinde," *Lüderitzbuchter Zeitung,* October 29, 1910.

45. Agreement (*Bergrezess*) of February 17, 1908, discussed in Matthias Erzberger, *Millionengeschenke: Die Privilegienwirtschaft in Südwestafrika* (Berlin: Germania, 1910), 21–30; agreement printed in full in Ludwig Sander, *Geschichte der deutschen Kolonial-Gesellschaft für Südwest-Afrika,* vol. 2 (Berlin, 1912), 271–276; original copy (April 2, 1908) in BAB R1002/42.

46. Nap, "Diamanten," 871. Wilhelm Regendanz, "Diamantenregie (I)," *Koloniale Rundschau* (1910), 237–238. Gallus, "Diamantvorkommen," 945. Curt Pasel's report, January 13, 1909, BAB R1001/1342. "'Konzessionen und Unterkonzessionen,'" *Lüderitzbuchter Zeitung,* June 12, 1909.

47. Sander, *Geschichte,* vol. 2, 265–279, 303. "Illusory," see DKSSWA to Dernburg, November 24, 1909; Schuckmann to RKA, October 25, 1909, BAB R1001/1528.

48. Notarial documents of Richard Irmler concerning proceedings of DKSSWA, February 6 and 12, 1909, BAB R1001/1528; "Du hast ja Diamanten . . . Aus unseren Kolonien," *Graf's Finanz-Chronik: Zeitschrift für Finanz- und Versicherungs-Praxis,* December 14, 1908, BAB R1001/1341; see "A. Goerz & Company, Limited," *African Review* 14, no. 276 (London, 1898): 354; see Rondo Cameron, *France and the Economic Development of Europe 1800–1914* (Princeton: Princeton University Press, 1961), 160.

49. Dernburg to Wilhelm II, January 7, 1909, BAB R1001/1341; cf. Rathenau to Dernburg, December 9, 1908, BAB R1001/1358. "Unworthy of civilization," see "Deutscher Reichstag," *Berliner Börsenzeitung,* January 26, 1910.

50. Matthias Erzberger, *Millionengeschenke* (Berlin: Germania, 1910), 34. German Colonial Corporation of SWA to Dernburg, September 18, 1908, Sander, *Geschichte,* vol. 2, 277–278.

51. Dernburg to Diamant-Schürfgesellschaft, August 17, 1908, BAK N1130/50; cf. Humboldt-Dachroeden, *Diamantenpolitik,* 29. Foreign investment figure, see Guillaume Daudin, Matthias Morys, and Kevin H. O'Rourke, "Globalization, 1870–1914," in *Cambridge Economic History of Modern Europe,* eds. Stephen Broadberry and Kevin H. O'Rourke, vol. 2 (Cambridge: Cambridge University Press, 2010), 10.

52. Cf. "Herrn Fürstenbergs 'Beklemmungen,'" *Berliner Tageblatt,* June 11, 1910. "Systemic harmony," see Hjalmar Schacht, "Diamant-Industrie," *Preußische Jahrbücher,* ed. Hans Delbrück, vol. 114 (Berlin, 1903), 301. "Lüderitzbucht," *Deutsch-Südwestafrikanische Zeitung,* July 28, 1908. Bernhard Dernburg, *Südwestafrikanische Eindrücke* (Berlin: Mittler, 1909), 28–31.

4. Conflict

1. Entry for June 28, 1915, Theodor Wolff, *Tagebücher 1914–1919,* vol. 1 (Boppard: Boldt, 1984), 243.

2. "Zum Vertragskonflikt der Deutschen Kolonialgesellschaft," *Berliner Börsen-Courier,* March 12, 1910. Markus Jahnel, *Das Bodenrecht in 'Neudeutschland über See'* (Frankfurt: Peter Lang, 2009), 328.

3. "Diamantenfunde," *Deutsche Kolonialzeitung* 25, no. 28 (1908): 504. "Diamond blessing," see Clara Brockmann, *Briefe eines deutschen Mädchen* (Berlin: Mittler, 1912), 205. "Zur Diamantengewinnung," *Frankfurter Zeitung,* November 6, 1909. "Deutsche Kolonialgesellschaft für Südwestafrika," *Berliner Börsen-Courier,* October 4, 1910. Apostolische Präfektur Groß-Namaland, "Neugründungen in Lüderitzbucht," *Die katholischen Missionen: Illustrierte Monatsschrift,* vol. 39, no. 7 (Freiburg: Herder, 1911), 176.

4. Anonymous report dated November 28, 1908, NAN BBL, 5, II.A.5.a,. Cf. Paul Range's report, July 19, 1908, NAN ZBU, 1484, R.II.e.2, vol. 1. Karl Helfferich to Paul von Schwabach, December 28, 1908, HID, Archives of Deutsche Bank Zentrale Berlin, Sekretariat (Frankfurt), S096. Cf. "Deutsche Kolonialgesellschaft für Südwestafrika," *Frankfurter Zeitung,* September 8, 1910.

5. G. Goldberg, "Technische Fortschritte," *Zeitschrift für Kolonialpolitik, Kolonialrecht und Kolonialwirtschaft* 14 (Berlin, 1912): 532; Hermann Thomsen, *Deutsches Land in Afrika* (München: Deutsche Alpenzeitung, 1911), 115. For image of "800-level": Lord Randolph S. Churchill, *Men, Mines and Animals in South Africa* (London: Sampson Low, Marston & Company, 1895), 43. Figures found in "Diamond Profit $25 per minute," *Chicago Daily Tribune,* September 27, 1908.

6. "Neugründungen in Lüderitzbucht," *Die katholischen Missionen* 39 (Freiburg, 1910); 176; "Zur Diamantengewinnung," *Frankfurter Zeitung,* November 6, 1909. Oberstleutnant Gallus, "Die Diamantvorkommen (Schluss)," *Zeitschrift für Kolonialpolitik, Kolonialrecht und Kolonialwirtschaft* 12 (1910): 32, 955.

7. Rudolf von Koch and Karl Helfferich to S. Bleichröder, December 24, 1908, HID, Archives of Deutsche Bank Zentrale Berlin, Sekretariat (Frankfurt), S096.

8. "Exclusive," see author's translation of original German order printed in Ludwig Sander, *Geschichte der deutschen Kolonial-Gesellschaft für Südwest-Afrika,* vol. 2 (Berlin,

1912), 279. "Steuern," *Windhuker Nachrichten,* December 19, 1908; see "Die südwestafrikanischen Diamantfunde," *Frankfurter Zeitung,* December 31, 1908; "Die Sperrverfügung," *Frankfurter Zeitung,* January 7, 1910. Breitmeyer to Hirschhorn, April 16, 1909, BW Wernher, Beit vol. 143.

9. "Der Aufklärung bedürftig," *Alldeutsche Blätter* 19, no. 2 (1909): 12. "Germany's Diamonds," *The Observer* (London), January 3, 1909. Dernburg's memorandum, April 30, 1909, BAB R1001/1424. Order of RKA, September 30, 1908 (eight days after the Sperrgebiet decree), Sander, *Geschichte,* vol. 2, 280. Wilhelm Regendanz, "Diamantenregie (I)," *Koloniale Rundschau* (1910), 238. F. Bugge and Henry Fowler to Dernburg, September 18, 1908, Sander, *Geschichte,* vol. 2, 277–278; "Zur Politik der Regierung in Lüderitzbucht," *Deutsch-Südwestafrikanische Zeitung,* December 5, 1908; "Die südwestafrikanischen Diamantfunde," *Frankfurter Zeitung,* December 31, 1908.

10. Hintrager to RKA, January 18, 1909; DKGfSWA to Dernburg, March 2, 1909, BAB R1001/1815; see Bruno Simmersbach, "Bergbau," *Zeitschrift für die gesamte Staatswissenschaft* 72 (1916), 420. C. Gagel, "Lagerstätten," *Zeitschrift für das Berg-, Hütten- und Salinenwesen im Preussichen Staate* 57 (Berlin, 1909): 182. Otto Wiemer and Wilhelm Lattmann to Reichstag, December 7, 1908, *Stenographische Berichte,* 6043 and 6059. Gallus, "Diamantvorkommen," 946; Peter Rainier, *African Hazard* (London: Murray, 1940), 35; "Aus den Kolonien," *Weser-Zeitung,* February 26, 1909. "Südwestafrikanische Kolonialschürfscheine," *Berliner Börsen-Courier,* March 2, 1909.

11. "Lüderitzbuchter Minenkammer," *Lüderitzbuchter Zeitung,* June 24, 1911. Christian Grotewold, *Unser Kolonialwesen* (Stuttgart: Moritz, 1911), 72. See Rainier, *African Hazard,* 28–32; "Diamond Way," *Louisville Courier-Journal,* April 2, 1911; Natty Rothschild (1st Lord Rothschild) to James Armand de Rothschild, June 27, 1909, RAL XI/130A/3/114.

12. Walter Moritz, *Die 'Sandwüste' hat eine Zukunft: Tagebuch und Zeichnungen des Malers Ernst Vollbehr 1910* (Windhoek: Meinert, 1994), 18. "Diamonds," *Yorkville Enquirer,* July 12, 1910. Harald Nestroy, *Duwisib* (Windhoek: Meinert, 2002), 70. See, e.g., Rainier, *African Hazard,* 36–37.

13. "Great population," see Müller to Grey, February 12, 1910, UKNA FO 403/414. "Von einem Freunde," *Berliner Börsenzeitung,* August 3, 1909. See H. F. B. Walker, *Doctor's Diary* (London: Arnold, 1917), 201. Judgment of November 28, 1923, *Entscheidungen des Reichsgerichts in Zivilsachen* 107 (Berlin: de Gruyter, 1924): 78. But see Louis Pink and Georg Hirschberg, *Das Liegenschaftsrecht in den deutschen Schutzgebieten,* vol. 1 (Berlin: Guttentag, 1912), 533.

14. Albert Herrlich, *Schwarze Reise* (Berlin: Oestergaard, 1937), 196. "City of Diamonds," *Times of India,* August 23, 1909. Captain Behntsch of SMS Panther to Wilhelm II, March 10, 1911, BAB R1001/1909. Reichskolonialamt, *Die deutschen Schutzgebiete in Afrika und der Südsee 1909/10: Amtliche Jahresberichte* (Berlin: Mittler, 1911), 129.

15. "German Diamond Fields," *The Sun* (New York), August 22, 1909. Brodersen-Manns, *Wie alles anders kam,* 7–10.

16. Dietrich Redeker, *Die Geschichte der Tagespresse Deutsch-Ostafrikas* (Berlin: Triltsch, 1937), 9. "Medieval feudalism," see "Die Abbaurechte," *Lüderitzbuchter Zeitung,* February 13, 1909.

17. Speech by Graf Friedrich Vitzthum von Eckstädt, December 1, 1909, *Mitteilungen über die Verhandlungen des Ordentlichen Landtages im Königreiche Sachsen während der Jahre 1909–1910, 2. Kammer,* vol. 1 (Dresden: Teubner, 1910), 319.

18. "Die deutschen Kolonien im Jahre 1909/10," *Vorwärts,* March 9, 1911. G. K. Anton, "La Politique Allemande et les Diamants," *Bulletin de colonisation comparée,* no. 6 (Bruxelles: Goemaere, 1910), 267.

19. "Rape," see "Bürger-Versammlung," *Windhuker Nachrichten*, February 20, 1909. "Gifted," see "Sitzung des Landesrates," *Windhuker Nachrichten*, May 4, 1910; cf. Deutsche Bank to Bergisch Märkische Bank, February 14, 1910, HID, Archives of Deutsche Bank Zentrale Berlin, Sekretariat (Frankfurt), So103.

20. Will Sellick (ed.), *Autobiography of Eugen Mansfeld* (London: Jeppestown Press, 2017), 77–78. "Spirit of *nouveau riche*" quoted in Winfried Baumgart, "Imperialism," in *Germans in the Tropics*, eds. Arthur J. Knoll and Lewis H. Gann (New York: Greenwood, 1987), 152; cf. Paul Singer to Reichstag, December 11, 1908, *Stenographische Berichte*, 6137.

21. "Dernburg," *Journal der Goldschmiedekunst* 29, no. 52 (Leipzig, 1908), unpaginated.

22. "Second DeBeers," see "Diamantenfrage," *Norddeutsche Allgemeine Zeitung*, January 29, 1909; "Der Kolonial-Courier," *Berliner Börsen-Courier*, May 25, 1909. Baer, "Diamantenpolitik," *Zeitschrift für Kolonialpolitik, Kolonialrecht und Kolonialwirtschaft* 14 (1912), 791.

23. Deutsche Gesandschaft Haag to Bethmann Hollweg, April 29, 1910, BAB R1001/1382. Karl von Lumm's report, May 22, 1918, 3, BAB N2181/86.

24. "Bankpraxis," *Bank-Archiv: Zeitschrift für Bank- und Börsenwesen* 6 (Berlin: Guttentag, 1907), 48. Stephan Rammeloo, *Corporations in Private International Law* (Oxford: Oxford University Press, 2001), 134. "Doubt De Beers Story," *New-York Tribune*, February 15, 1907. Dernburg to Wilhelm II, January 7, 1909, BAB R1001/1341; Nathaniel (1st Lord Rothschild) to Rothschild Cousins, Paris, April 8, 1907 and July 22, 1907, RAL XI/130A/1/68 and RAL XI/130A/1/140.

25. Jean Demuth, *Der Diamantenmarkt* (Karlsruhe: Braun, 1912), 58.

26. Godehard Lenzen, *History of Diamond Production and the Diamond Trade* (London: Barrie and Jenkins, 1970), 161. Percy Wagner, *Die diamantführenden Gesteine* (Berlin, 1909), 201–203; see Natty Rothschild to Rothschild Cousins in Paris, January 6, 1914, RAL, XI/130A/8/4. "Retrospect of 1908," *The Financial Review: Finance, Commerce, Railroads* (New York: Dana, 1909), 15. Arno Jollast, "Diamantenfieber," *Die Zukunft*, vol. 66 (Berlin: Zukunft, 1909), 81. Natty Rothschild to Rothschild Cousins in Paris, December 16, 1907, RAL, XI/130A/1/240. "Damned fools," see Humboldt to Bülow, January 7, 1909, BAB R1001/1408.

27. Dernburg to Wilhelm II, July 1, 1909, BAB R1001/1341. "Diamond Fields," *Rand Daily Mail*, November 24, 1908. "Staatssekretär Dernburg," *Journal der Goldschmiedekunst* 29, no. 52 (Leipzig, 1908): unpaginated. Ernest Oppenheimer to William Honnold, August 26, 1908, Box 3, Folder 15, William L. Honnold Papers, H.Mss.0381, CCL, Honnold Mudd Library. "Deutsches Reich," *Frankfurter Zeitung*, February 4, 1909. Wilhelm Freiherr von Humboldt-Dachroeden, *Die Deutsche Diamantenpolitik* (Jena: Fischer, 1918), 43; Gallus, "Diamantvorkommen (Schluss)," 40.

28. "Weltausstellung in Brüssel," *Allgemeines Journal der Uhrmacher-Kunst* 35, no. 19 (Halle: Knapp, 1910): 296; "Deutsche Diamanten," *Vorwärts*, November 30, 1913. Data (3.1 percent) from John Kay, *The Diamond: Its History, Importance and Value* (Detroit: John Kay & Co., 1908), 29.

29. Dernburg to Leo Weinthal, December 17, 1908, BAB R1001/1341; "Die südwestafrikanischen Diamanten," *Frankfurter Zeitung*, July 8, 1909; "Koloniales," *Tägliche Rundschau*, June 26, 1909; "Diamantfunde," *Globus* 96 (1909): 507. See "Diamanten-Abbau in Südwestafrika," *Berliner Börsen-Courier*, June 4, 1909. Gallus, "Diamantvorkommen (Schluss)," 39. Cf. Ernst Steiner, *Der internationale Diamantenmarkt* (Wien: Richards, 1933), 16. "Diamond Prices," *New York Times*, August 7, 1909. Richard Helm, *Zwischen Ankunft und Abschied: Einige Begebenheiten aus dem ehemaligen Südwestafrika* (Mannheim: Kolb, 2005), 60. "Limpidity," see "Vom Diamantenmarkt," *Frankfurter Zei-*

tung, November 7, 1909. See "Lüderitzbucht," *Diamond Fields Advertiser,* January 4, 1909; "Neueste Handels-Nachrichten," *Berliner Börsen-Courier,* January 16, 1910.

    30. C. Gagel, "Lagerstätten," 183. Twenty-seven percent, see "Erwiderung der Regie," *Lüderitzbuchter Zeitung,* September 4, 1909. "Diamond Trade," *New York Times,* March 10, 1912. Cf. Simmersbach, "Bergbau," 418.

    31. Leopoldus Laub to Dernburg, February 25, 1909, BAK N1130/32.

    32. Cf. *Berliner Tageblatt* no. 243, May 13, 1908, 9, excerpted in Walther Rathenau, *Briefe 1871–1913,* vol. 5, part 1, ed. Alexander Jaser, Clemens Picht, and Ernst Schulin (Düsseldorf: Droste, 2006), 847–848. Cf. Sigmund Schilder, *Entwicklungstendenzen der Weltwirtschaft,* vol. 2 (Berlin: Siemenroth, 1915), 199. "No Slump," *New York Times,* June 10, 1900. Cf. Humboldt-Dachroeden, *Die Deutsche Diamantenpolitik,* 39.

    33. Report by Bezirksamtmann Böhmer, November 22, 1910, BAB R1001/1386. "Die Diamantenfrage," *Frankfurter Zeitung,* June 25, 1909. Cf. Karl Helfferich's memorandum, December 22, 1908, HID, Archives of Deutsche Bank Zentrale Berlin, Sekretariat (Frankfurt), S096. Hirschhorn to Dernburg, October 14, 1908, BAK N1130/31; Hirschhorn to Dernburg, January 30, 1909, BAK N1130/32.

    34. Humboldt-Dachroeden, *Die Deutsche Diamantenpolitik,* 42; see Jana Moser, *Kartographiegeschichte* (Dresden: Universität Dresden, 2007), 93, 95; "Diamond Fields," *The Times,* December 26, 1908; "Spekulation in Kolonial-Werten," *Frankfurter Zeitung,* February 5, 1909; cf. W. G. Fitz-Gerald, "Mining the World's Diamonds," *The World To-Day,* vol. 12 (Chicago: Hearst, 1907), 528. "German Emperor's Diamond Fields," *The Globe,* October 19, 1909.

    35. "Diamond Smuggler," *Manchester Guardian,* October 6, 1909. "Ein neuer Schwindel," *Lüderitzbuchter Zeitung,* August 27, 1910. Polizeipräsident of Berlin to RKA, September 23, 1909, BAB R1001/1426; "Smuggler Keeps Secret," *St. Louis Post-Dispatch,* October 24, 1909. Cf. "Deutsche Kolonialgesellschaft für Südwestafrika," *Berliner Volkszeitung,* October 9, 1910. "German Emperor's Diamond Fields," *The Globe,* October 19, 1909.

    36. Humboldt-Dachroeden, *Die Deutsche Diamantenpolitik,* 41. Cf. "Diamond-Dealers," *New York Tribune,* July 18, 1896. Steiner, *Diamantenmarkt,* 13. "German Gems," *New York Times,* July 7, 1910. See Paul Rohrbach, *Kolonialwesen* (Leipzig: Gloeckner, 1911), 59.

    37. Arthur von Gwinner's memorandum, March 30, 1909, HID, Archives of Deutsche Bank Zentrale Berlin, Sekretariat (Frankfurt), S1370. "Diamantenfrage," *Norddeutsche Allgemeine Zeitung,* January 29, 1909. See Pomona-Minengesellschaft/Pomona-Diamanten-Gesellschaft records in BAB R1001/1413–1414. "De Beers," *Financial Times,* November 8, 1910.

    38. Demuth, *Diamantenmarkt,* 73.

    39. *Berliner Jahrbuch für Handel und Industrie: Bericht der Ältesten der Kaufmannschaft von Berlin, Jahrgang 1913,* vol. 1 (Berlin, 1914), 68. "Bergbau," *Glückauf* 49, no. 10 (Essen, 1913): 366.

    40. Decree of January 16 1909, NAN ZBU, 1612, R.XIV.f.1, Bd. 1. Protocol of *Regie* board meeting, February 10, HID, Archives of Deutsche Bank Zentrale Berlin, Sekretariat (Frankfurt), S097.

    41. BAB R1001/1341, Dernburg to Wilhelm II, January 7, 1909; cf. Robert Vicat Turrell, *Capital and Labour on the Kimberley Diamond Fields, 1871–1890* (Cambridge: Cambridge University Press, 1987), 132–134, 176–177, 186, 195. Paul Rettig, "Deutsche Diamanten," *Westermanns Monatshefte* 54, no. 108, part 2 (Braunschweig: Westermann, 1910): 472. Humboldt-Dachroeden, *Die Deutsche Diamantenpolitik,* 75; "Diamantendiebstähle und ihre Verhütung," *Lüderitzbuchter Zeitung* of July 30, 1910.

42. See Turrell, *Capital and Labour,* 181.

43. Ludwig Sander, *Geschichte,* vol. 1, 232. Regie to RKA, July 1, 1909, BAB R1001/1458a. NAN ZBU, 1612, R.XIV.f.1, Bd. 1.

44. Regendanz, "Diamantenregie (I)," 224. Karl Helfferich's memorandum, December 22, 1908, HID, Archives of Deutsche Bank Zentrale Berlin, Sekretariat (Frankfurt), S096.

45. J. Neumann, "Verwendung," *Abhandlungen des Hamburgischen Kolonialinstituts,* vol. 26 (Hamburg, 1914), 121. "In the best interests of producers," see Regendanz, "Diamantenregie (I)," 224; O. Stutzer, *Lagerstätten,* vol. 1 (Berlin, 1911), 145.

46. Fritz Blaich, *Kartell- und Monopolpolitik im Kaiserlichen Deutschland* (Düsseldorf: Droste, 1973), 185; Harm Schröter, "Cartelization," *Journal of European Economic History* 25, no. 1 (1996): 132. Friedrich Kleinwächter, *Kartelle* (Innsbruck, 1883), 143; see Erich Maschke, "German Cartels," in *Essays in European Economic History,* eds. F. Crouzet et al. (London, 1969), 228. Karl Helfferich's memorandum, December 22, 1908, HID, Archives of Deutsche Bank Zentrale Berlin, Sekretariat (Frankfurt), S096. "Diamanten-Regie-Gesellschaft," *Frankfurter Zeitung,* January 4, 1909. See Joseph Davies, *Trust Laws* (Washington, DC: Government Printing Office, 1916), 254. Otto Jöhlinger, "Diamantenpolitik," *Schmollers Jahrbuch für Gesetzgebung, Verwaltung, und Volkswirtschaft,* vol. 44 (Leipzig, 1920), 292.

47. Cf. Karl Helfferich's memorandum, January 15, 1910, HID, Archives of Deutsche Bank Zentrale Berlin, Sekretariat (Frankfurt), S096; Dernburg to Eugen Wolf, November 13, 1909, BAK N1130/35. Marburg, "Government," *Business History Review* 38 (1964): 82. Davies, *Trust Laws,* 260.

48. "How our economy may look," see Dernburg's foreword to Robert Liefmann, *Kartelle* (Berlin, 1918), 4. See Helga Nussbaum, "Versuche," *Jahrbuch für Wirtschaftsgeschichte,* vol. 9, no. 2 (1968), 124, 166–203; Fritz Fischer, "World Policy," *Origins of the First World War,* ed. H. W. Koch (London: Macmillan, 1984), 166. Cf. Hartmut Pogge von Strandmann, "Rathenau zwischen Politik und Wirtschaft," *Am Wendepunkt der europäischen Geschichte,* ed. O. Franz (Göttingen: Muster-Schmidt, 1981), 101. See Ann Laura Stoler and Frederick Cooper, "Between Metropole and Colony," in *Tensions of Empire,* eds. Ann Laura Stoler and Frederick Cooper (Berkeley: University of California Press, 1997), 5. Walther Rathenau, *Notes and Diaries 1907–1922,* ed. Hartmut Pogge von Strandmann (Oxford: Clarendon, 1985), 170.

49. Rudolf Hilferding, *Das Finanzkapital* (Wien: Ignaz, 1910), 475. See Maschke, "German Cartels," 239; see Andreas Resch, *Industriekartelle in Österreich vor dem Ersten Weltkrieg* (Berlin: Duncker & Humblot, 2002), 14.

50. Export between 1908 and 1913, see Horst Gründer, *Geschichte der deutschen Kolonien* (Paderborn: Brill, 2018), 139. Export in 1912, see Senate of the Parliament of the Union of South Africa, *Report from Select Committee on Establishment of Diamond Cutting Industry in South Africa* (Cape Town, 1913), 126. Export in 1913, see Walther Vogel, "Die territorialen und bevölkerungspolitischen Veränderungen," *Der Friedensvertrag,* ed. Deutsche Wirtschaftliche Gesellschaft (Berlin: Springer, 1921), 36; Cf. table 2.1 in Charles C. Stover, "Tropical Exports," *Tropical Development, 1880–1913,* ed. William Arthur Lewis (London: Allen & Unwin, 1970), 46.

51. Gallus, "Diamantvorkommen (Schluss)," 37; Baer, "Diamantenpolitik," 784. Schuckmann to Dernburg, January 6, 1909, BAB R1001/1342; "Diamantschmuggel," *Windhuker Nachrichten,* July 13, 1910.

52. For 57 million marks estimate, see Markus A. Denzel, "Die wirtschaftliche Bilanz," *Die Deutschen und ihre Kolonien,* eds. Horst Gründer and Hermann Hiery (Berlin: be.bra, 2018), 160. This datum comports with other published figures regarding Germa-

ny's trade *with* its colonies; cf. Percy Ernst Schramm, *Deutschland und Übersee* (Braunschweig: Westermann, 1950), 458. Export value between 243 and 302 million marks, cf. Kolonial-Wirtschaftliches Komitee, *Der Handel der deutschen Kolonien* (Berlin, 1915), 7–8; Gustav Stresemann, Englandswirtschaftskrieg gegen Deutschland (Stuttgart: Verlagsanstalt, 1915), 16. Cf. L. H. Gann and Peter Duignan, *Rulers of German Africa* (Stanford: Stanford University Press, 1977), 241. But see Hans-Ulrich Wehler, "Transnationale Geschichte," *Transnationale Geschichte,* eds. Gunilla Budde, Sebastian Conrad, Oliver Janz (Göttingen: V&R, 2007), 167–168.

53. "Rechtsverhältnisse der Deutschen Kolonialgesellschaft für Südwestafrika," *Berliner Börsen-Courier,* February 15, 1910. Humboldt-Dachroeden, *Die Deutsche Diamantenpolitik*), 163. "Labor Raises Price of Diamond," *New York Times,* August 30, 1925.

54. Cf. "In the Underground Way of the Diamond Trade," *New York Times,* October 3, 1906; League of Nations, *Memorandum on Balance of Payments and Foreign Trade Balances 1910–1924* (Geneva: Imp. réunies, 1925), 37. Carat total comes from statement of Walter N. Kahn, printed in House of Representatives Committee on Ways and Means, Seventieth Congress, Second Session, *Tariff Readjustment—1929,* vol. 12 (Washington, DC: Government Printing Office, 1929), 7458. Cf. Hermann Schumacher, "Germany's International Economic Position," *Modern Germany in Relation to the Great War* (New York: Kennerley, 1916), 107. "Periphery," see, e.g., Albert Wirz, *Sklaverei und kapitalistisches Weltsystem* (Frankfurt: Suhrkamp, 1984), 198.

5. Markets

1. "Homer," see "Briefkasten," *Kladderadatsch* 63, no. 11, 3rd supplement (Berlin, 1910): 3. See "Germany's Chamberlain," *Guyra Argus,* January 20, 1910. Cf. George Louis Beer, *African Questions at the Paris Peace Conference* (New York: Macmillan, 1923), 21. See, e.g., "Diamanten," *Berliner Volkszeitung,* May 3, 1912. Emil Merkel to Dernburg, May 25, 1909, BAK N1130/34. "Harzreise," *Hamburger Nachrichten,* January 29, 1910.

2. "Deutscher Reichstag," *Berliner Börsenzeitung,* January 26, 1910. Oberstleutnant Gallus, "Die Diamantvorkommen (Schluss)," *Zeitschrift für Kolonialpolitik, Kolonialrecht und Kolonialwirtschaft* 12 (1910), 37–39. Francis Oats to Dernburg, July 6, 1909, BAB R1001/1343. Cf. Karl Helfferich's memorandum, December 22, 1908, HID, Archives of Deutsche Bank Zentrale Berlin, Sekretariat (Frankfurt), S096. Frentzel and Co. to Government at Windhoek, September 1, 1909, BAB R151F, FC 15079.

3. Dernburg to Fürstenberg, December 14, 1908, BAB R1001/1358.

4. "World is a ring," see "Diamantlager," *Vorwärts,* February 16, 1914; Berthold Laufer, *Diamond* (Chicago, 1915), 49. Henri Polak to Jewelers' Circular, November 14, 1921, "Denies," *Jewelers' Circular,* December 7, 1921, 91.

5. Karl von Lumm's report, "Die Banque Generale Belge," May 22, 1918, 3, BAB N2181/86. See Otto Warburg, "Poskin," *Tropenpflanzer* 4 (1900): 625. See Emile Denekamp, *Diamantindustrie* (Heidelberg: Hörning, 1895), 19, 26–27. C. P. Kindleberger, *Economic Primacy* (Oxford: Oxford University Press, 1996), 94; A. Harou, "Diamant," *Société Royale Belge de Géographie: Bulletin* (Bruxelles, 1885), 480. Erik Hansen, "Labour," *Histoire Sociale* 10, no. 20 (1977): 398, 389; cf. "Gems and Jewels," *Atlanta Constitution,* December 28, 1890. National City Bank of New York, "Antwerp," *The Americas* 6, no. 1 (October 1919): 17; "Diamantindustrie," *Weltwirtschaftliches Archiv* 13 (1918): 33.

6. Denekamp, *Diamantindustrie,* 27, 30. See Hansen, "Labour," 397–398; "Holland," *Windhuker Nachrichten,* February 29, 1908. Rothschilds in London to Rothschild Cousins, Paris, April 10 and 30, 1908, RAL XI/130A/2/77 and XI/130A/2/84. Excerpt from newspaper marked "B.Z", June 23, 1909, BAB R1001/1423.

7. "Die südwestafrikanischen Diamanten," *Frankfurter Zeitung,* July 8, 1909. Natty Rothschild to Édouard de Rothschild, Paris, May 20, 1908, RAL XI/130A/2/96. "Vom Diamantenmarkt," *Frankfurter Zeitung,* November 7, 1909. Cf. Ernst Steiner, *Der internationale Diamantenmarkt* (Wien: Richards, 1933), 18. Cf. Deutsche Gesandschaft Haag to Bethmann Hollweg, April 29, 1910, BAB R1001/1382.

8. Figure of 16,000 cited in Godehard Lenzen, *History of Diamond Production and the Diamond Trade* (London: Barrie and Jenkins, 1970), 205, note 137. Ernst Falz, *Idar-Obersteiner Schmuckstein-Industrie* (Idar: Carl Schmidt Verlag, 1926), 170n1. "Diamond Industry of Antwerp," *The Times* (London), April 10, 1912. "Jewelry," *New-York Tribune,* June 8, 1919. "Fritz and the Antwerp Diamonds," *New-York Tribune,* May 18, 1919. Lotz's protocol, November 17, 1913, HID, Archives of Deutsche Bank Zentrale Berlin, Sekretariat (Frankfurt), S097. A. Guradze to Bethmann Hollweg, December 5, 1913, BAB R901/789.

9. Tariff figure, see Karl Helfferich's memorandum, December 29, 1908, HID, Archives of Deutsche Bank Zentrale Berlin, Sekretariat (Frankfurt), S096; Karl Kucklentz, *Zollwesen* (Halle, 1913), 46. Jean Demuth, *Der Diamantenmarkt* (Karlsruhe: Braun, 1912), 15. "Tages-Rundschau," *Frankfurter Zeitung,* April 19, 1912. Wilhelm Solf to Reichstag, May 2, 1912, *Stenographische Berichte,* 1627. "Open market," see Dernburg to Reichstag, January 25, 1910, *Stenographische Berichte,* 779.

10. Busch & Schwarz Diamantenschleiferei to Dernburg, December 26, 1908, BAB R1001/1351.

11. Vorstand Kolonialgesellschaft (Idar) to Dernburg, March 22, 1909, BAB N1130/33. RKA to Gottlieb von Jagow, April 2, 1913, R901/789. Robert Gerstenhauer, "Südwestafrikanische Diamantenpolitik," *Jahrbuch über die deutschen Kolonien* 7 (Essen: Baedeker, 1914): 177. "Neueste Handels-Nachrichten," *Berliner Börsen-Courier,* August 6, 1909.

12. Deutsche Diamanten-Gesellschaft to Helfferich, October 24, 1913, HID, Archives of Deutsche Bank Zentrale Berlin, Sekretariat (Frankfurt), S097. Cf. Hoch's speech, *Stenographische Berichte,* May 2, 1912, 1613.

13. Verband der Diamantschleiferei-Besitzer für Hanau to Lindequist, June 30, 1911, BAB R1001/1382. "Tages-Rundschau," *Frankfurter Zeitung,* April 19, 1912. Attachment to protocol of *Regie* board meeting on August 20, 1913, BAB R1001/1390. See "La taillerie de diamants," *Journal d'Ypres,* June 11, 1910. "German Diamonds," *San Francisco Call,* February 6, 1911. "No bread," see Gustav Hoch's speech, *Stenographische Berichte,* May 2, 1912, 1613. Clemens von Delbrück to Alfred von Kiderlen-Waechter, November 1, 1911, BAB R901/787.

14. "Office for social politics," see Felix Waldstein's speech to Reichstag, May 2, 1912, *Stenographische Berichte,* 1624. BAB N2181/86, Karl von Lumm's report, "Die Banque Generale Belge," May 22, 1918, 3–5.

15. Cf. Procotol of *Regie*'s boardmeeting, October 11, 1913, HID, Archives of Deutsche Bank Zentrale Berlin, Sekretariat (Frankfurt), S097. "Karatgewicht," *Frankfurter Zeitung,* October 7, 1911. Alfred Eppler, "Die Schmuckstein-Industrie," *Die Gartenlaube,* no. 14 (1910), 300.

16. Frankfurter Handelskammer to German State Minister for Trade in Berlin, August 14, 1911, R901/787. Figure of 200,000, cf. "Deutsches Reich," *Frankfurter Zeitung,* February 4, 1909. See Falz, *Idar-Obersteiner Schmuckstein-Industrie,* 146.

17. "Sight-holder" model, see language in "Telegramme: Frankfurt a.M.," *Berliner Börsenzeitung,* October 8, 1909. "Diamanten," *Vossische Zeitung,* June 7, 1913. Natty Rothschild to Édouard Rothschild, December 28, 1909, RAL XI/130A/3/224.

18. Cf. Ferreira Ramos, *Valorisation* (Antwerp: Buschmann, 1907).

19. Falz, *Idar-Obersteiner Schmuckstein-Industrie,* 169. Karl Helfferich's memorandum, December 22, 1908, HID, Archives of Deutsche Bank Zentrale Berlin, Sekretariat

(Frankfurt), S096. See Andrew Zimmerman, *Alabama in Africa* (Princeton: Princeton University Press, 2010).

20. "Briefe," *Allgemeines Journal der Uhrmacher-Kunst* 35, no. 19 (Halle: Knapp, 1910): 296. J. Neumann, "Verwendung," *Abhandlungen des Hamburgischen Kolonialinstituts* 26 (Hamburg, 1914): 121. Wilhelm Solf, "Colonial Policy," *Modern Germany*, ed. William Whitelock (New York: Kennerley, 1916), 153. Cf. "Diamonds in 1911," *American Jeweler* 31, no. 12 (Chicago, 1911): 461.

21. Rothschilds in London to Rothschild Cousins, Paris, April 10 and 30, 1908, RAL XI/130A/2/77 and XI/130A/2/84. See Frank Caestecker and Torsten Feys, "East European Jewish Migrants and Settlers in Belgium, 1880–1914," *East European Jewish Affairs* 40, no. 3 (2010): 261. Hermann Schumacher, *Antwerpen: seine Weltstellung und Bedeutung* (München: Duncker & Humblot, 1916), 41. Cf. "The Diamond Cutters' Case," *New-York Tribune*, April 3, 1895. "Alleged Diamond Smuggler," *New York Times*, February 17, 1896. Cf. "Belgian Moratorium," *Wall Street Journal*, July 9, 1915; Francis Bacon James, *Advertising and Other Addresses* (Cincinnati: Clarke, 1907), 95.

22. Wilhelm Solf's diary entry for July 29, 1912, BAK N1053/36; cf. "Beauty and Etiquette," *St. Louis Post-Dispatch*, July 14, 1901. "No diamond, no engagement," see "Price of Engagement Rings," *Chicago Daily Tribune*, November 27, 1904. "Fiancée's pocketbook," see "Society Chat by Lady Teazle," *San Francisco Chronicle*, May 25, 1910; cf. "Sure Cause," *Women's Wear Daily*, August 2, 1913.

23. "Diamond Engagement Rings Preferred," *St. Louis Post-Dispatch*, March 20, 1910. "Diamond Drummers," *Evening Star* (Washington, DC), November 15, 1908. "Betty Vincent's Advice to Lovers," *St. Louis Post-Dispatch*, November 24, 1914. "Buying Smaller Gems," *Los Angeles Times*, July 13, 1912. "Poor families," see "Stringency in Diamonds," *Wall Street Journal*, June 25, 1904. "Nurses' Rats Barred," *St. Louis Post-Dispatch*, February 12, 1911. "Little diamond engagement ring," see Jean Weidensall, *The Mentality of the Criminal Woman* (Baltimore: Warwick, 1916), 306.

24. "Diamonds and Prosperity," *Washington Post*, July 11, 1909. "Only $20 a week," see "Cuttll Fish as an Aid to Cupid," *San Francisco Chronicle*, February 11, 1912. "In the Good Old Summertime," *Pawtucket Times*, August 4, 1911; "The Month of Engagements," *The State* (South Carolina), April 30, 1910; "Diamonds Extraordinary," *Harrisburg Star-Independent*, December 14, 1914. "Third quality," see Sears, Roebuck and Co. Chicago, *Catalog No. 120, Spring 1910* (Philadelphia: Sears, Roebuck and Company, 1910), 464. "Tagesnachrichten," *Unterhaltungsblatt und Anzeiger für den Kreis Schleiden und Umgegend*, January 9, 1909.

25. For wage data, compare statistics in U.S. Department of Labor, *Bureau of Labor Statistics, Union Scale of Wages and Hours of Labor 1907 to 1912* (Washington, DC: Government Printing Office, 1913), 68. "Nice little dinner," see "What It Costs to Woo," *Chicago Daily Tribune*, June 11, 1911. "Handel und Verkehr," *Berliner Tageblatt*, December 27, 1910. "No knowledge," see Minute of Representatives' Meeting of J. Walter Thompson Company, November 22, 1927, David M. Rubenstein Rare Book and Manuscript Library, Duke University (hereafter RL) The John W. Hartman Center for Sales, Advertising and Marketing History, RL.00749 Box 1. "Easy payment," see "Price of Engagement Rings," *Chicago Daily Tribune*, November 27, 1904. "Precious Stones of Africa," *Atlanta Constitution*, October 11, 1908. "Diamond Engagement Rings," *St. Louis Post-Dispatch*, February 10, 1911.

26. "Perfect," "to suit all pockets," "perfection," cf. "Engagement Rings," *The Daily Gate City* (Keokuk, Iowa), June 9, 1912; "Diamond Rings to Suit all Pockets," *Daily Independent* (Elko, Nevada), December 27, 1912; "Seal the Promise with a Kiss," *The Prince George's Enquirer*, October 31, 1913. Robert M. Shipley, *Diamonds* (Los Angeles:

Gemological Institute of America, 1940), 168. "Constant source of pleasure," see "Diamond Engagement Rings," *The Liberal Democrat* (Liberal, Kansas), April 28, 1916. "Most perfect," see "Klein's Diamond Engagement Rings," *Montgomery Advertiser* (Alabama), October 22, 1913. "Diamond Engagement Rings," *St. Louis Post-Dispatch,* March 20, 1910; "Buying Smaller Gems," *Los Angeles Times,* July 13, 1912.

27. "The Engagement Ring," *Chicago Defender,* July 22, 1911. "Fads in Engagement Rings," *The Chicago Defender,* May 27, 1911; "What It Costs to Woo," *Chicago Daily Tribune,* June 11, 1911.

28. Cf. Paul H. Jacobson, *American Marriage and Divorce* (Rinehart: New York, 1959), table 2. Walter N. Kahn, printed in House of Representatives Committee on Ways and Means, Seventieth Congress, Second Session, *Tariff Readjustment—1929,* vol. 12 (Washington, DC: Government Printing Office, 1929), 7458. Arthur Norden, "Wochenschau," *Berliner Tageblatt,* June 11, 1910. Cf. Beckert, *Empire of Cotton,* 355. Cf. Erik Grimmer-Solem, *Learning Empire* (Cambridge: Cambridge University Press, 2019), 266.

29. "Eine, die vorsichtig geworden ist," *Kladderadatsch* 63, no. 15 (Berlin, 1910): 286. Cf. "Diamanten," *Deutsch-Südwestafrikanische Zeitung,* May 5, 1909. Cf. Georg Simmel, "Some Remarks on Prostitution," *Simmel on Culture,* eds. David Frisby and Mike Featherstone (London: Sage, 1997), 262. See Robert N. Proctor, "Anti-Agate: The Great Diamond Hoax and the Semiprecious Stone Scam," *Configurations* 9, no. 3 (2001): 408. "She Wanted to Know," *Washington Bee,* May 13, 1911; "She Took No Chances," *Savannah Tribune,* September 24, 1910; "The Test of Love," *Women's Wear Daily,* May 9, 1919. "Engagement Ring a Gift," *New York Times,* May 7, 1909; "Engagement Rings," *New-York Tribune,* April 4, 1910; "Betrothal Ring Hers," *Washington Post,* January 20, 1911.

30. O. Stutzer, *Lagerstätten,* vol. 1 (Berlin, 1911), 145; see BAB R1001/1384, "Diamanten-Sendungen," April 1912–April 1916. *Berliner Jahrbuch für Handel und Industrie: Bericht der Ältesten der Kaufmannschaft von Berlin, Jahrgang 1913,* vol. 1 (Berlin, 1914), 68. "Diamanten-Regie des SWA Schutzgebietes," *Deutsches Kolonialblatt* 25, no. 12 (Berlin: Mittler, 1914): 582–585.

31. Hermann Wendel, *August Bebel* (Berlin: Singer, 1913), 87. "Sankt Bernhard," *Die Zukunft* 18 (1910), 390. Cf. Rudolf Martin, *Deutsche Machthaber* (Berlin: Schuster, 1910), 502. "Dernburg wird geadelt," *Prager Tagblatt,* January 22, 1910. Abbé Wetterlé, *Behind the Scenes* (New York: Doran, 1918), 145. "Dernburg's diamonds," see Zedlitz-Trützschler, *Zwölf Jahre,* 202, 210. See marginalia of Dernburg to Bülow, January 2, 1909; Valentini to Dernburg, January 4, 1909, BAB R1001/1341. Wilhelm II to Bülow, August 12, 1908, *Bilder aus der letzten Kaiserzeit,* 140. Dernburg to Zedlitz, January 4, 1927, BAK N1207/8. Credit for source (elevation of Dernburg) to Katharine Lerman. Cf. Martin, *Machthaber,* 501.

32. Fritz Diepenhorst, "Bevölkerungslehre," *Jahrbücher für Nationalökonomie und Statistik,* vol. 115 (Jena 1920), 172. Max Warburg, *Aus meinen Aufzeichnungen* (Glückstadt, 1952), 24–35. Siegfried Passarge, "Dernburgs Rücktritt," *Koloniale Rundschau* (Berlin, 1910), 418. Figure of 1.5 million, see Gallus, "Diamantvorkommen (Schluß)," 37. Cf. "Deutsche Kolonialgesellschaft für Südwestafrika," *Berliner Börsen-Courier,* August 20, 1911, and August 11, 1913. Dernburg to Stresemann, February 17, 1911, PAAA NL Stresemann 120. "Das Duell," *Montagsblatt aus Böhmen,* May 2, 1910.

33. Cf. L. H. Gann and Peter Duignan, *Rulers of German Africa* (Stanford: Stanford University Press, 1977), 183–193; Werner Schiefel, *Dernburg 1865–1937* (Zürich: Atlantis, 1974), 132–142. See Passarge, "Dernburgs Rücktritt," 418. Dernburg to Stresemann, February 17, 1911, PAAA NL Stresemann 120. Wilhelm Langheld, *Zwanzig Jahre* (Berlin: Weicher, 1909), 150. Figures from Ernst Jacob, *Kolonialkunde* (Dresden: Ehlermann, 1934),

40. Hellmuth Forkel, *Küstengebiet* (Rostock: Beckmann, 1926), 78. Louis Hogrefe, ed., *Auslandsbuch für Kaufleute*, vol. 1 (Leipzig: Handlungsgehilfen, 1913), 19.

34. Cf. Harry F. Young, *Maximillian Harden* (The Hague: Nijhoff, 1959), 171. "Preached to the Reichstag," see Arno Jollast, "Diamantenfieber," *Die Zukunft*, vol. 66 (Berlin: Zukunft, 1909), 79–81.

35. "Capitalistic colonial policy," see Christian Stuart Davis, "Colonialism and Anti-semitism during the Kaiserreich: Bernhard Dernburg and the Antisemites," *Leo Baeck Institute Year Book* 53, no. 1 (2008): 50. See Peter Pulzer, *The Rise of Political Anti-Semitism* (New York: Wiley, 1964), 192.

36. "Bloodsuckers" and "foreign bodies," see "Rücktritt Dernburgs," *Mitteilungen aus dem Verein zur Abwehr des Antisemitismus* 20, no. 25 (Berlin, 1910): 195. "Südwest unter Dernburg," *Windhuker Nachrichten*, March 3, 1909. "Nose," see "Ein Wort," *Mecklenburger Warte (Wismar)*, August 23, 1910. "Diamantenregie," *Berliner Börsenzeitung*, October 12, 1913. Page 2 of anonymous, unattributed memo, BAK N1138/51.

37. See Harold James, *Globalization* (Cambridge, MA: Harvard University Press, 2001), 19. Werner Sombart, *Die Juden und das Wirtschaftsleben* (Leipzig: Duncker & Humblot, 1911), 84. "Capitalistically than nationalistically," see *Deutsche Tageszeitung* as quoted in "Dernburg," *Hamburgischer Correspondent*, January 10, 1910. "Diamond princes," see Dusé Mohamed Ali, *In the Land of Pharaohs* (London: Paul, 1911), 216.

38. See Alan Temple, "Lure of Diamond," *Commerce and Finance* 8, no. 31 (New York: Price, 1919): 1022. Hue de Grais, *Handbuch der Verfassung* (Berlin: Springer, 1908), 136. "German Hong Kong," see Russell Berman, "Der ewige Zweite," in *Phantasiereiche*, ed. Birthe Kundrus (Frankfurt: Campus, 2003), 28. Jakob Zollmann, "Colonial Law," *Entanglements*, ed. Thomas Duve (Frankfurt: Max Planck, 2014), 253.

39. See Thorstein Veblen, *Theory of the Leisure Class* (London: Macmillan, 1899), 68–101. See Norbert Elias, *Court Society* (New York: Blackwell, 1983), 38. See Joseph Schumpeter, *Imperialism and Social Classes* (New York: Meridian, 1955; rpt. 1966), 54–64.

40. Moritz J. Bonn, *Wandering Scholar* (New York: John Day Company, 1948), 143. Hyam, *Failure*, 30. "Deutsche Reichspolitik," *Grazer Tagblatt*, January 4, 1910. See Hans-Otto Meissner, *Traumland* (Stuttgart, 1968), 371. "Financial future of Southwest," see Clara Brockmann, *Briefe eines deutschen Mädchen* (Berlin: Mittler, 1912), 176. Cf. "Kolonial-Abteilung," *Jahrbuch der Deutschen Landwirtschafts-Gesellschaft* 27 (Berlin, 1912), 407. Paul Barth, *Südwestafrika* (Windhoek: Meinert, 1926), 51. Oskar Hintrager, *Südwestafrika in der deutschen Zeit* (München: Oldenbourg, 1955), 108. Hintrager to Beth-mann, November 12, 1909, BAK N1037/8. Speech given on March 28, 1908, BAB R1001/2175. "Dernburgs Rücktritt," *Hamburger Fremdenblatt*, June 9, 1910.

41. See "Maßgebliches und Unmaßgebliches," *Die Grenzboten*, 67 (1908): 396. J.E. Mackenzie, "Colonial Aspirations," *Sea Commonwealth and Other Papers*, ed. A.P. Newton (London: Dent, 1919), 40. Moritz J. Bonn, *Die Neugestaltung unserer kolonialen Aufgaben* (Tübingen: Mohr, 1911), 3. See Karl Gerich, *Außenhandel und Handelspolitik der Südafrikanischen Union unter besonderer Berücksichtigung der Wirtschaftsexpansion der Union* (Leipzig: Breuer, 1938), 1.

42. Cf. data from Andrew Carlson, *German Foreign Policy, 1890–1914, and Colonial Policy to 1914* (Metuchen, NJ: Scarecrow Press, 1970), 57. I. Goldblatt, *History of South West Africa* (Cape Town: Juta, 1971), 171, 174. Bley, *Kolonialherrschaft*, 131. See Bonn, *Wandering Scholar*, 148. Cf. Goldblatt, *South West Africa*, 175.

43. See Ute Hagen et al., "Schutzgebiete," in *Verwaltungsgeschichte*, ed. Walther Hubatsch, vol. 22 (Marburg: Herder, 1983), 425. "Non-German," see "Deutsche Ortsnamen,"

Alldeutsche Blätter 19, no. 46 (1909): 393. Eugen Fischer, "Deutsch-Südwestafrika," *Tägliche Rundschau,* April 3, 1909. See Lora Wildenthal, *German Women for Empire* (Durham: Duke University Press, 2001), 79–130.

44. For economic sectors, see table in W. O. Henderson, *Studies in German Colonial History* (Chicago: Quadrangle, 1962), 132. See table A.II.2 in Reichskolonialamt, *Schutzgebiete in Afrika und der Südsee 1912/1913: Amtliche Jahresberichte* (Berlin: Mittler, 1914), 24. "Wähler des Erzgebirges!" (Campaign pamphlet, undated 1910–1911), PAAA NL Stresemann 120.

45. Schumpeter, *Imperialism,* 54–64. Poultney Bigelow, *Children of Nations* (New York: McClure, 1901), 114. Cf. Adolf Zimmermann, *Mit Dernburg nach Ostafrika* (Berlin: Schwetschke, 1908), 38.

46. Figure of 64 percent, see Rudolf Martin, *Unter dem Scheinwerfer* (Berlin: Schuster, 1910), 27. "Von einem Freunde," *Berliner Börsenzeitung,* August 3, 1909.

47. Matthew Fitzpatrick, "Wilhelm II," *Crowns and Colonies,* eds. Robert Aldrich et al. (Manchester: Manchester University Press, 2016), 77. "Domestic" vs. "foreign," see Ignacio Czeguhn, "Kolonialgesetzgebung," *Jahrbuch für Juristische Zeitgeschichte,* ed. Thomas Vormbaum, vol. 8 (Berlin: BWV, 2007), 174–202. Marc Grohmann, *Exotische Verfassung* (Tübingen: Mohr, 2001), 94.

48. Percentage cited in Meissner, *Traumland,* 74.

49. "Steam-engine of diamond," see *Selections from Émile Zola,* ed. Guyot Cameron (New York: Holt, 1905), liii. Figure of 3,900 kilometers, see Politicus, "Empire," *Fortnightly Review* 98 (August 1915): 308.

50. Wolfe Schmokel, "Myth," *International Journal of African Historical Studies* 18, no. 1 (1985): 96. Compare Bernhard Voigt, "Geschichte," in *Afrika spricht zu Dir,* ed. Paul Ritter (Mühlhausen, 1938), 266.

51. "Repay Germany," see "Südwestafrika," *Kolonialreich,* ed. Hans Meyer, vol. 2 (Leipzig, 1910), 286. William Morton Fullerton, *Problems of Power* (New York: Scribner's, 1914), 238.

52. "Ausland," *Das Vaterland* (Vienna), February 1, 1910. "Maßgebliches und Unmaßgebliches," *Die Grenzboten* 69 (1910): 499.

53. Nils Ole Oermann, *Mission, Church and State Relations in South West Africa Under German Rule (1884–1915)* (Stuttgart: Steiner, 1999), 212. See Winfried Baumgart, *Imperialism: The Idea and Reality of British and French Colonial Expansion* (Oxford: Oxford University Press, 1983), 115. "Anregungen zur Selbstverwaltungsfrage," *Lüderitzbuchter Zeitung,* December 18, 1909. Cf. Protocol of meeting between Solf, Seitz, Hintrager, et al., July 15, 1912, BAB R1001/2087.

54. Grohmann, *Exotische Verfassung,* 205–206. Cf. Bley, *Kolonialherrschaft,* 223–239.

55. Anonymous, "Südwestafrikaner," *Zeitschrift für Kolonialpolitik, Kolonialrecht und Kolonialwirtschaft* 12 (Berlin, 1910), 385–386. See Woodruff Smith, *German Colonial Empire* (Chapel Hill: UNC Press, 1978), 167; Woodruff Smith, *Ideological Origins of Nazi Imperialism* (Oxford: Oxford University Press, 1989), 128.

56. Schuckmann to Dernburg, May 18, 1909, BAB R1001/1397. F. Bertie to E. Grey, December 1, 1909, UKNA FO 800/51. "Landesverräter," *Königsberger Allgemeine Zeitung,* August 27, 1910.

57. Otto Mathies, *Beschränkungen der Gewerbe- und Handelsfreiheit* (Hamburg: Friederichsen, 1916), 122. "Bringing the attention," see Erzberger to Reichstag, March 2, 1909, *Stenographische Berichte,* 7277. Gerstenhauer, "Südwestafrikanische Diamantenpolitik," 175.

58. Paul Rohrbach, *Dernburg und die Südwestafrikaner* (Berlin: Kolonialverlag, 1911), 66. "Deutsche Kolonialgesellschaft für Südwestafrika," *Berliner Börsen-Courier,* February 19, 1909. "Dernburg Accused," *New York Times,* January 21, 1910.

59. Kenneth D. Barkin, *The Controversy Over German Industrialization 1890–1902* (Chicago: University of Chicago Press, 1970), 150. David Blackbourn and Geoff Eley, *Peculiarities of German History* (Oxford: Oxford University Press, 1984), 114. US Department of Commerce, *Commercial Organizations in Germany* (Washington, DC: Government Printing Office, 1914), 25. "Dernburgs Rücktritt," *Hamburger Fremdenblatt,* June 9, 1910. Max Warburg to Dernburg, September 4, 1909, BAK N1130/36.

60. Control of board seats, see Morten Reitmayer, *Bankiers* (Göttingen, 2011), 60–61. See Dolores Augustine, "The Banker in German Society," 162. Rudolf Martin, *Jahrbuch des Vermögens und Einkommens der Millionäre in der Provinz Brandenburg* (Berlin: Rudolf Martin, 1913), 49. Bernhard Dernburg, "Erlebnisse," *8Uhr-Abendblatt,* May 2, 1929. Adolf Wermuth, *Beamtenleben* (Berlin: Scherl, 1922), 283.

61. Compare Birthe Kundrus, *Moderne Imperialisten* (Köln: Böhlau, 2003), 180. "Diamantenregie," *Berliner Tageblatt,* May 13, 1911. Lenzen, *History of Diamond Production,* 163.

62. Wilhelm Regendanz, "Diamantenregie (II)," *Koloniale Rundschau* (1911), 299–302. Rolf Lüke, *Handels-Gesellschaft* (Berlin: Hartmann, 1956), 133. Fürstenberg to Helfferich, May 11, 1909, HID, Archives of Deutsche Bank Zentrale Berlin, Sekretariat (Frankfurt), S097.

6. Labor

1. Loftis Bros. & Co., *Some Interesting Facts About Diamonds* (Chicago, 1904), 1–2, UCSB, Lawrence B. Romaine Trade Catalogue Collection (Mss 107), Series 1, Subseries A, Box 8.

2. "General v. Trothas Rechtfertigung," *Berliner Tageblatt,* February 5, 1909. Max Warnack, *Die Bedeutung kolonialer Eigenproduktion für die deutsche Volkswirtschaft* (Berlin: Kolonial-Wirtschaftliches Komitee, 1926), 8. Milton S. J. Wright, *Die Wirtschaftsentwicklung und die Eingeborenenpolitik in den ehemaligen afrikanischen Schutzgebieten Deutschlands von 1884 bis 1918* (Wertheim am Main: Bechstein, 1932), 13. See Oberstabsarzt Mankiewitz, *Kohlstocks Ratgeber für die Tropen* (Stettin: Hermann Peters, 1910), 49. Compare Karl Helfferich, *Deutschlands Volkswohlstand 1888–1913* (Berlin: Stilke, 1914), 82. See Juhani Koponen, *Development for Exploitation* (Helsinki: Tiedekirja, 1994), 669.

3. Cf. Tilman Dedering, "German-Herero War," *Journal of Southern African Studies* 19, no. 1 (1993): 80; Horst Gründer, "Feind überall," *Historische Zeitschrift* 273 (2001): 802. "The peace of the graveyard," see Horst Drechsler, *'Let Us Die Fighting': The Struggle of the Herero and Nama Against German Imperialism, 1884–1915* (London: Zed, 1980), 214, 231. Union of South Africa, *Report on the Natives of South-West Africa and their Treatment by Germany* (London, 1918), 140.

4. Dernburg to Wilhelm II, December 22, 1908, BAB R1001/1341. Wilhelm von Humboldt-Dachroeden, *Diamantenpolitik* (Jena: Fischer, 1915), 27. "Arbeiterbeschaffung," *Deutsch-Südwestafrikanische Zeitung,* December 3, 1910. Protocol of Dernburg's meeting, August 12, 1908, BAB R1001/2086. Hintrager's decree, February 15, 1909, BAB R1001/2040. Hubert Henoch, "Tagung des Deutsch-Südwestafrikanischen Landesrats," *Zeitschrift für Kolonialpolitik, Kolonialrecht und Kolonialwirtschaft,* no. 9 (1912), 674. See Jürgen Zimmerer, *Deutsche Herrschaft über Afrikaner* (Münster: LIT, 2004), 269–283.

5. "Property," see G. Glockemeier to Deutsche Diamanten-Gesellschaft, June 2, 1915, BAB R1001/1396; "Diamantfunde," *Frankfurter Zeitung*, December 31, 1908. See Gesine Krüger, *Kriegsbewältigung und Geschichtsbewußtsein* (Göttingen: Vandenhoeck & Ruprecht, 1999), 143. See also Philipp Prein, "Guns," *Journal of Southern African Studies* 20, no. 1 (March 1994): 99–121. Charles Dawbarn, *My South African Year* (London: Mills & Boon, 1921), 149. Carl Uhlig, "Der südafrikanische Bundesstaat und Deutsch-Südwestafrika," *Geographische Zeitschrift* 21, no. 4 (1915): 222. "Goldshares," *Frankfurter Zeitung*, April 24, 1912.

6. "Deutsche Kolonialgesellschaft für Südwestafrika," *Frankfurter Zeitung*, September 4, 1911. Wilhelm Külz, "Arbeiternot," *Deutsche Kolonialzeitung* 28, no. 17 (1911): 281. Otto Jöhlinger, "Kolonialwirtschaft," *Koloniale Rundschau* (1913), 50. Robert Gordon, *The Bushman Myth* (Boulder: Westview, 1992), 72.

7. See Ulrike Lindner, *Koloniale Begegnungen* (Frankfurt: Campus, 2011), 385–408. See Jürgen Osterhammel, *Die Verwandlung der Welt* (Munich, 2010), 229. See Charles van Onselen, *Chibaro* (London: Pluto Press, 1976). See Colin Bundy, "Rhodes," in *Hidden Struggles*, eds. William Beinart and Colin Bundy (Johannesburg: Ravan, 1987), 138–165.

8. German consulate at Johannesburg to Bethmann Hollweg, February 27, 1912, BAB R901/787. See Vivian Bickford-Smith, *Emergence of the South African Metropolis* (Cambridge: Cambridge University Press, 2016), 112. "Deutsche Arbeiter in deutschen Kolonien," *Alldeutsche Blätter* 19, no. 13 (1909): 111.

9. H. A. Lerchen to Baron von Humboldt-Dachroeden, July 19, 1912, BAB R1001/1232. Cf. Hartmut Pogge von Strandmann, ed., *Walther Rathenau: Industrialist, Banker, Intellectual, and Politician: Notes and Diaries 1907–1922* (Oxford: Clarendon, 1985), 69. Alex La Guma, *Jimmy La Guma* (Cape Town: South African Library, 1997), 10–21. German consulate at Johannesburg to Bethmann Hollweg, February 27, 1912, BAB R901/787.

10. Female wages taken from Leonore Niessen-Deiters, *Die deutsche Frau* (Berlin: Fleischel, 1913), 62. Compare wages cited in Reichsstelle für das Auswanderungswesen to Eduard Grosser, April 25, 1910, BAB R1505/10. "From a well-informed source," see "Ovambohn," *Deutsch-Südwestafrikanische Zeitung*, October 27, 1909. "Zur Arbeiterfrage," *Deutsch-Südwestafrikanische Zeitung*, October 20, 1909. Birthe Kundrus, *Moderne Imperialisten* (Köln: Böhlau, 2003), 116–117.

11. "Sitzung des Landesrates," *Windhuker Nachrichten*, May 4, 1910. Cf. Alfred Mansfeld, ed., *Englische Urteile über die deutsche Kolonisationsarbeit* (Berlin: Reimer, 1919), 6. See Norbert Aas and Harald Sippel, *Koloniale Konflikte im Alltag* (Bayreuth: Breitinger, 1997), 66.

12. Curt Pasel to Koloniale Bergbau-Gesellschaft, June 1, 1909, BAB R1001/1343. See William Beinart, "Cape Workers in German South-West Africa, 1904–1912," *Societies of Southern Africa in the 19th and 20th Centuries: Collected Seminar Papers*, 27 (London, Institute of Commonwealth Studies, 1981), 48–65. See Zimmerer, *Deutsche Herrschaft*, 228–229. Meyer-Gerhard's report, December 9, 1912, BAB R1001/2162.

13. Cf. Betriebskonsortium Bachstein-Koppel to RKA, November 2, 1910, BAB R1001/1230. See marginalia of Bezirksamt Swakopmund to RKA, October 27, 1910, BAB R1001/1230. "Asiatic Labour," *Rand Daily Mail*, July 30, 1912. Richard von Kühlmann to Bethmann Hollweg, May 1, 1912, BAB R1001/1232. Ulrike Lindner, "Indentured Labour in Sub-Saharan Africa (1880–1918): Circulation of Concepts between Imperial Powers," in *Bonded Labour: Global and Comparative Perspectives (18th–21st Century)*, eds. Sabine Damir-Geilsdorf et al. (Bielefeld: Transcript, 2016), 59, 70–71. "Hilfskräfte," *Deutsche Kolonialzeitung* 25, no. 46 (1908): 809. Walter Moritz, *Die 'Sandwüste' hat eine Zukunft:*

Tagebuch und Zeichnungen des Malers Ernst Vollbehr 1910 (Windhoek: Werther, 1994), 17. G. Goldberg, "Diamantenabbau," *Dinglers Polytechnisches Journal* 329, no. 34/35 (Berlin: Dietze, 1914): 532–33. "Nachweisung der in den Haupt-Bergbaubezirken Preußens im II. Vierteljahre 1908 verdienten Bergarbeiterlöhne," *Zeitschrift für das Berg, Hütten- und Salinen-Wesen im Preussischen Staate* 56 (Berlin: Ernst, 1908): 74. Speech by Ludwig Quessel to Reichstag, March 8, 1913, *Stenographische Berichte*, 4417. Kurd Schwabe and Philalethes Kuhn, eds., *Taschenbuch für Südwestafrika 1908* (Leipzig: Weicher, 1907), 35.

14. "Die Ovambo," *Hamburgischer Correspondent*, July 24, 1911. Dernburg to Wilhelm II, December 22, 1908, BAB R1001/1341. Bernhard Dernburg, *Zielpunkte* (Berlin: Mittler und Sohn, 1907), 16.

15. "Aus dem Schutzgebiet," *Deutsch-Südwestafrikanische Zeitung*, February 3, 1909. German Colonial Office, *The Treatment of Native and other Populations in the Colonial Possessions of Germany and England* (Berlin: Engelmann, 1919), 110. Franz Baltzer, *Kolonialbahnen* (Berlin: Göschen, 1916), 94. Cf. "Verschiedenes," *Windhuker Nachrichten*, October 19, 1910. Seitz to RKA, April 20, 1912, BAB R1001/1232. The most comprehensive account of Ovambo migrant labor during these years is Regina Strassegger, *Die Wanderarbeit der Ovambo* (Graz: Universität Graz, 1988).

16. A. P. Walshe and Andrew Roberts, "Southern Africa," *Cambridge History of Africa*, vol. 7 (Cambridge: Cambridge University Press, 1986), 559. Compare statistics in Fritz Wege, "Anfänge," *Jahrbuch für Wirtschaftsgeschichte*, no. 1 (1969), 191. See Meredith McKittrick, *To Dwell Secure* (Portsmouth, NH: Heinemann, 2002), 275. "Botschaft aus Südwest," *Kolonialpolitische Handels-Korrespondenz*, March 9, 1909. Dernburg to Wilhelm II, December 22, 1908, BAB R1001/1341.

17. See Hermann Tönjes, *Ovamboland* (Berlin, 1911), 108–132. See Randolph Vigne, "Moveable Frontier," in *Namibia under South African Rule*, ed. Patricia Hayes et al. (Oxford: James Currey, 1998), 289–304. Martti Eirola, *The Ovambogefahr* (Rovaniemi: Ponjois-Suomen Historiallinen Yhdistys, 1992), 222–240.

18. "Die sieben Tage," *Die Woche* 10, no. 29 (Berlin: Scherl, 1908): 1235. Dernburg to Schuckmann, February 27, 1909, NAN, BGR F.9.b. "Was wird aus der Ovambofrage?" *Deutsch-Südwestafrikanische Zeitung*, December 9, 1908. R.J. Gordon, "Variations in Migration Rates: The Ovambo Case," *Journal of Southern African Studies* 3 (1978): 273. For a comparison with South Africa, see Patrick Harries, *Work, Culture, and Identity: Migrant Laborers in Mozambique and South Africa, c. 1860–1910* (Portsmouth, NH: Heinemann, 1994). "Die Ovambo," *Hamburgischer Correspondent*, July 24, 1911. Eirola, *Ovambogefahr*, 273–274. Cf. "Deutsche Kolonialgesellschaft," *Frankfurter Zeitung*, September 4, 1911.

19. "Bergbau," *Glückauf* 49, no. 10 (Essen, 1913): 366. W. G. Clarence-Smith and Richard Moorsom, "Underdevelopment," in *Roots of Rural Poverty*, eds. Robin Palmer et al. (Berkeley: University of California Press, 1977), 107. Eirola, *Ovambogefahr*, 135, 137. "Native Location" mentioned in Gysbert Hofmeyr to Jan Smuts, June 18, 1923, *Marcus Garvey and Universal Negro Improvement Association Papers*, ed. Robert Hill, vol. 10 (Berkeley: University of California Press, 2006), 82. "Lüderitzbucht," *Diamond Fields Advertiser*, November 25, 1908.

20. Jan-Bart Gewald, "Near Death in the Streets of Karibib," *Journal of African History* 44, no. 2 (2003): 211–239. Johannes Paul, "Wirtschaft," *Wissenschaftliche Veröffentlichungen des Museums für Länderkunde zu Leipzig* (1933), 101. "Bergbau," *Glückauf* 49, no. 10 (Essen, 1913): 366.

21. Dörte Lerp, *Imperiale Grenzräume* (Frankfurt: Campus, 2016), 138. Otavi Minen-Gesellschaft to Schuckmann, December 20, 1909, NAN ZBU 2064, W.IV.h.2. Woermann & Co. to Wellmann, July 5, 1910, NAN ZBU 2064, W.IV.h.1. See also Pasel to Böhmer, July 1, 1910, NAN ZBU 2061, W.IV.h.1. Resident Commissioner in Ovamboland to Secre-

tary of the Protectorate, September 24, 1917, NAN RCO [2] 2/1916/1. District Officer at Outjo to Government in Windhoek, July 29, 1914, NAN ZBU [2066] W.IV.h.13, "Regelung des Nachlasses verstorbener Ovambo."

22. On six-month stints: Zimmerer, *Deutsche Herrschaft*, 211–238. Otavi Minen-Gesellschaft to Schuckmann, December 20, 1909, NAN ZBU 2064, W.IV.h.2. Compare Lerp, *Grenzräume*, 138. District Officer at Outjo to Schuckmann, January 19, 1910, NAN ZBU 2064, W.IV.h.2.

23. Alfred Henke's address to Reichstag, March 20, 1914, *Stenographische Berichte*, 8154. Otavi Gesellschaft to Governor of SWA, August 26, 1911, NAN ZBU 2065, W.IV.h.7. Hannus Haahtz to Theodor Seitz, January 27, 1912, NAN ZBU 2073, W.IV.n.2.

24. Südwestafrikanische Bodenkredit-Gesellschaft to Rechnungsrat Hintze, March 2, 1914, BAB R1001/6427. Hanno Haahti to Seitz, January 27, 1912, BAB R1001/1231. "Arbeiternot," *Deutsche Kolonialzeitung* 28, no. 17 (1911): 283. Cf. "Die Ovambo," *Hamburgischer Correspondent,* July 24, 1911.

25. See Strassegger, *Wanderarbeit*, 85–100. Baltzer, *Kolonialbahnen*, 94. Cf. "Deutsche Kolonialgesellschaft," *Frankfurter Zeitung*, September 4, 1911.

26. See Zimmerer, *Deutsche Herrschaft*, 219–228. "Versammlung der Lüderitzbuchter Minenkammer," *Lüderitzbuchter Zeitung*, August 20, 1910. "Deutsche Schutzgebiete," *Hamburger Nachrichten*, October 1, 1910.

27. Cf. A. P. J. Beris, *Making the Desert Bloom*, vol. 1 (Windhoek: Diocese of Keetmanshoop, 2001), 151. "The Diamond Way," *Louisville Courier-Journal*, April 2, 1911. Hermann Tönjes' report, February 14, 1912, NAN ZBU 2079, W.IV.V.2. Cf. Hermann Freyberg, *Diamanten in der Namib* (Kempen: Thomas, 1943), 208–209. "Scherer: Über Skorbut," *Centralblatt für Bakteriologie, Parasitenkunde und Infektionskrankheiten, Erste Abteilung* 58 (Jena, 1913): 540. Cf. Ian Phimister and Charles van Onselen, *Studies in the History of African Mine Labour* (Gwelo: Mambo, 1978), 125. "A lot of coughing," see Peter Conze's report, October 12, 1909, BAB R1001/1500.

28. Strassegger, *Wanderarbeit*, 132. Erich Kaiser and Werner Beetz, "Wassererschließung," *Zeitschrift für praktische Geologie* 27, no. 12 (1919): 188. G. Nachtigall, "Bedeutung des Bodens in der Hygiene," in *Die Technische Ausnutzung des Bodens,* eds. F. Giesecke et al. (Heidelberg: Springer, 1932), 230. Richard Pfalz, *Hydrologie der deutschen Kolonien in Afrika* (Berlin: Reimer, 1944), 83. Strassegger, *Wanderarbeit*, 130.

29. See Charlotte Cameron, *A Woman's Winter in Africa* (London: Stanley Paul & Co., 1913), 223–230. Report of Brenner, July 1913, NAN ZBU 2079, Überwachung und Revisionen der Eingeborenen-Arbeiter-Verhältnisse, 1911–1914, v.1–2. Seitz to Solf, March 26, 1912, BAB N1053/134.

30. Zimmerer, *Deutsche Herrschaft,* 227. Strassegger, *Wanderarbeit,* 145–162. "Bereisung des Ambolandes Juli bis August 1912," c. September 11, 1912, BAB R1001/2162. Kurd Schwabe, *Im Diamantenlande,* 421. "Quickly," see Hermann Tönjes' report, February 14, 1912, NAN ZBU 2079, W.IV.V.2.

31. Reichskolonialamt, *Schutzgebiete in Afrika und der Südsee 1910/1911: Amtliche Jahresberichte* (Berlin, 1912), 111, 128. Reichskolonialamt, *Die Behandlung der einheimischen Bevölkerung in den kolonialen Besitzungen Deutschlands* (Berlin: Engelmann, 1919), 64. "Most precious resource," see Otto Peiper, "Tuberkulinreaktion," *Beihefte zum Archiv für Schiffs- und Tropenhygiene* 15, no. 1 (Leipzig: Barth, 1911): 23. "Too valuable," see "Koloniale Rundschau," *Die Grenzboten* 67 (1908): 395. Cf. "Deutsche Schutzgebiete," *Hamburger Nachrichten*, October 1, 1910. See German Colonial Office, *Treatment of Native and other Populations* (Berlin: Engelmann, 1919), 111. Compare Goldberg, "Diamantenabbau," 532–533.

32. More information in NAN Berzirksamt Lüderitzbucht BLU [168] O.7.a vol.1–3; and ZBU [2066] W.IV.h.13. Compare W. S. Rayner, *Botha and Smuts* (London: Simpkin, 1916), 65. Protocol of meeting between Solf, Seitz, Hintrager et al., July 15, 1912, BAB R1001/2087. Charles Berndes to RKA, August 27, 1910, BAB R1001/2162.

33. Solf's diary entry, June 20, 1912, BAK N1053/36. See Lüderitzbuchter Minenkammer to Kaiserliches Gouvernement Windhuk, June 18, 1912, NAN Zentralbureau des Kaiserlichen Gouvernements Windhuk W III R 2 Bd. 1 Bl. 116a–117a. Figures from Jöhlinger, "Rundschau," *Koloniale Rundschau, Jahrgang 1914* (Berlin, 1914), 317. Strassegger, *Wanderarbeit,* 142–143.

34. Kolmanskop and Phoenix Diamond statistics, see Meyer-Gerhard report, December 9, 1912, BAB R1001/2162. "A policy of extermination," see Isabel Hull, *Absolute Destruction* (Ithaca: Cornell University Press, 2005), 187. "'Ombepera i koza—Die Kälte tötet mich,'" Joachim Zeller, *Völkermord in Deutsch-Südwestafrika,* eds. Jürgen Zimmerer and Joachim Zeller (Berlin: Links, 2016), 76.

35. "Know their rights," see "Zur Arbeiterfrage," *Deutsch-Südwestafrikanische Zeitung,* October 20, 1909. "Truly high," see Hintrager to Solf, November 22, 1912, BAB R1001/2162. Cf. Heiligbrunner to the Kaiserliches Gouvernement Windhuk, June 14, 1911, Union of South Africa, *Report on the natives of South-west Africa and their treatment by Germany* (London: His Majesty's Stationery Office, 1918), 204. Kaiserliches Gouvernement Windhuk to Lüderitzbuchter Minenkammer, May 25, 1912, NAN, Zentralbureau des Kaiserlichen Gouvernements Windhuk, W.III.R.2 Bd. 1, Bl. 112a–113a. "Diamond sorters," see Rudolf Boehmer to Kaiserliches Gouvernement Windhuk, April 21, 1913, printed in Jerermy Silvester and Jan-Bart Gewald, *Words Cannot Be Found: German Colonial Rule in Namibia: An Annotated Reprint of the 1918 Blue Book* (Brill: Leiden, 2003), 340. Bezirksamt Lüderitzbucht to Kaiserliches Gouvernement Windhuk, July 25, 1913, NAN ZBU Geheimakten, VII.m, Bd. 1, Bl. 4.

36. On Ovambo laws in 1910: Decree of August 17, 1910, NAN ZBU 2064, W.IV.h.1. Decree of German colonial governor, effective 16 December 1911, printed in Kaiserliches Gouvernement in Windhuk, *Amtsblatt für das Schutzgebiet Deutsch-Südwestafrika,* vol. 3, no. 1 (Windhuk: Windhuker Druckerei, 1913), 2–4. See Wege, "Anfänge," 188.

37. "A certain right to punish," see "Versammlung der Lüderitzbuchter Minenkammer," *Lüderitzbuchter Zeitung,* August 20, 1910. See Benjamin Madley, "From Africa," *European History Quarterly* 35, no. 3 (2005): 437. Cf. Jan-Georg Deutsch, *Emancipation without Abolition in German East Africa* (Athens, OH: Ohio University Press, 2006). Max Ewald Baericke, *Lüderitzbucht: Historische Erinnerungen eines alten Diamantensuchers* (Windhoek: Namibia Wissenschaftliche Gesellschaft, 2001), 138.

38. "Koloniales," *Deutsche Tageszeitung,* May 6, 1911. Böhmer's report, April 1919, BAB R1001/9651. Helmut Bley, *Kolonialherrschaft* (Hamburg: Leibniz, 1968), 296. Acting magistrate Heilingbrunner to Governor of SWA, June 14, 1911, *Parliamentary Papers, House of Commons: Session 12 February 1918–21 November 1918,* vol. 17 (London, 1918), 161. "Koloniales," *Tägliche Rundschau* (Berlin), December 14, 1909. On corporal punishment, see Ralf Schlottau, *Deutsche Kolonialrechtspflege* (Frankfurt: Peter Lang, 2007). Bahnfelder Diamantengesellschaft to Lüderitzbuchter Minenkammer, October 12 and 26, 1912, NAN ZBU 2063, W.IV.f.2.

39. "Addicted to gossip," see Rechtsanwalt Traumann to Bethmann Hollweg, April 19, 1911, BAB R1001/4847. "Utterly useless," see Boehmer to Kaiserliches Gouvernement Windhuk, April 21, 1913, printed in Silvester and Gewald, *Words Cannot Be Found,* 340. Wilhelm Külz's protocol, August 12, 1908, BAB R1001/4760. "Meant very little," see Seitz to Colonial Office, July 31, 1911, BAB R1001/4847.

40. "Die Ovambo als Arbeiter," *Berliner Tageblatt,* July 28, 1911. Lüderitzbuchter Minenkammer to Solf, August 3, 1912, BAK R1053/34. Cf. Beris, *Making the Desert Bloom,* 151.

41. Hermann Tönjes to Governor of SWA, October 31, 1912, NAN ZBU 2063, W.IV.f.2.

42. Attachment in Seitz to Colonial Office, October 17, 1911, BAB R1001/5553. On wage: Reichsstelle für das Auswanderungswesen to Eduard Grosser, April 25, 1910, BAB R1505/10. Juvera was kept outside the courtroom throughout the trial and only allowed to enter when the judge summarized the verdict for him through an interpreter. Kaiserlicher Gouverneur von SWA to Redaktion der Täglichen Rundschau, Berlin, August 28, 1911, BAB R1001/5553. "Koloniale Neuigkeiten," *Kolonie und Heimat* 4, no. 45 (Berlin, 1910): 17. "Not know the conditions," see Boehmer to Kaiserliches Gouvernement Windhuk, April 21, 1913, printed in Silvester and Gewald, *Words Cannot Be Found,* 340.

43. See Marie Muschalek, *Violence as Usual* (Ithaca: Cornell University Press, 2019). Hull, *Absolute Destruction,* 65–66, 86–87.

44. 'Mißhandlung von Eingeborenen durch Weiße', NAN Specialia, Zentralbureau des Kaiserlichen Gouvernements Windhuk 2054, WIIr2, Bd.1, Bl. 68. Humboldt-Dachroeden, *Diamantenpolitik,* 75. Bezirksamt Lüderitzbucht to Kaiserliches Gouvernement Windhuk, June 6, 1913, NAN, Zentralbureau des Kaiserlichen Gouvernements Windhuk, W.III.R.2. Bd. 1, Bl. 169a–170b. Egon Freiherr von Dalwigk zu Lichtenfels, *Dernburgs Amtliche Tätigkeit* (Berlin: Reimer, 1911), 12. Hermann Tönjes' report, October 31, 1912, NAN ZBU 2063, W.IV.f.2. Angelo Golinelli to Schuckmann, November 27, 1909; Rudolf Böhmer to Imperial Mining Office, March 15, 1909, BAB R1001/1324. Bezirksamt Lüderitzbucht to Kaiserliches Gouvernement Windhuk, April 21, 1913, NAN, Zentralbureau des Kaiserlichen Gouvernements Windhuk, W.III.R.2. Bd. 1, Bl. 156a–159a. See Strassegger, *Wanderarbeit,* 114–117.

45. Ernest Oppenheimer and Alpheus F. Williams, *Diamond Deposits of German South West Africa* (Kimberley, 1914), 13. Cf. Baltzer, *Kolonialbahnen,* 94.

46. Jakob Zollmann, "Communicating Colonial Order," *Crime, Histoire & Sociétés* 15, no. 1 (2011): 35, 36–37, 39n33. "Madness for control," see Krüger, *Kriegsbewältigung,* 144.

47. "Bergbau," *Glückauf* 49, no. 10 (Essen, 1913): 366. See David Blackbourn, "Das Kaiserreich transnational: eine Skizze," in *Das Kaiserreich transnational: Deutschland in der Welt 1871–1914,* eds. Sebastian Conrad and Jürgen Osterhammel (Göttingen: V&R, 2006), 303. See Andreas Eckert, "Verheißungen," in *Die Grenzen der Zivilisierungsmissionen,* eds. Boris Barth and Jürgen Osterhammel (Konstanz: UVK Verlag, 2005), 269. "Schizophrenic nature," see Jeffrey Herbst, *States and Power in Africa* (Princeton: Princeton University Press, 2000), 58, 90.

48. Kleinwächter (1883), quoted in translation in Erich Maschke, "Outline of the History of German Cartels from 1873 to 1914," in *Essays in European Economic History,* eds. F. Crouzet et al. (London: St. Martin's, 1969), 238.

49. Compare Günther Karl Anton, "Diamantenpolitik," *Koloniale Rundschau,* March 1910, 129–161, 146. "Everything else," see Lüderitzbuchter Minenkammer to Bezirksamt Lüderitzbucht, May 11, 1912, NAN, ZBU Windhuk, W.III.R.2. Bd. 1, Bl. 67a–68a.

50. "Deutscher Reichstag," *Neue Hamburger Zeitung,* March 9, 1913. "Fade away," see Adolf Damaschke, *Geschichte der Nationalökonomie* (Jena: Fischer, 1909), 402. Werner Schiefel, *Dernburg 1865–1937* (Zürich: Atlantis, 1974), 131. Cf. "Deutsche Kolonialgesellschaft für Südwestafrika," *Berliner Börsen-Courier,* February 11, 1910. "Rechtsverhältnisse," *Berliner Börsen-Courier,* February 15, 1910. Cf. "Bergrechte," *Berliner Börsen-*

Courier, February 9 and 15, 1910. Carl Peters, "Kolonialkonzessionen," *Der Tag,* October 30, 1906. Dernburg to Schuckmann, November 27, 1909, BAB R1001/1324. "Die Bergrechte der Kolonialgesellschaft," *Neue Hamburgische Börsen-Halle,* January 30, 1910. Cf. "Zwanzigmeilen-Streifen," *Lüderitzbuchter Zeitung,* December 23, 1911.

51. "Dernburgs südwestafrikanische Politik," *Alldeutsche Blätter* 20, no. 21 (1910): 173–176. Dernburg to Schuckmann, June 6, 1910, BAB R1001/1326. Unsigned RKA memo of November 16, 1911, BAB R1001/1940.

52. Kaiserlicher Gouverneur to RKA, April 26, 1910, BAB R1001/2064. Otto Jöhlinger to Dernburg, January 16, 1910, BAK N1130/36. "Increasingly mountainous literature," see Karl Radek, "Literarische Rundschau," *Die neue Zeit* 30, no. 32 (1912): 213. *Berliner Börsen Courier* to Dernburg, January 21, 1909, BAB R1001/1662.

7. Stocks

1. "Investment grade," see Herbert Beckerath, *Kapitalmarkt und Geldmarkt* (Jena: Fischer, 1916), 154. "Berliner Börsenverkehr in Kolonialwerten," *Frankfurter Zeitung,* January 29, 1909. Pluto, "Finanzpolitisches," *Morgen: Wochenschrift für deutsche Kultur,* July 1, 1909, 902. Oskar Geck's speech to Reichstag, November 14, 1911, *Stenographische Berichte,* 7848. "Kaffirs," see Hugo Lustig, *Südafrikanische Minenwerte* (Berlin: Minenverlag, 1909), 749. Alfred Schirmer, *Kaufmannssprache* (Leipzig: Gloeckner, 1925), 88.

2. Compare Andreas Eckert, *Grundbesitz, Landkonflikte und kolonialer Wandel* (Stuttgart: Steiner, 1999), 74. Hjalmar Schacht, "Kapitalbeschaffung," *Verhandlungen des Deutschen Kolonialkongresses 1910* (Berlin, 1910), 1160. See Boris Barth, *Die deutsche Hochfinanz und die Imperialismen* (Stuttgart: Steiner, 1995), 64. Arthur Raffalovich, "Les Colonies," *L'Économiste Français* 34, no. 37 (Paris, 1906), 379. John S. Galbraith, *Mackinnon and East Africa* (Cambridge: Cambridge University Press, 1972), 9. "Die Kolonialgesellschaften," *Berliner Börsen-Courier,* February 23, 1909. "Unsere afrikanischen Colonien," *Leipziger Neueste Nachrichten,* November 13, 1900. "Kolonialwerte," *Berliner Tageblatt,* November 8, 1906. Dernburg to Dr. Friedrich, February 9, 1909, BAK N1130/32. "Kolonialwerte," *Neue Hamburger Zeitung,* November 2, 1906.

3. Schacht, "Kapitalbeschaffung," 1154–1161. "Otavi," *Allgemeine Zeitung* (Munich), July 17, 1909. Cf. "Spekulation in Kolonial-Werten," *Frankfurter Zeitung,* February 5, 1909.

4. Raghuram Rajan et al., "Reversals," *Journal of Financial Economics* 69, no. 1 (2003): 17. Konrad Mellerowicz, *Kapitalverkehr* (Wiesbaden: Gabler, 1950), 52. Cf. Berliner Handelsgesellschaft to Deutsche Bank, January 29, 1909, HID, Archives of Deutsche Bank Zentrale Berlin, Sekretariat (Frankfurt), S096; "Conceptionsbuch Diamanten-Gesellschaft," *Frankfurter Zeitung,* January 10, 1911.

5. "Kolonialwerte," *Berliner Tageblatt,* November 8, 1906. "Kolonial-Werte," *Der Kolonial-Courier (Beilage des Berliner Börsen-Courier),* January 19, 1909. Arthur Norden, "Wochenschau," *Berliner Tageblatt,* February 26, 1910.

6. "Kolonialwerte," *Deutsches Kolonialblatt* 18 (Berlin: Mittler, 1907): 788. "Berliner Börsenverkehr in Kolonialwerten," *Frankfurter Zeitung,* January 29, 1909.

7. Gottfried Zoepfl, "Koloniales Börsenwesen," *Deutsches Kolonial-Lexikon* 2 (1920): 327. Cf. "Berliner Börsenverkehr in Kolonialwerten," *Frankfurter Zeitung,* January 29, 1909. "Zur Organisation der Deutschen Diamantenproduktion," *Frankfurter Zeitung,* March 16, 1909. Cf. Die Ältesten der Kaufmannschaft von Berlin, *Berliner Jahrbuch für Handel und Industrie,* vol. 1 (Berlin: Reimer, 1910), 281.

8. Calmann to Berliner Handelsgesellschaft, January 6, 1913, BAB R8127/14155. For example, see Leopold Hamburger (Banking House) to RKA, July 24, 1909, BAB R1001/1528.

9. "Handelskammer Windhuk," *Berliner Börsen-Courier,* May 30, 1911. E. Lübbert to Berliner Handelsgesellschaft, December 27, 1912, R8127/14155. "Local," see advertisements for "Edmund Rust" and "Friedr. Knacke," *Adreßbuch für Stadt und Bezirk Lüderitzbucht 1914* (Leipzig: Koehler, 1914), 68, 73.

10. Otto Köbner, *Organisation der Rechtspflege* (Berlin: Mittler, 1903), 2. Bankhaus Heinrich Emden & Co., "Kolonialwerten," in *Koloniale Zeitschrift,* ed. A. Herfurth, vol. 8 (Berlin, 1907), 17. Hugo Linschmann, *Reichsfinanzreform* (Berlin: Nagel, 1909), 123.

11. On colonial uncertainty, see Zollmann, "German Colonial Law," 264. Matthias Deeken, *Geldwesen* (Münster: Vereinsdruckerei, 1913), 20. Eugen Fischer, "Deutsch-Südwestafrika," *Tägliche Rundschau,* April 3, 1909. H. A. Behrens, "Kreditverhältnisse," *Taschenbuch für Südwestafrika,* eds. Philalethes Kuhn and Kurd Schwabe (Leipzig: Weicher, 1908), 78.

12. "Börsenspiel," *Der Tag,* March 1, 1910. Siegfried Wolff, *Gründungsgeschäft* (Stuttgart: Cotta, 1915), 200. "Spekulation in Kolonial-Werten," *Frankfurter Zeitung,* February 5, 1909.

13. "Kolonialfieber," *Berliner Volkszeitung,* June 22, 1909. "Deutsche Kolonialgesellschaft für Südwestafrika," *Frankfurter Zeitung,* May 22, 1909, and August 24, 1910. Figure of 410 percent, see Regierungskommissar Fischer's report, September 29, 1910, BAB R1001/1535. Figure of 500 percent, see "Zur Abwehr-Aktion," *Frankfurter Zeitung,* February 9, 1909.

14. Figure of 2020 percent, see "Börsen- und Handelsteil," *Dresdner Nachrichten,* June 19, 1909. "Kolonialfieber," *Berliner Volkszeitung,* June 22, 1909. For values, see Artur Nap, "Diamanten," *Das Freie Wort,* vol. 11 (Frankfurt am Main: Neuer Frankfurter Verlag, 1912), 871.

15. Arthur Norden, "Wochenschau," *Berliner Tageblatt,* February 26, 1910. Thirty million pounds sterling, see Deutsche Kolonialgesellschaft to Deutsche Bank, May 14, 1909, HID, Archives of Deutsche Bank Zentrale Berlin, Sekretariat (Frankfurt), S0103. Hintrager to RKA, December 29, 1908, BAB R1001/1341. For market capitalization, see "Der Kolonial-Courier," *Berliner Börsen-Courier,* May 25, 1909. One billion, see Natty Rothschild to Rothschild Cousins, Paris, July 5, 1909, RAL XI/130A/3/119. "Gobsmacked," see Carl Weiss to Rudolf von Bennigsen Jr., February 15, 1909, BAB R1001/1529. Compare data in Ken Post, *Revolution and the European Experience* (New York: St. Martin's Press, 1999), 125; Rudolf Martin, *Unter dem Scheinwerfer* (Berlin: Schuster, 1910), 26–27; Rudolf Martin, *Die Zukunft Deutschlands: Eine Warnung* (Leipzig: Hirschfeld, 1908), 45.

16. "Diamond Share Speculation," *Financial Times,* May 25, 1909. "Spekulation in Kolonial-Werten," *Frankfurter Zeitung,* February 5, 1909. "Englische 'Schiebungen,'" *Leipziger Tageblatt,* September 6, 1909. "Spielpapiere," *Allgemeine Zeitung* (Munich), January 30, 1909. See Horst Drechsler, *Südwestafrika unter deutscher Kolonialherrschaft: Die großen Land- und Minengesellschaften (1885–1914)* (Stuttgart: Steiner, 1996), 273–4. Figures for South African Territories Ltd., see Norden, "Wochenschau," *Berliner Tageblatt,* February 26, 1910. "Dezember 1908," *Die Bank: Monatshefte für Finanz- u. Bankwesen* (Berlin-Charlottenburg, 1909), 46. "Kolonialschätze und Kolonialspekulation," *Frankfurter Zeitung,* August 30, 1909.

17. Die Ältesten der Kaufmannschaft von Berlin, *Berliner Jahrbuch für Handel und Industrie,* vol. 1 (Berlin: Reimer, 1910), 280. Wernher to Hirschhorn, August 6, 1909, BW

Wernher, Beit vol. 143. See "Geschichte," *Deutsche Goldschmiede-Zeitung* 13 (1910): 140. See Wolff, *Gründungsgeschäft*, 202.

18. "Börsen-Kritik," *Plutus: Kritische Wochenschrift*, February 10, 1906, 105. For explanation of dividend, see "Deutsche Diamant-Gesellschaft," *Berliner Börsen-Courier*, November 2, 1909. For *Bergbaugesellschaft* dividends, see Matthias Erzberger, *Millionengeschenke: Die Privilegienwirtschaft in Südwestafrika* (Berlin: Germania, 1910), 71, and "Pays 2,500 Per Cent," *New York Times*, March 28, 1914.

19. W. Schmidt, *Geschichte der Deutschen Post in den Kolonien und im Ausland* (Leipzig: Konkordia, 1939), 54. Sebastian Mantei, *Entwicklungsgeschichte* (Halle: Universität Halle-Wittenberg, 2004), 155. "Greatest cut in dividends," see "Dividends Worth While," *Wall Street Journal*, May 5, 1914. "Diamantenprozess," *Berliner Tageblatt*, November 29, 1913.

20. "Deutsche Kolonialgesellschaft für Südwestafrika," *Frankfurter Zeitung*, June 19, 1909. Jöhlinger, "Rundschau," *Koloniale Rundschau, Jahrgang 1914* (Berlin, 1914), 316. "Kolonialgründungen," *Frankfurter Zeitung*, December 24, 1909. Cf. "Goerz & Co.," *Der Wächter auf dem Kapitalmarkt*, October 30, 1909, HID, Archives of Deutsche Bank Zentrale Berlin, Sekretariat (Frankfurt), S0323. Cf. "Dividendensteuer," *Zeitfragen: Wochenschrift für deutsches Leben*, December 25, 1908.

21. "Das heimische Kapital und die Schutzgebiete," *Berliner Tageblatt*, June 9, 1910. Bergisch Märkische Bank to Deutsche Bank, February 11, 1910; Deutsche Bank to Rheinische Creditbank, April 7, 1914, HID, Archives of Deutsche Bank Zentrale Berlin, Sekretariat (Frankfurt), S0103. Wolff, *Gründungsgeschäft*, 202. Arthur Norden, "Wochenschau," *Berliner Tageblatt*, February 26, 1910.

22. "Cold shower," see "Dernburgs Märchen," *Vorwärts*, February 7, 1909. "Swarm of speculators," see "Diamanten," *Der wahre Jacob* 26, no. 590 (Stuttgart: Singer, 1909); 6147. See "Hochschulkurse," *Zeitschrift für Handelswissenschaft und Handelspraxis* 2, no. 8 (Leipzig: Poeschel, 1909): 296. "German South West Africa Diamond Co.," *Frankfurter Zeitung*, August 27, 1909. "Vorsicht bei Kolonialgründungen," *Berliner Lokal-Anzeiger*, August 27, 1909.

23. For factor of four, I extrapolate on the basis of share prices for the Colonial Corporation of Southwest Africa, as reported in "Börse und Kolonien," *Vorwärts*, February 4, 1909. "Deutsche Kolonialgesellschaft für Südwestafrika," *Frankfurter Zeitung*, May 22, 1909. "Die Bedeutung und Entwicklung unserer Kolonien," January 22, 1909, BAK N1130/33. Schriftleitung der *Täglichen Rundschau* to RKA, December 31, 1908, BAB R1001/1341. "Englisch-Deutsche Kolonialgründungen," *Berliner Börsen-Courier*, August 25, 1909. Cf. "Neue Diamantfunde bei Lüderitzbucht," *Berliner Börsen-Courier*, February 12, 1909. See Robert Radu, *Auguren des Geldes* (Göttingen: V&R, 2017), 332, see generally 147. "Goerz & Co.," *Der Wächter auf dem Kapitalmarkt*, October 30, 1909, HID, Archives of Deutsche Bank Zentrale Berlin, Sekretariat (Frankfurt), S0323. Paul Rohrbach, "Diamanten," *Frankfurter Zeitung*, July 29, 1910. "Kolonialschätze und Kolonialspekulation," *Frankfurter Zeitung*, August 30, 1909; "Verbot der Preisnotierung von Kolonialwerten," *Lüderitzbuchter Zeitung*, October 23, 1909.

24. "Kolonialschätze und Kolonialspekulation," *Frankfurter Zeitung*, August 3, 1909. "Harden," *Koloniale Rundschau 1910*, no. 7 (Berlin, 1910), 443. Johann Plenge, *Von der Diskontpolitik zur Herrschaft über den Geldmarkt* (Berlin: Springer, 1913), 100. Cf. the *Effekten-Kursblatt* of the Schweizerische Kreditanstalt (Credit Suisse), December 30, 1908, BAK N1130/32. Bernhard von Bülow to Wilhelm II, July 15, 1908, *Letters of Prince von Bülow*, ed. Frederic Whyte (London: Hutchinson & Co., 1930), 250.

25. See Heinrich Graf Schlieffen, *Reichsbank* (Leipzig: Weicher, 1909), 9. "Spielpapiere," *Allgemeine Zeitung* (Munich), January 30, 1909. Cf. W. Schütze, *Strafbarkeit des*

bucket-shop-Systems (Berlin: Heymanns, 1911), 8. "Eingesandt: Von Lüderitzbucht nord-wärts," *Beilage zur Lüderitzbuchter Zeitung,* July 24, 1909. Willi Prion, *Preisbildung* (Leipzig: Duncker & Humblot, 1910), ix. "Spekulation in Kolonial-Werten," *Frankfurter Zeitung,* February 5, 1909.

26. "Diamantenfieber," *Volksstimme,* January 10, 1909. "Verkauf der Diamanten-felder," *Hamburger Nachrichten,* January 27, 1909. Egon Freiherr von Dalwigk zu Lich-tenfels, *Dernburgs amtliche Tätigkeit* (Berlin: Reimer, 1911), 11. Deutsche Bank to Julius Brabant, July 16, 1910, HID, Archives of Deutsche Bank Zentrale Berlin, Sekretariat (Frank-furt), S0103. Arthur Norden, "Wochenschau," *Berliner Tageblatt,* February 26, 1910. "Kharas Exploration," *The Economist,* August 28, 1909, 430. Judgment of July 3rd, 1918, *Entscheidungen des Reichsgerichts in Zivilsachen,* vol. 93 (Leipzig, 1918), 231. Pluto, "Fi-nanzpolitisches," *Morgen: Wochenschrift für deutsche Kultur,* May 29, 1909, 792. "Der Kolonial-Courier," *Berliner Börsen-Courier,* October 8, 1910. Cf. Deutsche Bank to Char-lotte Sprandel, May 14, 1912, HID, Archives of Deutsche Bank Zentrale Berlin, Sekretariat (Frankfurt), S0103.

27. Hugo Gerisch & Co. to Lindequist, September 15, 1910, September 19, 1910, BAB R1001/1529. "Der südwestafrikanische Nachtragsetat," *Berliner Tageblatt,* Jan-uary 26, 1910. "Spekulation in Kolonial-Werten," *Frankfurter Zeitung,* February 5, 1909. "Wirtschaftliches aus Deutsch-Südwestafrika," *Frankfurter Zeitung,* August 9, 1909.

28. "Handelskammer Windhuk," *Berliner Börsen-Courier,* May 30, 1911. RKA to Rosenbaum and Wolf (Hamburg), June 25, 1909, BAB R1001/6427. Cf. "Telegraphischer Kursbericht," *Deutsch-Südwestafrikanische Zeitung,* May 12, 1909. "Telegraphischer Kursbericht," *Lüderitzbuchter Zeitung,* October 30, 1909.

29. Founding of companies, see "Kolonialgründungen," *Der Tag,* August 24, 1909; Otto Jöhlinger, *Die wirtschaftliche Bedeutung unserer Kolonien* (Berlin: Reimer, 1910), 114; "Kapital und die Schutzgebiete," *Berliner Tageblatt,* June 9, 1910. "Three men," see Eugen Hobein, *Ungeschminktes Afrika* (Essen: Verlagsanstalt, 1938), 145. Cf. "Wirtschaftli-ches aus Deutsch-Südwestafrika," *Frankfurter Zeitung,* August 9, 1909. "Nearly every day," see "German South West Africa Diamond Co.," *Frankfurter Zeitung,* August 27, 1909. "Founding fever," see Otto Warburg, "A. Poskin," *Der Tropenpflanzer* 4 (1900); 625; Catherine Coquery-Vidrovitch, *Le Congo au temps des grands compagnies concession-naires* (Paris: Mouton, 1972), 46.

30. "Die Wirtschaftskrisis in Südwest," *Deutsche Tageszeitung,* May 4, 1911.

31. See Prion, *Preisbildung,* 2–76; Heinrich Göppert, *Börsentermingeschäft* (Berlin: Springer, 1914), 52. Cf. "Deutsche Kolonialgesellschaft für Südwestafrika," *Frankfurter Zeitung,* May 26, 1909.

32. "Berliner Börsenverkehr in Kolonialwerten," *Frankfurter Zeitung,* January 29, 1909. See *Das Reichsstempelgesetz vom 15. Juli 1909* (Berlin: Springer, 1912). Jeffrey Fear and Daniel Wadwani, "Populism," in *Business in the Age of Extremes,* eds. Hartmut Berg-hoff et al. (Cambridge: Cambridge University Press, 2013), 99. See Jonathan Levy, "Con-templating," *American Historical Review* 111 (2006): 307–335.

33. See Hermann Mauer, "Kompetenzbeschränkung," *Bank-Archiv: Zeitschrift für Bank- und Börsenwesen* 7 (Berlin: Guttentag, 1908), 120. Cf. "Handelskammer Windhuk," *Berliner Börsen-Courier,* May 30, 1911. "Kolonialschwindel," *Frankfurter Zeitung,* De-cember 9, 1909.

34. Schnee to Königliches Amtsgericht in Kiel, January 9, 1912, BAB R1001/1346. Lindequist to Theodor Seitz, Arthur Dieseldorf, August 19, 1911, BAB R1001/1346. Bes-cheinigung des Kaiserichen Bezirksrichters, November 3, 1910, BAB 1001/4918.

35. "News," see "Einer in diesen Tagen veröffentlichten Denkschrift . . ." *Berliner Börsenzeitung,* October 12, 1909. "Anglo German Territories Co.," *Berliner Tageblatt,* Au-

gust 31, 1909. "Lüderitzbucht," *Diamond Fields Advertiser,* September 3, 1909. Arthur Dieseldorff to Geheimrat von Jacobs, August 30, 1911, BAB R1001/1346.

36. "Entirely true," see "Die Diamantenfrage," *Frankfurter Zeitung,* July 5, 1909.

37. Lindequist to Dernburg, July 30, 1909, BAK N1130/10. "Credible," see "Organisation der deutschen Diamanteninteressen in Südwestafrika," *Frankfurter Zeitung,* April 19, 1909. "Kolonialschätze und Kolonialspekulation," *Frankfurter Zeitung,* August 30, 1909. Cf. "Anglo German Territories Ltd.," *Berliner Tageblatt,* August 24, 1909. Cf. "Deutsche Kolonialgesellschaft für Südwestafrika," *Frankfurter Zeitung,* June 19, 1909. "Anglo German Territories Co.," *Frankfurter Zeitung,* August 27, 1909.

38. "Unregelmässigkeiten," *Berliner Tageblatt,* October 31, 1911. "Publizität der Kolonialunternehmungen," *Frankfurter Zeitung,* July 15, 1909. See Lene Haase, *Raggys Fahrt nach Südwest* (Berlin: Fleischel, 1910), 190.

39. Dernburg to Dr. Friedrich, February 9, 1909, BAK N1130/32. "Otavi-Minen," *Berliner Börsen-Courier,* February 2, 1909. "Illusory and real values," see Carl Meinhof, "Dernburg," *Koloniale Rundschau 1910,* no. 7 (1910), 414. Prion,, vii. See Eley, *Reshaping the German Right* (New Haven: Yale University Press, 1980), 49; Roger Chickering, *We Men Who Feel Most German* (Boston: Allen & Unwin, 1984), 52, 225. "Kolonialwerten," *Deutsche Kolonialzeitung* 26, no. 5 (1909): 77. Cf. "Kolmanskop Diamond Mines," *Berliner Börsen-Courier,* November 2, 1909. Protocol of Regie's board meeting, February 10, 1909, HID, Archives of Deutsche Bank Zentrale Berlin, Sekretariat (Frankfurt), S097.

40. Enclosure to Reichsjustizamt to RKA, August 19, 1911; RKA to Deutsch-Ostafrikanische Gesellschaft et al., December 30, 1911, BAB R1001/5353. Rönnecke's protocol, May 29, 1912, BAK N1138/51. Wilhelm Dyes, "Bergbau," *Metall und Erz* 4, no. 5 (Halle: Knapp, 1916): 125.

41. "Founding factories," see "Spekulation in Kolonial-Werten," *Frankfurter Zeitung,* February 5, 1909. "Concessions," see "Eigentümliche Vorgänge," *Hannoverscher Courier,* September 2, 1909. "Achtung!" *Hamburger Nachrichten,* August 25, 1909. Cf. Disconto-Gesellschaft to Deutsche Bank, January 23, 1909, HID, Archives of Deutsche Bank Zentrale Berlin, Sekretariat (Frankfurt), S1370. "Kolonialschätze und Kolonialspekulation," *Frankfurter Zeitung,* August 30, 1909.

42. Robert Edgcumbe to Edward Grey, September 16, 1914, CO 163, 1914, MS Selected Colonial Office Files on Africa, UKNA, Gale Nineteenth Century Collections Online, Europe and Africa, Colonialism and Culture, http://tinyurl.galegroup.com.stanford .idm.oclc.org/tinyurl/6voCG4. Accessed 21 August 2018. Rudolf Martin, *Deutsche Machthaber* (Berlin: Schuster, 1910), 507. Cf. data in Disconto-Gesellschaft in Berlin, *Geschäftsbericht für das Jahr 1910* (Berlin: Discontogesellschaft, 1911), 7. "Spielpapiere," *Allgemeine Zeitung* (Munich), January 30, 1909. See Horst Gericke, *Börsenzulassung* (Wiesbaden: Gabler, 1961), 85.

43. "Internal," "foreign," see Bernhard Dernburg, *Kapital und Staatsaufsicht: eine finanzpolitische Studie* (Berlin: Mittler, 1911), 3. "Inside," see "Diamantenfieber," *Volksstimme,* January 10, 1909.

44. "Kolonialwerte," *Neue Hamburgische Börsen-Halle,* June 16, 1910. "Der südwestafrikanische Nachtragsetat," *Berliner Tageblatt,* January 26, 1910. "Hamburger Börse," *Hamburgischer Correspondent,* March 2, 1910.

45. Cf. "Deutsche Kolonialgesellschaft für Südwestafrika," *Frankfurter Zeitung,* October 12, 1910. Siegfried Strzelecki to RKA, September 9, 1913, BAB R1001/5508.

46. Clara Brockmann, *Briefe eines deutschen Mädchen* (Berlin: Mittler, 1912), 206. Margarethe von Eckenbrecher, *Was Afrika mir gab und nahm: Erlebnisse einer deutschen Frau in Südwestafrika 1902–1936* (Berlin: Mittler, 1940), 320–321. "Verschiedenes,"

Berliner Börsenzeitung, March 13, 1909. "Business of the utmost importance," see "Diamond Way," *Louisville Courier-Journal,* April 2, 1911.

47. See "In the Underground Way," *New York Times,* October 3, 1906. "The Diamond Trade," *New York Times,* July 30, 1893. "Dropped $172,000 in Diamond Deal," *New York Times,* March 12, 1908. "Diamond Importer Fined as Smuggler," *New York Times,* June 30, 1910. "Importers Resent Diamond Trickery," *New York Times,* March 23, 1913.

48. "Kolonialwerte," *Berliner Tageblatt,* November 8, 1906. Oskar Geck's speech to Reichstag, November 14, 1911, *Stenographische Berichte,* 7848. Speech by Johannes Kaempf, April 25, 1910, *Reden und Aufsätze von Johannes Kaempf* (Berlin: Reimer, 1912), 567. Minister für Handel und Gewerbe to Bülow, April 5, 1909, BAB R1001/1663.

49. "Otavi," *Allgemeine Zeitung* (Munich), July 17, 1909. "Flesh of their flesh," see August Bebel's speech of December 1, 1906, *Ausgewählte Reden und Schriften,* vol. 8/1 (München: Saur, 1997), 93. Harden to Rathenau, September 27, 1911, *Walther Rathenau/Maximilian Harden Briefwechsel,* 637. "There must be an end," see "Dernburg," *Sydney Morning Herald,* June 8, 1910.

50. Deutsche Bank to Joseph Bremer, August 19, 1909, HID, Archives of Deutsche Bank Zentrale Berlin, Sekretariat (Frankfurt), S096. "'Konzessionen und Unterkonzessionen,'" *Lüderitzbuchter Zeitung,* June 12, 1909.

51. "Aus Lüderitzbucht," *Lüderitzbuchter Zeitung,* February 27, 1909. RKA to German Foreign Office, February 15, 1910; Börsenverein Lüderitzbucht to RKA, September 3, 1909, BAB R1001/5353.

52. "Lüderitzbucht," *Diamond Fields Advertiser,* July 21, 1909. Drechsler, *Kolonialherrschaft,* 254–255. Dieseldorff to Reichskolonialamt, August 18, 1911; Bezirksamtsmann Böhmer to Kaiserliches Gouvernement Windhuk, May 13, 1911, BAB R1001/1346. G. K. Anton to Dernburg, May 25, 1909, BAK N1130/34.

53. Cf. "Handelsteil," *Berliner Volkszeitung,* October 14, 1910. "Particularly difficult," see Bezirksrichter Werner to Governor of Southwest, December 30, 1910, BAB R1001/4847. William Eveleigh, *South-West Africa* (London: Unwin, 1915), 219.

54. "Kurssturz der Kolonialanteile," *Berliner Volkszeitung,* August 24, 1910. "Kolonialfieber," *Berliner Volkszeitung,* June 22, 1909; "Deutsche Kolonialgesellschaft für Südwestafrika," *Berliner Börsen-Courier,* January 27, 1911. "Be everybody's thing," see "Deutsche Kolonialgesellschaft für Südwestafrika," *Frankfurter Zeitung,* May 22, 1909.

55. Cf. Grete Meisel-Heß, *Betrachtungen zur Frauenfrage* (Berlin: Prometheus, 1914), 26; Marianne Westerlind, *Du heiliges Land!* (Hamburg: Broschek, 1914), 61. Hans Merensky to RKA, September 6, 1909, BAB R1001/1529. "Hunger im Diamantenlande," *Vorwärts,* February 3, 1910. Cf. "Deutsch-Südwestafrika im Reichstage," *Windhuker Nachrichten,* April 21, 1909.

56. Anonymous, *Berlin und die Berliner* (Karlsruhe: Bielefelds, 1905), 158. "Finanzwelt Berlins," *Allgemeine Zeitung* (Munich), January 1, 1910. "The only ones," see ""Dezember 1908," *Die Bank: Monatshefte für Finanz- u. Bankwesen* (Berlin-Charlottenburg, 1909)," 46. Cf. Lazard Speyer-Ellissen to Deutsche Bank, February 1, 1909, HID, Archives of Deutsche Bank Zentrale Berlin, Sekretariat (Frankfurt), S1374. Oskar Geck's speech to Reichstag, November 14, 1911, *Stenographische Berichte,* 7848. Deutsche Bank to Bergisch Märkische Bank, February 14, 1910, HID, Archives of Deutsche Bank Zentrale Berlin, Sekretariat (Frankfurt), S0103.

57. "Well-priced colonial shares," see Georg von Rechenberg, quoted incidentally in Anne Dreesbach, *Gezähmte Wilde* (Frankfurt: Campus, 2005), 226. "Unhealthy," see Schlieffen, *Reichsbank,* 14. "Zur Verstaatlichung der Otavibahn," *Lüderitzbuchter Zeitung,* June 5, 1909. Johannes Tesch, *Kolonialbeamten* (Berlin, 1912), 4–14. "Illusory," see Schuckmann to Bezirksamt Lüderitzbucht, June 19, 1909, BAB R1001/1343.

58. Will Sellick (ed.), *Autobiography of Eugen Mansfeld* (London: Jeppestown Press, 2017), 33. Charles van Onselen, *New Babylon* (Johannesburg: Ball, 2001), 49. Max Warnack, "Alkoholkonsum," *Deutsche Kolonialzeitung* 30, no. 12 (1913): 196. Hence Schuckmann's decree, April 30, 1908, BAB R1001/2040. Cf. Charles Dawbarn, *My South African Year* (London: Mills & Boon, 1921), 147.

59. Walther Rathenau, "Notizen zur Afrikareise 1908," in *Schriften der Wilhelminischen Zeit 1885–1914,* ed. Alexander Jaser (Düsseldorf: Droste, 2015), 683. "City of Diamonds," *Times of India,* August 23, 1909. Westerlind, *Du heiliges Land!,* 107. Max Fiebig, *Alkoholfrage* (Berlin: Süsserott, 1908), 50.

60. "German Diamond Fields," *The Sun* (New York), August 22, 1909. "Insel der Pinguine, *Berliner Tageblatt,* November 1, 1925.

61. "Flask post," see Emil Zimmermann, *Unsere Kolonien* (Berlin: Ullstein, 1912), 139. Max Fleischmann, *Die Verwaltung* (Essen: Baedeker, 1908), 42. Walther Rathenau, "Denkschrift über den Stand des Südwestafrikanischen Schutzgebietes," *Schriften der Wilhelminischen Zeit 1885–1914,* ed. Alexander Jaser (Düsseldorf: Droste, 2015), 657. Schuckmann's decree, December 2, 1909, BAB R1001/4730.

62. "Munich" beer, see "Apotheken," *Apothekenbilder von Nah und Fern,* vol. 5, ed. Hans Heger (Wien: Brück, 1912), 115. Christian Schäder, *Brauindustrie* (Marburg: Tectum, 1999), 177. Hans Grimm, *Afrikafahrt West* (Frankfurt: Hendschel, 1913), 91. Cf. "Die Geldnöte des Reiches," *Windhuker Nachrichten,* January 25, 1908. Bernhard Dernburg, *Vorbedingungen* (Berlin: Borngräber, 1912), 17. Rheinische Weinkelterei Gebrüder Wagner to RKA, March 7, 1910, BAB R1001/5466. "Habit drinkers," see Oberstabsarzt Mankiewitz, *Kohlstocks Ratgeber für die Tropen* (Stettin: Hermann Peters, 1910), 6.

63. "Reichsspiegel," *Die Grenzboten,* vol. 70 (1911), 185. "Heulendes Elend in Südwestafrika," *Vorwärts,* May 2, 1911. "Handelsteil," *Altonaer Nachrichten,* August 16, 1909. "Kursbericht," *General-Anzeiger für Hamburg-Altona,* March 14, June 6, and August 22, 1909.

64. "Telegraphische Nachrichten," *Lüderitzbuchter Zeitung,* May 8, 1909. Wilhelm II to Bernhard von Bülow, December 13, 1908, *Letters of Bülow* (London: Hutchinson, 1930), 281. See Peter-Christian Witt, *Finanzpolitik* (Hamburg: Matthiesen, 1970). Cf. Martin, *Scheinwerfer,* 26.

65. "Singular," see Disconto-Gesellschaft in Berlin, *Geschäftsbericht für das Jahr 1909* (Berlin: Discontogesellschaft, 1910), 6. Richard Müller to Reichstag on June 21, 1909, *Stenographische Berichte,* 8732–8733. "Internationale Börsenschau," *Deutsche Wirtschafts-Zeitung: Zentralblatt für Handel, Industrie und Verkehr,* vol. 5 (Berlin: Teubner, 1909), 567.

66. *Reden und Aufsätze von Johannes Kaempf,* ed. Die Ältesten der Kaufmannschaft von Berlin (Berlin: Reimer, 1912), 54. Disconto-Gesellschaft in Berlin, *Geschäftsbericht für das Jahr 1910,* 7. Cf. the *Effekten-Kursblatt* of the Schweizerische Kreditanstalt (Credit Suisse), December 30, 1909, BAK N1130/36. Otto Pommer, *Die Konservativen* (Berlin: Fortschritt, 1912), 52; Martin, *Scheinwerfer,* 31.

67. Tax code, see Fritz Kestner, *Ausführungsbestimmungen zu den Reichssteuergesetzen auf Grund der Reichsfinanzreform von 1909* (Leipzig: Hirschfeld, 1910). Witt, *Finanzpolitik,* 313. "Reichsfinanzreform," *Lüderitzbuchter Zeitung,* July 3, 1909. Paul Beusch, *Steuerarten und Steuersysteme* (Mönchengladbach: Volksverein, 1911), 71.

68. "Kolonialfieber," *Berliner Volkszeitung,* June 22, 1909. See US Senate, 61st Congress, 1st Session, Document No. 68, Pt. 2: *Wages in Germany: Message from the President of the United States* (Washington, DC, 1909), 80 and 114. "Wirtschaftsjahr," *Deutsche Bäcker- und Konditoren-Zeitung,* January 1, 1910. Christof Böhm to RKA, October 26, 1912, BAB R1001/1353.

69. "German Diamond Scandal," *New York Times,* January 30, 1910. "Zum Deutsch-Südwestafrikanischen Diamantenstreit," *Berliner Börsen-Courier,* January 19, 1911.

70. Arnold Wahnschaffe to Dernburg, January 29, 1910, BAB R1001/1324. "Small men," see editorials in *Lüderitzbuchter Zeitung,* March 20, 1909; "Staatssekretär Dernburg," *Windhuker Nachrichten,* June 16, 1910. "Finanzwelt Berlins," *Allgemeine Zeitung* (Munich), January 1, 1910. Cf. Ashok Desai, *Real Wages in Germany* (Oxford: Oxford University Press, 1968), 112–125.

71. DKGfSWA to Dernburg, January 26, 1910, BAB R1001/1324. Carl Fürstenberg's memorandum, December 22, 1908, HID, Archives of Deutsche Bank Zentrale Berlin, Sekretariat (Frankfurt), S096. For royalty fees, see Schuckmann to RKA, October 12, 1909, BAB R1001/1324. O. Stutzer, *Lagerstätten,* vol. 1 (Berlin, 1911), 145. See Georg Wunderlich, "Wertzuwachssteuern," *Zeitschrift für Kolonialrecht* 16, no. 1 (Berlin: Deutsche Kolonialgesellschaft, 1914): 2.

72. "Glowed with diamonds," see "Diamanten," *Deutsche Kolonialzeitung* 25, no. 40 (1908): 710. See Brockmann, *Briefe,* vi. Cf. Hans Grimm, *Die dreizehn Briefe* (Munich: Langen, 1928), 35. "Died for the Fatherland," see Cf. Noske to Reichstag, *Stenographische Berichte,* May 1, 1912, 1596. "Counting-house," see Erzberger, *Millionengeschenke,* 72.

73. "Tears," see Max Bewer, "Diamanten," *Kolonie und Heimat,* October 10, 1909, 11. "Being used," "Ein Wort," *Mecklenburger Warte,* August 23, 1910. "Omnipotence of money," see "Trotha gegen Dernburg," *General-Anzeiger für Hamburg-Altona,* February 5, 1909.

74. "Not get a solitary diamond," see Session of July 24, 1914, Garton Foundation, *International Polity Summer School Report* (London: Harrison, 1915), 237. "Plundering of the German Empire," see Sozialdemokratische Partei Deutschlands, *Protokoll über die Verhandlungen des Parteitages, abgehalten in Magdeburg* (Berlin: Vorwärts, 1910), 134–136.

8. Underworld

1. "Father in heaven," see Hans Paul von Humboldt-Dachroeden (Consul at Cape Town) to Government at Windhoek, March 15, 1909, BAB R901/785.

2. Hans Paul von Humboldt-Dachroeden (Consul at Cape Town) to Government at Windhoek, March 15, 1909, BAB R901/785. Diamanten-Regie to Angelo Golinelli, June 9, 1909, BAB R1001/1423. Generalkonsulat Antwerpen to Bethmann Hollweg, July 19, 1909, BAB R1001/1425. See Natty Rothschild (1st Lord Rothschild) to Édouard de Rothschild, Paris, August 21, 1909, RAL XI/130A/3/150. Schuckmann to Dernburg, January 6, 1909, BAB R1001/1342. "Diamantschmuggel," *Windhuker Nachrichten,* July 13, 1910. "Uebertreibungen," *Lüderitzbuchter Zeitung,* August 27, 1910. "Geschichte," *Deutsche Goldschmiede-Zeitung* 13 (Leipzig, 1910): 140. Cf. figures in Sigmund Schilder, *Entwicklungstendenzen der Weltwirtschaft,* vol. 2 (Berlin, 1915), 190. Bruno Simmersbach, "Bergbau," *Zeitschrift für die gesamte Staatswissenschaft* 72 (1916): 418. Cf. estimates in "Diamant-Schmuggel," *Windhuker Nachrichten,* August 24, 1910.

3. Duty figure, see Hintrager to RKA, December 31, 1909, BAB R1001/1918. Adolf Kaminsky's statement, June 15, 1909, BAB R1001/1425. "Diamantfelder," *Swakopmunder Zeitung,* November 3, 1909.

4. "Diamantendiebstähle," *Lüderitzbuchter Zeitung,* July 30, 1910. "No one would deny," see "Von einer Berliner Mittagszeitung ist heute die Meldung . . ." *Berliner Tageblatt,* July 9, 1910. Bernhard Voigt, "Geschichte des langen Tom," in *Afrika spricht,* ed. Paul Ritter (Mühlhausen, 1938), 264.

5. "Frankreich und die deutschen Handelsinteressen," *Windhuker Nachrichten,* June 20, 1908. Schilder, *Entwicklungstendenzen,* vol. 2, 712. "In the Underground Way of the Diamond Trade," *New York Times,* October 3, 1906.

6. "Big Plot to Smuggle Gems," *New York Times,* July 11, 1910. "Must Take Punishment," *New-York Tribune,* May 11, 1903. "Juwelen-Einfuhr," *Lüderitzbuchter Zeitung,* August 27, 1910. "Slope Briefs," *Los Angeles Times,* December 29, 1910. "War Declared on the Smuggler of Diamonds," *New York Times,* January 2, 1910.

7. Hintrager to RKA, December 31, 1909, BAB R1001/1918. See Charles van Onselen, *The Fox and the Flies* (New York: Walker, 2007), 269, 301, 328. "Cockaigne," see Breitmeyer to Hirschhorn, April 16, 1909, BW Wernher, Beit vol. 143. "Land of," see "Sun, Sand, and Sin," *New York Tribune,* April 29, 1917.

8. Hintrager to RKA, December 31, 1909, BAB R1001/1918. Cf. Richard Helm, *Zwischen Ankunft und Abschied: Einige Begebenheiten aus dem ehemaligen Südwestafrika* (Mannheim: Kolb, 2005, 17. Cf. "Diamant-Schmuggel," *Windhuker Nachrichten,* August 24, 1910. Dernburg to Paul Schmitz, December 19, 1908, BAB R1001/1351.

9. Hintrager's memo, March 12, 1910, BAB R1001/1423. German Foreign Office to German Colonial Office, March 17, 1911, BAB R1001/5553. Gouverneur to RKA, June 10, 1911, BAB R1001/1424. Cf. Mayor of Reinickendorf to Colonial Office, September 15, 1909, BAB R1001/4767. "Aus Lüderitzbucht," *Lüderitzbuchter Zeitung,* August 20, 1910. "Bekanntmachung," October 9, *Deutsches Kolonialblatt* 23 (Berlin: Mittler, 1912): 989. "Einziehung der Zollhebestellen," *Deutsch-Südwestafrikanische Zeitung,* December 9, 1908.

10. Hans Rafalski, *Niemandsland* (Berlin: Wernitz, 1930), 318–319. Hans-Otto Meissner, *Traumland* (Stuttgart, 1968), 371. *Denkschrift über die Entwicklung der deutschen Schutzgebiete in Afrika und der Südsee, Berichtsjahr 1908/09,* printed in *Stenographische Berichte über die Verhandlungen des deutschen Reichstages, XII. Legislaturperiode, II. Session,* vol. 271 (Berlin, 1911), 783. "Aus Lüderitzbucht," *Lüderitzbuchter Zeitung,* June 26, 1909. Hans Grimm, *Afrikafahrt West* (Frankfurt: Hendschel, 1913), 191. Schuckmann to Dernburg, January 6, 1909, BAB R1001/1342. Sarah Gertrude Millin, *General Smuts* (New York: Faber, 1936), 294. "Deutsche Diamantengesellschaft," *Berliner Börsen-Courier,* August 26, 1911.

11. See Jakob Zollmann, "Communicating Colonial Order," *Crime, History & Societies* 15, no. 1 (2011): 33–57. "Day and night," see "Deutsche Schutzgebiete," *Hamburger Nachrichten,* October 1, 1910. Hermann Freyberg, *Diamanten in der Namib* (Kempen: Thomas, 1943), 32–33. Rafalski, *Niemandsland,* 329.

12. "Out on patrol," see "Versammlung der Lüderitzbuchter Minenkammer," *Lüderitzbuchter Zeitung,* August 20, 1910. Böhmer's memo, March 16, 1912, BAB R1001/1914. Page 91 of "Denkschrift über die Massnahmen zur Bekämpfung des Diamantdiebstahls," undated (likely late 1910), BAB R1001/1424. Freyberg, *Diamanten,* 32–33.

13. Gibeon Schürf und Handelsgesellhaft to German Foreign Office, March 1, 1905, BAB R1001/1679. Charles van Onselen, "Hasenfus," *History Workshop Journal* 67 (Spring 2009): 2.

14. Freyberg, *Diamanten,* 208–209, 224–225. Reichsstelle für Auswanderungswesen to Eduard Grosser, April 25, 1910, BAB R1505/10.

15. Sydney Buxton's report, April 1915, UKNA, CAB 37/127/51.

16. Gouverneur to RKA, November 14, 1910; Page 100 of "Denkschrift über die Massnahmen zur Bekämpfung des Diamantdiebstahls," undated (likely late 1910), BAB R1001/1424.

17. Cf. Ulrike Schaper, *Koloniale Verhandlungen* (Frankfurt: Campus, 2012), 68–86. See section 14 of Hintrager's decree, February 25, 1913, BAB R1001/4730. Hermann Riedl, *Rund um Afrika* (Linz: Riedl, 1911), 43. "Aus Swakopmund," *Deutsch-Südwestafrikanische Zeitung,* June 20, 1908. "Staatssekretär Dernburg," *Windhuker Nachrichten,* June 16, 1909. "Zum Besuche des Herrn Oats," *Windhuker Nachrichten,* June 16, 1909. Erwin Rupp, *Soll und Haben in Deutsch-Südwest-Afrika* (Berlin: Reimer, 1904), 52.

18. "International," see "Diamantendiebstähle," *Lüderitzbuchter Zeitung,* July 30, 1910; "Alleged I. D. B.," *Diamond Fields Advertiser,* August 24, 1909 and January 5, 1910. "Partly Jewish," see Grimm, *Afrikafahrt West,* 191. Bezirkshauptmann Brill to Hintrager, December 9, 1908, NAN ZBU, 1617-R.XIV.G Bd. 1. Rafalski, *Niemandsland,* 339. See Marianne Westerlind, *Du heiliges Land!* (Hamburg: Broschek, 1914), 98; Lene Haase, *Raggys Fahrt* (Berlin: Fleischel, 1910), 162–164. "Know how to get around," see Erich Schroetter to Schuckmann, May 11, 1909, BAB R901/785. "International trash," see Hintrager to RKA, December 31, 1909, BAB R1001/1918. "Inclination to diamonds," quoted in Christian Stuart Davis, *Colonialism, Antisemitism, and Germans of Jewish Descent in Imperial Germany* (Ann Arbor: University of Michigan Press, 2012), 241.

19. Cf. Sarah Stein, *Plumes* (New Haven: Yale University Press, 2008), 151; Boris Barth, "Weder Bürgertum noch Adel," *Geschichte und Gesellschaft* 25, no. 1 (1999): 94–122. Page 2 of anonymous, unattributed memo, BAK N1138/51. "Jews and the Diamond Trade," *American Israelite,* May 1, 1924. See Jean-Philippe Schreiber, *L'immigration juive en Belgique du moyen âge à la première guerre mondiale* (Bruxelles: Éditions de l'Université de Bruxelles, 1996), 97, 203.

20. Cf. Bernhard Dernburg, *Search-Lights on the War* (New York: Fatherland, 1915), 12. Robert Vicat Turrell, *Capital and Labour on the Kimberley Diamond Fields, 1871–1890* (New York: Cambridge University Press, 1987), 75. "Aus London wird uns unterm 6. d. M. geschrieben," *Berliner Börsenzeitung,* December 8, 1910. See John C. G. Röhl, *Wilhelm II: Into the Abyss* (Cambridge: Cambridge University Press, 2014), 410. Paul Kennedy, *The Rise of the Anglo-German Antagonism, 1860–1914* (London: Allen & Unwin, 1980), 304. Stanley Chapman, *Merchant Enterprise in Britain* (New York: Cambridge University Press, 1992), 276. "Randlords," see Eric Hobsbawm, *Age of Empire* (New York: Vintage, 1989), 74.

21. Cf. Franz Schuster, *Diamanten-Politik* (Altenburg: Geibel, 1910), 8. Cf. Julius Wernher to Dernburg, December 2, 1908, BAB R1001/1341. See Wilhelm Lattmann as quoted in "Deutscher Reichstag," *Berliner Tageblatt,* March 19, 1905. Cf. Walter Frank, "Der Geheime Rat," *Historische Zeitschrift* 168, no. 2 (1943): 305–306. More on this dynamic in Davis, *Colonialism.* Cf. "Der Landwirtschaftsminister v. Podbielski" and "Staatsstellungen," *Mitteilungen aus dem Verein zur Abwehr des Antisemitismus* 16, no. 39 (Berlin, 1906): 302–303. Alfred Lichtenstein, *Persönlichkeiten,* vol. 6 (Charlottenburg: Virgil, 1908), 14. See Werner Mosse, *Jews in the German Economy* (Oxford: Clarendon, 1987), 130. "Diamanten," *Graf's Finanz-Chronik: Zeitschrift für Finanz- und Versicherungs-Praxis,* December 14, 1908, BAB R1001/1341. "Kolonialdirektor," *Allgemeine Zeitung* (Munich), September 5, 1906. Cf. Con Weinberg, *Fragments of a Desert Land* (Cape Town: Timmins, 1975), 81.

22. Peter Pulzer, *Jews and the German State* (Cambridge: Blackwell, 1992), 183. "Dernburg Denies," *New York Times,* May 4, 1915. E. Ekkehard, ed., *Sigilla Veri (Ph. Stauff's Semi-Kürschner,* vol. 1 (Erfurt: Bodung, 1929), 1164. "At the wrong address," see Frederic Wile, *The Assault* (Indianapolis: Bobbs-Merrill, 1916), 219. "Banks, stocks, Jews," see Edgar Kirsch, *Hans Grimm als Wegbereiter nordischer Gesamtschau* (Leipzig: Noske, 1937), 32.

23. "A Jew," see Heinrich Köhler, *Lebenserinnerungen* (Stuttgart: Kohlhammer, 1964), 214. "Women of Jewish high finance," see "Das amerikanische Judenthum," *Die*

Zukunft 67 (1909): 285. Cf. Robert N. Proctor, "Anti-Agate: The Great Diamond Hoax and the Semiprecious Stone Scam," *Configurations* 9, no. 3 (2001): 407.

24. "Verfassungskommission," *Lüderitzbuchter Zeitung,* September 19, 1935. "Interview with Mr. F. Ginsberg," *Mining Journal* 84, no. 3826 (London, 1908): 777. See Margaret Lavinia Anderson, "Interdenominationalism," *Central European History* 21, no. 4 (1988): 351.

25. "Bad elements," see anonymous, "Juden und die deutschen Kolonien," *Im deutschen Reich* 16, no. 11 (Berlin, 1910): 724. "Especially strong national sentiment," see Birthe Kundrus, *Moderne Imperialisten* (Köln: Böhlau, 2003), 114n241. Otto Rheinen, *Die Selbstverwaltung* (Berlin: Gutenberg, 1913), 55.

26. "Jewish" crooks, see Grimm, *Afrikafahrt West,* 191. Brill to Hintrager, December 9, 1908, NAN ZBU, 1617-R.XIV.G Bd. 1. Erich Schroetter to Bülow, June 9, 1909, BAB R901/785. Cf. Consul Müller to Foreign Office, July 17, 1911, UKNA CO 879/107.

27. Stephen to Müller, August 24, 1911; Boehmer to Müller, September 13, 1911, UKNA FO 403/422. Cf. Ulrike Lindner, *Koloniale Begegnungen* (Frankfurt: Campus, 2011), 394. "Deutsche Schutzgebiete," *Hamburger Nachrichten,* October 1, 1910. Fred Cornell, *Glamour of Prospecting* (London: Unwin, 1920), 12. "Deutsche Diamantengesellschaft," *Berliner Börsen-Courier,* August 26, 1911.

28. "Kolonial-Courier," *Berliner Börsen-Courier,* October 8, 1910. "Clever Cape boys," see Walter Moritz, *Die 'Sandwüste' hat eine Zukunft: Tagebuch und Zeichnungen des Malers Ernst Vollbehr 1910* (Windhoek: Meinert, 1994), 16. Clara Brockmann, *Briefe eines deutschen Mädchen* (Berlin: Mittler, 1912), 175–176. Cf. "Deutsche Schutzgebiete," *Frankfurter Zeitung,* September 5, 1909; "Deutsche Diamantengesellschaft," *Frankfurter Zeitung,* August 25, 1911.

29. "Not so advanced culturally," see Kaiserlicher Gouverneur von Südwestafrika to Colonial Office, August 17, 1910, BAB R1001/1229. Cf. "Sitzung des Landesrates," *Windhuker Nachrichten,* May 4, 1910. Schuckmann to Dernburg, June 15, 1909, BAK N1130/51.

30. See Sebastian Mantei, *Entwicklungsgeschichte* (Halle: Universität Halle-Wittenberg, 2004), 141. Cf. Frank G. Carpenter, *How the World Is Clothed* (Chicago: American, 1908), 269. Cf. Emily Osborn, "'Rubber Fever,'" *Journal of African History* 45, no. 3 (2004): 445–465. Cf. Schuckmann to Dernburg, January 6, 1909, BAB R1001/1342. "Jagd nach Diamanten," *Der wahre Jacob* 27, no. 616 (1910): 6546.

31. "Diamanten," *Deutsche Kolonialzeitung* 25, no. 40 (1908): 710. "The different ways," see "Diamonds More Dear," *New-York Tribune,* October 16, 1904. "To Catch Diamond Thieves," *Evening Star* (Washington, DC), October 4, 1908. "Foulger to Deliver a Lecture," *The Evening Standard* (Ogden City, UT), November 1, 1910. "The necessary evil," *Massenmord,* see "Diamantschmuggel," *Windhuker Nachrichten,* July 13, 1910.

32. "Diamond Smuggling," *New York Tribune,* August 7, 1910. "Diamanten-Schmuggel," *Windhuker Nachrichten,* August 24, 1910. "Wie man Diamanten schmuggelt," *Berliner Börsenzeitung,* August 7, 1910. Brockmann, *Briefe,* 178.

33. "Diamantschmuggel," *Windhuker Nachrichten,* July 13, 1910. "Care packages," see RKA to Kreplin, April 20, 1922, BAB R1001/1438.

34. Max Ewald Baericke, *Lüderitzbucht: Historische Erinnerungen eines alten Diamantensuchers* (Windhoek: Namibia Wissenschaftliche Gesellschaft, 2001), 67. Cornell, *Glamour,* 10. Cf. Charles van Onselen, *Studies in the Social and Economic History of Witwatersrand, 1886–1914,* vol. 1 (London: Longman, 1982). Lindequist to Foreign Office, July 31, 1906, BAB R1001/4846. Karl Dove, *Kolonien* (Leipzig: Göschen, 1913), 65. Ludwig Kastl's memo on "Belastung der weißen Bevölkerung," undated 1911, BAK N1138/41.

35. See Harald Nestroy, *Duwisib* (Windhoek: Meinert, 2002), 70. "Problem," see Wollmann to Bülow, August 8, 1909, BAB R1001/1918. Cf. Elizabeth Siegfried to

Dernburg, March 24, 1909, BAK N1130/33. Hintrager to Solf, September 29, 1912, BAB R1001/4847.

36. "Smuggling by Airship," *San Francisco Call,* June 13, 1909. "Verhaftung von Diamantenschmugglern," *Karlsruher Tageblatt,* July 10, 1914.

37. See Sears, Roebuck and Co. Chicago, *Catalog No. 120, Spring 1910* (Philadelphia: Sears, Roebuck and Company, 1910). Cf. Proctor, "Anti-Agate," 402. "Big Plot to Smuggle Gems," *New York Times,* July 11, 1910.

38. "Must Take Punishment," *New-York Tribune,* May 11, 1903. Cf. Natty Rothschild to Rothschild Cousins in Paris, December 16, 1907, RAL XI/130A/1/240. Regarding markup, I extrapolate from the data included in "Price of Diamonds," *Cincinnati Enquirer,* December 1, 1912. "No Slump," *New York Times,* June 10, 1900.

39. Import toll, see Schilder, *Entwicklungstendenzen,* vol. 2, 713, 202. "Diamond Duties and Smuggling," *The Observer* (London), June 1, 1913. "Diamantenschmugglerinnen," *Berliner Börsenzeitung,* June 14, 1914. "His Diamonds Held," *New York Times,* June 9, 1913. "War Declared on the Smuggler," *New York Times,* January 2, 1910.

40. "German Gems," *New York Times,* July 7, 1910. Karl Helfferich's memorandum, December 22, 1908, HID, Archives of Deutsche Bank Zentrale Berlin, Sekretariat (Frankfurt), S096. Gouverneur to RKA, July 20, 1910, BAB R1001/1425. Extrapolation based on equivalence given in "Diamanten," *Vossische Zeitung,* May 29, 1913.

41. Moritz, *Sandwüste,* 15. "Sort Diamonds with a Sieve," *Washington Post,* January 24, 1909. "Diamond Smugglers," *New York Times,* July 10, 1910. "Entirely simple thing," see Brockmann, *Briefe,* 175.

42. Cf. Proctor, "Anti-Agate," 397. Figures for 1909, see Alexander Fersman, *Der Diamant* (Heidelberg: Winter, 1911), iii.

43. Baron de Bodman to A. A., November 5, 1910, BAB R1001/1435. A. A. to RKA, November 15, 1910; Telegram from Windhoek to A. A., November 11, 1910, BAB R1001/1435. See Lindner, *Koloniale Begegnungen,* 390. Dernburg to Secretary of A. A., December 22, 1909, R901/786. Brill to Hintrager, December 9, 1908, NAN ZBU, 1617-R. XIV.G Bd. 1.

44. "Diamantenfrage," *Norddeutsche Allgemeine Zeitung,* January 29, 1909. See "Verordnung über den Handel mit südwestafrikanischen Diamanten," Staatsarchiv Hamburg, 132–1 I_1666. Verband deutscher Juweliere, Gold- und Silberschmiede, "Die Berliner Kriminal-Polizei meldet soeben [. . .]," *Journal der Goldschmiedekunst* 29, no. 28 (Leipzig, 1908): unpaginated. Alfred Henke's address to Reichstag, March 20, 1914, *Stenographische Berichte,* 8154.

45. Meissner, *Traumland,* 371. Baericke, *Lüderitzbucht,* 67. "Diamantenregie," *Frankfurter Zeitung,* November 15, 1910.

46. "Landesrat," *Lüderitzbuchter Zeitung,* May 9, 1913. Cf. Report of Diamanten-Regie for 1912/13, HID, Archives of Deutsche Bank Zentrale Berlin, Sekretariat (Frankfurt), S097.

47. Paul Leutwein, *Die Leistungen der Regierung in der südwestafrikanischen Land- und Minenfrage* (Berlin: Universität Berlin, 1911), 125. Peter Conze's report, October 12, 1909, BAB R1001/1500. "Parlamentarisches," *Die Presse* (Thorn), January 21, 1910. "Landesrat," *Lüderitzbuchter Zeitung,* June 20, 1913.

48. Leutwein, *Die Leistungen,* 126. Total police budget, see Grimm, *Afrikafahrt West,* 192. Cf. Karl Helfferich's memorandum, December 22, 1908, HID, Archives of Deutsche Bank Zentrale Berlin, Sekretariat (Frankfurt), S096. Felix Waldstein's speech to Reichstag, May 2, 1912, *Stenographische Berichte,* 1646. But see "Aufzeichnung zur Frage der Umgestaltung der Landespolizei in SWA," undated (c. 1912), BAB R1001/1914. Deutsche Dia-

mantengesellschaft to Solf, October 22, 1913, HID, Archives of Deutsche Bank Zentrale Berlin, Sekretariat (Frankfurt), S097.

49. Cf. "Diamantschmuggel," *Windhuker Nachrichten,* July 13, 1910. Diamanten-Regie to Angelo Golinelli, June 9, 1909, BAB R1001/1423. Generalkonsulat Antwerpen to Bethmann Hollweg, July 19, 1909, BAB R1001/1425.

50. Statement by Anton Jost, printed as part of court transcript in "Gerichtsverhandlungen," *Lüderitzbuchter Zeitung,* October 30, 1909. Generalkonsulat Antwerpen to Bethmann Hollweg, July 11, 1911, BAB R1001/1425.

51. Cf. "Warnung," *Windhuker Nachrichten,* December 30, 1908. German Colonial Corporation to Dernburg, October 30, 1909, BAB R1001/2054. Hermann Lisco to Wilhelm von Schoen, February 25, 1909, BAB R1001/2054. Lindequist to Hermann Lisco, July 6, 1910, and Dernburg's memo, July 2, 1910, BAB R1001/1357. Cf. Hintrager to RKA, March 17, 1910, BAB R1001/1345.

52. Consul Müller to Sir Edward Grey, February 12, 1910, UKNA FO 403/414. "Preserve the dignity of the empire," see "Dernburg Resigns," *Sydney Morning Herald,* June 8, 1910. Tirpitz to Dernburg, February 10, 1909; Dernburg to Hintrager, February 17, 1909, BAB R1001/1342.

53. Voigt, "Geschichte," 266. "Theft is easy," see Politicus, "Empire," *Fortnightly Review* 98 (August 1915): 310. See "Bekanntmachung" attached to Gouverneur to RKA, November 14, 1910, BAB R1001/1424. "Perpetual," "monstrous," see Böhmer's memo, March 16, 1912, BAB R1001/1914.

54. See, e.g., Schuckmann to RKA, October 12, 1909, BAB R1001/1324. "Deutsche Kolonialgesellschaft für Südwestafrika," *Frankfurter Zeitung,* November 1, 1910.

55. Rohland to Bethmann Hollweg, July 19, 1909; Gouverneur to RKA, July 20, 1910, BAB R1001/1425. Cf. "Price of Diamonds," *Cincinnati Enquirer,* December 1, 1912. "Jeweler and Wife Caught," *New York Times,* September 26, 1911. "Gems Seized," *New York Tribune,* May 7, 1913. Baericke, *Lüderitzbucht,* 63, 68–69. "Wie man Diamanten schmuggelt," *Berliner Börsenzeitung,* August 7, 1910. "Dodges of Smugglers," *Washington Post,* August 21, 1910. Henry John May, *Murder by Consent* (London: Hutchinson, 1968), 39. Heilingbrunner to Pomonaporte Police Station, May 8, 1912, NAN BLU 267--IV.G.15.II.

56. "Central-Kinematograph," *Salzburger Wacht,* December 22, 1913. See "Schürfrecht," *Entscheidungen des Reichsgerichts in Zivilsachen,* vol. 81 (Leipzig: Veit, 1913), 237–241. Geheime Registratur to RKA, April 30, 1913; Hintrager to Solf, May 9, 1913, BAB R1001/1346. See, e.g., German Foreign Office to Kolonialhauptkasse, June 8, 1910; Generalkonsul London to RKA, April 22, 1910, BAB R1001/1434.

57. Seitz to RKA, May 15, 1911; Judgement of Kaiserliches Bezirksgericht, December 16, 1910, BAB R1001/5521.

58. Kaiserliches Bezirksgericht (Bischof) at Lüderitzbucht, May 30, 1912; Freyberg to Staatsanwaltschaft, Königliches Landgericht, Berlin, February 19, 1913, BAB R1002/2346. Kaiserliches Bezirksgericht Lüderitzbucht to Staatsanwalt beim Königlichen Landgericht, Berlin, September 27, 1912, BAB R1002/2346.

59. Peter Conze to Ersten Staatsanwalt bei dem Königlichen Landgericht, Berlin, January 6, 1913, BAB R1002/2346. Sekretariat der Staantsanwaltschaft, Berlin to Hermann Freyberg, January 30, 1913, BAB R1002/2346. "Spa cures," see Hermann Freyberg to Königliches Landgericht, April 30, 1914, BAB R1002/2346. Kostenrechnung of Königliches Landgericht at Berlin, September 6, 1915, BAB R1002/2346. Freyberg, *Flasche mit den Teufelssteinen* (Leipzig: Schmidt & Spring, 1938); Freyberg, *Verrat in der Wüste* (Gütersloh: Bertelsmann, 1941).

60. Hintrager to Solf, November 2, 1912, BAB R1001/4847. Hinz to Seitz in Windhoek, April 7, 1913, BAB R1001/1346.

61. "Diamond Pie," *Answers* 45, no. 15 (London 1910): 366. Generalkonsul Falcke to Bethmann Hollweg, May 8 and 29, 1914; Diamanten-Regie to RKA, May 25, 1914; K. B. G. to Solf, May 20, 1914; Stauch's affidavit, October 31, 1914, BAB R1001/1436. "'Grub Stake," *Washington Post,* July 19, 1914. "Gem Importer of Steerage Freed," *New York Tribune,* July 22, 1914.

62. "Schürfrecht," *Entscheidungen des Reichsgerichts in Zivilsachen,* vol. 81 (Leipzig: Veit, 1913), 238. State fisc of Southwest Africa against Frau Klara Heim, February 24, 1913, BAB R1001/5591. "Stadtgemeinde Lüderitzbucht," *Lüderitzbuchter Zeitung,* October 29, 1910. Protocol of meeting between Solf, Seitz, Hintrager et al., July 15, 1912, BAB R1001/2087. "Bergbau," *Glückauf* 48, no. 8 (Essen, 1912): 305. Cf. Dernburg to Schuckmann, November 27, 1909, BAB R1001/1324. Will Sellick, ed., *Autobiography of Eugen Mansfeld* (London: Jeppestown Press, 2017), 96.

63. "Uebertreibungen," *Lüderitzbuchter Zeitung,* August 27, 1910. Willy Schmidt to Dernburg, November 14, 1908, BAB R1001/4760. Hintrager's decree, December 16, 1908, BAB R1001/2040. See Schilder, *Entwicklungstendenzen,* vol. 2, 189. Cf. the story of "Becker" in Rafalski, *Niemandsland,* 338.

64. See page 18 of Abgeordneter Dr. Goller, "Bericht der Kommission zur Besprechung der bergrechtlichen Verhältnisse und der Diamantenfrage in Südwestafrika," November 2, 1911, BAB R1001/1346. Baericke, *Lüderitzbucht,* 62.

65. Polizeipräsident of Berlin to RKA, September 23, 1909, BAB R1001/1426. Meldung gegen Slottke, July 9, 1911; Edgar Lange to Georg Sprenkmann, July 17, 1911, BAB R1001/1425. Cf. Schlepps to Müller, September 6, 1911, NAN, BCL 22. Diamanten-Regie to Angelo Golinelli, June 9, 1909, BAB R1001/1423. "Uebertreibungen," *Lüderitzbuchter Zeitung,* August 27, 1910. Schuckmann to Dernburg, January 6, 1909, BAB R1001/1342. "Scharfe Maßregeln," *Berliner Börsenzeitung,* August 9, 1910. "Diamantschmuggel," *Windhuker Nachrichten,* July 13, 1910.

66. See Kundrus, *Moderne Imperialisten,* 118–119. Voigt, "Geschichte," 264. Seitz's decree, September 8, 1911, BAB R1001/1424.

67. Peter Rainier, *African Hazard* (London: Murray, 1940), 30. See Meissner, *Traumland,* 372. "Diamantfelder," *Swakopmunder Zeitung,* November 3, 1909.

68. "Scharfe Maßregeln," *Berliner Börsenzeitung,* August 9, 1910. Pages 91–92 of "Denkschrift über die Massnahmen zur Bekämpfung des Diamantdiebstahls," BAB R1001/1424. "Gerichtsverhandlungen," *Lüderitzbuchter Zeitung,* October 23, 1909.

69. Affidavit of Erich Schroetter at German consulate in Cape Town, January 17, 1910, BAB R1001/1424. Lindequist to Secretary of A. A., March 4, 1910, BAB R901/786. Polizei-Präsident, Abteilung IV (Berlin) to RKA, April 20, 1911, BAB R1001/1425. Paul Etling to Bezirksamt at Lüderitzbucht, April 2, 1913, BAB R901/789.

70. Erich Schroetter to Schuckmann, May 11, 1909, BAB R901/785.

71. Kaiserliches Gouvernement Windhuk to RKA, February 27, 1911, NAN ZBU 1617-R.XIV.G. Regie to Secretary of A. A., June 5, 1914, BAB R1001/1436.

72. Stauch's "Abtretung" at American Consulate, October 31, 1914; Fritz Schlepps to Carl Schurz, October 22, 1914; Falcke to Bethmann Hollweg, May 29, 1914, Anlagen 9 und 10; Meyer-Gerhard to Solf, December 30, 1914; Compare fee quoted in Fritz Schlepps to Carl Schurz, October 22, 1914, BAB R1001/1436.

73. "Gerichtsverhandlungen," *Lüderitzbuchter Zeitung,* October 23, 1909.

74. "Human weakness," see "Aus Lüderitzbucht," *Lüderitzbuchter Zeitung,* June 26, 1909. "Gerichtsverhandlungen," *Lüderitzbuchter Zeitung,* October 30, 1909.

75. Diamanten-Regie to Angelo Golinelli, June 9, 1909, BAB R1001/1423. Paul Rohrbach, *Dernburg und die Südwestafrikaner* (Berlin: Kolonialverlag, 1911), 215, 266. This according to Paul Etling, Secretary to Boehmer, Chief Magistrate at Lüderitzbucht. Voigt, "Geschichte," 266. "Diamantendiebstähle," *Deutsche Tageszeitung*, October 27, 1910; "Uebertreibungen," *Lüderitzbuchter Zeitung*, August 27, 1910.

76. "Jewish" connection, see *Die deutschen Diamanten und ihre Gewinnung* (Berlin: Reimer, 1914), 29. Ludwig Sander, *Geschichte der deutschen Kolonial-Gesellschaft für Südwest-Afrika*, vol. 1 (Berlin, 1912), 232. "Deutsche Kolonialgesellschaft für Südwestafrika," *Frankfurter Zeitung*, October 12, 1910. See Carl Schmidt, *Europäersiedelungen* (Jena: Fischer, 1922), 96.

9. Politics

1. Paul Rohrbach, *Dernburg und die Südwestafrikaner* (Berlin: Kolonialverlag, 1911), 154–156. "A big fellow," see Abbé Wetterlé, *Behind the Scenes in the Reichstag* (London: Hodder and Stoughton, 1918), 105, 145. "Rede Erzbergers," *Salzburger Chronik*, April 25, 1912.

2. See Klaus Epstein, *Matthias Erzberger and the Dilemma of German Democracy* (Princeton: Princeton University Press, 1959), 55.

3. Richard Lewinsohn, *Das Geld in der Politik* (Berlin: S. Fischer, 1930), 38–39. See, e.g., Peter Conze to A. A., November 8, 1907, BAB R1001/6427. "Woermann gegen Simplizissimus," *Deutsch-Südwestafrikanische Zeitung*, June 20, 1908.

4. Protection statistic, see Dernburg to Wilhelm II, December 22, 1908, BAB R1001/1341. George D. Crothers, *The German Elections of 1907* (New York: Columbia University Press, 1941), 36–38. Compare Rohrbach, *Dernburg und die Südwestafrikaner*, 285.

5. Erzberger's speech to Reichstag, *Stenographische Berichte*, November 30, 1906, 4035. See Lascelles to Grey, September 14, 1906, UKNA, FO 800/19.

6. See Volker Berghahn, *Der Tirpitz-Plan* (Düsseldorf: Droste, 1971), 501.

7. See "Maßgebliches," *Die Grenzboten* 66 (1907): 162. Cf. "Unter den Auserwählten," *Berliner Tageblatt*, August 14, 1913. "Kolonialberufe," *Stimmen aus Maria-Laach*, vol. 84 (Freiburg: Herder, 1913), 578. Margaret Lavinia Anderson, "Interdenominationalism," *Central European History* 21, no. 4 (1988): 356. "Systematically sabotaged," see Werner Jochmann, ed., *Im Kampf um die Macht: Hitlers Rede vor dem Hamburger Nationalklub von 1919* (Frankfurt: Verlagsanstalt, 1960), 46.

8. Cf. Freisinnige Volkspartei, *Die Freisinnige Volkspartei und die Reichssteuerpolitik* (Berlin: Deutsche Presse, 1910), 17–20. See Wilfried Loth, *Katholiken im Kaiserreich* (Düsseldorf: Droste, 1984), 166–180.

9. "Agrarier gegen Dernburg," *Vorwärts*, September 16, 1909. Thomas H. Wagner, *"Krieg oder Frieden—Unser Platz an der Sonne": Gustav Stresemann und die Außenpolitik des Kaiserreichs* (Paderborn: Schöningh, 2007), 72. Bethmann sought to distance himself, as recalled in speech by Georges Weill to Reichstag, March 7, 1913, *Stenographische Berichte*, 4374. "Dernburgs Rücktritt," *Berliner Tageblatt*, June 7, 1910. Protocol of Staatsministerium on January 10, 1910, BAB R 43/927. See Helmut Walser Smith, *German Nationalism and Religious Conflict* (Princeton: Princeton University Press, 1995), 143. "Con," see "Wahlkampf," *Reichspost* (Vienna), January 22, 1907. "Das Duell," *Montagsblatt aus Böhmen*, May 2, 1910. Hermann Hillger, *Hillgers Wegweiser für die Reichstagswahl* (Berlin: Hillger, 1907), 126. "Only" a schoolteacher, see Felix Pinner, "Dernburg," *Die Weltbühne* 18, no. 2: 472. Epstein, *Erzberger*, 58. "Deutscher Reichstag," *Neue Hamburger Zeitung*, May 5, 1910.

10. "Erzberger," *General-Anzeiger für Hamburg-Altona,* February 20, 1913. Jöhlinger, "Koloniale Rundschau," *Nord und Süd* 141 (1912): 124. "Der schweigende Erzberger," *Der wahre Jacob,* August 23, 1913, 8026. William Harbutt Dawson, *Evolution of Modern Germany* (London: Unwin, 1909), 386. "Staatssekretär Dernburg," *Berliner Volkszeitung,* April 22, 1910. See "Schwurzeuge," *Windhuker Nachrichten,* June 19, 1914.

11. Stig Förster, *Der doppelte Militarismus* (Stuttgart: Franz Steiner, 1985), 108. Horst Gründer, "Nation," in *Katholizismus,* ed. Albrecht Langner (Paderborn: Schöningh, 1985), 65–88. "Giving up," see Johannes Semler's speech to Reichstag, April 29, 1910, *Stenographische Berichte,* 2770. Wetterlé, *Behind the Scenes,* 105. Extermination order, see Frank Sobich, *"Schwarze Bestien, rote Gefahr"* (Frankfurt am Main: Campus, 2006), 106.

12. Matthias Erzberger, *Glänzende Rechtfertigung der Kolonialpolitik des Zentrums* (Berlin: Germania, 1908).

13. "No convictions, only appetites," see Wetterlé, *Behind the Scenes,* 144. Georg Ledebour, "Südwestafrika (Schluß)," *Die neue Zeit* 28, no. 43 (Stuttgart, 1910): 579. See Herbert Jäckel, *Landgesellschaften* (Halle: Saale, 1909), 5. "Deutsche Kolonialgesellschaft für Südwestafrika," *Frankfurter Zeitung,* October 12, 1910.

14. Erzberger to Reichstag, December 2, 1905, *Stenographische Berichte,* 82. "Deutscher Reichstag," *Berliner Tageblatt,* January 26, 1910. "Staatssekretär Dernburg," *Berliner Volkszeitung,* April 22, 1910.

15. Wetterlé, *Behind the Scenes,* 145. "Koloniale Rundschau," *Nord und Süd* 143 (Breslau, 1912): 127. Matthias Erzberger, *Millionengeschenke: Die Privilegienwirtschaft in Südwestafrika* (Berlin: Germania, 1910), 32. Oskar Hintrager, *Südwestafrika in der deutschen Zeit* (München: Oldenbourg, 1955), 117. Bernhard von Bülow, *Denkwürdigkeiten,* vol. 2 (Berlin: Ullstein, 1930), 267. "A complete fiasco," see "Deutscher Reichstag," *Berliner Börsenzeitung,* January 25, 1910. "La démission de M. Dernburg," *Le Figaro,* June 8, 1910. Matthias Erzberger, "Erfolge," *Kolonialpolitik vor dem Gerichtshof* (Basel: Finckh, 1918), 12.

16. On the last point see, e.g., Fürstenberg to Angelo Golinelli, June 10, 1909, BAB R1001/1397. Stanley Suval, *Electoral Politics in Wilhelmine Germany* (Chapel Hill: University of North Carolina Press, 1985), 81.

17. "Abbaurechte," *Lüderitzbuchter Zeitung,* February 13, 1909. See Theodor Eschenburg, *Matthias Erzberger* (München: Piper, 1973), 29. See Frank Bösch, *Öffentliche Geheimnisse: Skandale, Politik und Medien in Deutschland und Großbritannien 1880–1914* (München: Oldenbourg, 2009), 448. Cf. "Der liberale Kongreß in München," *Gießener Anzeiger,* July 8, 1908.

18. "In the budget," see Rudolf Goldscheid, *Staatssozialismus* (Wien: Anzengruber, 1917), 129. Joseph Davies, *Trust Laws* (Washington, DC: Government Printing Office, 1916), 265. Cf. Edward Dickinson, "German Empire," *History Workshop Journal* 66 (2008): 131. See Centralbureau der Nationalliberalen Partei, *Kolonialpolitik seit der Reichstagsauflösung* (Berlin: Nationalliberale Partei, 1909), 8. Speech by Hermann Paasche, March 23, 1911, *Stenographische Berichte,* 5803.

19. *Deutscher Kolonialatlas,* eds. P. Sprigade and M. Moisel (Berlin: Reimer, 1911), 23. See Dörte Lerp, "Prairie," *Journal of Modern European History* 14, no. 2 (2016): 234. "Die Nachverzollung in Südwestafrika," *Hamburger Nachrichten,* March 4, 1910.

20. Erzberger, *Millionengeschenke,* 35. Cf. "Deutsche Kolonialgesellschaft für Südwestafrika," *Berliner Börsen-Courier,* December 8, 1908. Wetterlé, *Behind the Scenes,* 146. Consul-General Oppenheimer to Sir F. Lascelles, March 12, 1907, British Library, India Office Records, IOR/R/15/1/507. "Lindequist geht," *Breslauer Zeitung,* November 4, 1911.

21. See Launspach (of South African Territories' office in London) to Baudissin (of South African Territories' office in Berlin), August 1908, BAB R1001/1646. Bezirksgericht Lüderitzbucht to RKA, November 3, 1910, BAB R1001/4918. "The boys from the stock exchange," see "Koloniale Stimmen," *Usambara Post,* January 30, 1909. Cf. Bankier von Finck to Dernburg, January 9, 1909; Fr. Hincke to Dernburg, February 2, 1909, BAK N1130/32. "Deutscher Reichstag," *Berliner Börsenzeitung,* January 26, 1910.

22. Deutsche Bank to Emil Lehmann, July 15, 1914, HID, Archives of Deutsche Bank Zentrale Berlin, Sekretariat (Frankfurt), S0103. "Bodenkreditfrage," *Deutsche Kolonialzeitung* 25, no. 10 (1908): 159. "Sache des Reichstages," *Berliner Volkszeitung,* April 22, 1910. "Aus dem Reichstage," *Hamburger Nachrichten,* May 5, 1910. "Question of millions," see "Deutscher Reichstag," *Neue Hamburger Zeitung,* May 5, 1910.

23. See editorial in *Lüderitzbuchter Zeitung,* December 4, 1909; "Die Lüderitzbuchter Denkschrift," *Berliner Börsenzeitung,* April 27, 1910. "Diamantenfunde," *Neues Wiener Tagblatt,* January 26, 1910. Cf. "Deutscher Reichstag," *Neue Hamburger Zeitung,* May 5, 1910.

24. Cf. Christoph Nonn, "Fleischteuerungsprotest und Parteipolitik," *Der Kampf um das tägliche Brot,* eds. Manfred Gailus and Heinrich Volkmann (Opladen: Westdeutscher, 1994), 314. Paul Busching, "Dernburg," *Süddeutsche Monatshefte* 7, no. 2 (München 1910), 580. Erzberger, *Millionengeschenke,*36. See Fritz Blaich, *Kartell- und Monopolpolitik im Kaiserlichen Deutschland* (Düsseldorf: Droste, 1973), 166.

25. "Dernburgs Rücktritt," *Lüderitzbuchter Zeitung,* July 30, 1910. Figures from Wilhelm von Humboldt-Dachroeden, *Diamantenpolitik* (Jena: Fischer, 1915), 55, and Bernhard von König, "Entwicklung," *Zeitschrift für Kolonialpolitik, Kolonialrecht und Kolonialwirtschaft* 12 (Berlin 1910): 600.

26. Cf. "Les Diamants," *Notes financières: Circulaire hebdomadaire de la Caisse commerciale de Roubaix,* July 10, 1909. This estimate from Dernburg to Schuckmann, November 29, 1909, BAB R1001/1324.

27. "One-way" grants, see Christian von Bornhaupt, "Stengel," *Zeitschrift für Kolonialpolitik, Kolonialrecht und Kolonialwirtschaft* 6, no. 5 (Berlin 1904): 539–569. See Karl Romberg, "Natur," *Zeitschrift für Kolonialpolitik, Kolonialrecht und Kolonialwirtschaft* 10 (Berlin, 1908): 369, 374. Dernburg's memo on Reichstag budget commission meeting, January 1910, BAB R1001/1324. Friedrich Giese, "Fortschritte," *Zeitschrift für Kolonialpolitik, Kolonialrecht und Kolonialwirtschaft* 11 (Berlin, 1908): 534. Rohrbach, *Dernburg und die Südwestafrikaner,* 52.

28. Schuckmann to Dernburg, October 12, 1909, BAB R1001/1324. "Der Kolonial-Courier," *Berliner Börsen-Courier,* January 28, 1910. Cf. Wilhlem Kögel to Dernburg, March 7, 1910, BAK N1130/37.

29. German Colonial Corporation to Dernburg, March 5, 1910, BAB R1001/1325. "Rechtsverhältnisse der Deutschen Kolonialgesellschaft für Südwestafrika," *Berliner Börsen-Courier,* February 15, 1910. "Wähler des Erzgebirges! Wählt am 12. Januar den Kandidaten der Vereinigten liberalen Parteien: Herrn Dr. Stresemann!" (Campaign pamphlet, undated 1910–1911), PAAA NL Stresemann 120. Cf. Dernburg to Schuckmann, November 27, 1909, BAB R1001/1324. Jürgen Kocka et al., *Sozialgeschichtliches Arbeitsbuch* (München: Beck, 1975), 132. Gerhard Bry, *Wages in Germany, 1871–1945* (Princeton: Princeton University Press, 1960), 32. "Streiks und Aussperrungen in Deutschland im Jahre 1909," *Norddeutsche Allgemeine Zeitung,* June 1, 1910. Cf. Rudolf Martin, *Unter dem Scheinwerfer* (Berlin: Schuster, 1910), 125. "Die Hetze gegen Dernburg," *Berliner Volkszeitung,* January 21, 1910. Slippery slope, see Leonard Seabrooke, *Social Sources of Financial Power* (Ithaca: Cornell University Press, 2006), 98.

30. "Sander, Karl," *Deutsches Kolonial-Lexikon,* ed. Heinrich Schnee, vol. 3 (Leipzig, 1920), 248. Horst Drechsler, *Südwestafrika unter deutscher Kolonialherrschaft: Die großen Land- und Minengesellschaften* (Stuttgart: Steiner, 1996), 311. Protocol of Regie's board meeting, February 10, 1909, HID, Archives of Deutsche Bank Zentrale Berlin, Sekretariat (Frankfurt), S097. Fürstenberg to Regie board, November 29, 1912, HID, Archives of Deutsche Bank Zentrale Berlin, Sekretariat (Frankfurt), S097. "Deutsche Kolonialgesellschaft für Südwestfrika," *Berliner Börsen-Courier,* July 24, 1909.

31. F. Bugge and Henry Fowler, "Bericht des Vortstandes der Deutschen Kolonial-Gesellschaft für Südwest-Afrika über das vierundzwanzigste Geschäftsjahr," 4, BAB R1001/1544. See emendations to Dernburg to German Colonial Corporation for Southwest Africa, February 27, 1909, BAB R1001/1815. Karl Helfferich's memorandum, December 29, 1908, HID, Archives of Deutsche Bank Zentrale Berlin, Sekretariat (Frankfurt), S096.

32. "Considerable" sum, see DKSSWA to Dernburg, December 22, 1909, and January 26 and 31, 1910, BAB R1001/1324.

33. "Zum Vertragskonflikt der Deutschen Kolonialgesellschaft," *Berliner Börsen-Courier,* March 12, 1910. See Georg Ledebour, "Interessenkämpfe," *Die neue Zeit* 2, no. 43 (1910): 582. Wolfgang Werner, "A Brief History of Land Dispossession in Namibia," *Journal of Southern African Studies* 19, no. 1 (1993): 139. Jürgen Zimmerer and Joachim Zeller, *Völkermord* (Berlin: Links Verlag, 2003), 32, 140.

34. See Lawrence Green, *Like Diamond Blazing* (London: Hale, 1967), 160. See also Robbie Aitken, *Exclusion* (New York: Peter Lang, 2007), 82n87. "The worst in the history of the world," quoted in "Rebellen im Busch," *Der Spiegel,* August 28, 1957, 33.

35. "Die Bergrechte der Deutschen Kolonialgesellschaft," *Kölnische Zeitung,* January 29, 1910. "Die Bergrechte der Kolonialgesellschaft," *Börsen-Halle,* January 30, 1910.

36. See treaty of January 28, 1909, "Gesetze," *Deutsches Kolonialblatt* 20 (Berlin, 1909): 569. "Der Erzbergersche Antrag," *Berliner Tageblatt,* April 22, 1910. Revenue target, see "Telegraphische Nachrichten," *Windhuker Nachrichten,* April 23, 1910. "Dernburg gegen Erzberger," *Berliner Volkszeitung,* April 22, 1910. W. Hahn, "Abänderung," *Verhandlungen des Deutschen Kolonialkongresses 1910* (Berlin, 1910), 516. Robert Gerstenhauer, "Südwestafrikanische Diamantenpolitik," *Jahrbuch über die deutschen Kolonien* 7 (Essen: Baedeker, 1914): 172–173. Protocol of Budget Commission's meeting, January 26, 1910, BAB R1001/1324.

37. Erzberger, "Bedeutung des Zentrums," *Zeitschrift für Politik* 2 (1909): 224. "Abscess," see Otto Hammann, *Um den Kaiser* (Berlin: Hobbing, 1919), 12. See Carl Peters, "Wie der gegenwärtige Krieg entstand," *Gesammelte Schriften,* ed. Walter Frank, vol. 3 (München: Beck, 1944), 464. Cf. Dernburg to Herbert Schmidt, August 27, 1908, N1130/35. Erich Ekkehard, ed., *Sigilla Veri (Ph. Stauff's Semi-Kürschner),* vol. 1 (Erfurt: Bodung, 1929), 1158. "His Excellency the money-maker," see Philipp Scheidemann, *Memoiren eines Sozialdemokraten,* vol. 1 (Dresden: Reissner, 1928), 155. Woodruff Smith, *Ideological Origins of Nazi Imperialism* (Oxford: Oxford University Press, 1989), 124.

38. Reichskolonialamt, *Schutzgebiete in Afrika und der Südsee 1910/1911: Amtliche Jahresberichte* (Berlin: Mittler, 1912), 134.

39. "For days and years," see Louis Hamilton, "Herr Dernburg and German Colonial Policy," *United Empire: The Royal Colonial Institute Journal* 1 (London: Isaac Pitman, 1910): 648. "Dernburgs südwestafrikanische Politik," *Alldeutsche Blätter* 20, no. 21 (1910); 175. "Work for the benefit of 250 people," see "German Diamond Scandal," *New York Times,* January 30, 1910. Cf. Eugen Wolf to Dernburg, January 17, 1910, BAK N1130/36. "Staub," "Desert-King," see Hans-Otto Meissner, *Traumland Südwest: Südwest-Afrika— Tiere, Farmen, Diamanten* (Stuttgart: Cotta, 1968), 372. See Dernburg to Schuckmann, November 27, 1909, BAB R1001/1324. "Dernburg," *Berliner Tageblatt,* April 25, 1910.

40. "Woermann-Ballin," *Die Zukunft* 59 (Berlin: Bernstein, 1907): 76. Edgar Allen Forbes, "Frenchman and German in Africa," *American Review of Reviews*, ed. Albert Shaw, vol. 44 (New York: Review of Reviews Co., 1911), 316. Max Schippel, "Kolonial-debatten," *Sozialistische Monatshefte*, ed. Josef Bloch, vol. 1 (Berlin, 1908), 440. Bettina Zurstrassen, *"Ein Stück deutscher Erde schaffen"* (Frankfurt: Campus, 2008), 107. "Germany's Chamberlain," *Guyra Argus*, January 20, 1910.

41. Cf. "Zum Diamantenstreit," *Berliner Tageblatt*, April 18, 1912. Stauch to German Colonial Office, BAB R1001/1325. Consul Müller at Lüderitzbucht to John Merriman, May 6, 1910, UKNA FO 403/414. "Politische Nachrichten," *Berliner Börsenzeitung*, February 24, 1910. "Deutsche Kolonialgesellschaft für Südwestafrika," *Frankfurter Zeitung*, February 25, 1910. "Little Bernhard," see "Dernburgs Rücktritt," *Namslauer Zeitung*, June 11, 1910; "Hamburg, 7. Juni," *Darmstädter Zeitung*, June 8, 1910; "Zu Dernburgs Rücktritt," *Hamburger Fremdenblatt*, June 9, 1910. "The man . . . must go," see "Dernburg-Krise," *Allgemeine Zeitung* (Munich), May 7, 1910; "Dernburgs Rücktritt," *Hamburger Fremdenblatt*, June 9, 1910.

42. "Rücktritt Dernburgs," *Mitteilungen aus dem Verein zur Abwehr des Antisemitismus* 20, no. 25 (Berlin, 1910): 194. See, e.g., "Kapital und die Schutzgebiete," *Berliner Tageblatt*, June 9, 1910. Felix Pinner, *Emil Rathenau* (Leipzig: Verlagsgesellschaft, 1918), 341. "The lesser evil," see "Diamanten," *Frankfurter Zeitung*, January 5, 1912. German consul at Johannesburg to Bethmann Hollweg, July 26, 1909, BAB R901/785. "Money, Mines, and Markets," *African World and Cape-Cairo Express* 49, no. 634 (London, 1915): 283.

43. See Hans-Christoph Schröder, *Gustav Noske und die Kolonialpolitik* (Bonn: Dietz, 1979), 63, 22. Hans Spellmeyer, *Deutsche Kolonialpolitik im Reichstag* (Stuttgart: Kohlhammer, 1931), 124–140. But see "Dernburgs Rücktritt," *Vorwärts*, June 7, 1910. "Dernburg's powerful initiative," see Ernst Friedegg, *Millionen und Millionäre* (Berlin: Vita, 1914), 293. Speech by Gustav Noske, May 2, 1912, *Stenographische Berichte*, 1639–1641. Cf. "Politische Nachrichten," *Berliner Börsenzeitung*, January 26, 1910. Cf. Wolfgang Reinhard, "'Sozialimperialismus' oder 'Entkolonialisierung der Historie?': Kolonialkrise und 'Hottentottenwahlen', 1904–1907," *Historisches Jahrbuch* 97/98 (1978), 406.

44. "Das 'Opfer' der Zentrumsrache," *Sächsische Volkszeitung*, June 10, 1910. "La démission de M. Dernburg," *Le Figaro*, June 8, 1910. "First-rate position," see Erzberger, "Erfolge," 12. "Die Hetze gegen Dernburg," *Berliner Volkszeitung*, January 21, 1910. "Erzbergers Raid," *Berliner Tageblatt*, April 23, 1910. Cf. "Politischer Tagesbericht," *Norddeutsche Allgemeine Zeitung*, June 10, 1910. See speech by Paasche, March 23, 1911, *Stenographische Berichte*, 5803. Cf. Dernburg to Stresemann, February 17, 1911, PAAA NL Stresemann 120. "Reichsfinanzreform," *Lüderitzbuchter Zeitung*, July 3, 1909.

45. "Aus dem Reichstag," *Berliner Tageblatt*, February 1, 1910. Norden, "Wochenschau," *Berliner Tageblatt*, February 26, 1910. "Katzenjammerstimmung im Reichstag," *Berliner Tageblatt*, January 31, 1910; "Zum Kurssturz der Kolonialanteile," *Berliner Tageblatt*, February 25, 1910. Share price, see "Neueste Handels-Nachrichten," *Berliner Tageblatt*, February 21 and 26, 1910.

46. "Die Börse," *Berliner Börsenzeitung*, February 24, 1910. "Sad list of colonial disappointments," see "Reichsspiegel," *Die Grenzboten* 70 (1911), 245. "64% Dividende!" *Neue Börsenzeitung*, September 16, 1910; "Eine nette Moral," *Lüderitzbuchter Zeitung*, December 3, 1910; "Berliner Börsenbericht," *Die Presse* (Thorn), November 11, 1911. "Wien, 6. Juni," *Neue Freie Presse*, June 7, 1910. Wetterlé, *Behind the Scenes*, 145. "Großbanken und Handelspresse," *März: Eine Wochenschrift* 5, no. 1 (München: Langen, 1911): 503. Drop in stock figures, see Rudolf Staab, *Die Unternehmertätigkeit deutscher Banken im Auslande* (Lörrach: Wisentaler, 1912), 54; "Gründungsmethoden," *Frankfurter*

Zeitung, February 4, 1911. "Kolonialgesellschaft," *Frankfurter Zeitung,* September 8, 1910. "Lindequist geht," *Breslauer Zeitung,* November 4, 1911. Otto Jöhlinger, "Kolonialwirtschaft," *Koloniale Rundschau* (Berlin, 1914), 45.

47. Hugo Gerisch & Co. to Lindequist, September 15, 1910; RKA to Hugo Gerisch & Co., September 19, 1910, BAB R1001/1529. "Handel, Industrie und Verkehr," *Deutsch-Südwestafrikanische Zeitung,* December 7, 1910. "Reichsspiegel," *Die Grenzboten* 70 (1911): 246. Georg Obst, *Kapitalsanlage und Vermögensverwaltung* (Leipzig: Poeschel, 1911), 37. "The people . . . had sacrificed," see Alfons Goldschmidt, "Kolonialspekulanten," *Zeit im Bild* (Berlin), September 17, 1912. Cf. Dernburg to Georg Heydner, March 2, 1910, BAK N1130/37. "Koloniale Rundschau," *Nord und Süd* 143 (Breslau, 1912): 125. "Dernburg und Erzberger," *Das Vaterland* (Vienna), April 23, 1910.

48. See Fritz André, *Pomona-Gebiet* (Berlin: Reimer, 1910), 5. Decline of dividends, see Rudolf von Koch's protocol of board meeting of September 12, 1914 (dated September 17, 1914), BAB R1001/1536. "Dernburg," *Berliner Börsenzeitung,* December 14, 1910.

49. Kurt Rein, *Wie England die Deutschen Kolonien bewertet* (Berlin: Reimer, 1918), 36. Otto Jöhlinger, "Kolonien," *Koloniale Rundschau* (Berlin, 1914), 123. Paul Schütte, *Wertpapiereinfuhr* (Iserlohn: Geldsetzer, 1914), 32. Reichskolonialamt memo, June 1914, BAB R1001/7001. Hartmut Pogge von Strandmann, "Purpose of German Colonialism," *German Colonialism,* eds. Volker Langbehn and Mohammad Salama (New York: Columbia University Press, 2011), 205.

50. "Excessive quantity of paper," see "Lüderitzbucht," *Diamond Fields Advertiser,* September 27, 1909. Wilhlem Kögel to Dernburg, March 7, 1910, BAK N1130/37. Between 1910 and 1913, the word "agiotage" made nine appearances in the *Stenographische Berichte.* Six of these appearances touched on colonial stocks.

51. "Too high," see "Diamantenfunde," *Neues Wiener Tagblatt,* January 26, 1910; "Deutsche Kolonialgesellschaft," *Berliner Börsen-Courier,* January 11, 1910. "Dernburg und Erzberger," *Das Vaterland,* April 23, 1910. Cf. "Unter den Auserwählten," *Berliner Tageblatt,* September 7 and 24, 1913. "Nochmals der 'berühmte' Vertrag," *Lüderitzbuchter Zeitung,* March 12, 1910. "Millionengeschenke," *Salzburger Chronik,* August 9, 1910. Zmarzlik, *Bethmann* (Düsseldorf: Droste, 1957), 17. "Dernburg," *Berliner Börsenzeitung,* December 14, 1910. "Kolonialkrieg," *Allgemeine Zeitung* (Munich), May 28, 1910. "Dernburgs Rücktritt," *Vorwärts,* June 8, 1910. Diary entry of July 19, 1910, Kurt Riezler, *Tagebücher, Aufsätze, Dokumente,* 167. Entry of June 19, *Tagebuch der Baronin Spitzemberg* (Göttingen: V&R, 1963), 522. Das 'Opfer,'" *Sächsische Volkszeitung,* June 10, 1910.

52. Solf to Vizeadmiral Grapow, June 10, 1912, BAK N1053/36. Cf. "Die Südwestafrikaner und die Reichsregierung," *Berliner Börsenzeitung,* May 12, 1910.

53. Lennox Ward to Inspector of Mines at Windhoek, September 7, 1921, Brenthurst Library (hereafter BL) MS/OPP/EO/K1.11.32. Entry of January 30, 1910, *Tagebuch der Baronin Spitzemberg,* 518. Bernhard Huldermann, *Ballin* (London: Cassell, 1922), 108.

54. "Assailed at every turn," see "Dernburg," *Le Figaro,* June 8, 1910. Cf. "Dernburgs Kolonialpolitik," *Berliner Börsen-Courier,* February 22, 1911; "Staatssekretär Dernburg," *Berliner Volkszeitung,* April 22, 1910. "Südafrika und Diamantenschleiferei," *Koloniale Rundschau, Jahrgang 1914* (Berlin, 1914), 168. "Endless," see "Dernburg," *Deutsche Tageszeitung* (Berlin), December 14, 1910. Pinner, *Emil Rathenau,* 49. "Dernburg's Fall," *New York Times,* June 12, 1910. "Dernburg," *Deutsche Tageszeitung* (Berlin), December 14, 1910.

55. Dernburg to Stresemann, February 17, 1911, PAAA NL Stresemann 120. See "Opfer der Wohltätigkeit," *Kladderadatsch* 63, no. 5 (Berlin, 1910): 18. "Dernburgs Abschied," *Simplicissimus* 15, no. 13 (1910): 213. Cf. "Dernburg," *Jugend* 15, no. 25 (1910): 603. "Dernburg," *Le Soir,* August 16, 1910. "Japan," *Der Ostasiatische Lloyd,* September 9,

1910. Dernburg to Solf, December 22, 1911, BAB R1001/1447. Bernhard Dernburg, *Kolonialwirtschaft* (Berlin: Hansa-Bund, 1924), 4. "The world . . . forgets," see Dernburg to Stresemann, February 17, 1911, PAAA NL Stresemann 120. "Dernburg," *Deutsche Tageszeitung* (Berlin), December 14, 1910.

56. Alexander von Benckendorff to Alexander Izvolsky, October 28/November 10, 1909, *Diplomatische Aktenstücke zur Geschichte der Ententepolitik der Vorkriegsjahre*, ed. B. von Siebert (Berlin: de Gruyter, 1921), 729. Cf. Roger Chickering, *Imperial Germany and a World Without War* (Princeton: Princeton University Press, 1975); Christopher Clark, *The Sleepwalkers* (London: Allen Lane, 2012), 334–335; Werner Schiefel, *Dernburg 1865– 1937* (Zürich: Atlantis, 1974), 120–127; Walther Rathenau, *Notes and Diaries 1907–1922*, ed. Hartmut Pogge von Strandmann (Oxford: Clarendon, 1985), 151. Cf. John C. G. Röhl, "The Curious Case," *An Improbable War? The Outbreak of World War I and European Political Culture Before 1914*, eds. Holger Afflerbach and David Stevenson (New York: Berghahn, 2007), 75–92. Dernburg to Bethmann Hollweg, January 3, 1912, R43/929. Theodor Wolff, *Tagebücher 1914–1919*, vol. 1 (Boppard: Boldt, 1984), 243, 249. But cf. Jules Cambon to Justin de Selves, July 13, 1911, *Documents diplomatiques français*, series 2, vol. 14 (Paris: Imprimerie Nationale, 1955), 62.

57. "Labor not to be rich," see "Millionengeschenke," *Salzburger Chronik*, August 9, 1910. Diary entry for November 11, 1910, Hedwig Pringsheim, *Tagebücher*, vol. 4 (Göttingen: Wallstein, 2015), 559. Egon Krull to Dernburg, August 28, 1913, BAK N1130/10. Harden to Rathenau, September 27, 1911, *Walther Rathenau/Maximilian Harden Briefwechsel, 1897–1920*, ed. Hans Dieter Hellige (G. Mueller Verlag, 1983), 637. "Inciting class hatred," see "Exzellenz—'Aufreizer,'" *Illustrierte Kronen-Zeitung*, May 21, 1912. See Ute Frevert and Anne Schmidt, "Geschichte, Emotionen und die Macht der Bilder," *Gechichte und Gesellschaft* 37, no. 1 (2011): 21.

58. Harden to Rathenau, Christmas 1910, *Walther Rathenau/Maximilian Harden Briefwechsel*, 627. Compare Zurstrassen, *"Ein Stück,"* 107–108. Erich Schmidt, *Jahrhundertfeier der Königlichen Friedrich-Wilhelms-Universität* (Berlin, 1911), 131. "Watered down," see Pinner, "Dernburg," 471; "Dernburgs Rücktritt," *Münchner Neueste Nachrichten*, June 9, 1910; Wolff, *Tagebücher 1914–1919*, vol. 1, 305. "The man who served up the colonies," etc., see "Dernburg," *Deutsche Tageszeitung*, February 13, 1912; "Nach dem Rücktritt," *Hamburgischer Correspondent*, August 26, 1912; "Deutschnationales Schatzkästlein," *Berliner Tageblatt*, January 30, 1919; Houston Stewart Chamberlain to Max von Baden, April 28, 1916, Karina Urbach and Bernd Buchner, "Prinz Max von Baden und Houston Stewart Chamberlain: Aus dem Briefwechsel 1909–1919," *Vierteljahrshefte für Zeitgeschichte* 52, no. 1 (2004): 154.

59. "Wien, 6. Juni," *Neue Freie Presse*, June 7, 1910. "Smart," see "Erzberger-Nudeln," *Neues Wiener Journal*, July 25, 1912. "Erzberger und Kiderlen-Waechter," *Allgemeiner Tiroler Anzeiger*, November 14, 1911. Reinhold Sydow to Klemens Delbrück, September 2, 1913, *Quellensammlung zur Geschichte der Deutschen Sozialpolitik 1867 bis 1914*, vol. 4, pt. 4 (Mainz: WBG, 2008), 451. See Alastair Thompson, "Honours Uneven," *Past & Present*, no. 144 (1994), 192.

60. "Political and moral victory," see Paul Rohrbach, "Diamantlager," *Velhagen & Klasings Monatshefte, Jahrgang 1910/1911*, vol. 1 (Berlin: Verlhagen & Klasing, 1911), 463.

10. Takeover

1. "German South West Africa," *Rhodesia Herald*, July 4, 1913. Compare Emil Zimmermann, *Unsere Kolonien* (Berlin: Ullstein, 1912), 238, with G. Goldberg, "Diamanten-

abbau," *Dinglers Polytechnisches Journal* 329, no. 34/35 (Berlin: Dietze, 1914): 532. Cf. Bezirksamt Lüderitzbucht to Kaiserliches Gouvernement Windhuk, May 27, 1913, NAN ZBU Geheimakten, VII.m, Bd. 1, Bl. 11. Carl Hagemann, *Weltfahrt: ein unempfindsames Reisebuch* (Berlin: Schuster & Loeffler, 1921), 59. "Modeneuheiten," *Maiser Wochenblatt*, March 29, 1914.

2. "Deutscher Reichstag," *Jenaer Volksblatt*, March 21, 1914. "Handelsteil," *Berliner Volkszeitung*, September 13, 1910. Lindequist's speech to Reichstag, December 12, 1910, *Stenographische Berichte*, 3596. "Zum Deutsch-Südwestafrikanischen Diamantenstreit," *Berliner Börsen-Courier*, January 19, 1911.

3. Lennox Ward to Inspector of Mines at Windhoek, September 7, 1921, BL MS/OPP/EO/K1.11.32. "Südwestafrika," *Berliner Volkszeitung*, March 20, 1914. "Siedelungen," *Berliner Tageblatt*, March 5, 1914. Dr. Goller's report, November 2, 1911, BAB R1001/1346. "Deutsche Schutzgebiete," *Frankfurter Zeitung*, August 22, 1911. "Deutscher Reichstag," *Dresdner Neueste Nachrichten*, December 11, 1912.

4. "Ost- und Südwestafrika im Reichstage," *Berliner Volkszeitung*, March 20, 1914.

5. Lora Wildenthal, *German Women for Empire* (Durham: Duke University Press, 2001), 100. "Incapable," see Paul Rohrbach, *Deutsche Kolonialwirtschaft*, vol. 1 (Berlin: Seitz, 1907), 349.

6. For example, Paul Rohrbach, "Diamantlager," *Velhagen & Klasings Monatshefte, Jahrgang 1910/1911*, vol. 1 (Berlin: Verlhagen & Klasing, 1911), 456. See Walter Mogk, *Paul Rohrbach* (Munich: Goldmann, 1972). Theodor Heuss to Friedrich Naumann, July 18, 1910, *Theodor Heuss: Aufbruch im Kaiserreich: Briefe 1892–1917*, ed. Frieder Günther (Munich: Saur, 2009), 301. "Rohrbachs Kampf," *Berliner Tageblatt*, January 11, 1911. Coloniensis, "Koloniale Rundschau: Millionengeschenke und Millionenverluste!" *Nord und Süd* 143 (Breslau, 1912): 126.

7. See three-part series of essays published by the *Frankfurter Zeitung:* "Diamanten von Südwestafrika," July 17, 20, and 29, 1910. "Diamond Field," *Aberdeen Herald*, August 4, 1910.

8. "Die deutschen Diamanten," *Frankfurter Zeitung*, January 5, 1912. "Diamantenregie," *Handels-Zeitung des Berliner Tageblatts*, October 8, 1913. Fürstenberg to Helfferich, April 19, 1912, HID, Archives of Deutsche Bank Zentrale Berlin, Sekretariat (Frankfurt), S097. Cf. Walther Rathenau, "Notizen zur Afrikareise 1908," in *Schriften der Wilhelminischen Zeit 1885–1914*, ed. Alexander Jaser (Düsseldorf: Droste, 2015), 683. "Das Duell," *Montagsblatt aus Böhmen*, May 2, 1910. Paul Willemsen, *Das Credit- und Bankwesen in den Deutschen Kolonien Afrikas* (Haselünne: Lammersdorf, 1915), 38. Curt Pasel's memo, November 17, 1913, BAB R1001/1347. Judgement of Prussian Kammergericht in case of Kolmanskop Diamond Mines, et al. against State Fisc, November 21, 1912, BAB R1001/5591.

9. Cf. Dernburg to Schuckmann, November 27, 1909, BAB R1001/1324. Ernest Oppenheimer's memorandum, April 12, 1932, BL MS/OPP/EO/K1.11.36. Paul Rohrbach, *Gedanke* (Leipzig: Königstein, 1912), 142–146. "Südwest unter Dernburg," *Windhuker Nachrichten*, March 3, 1909. "Als Vertreter der Südwestafrikanischen Diamanteninteressenten . . ." *Frankfurter Zeitung*, August 25, 1911. See Carl Bödiker & Co. to RKA, July 22, 1912, BAB R1001/1232. "Reichskolonialamt und Diamantenfelder," *Berliner Börsen-Courier*, February 26, 1910. "£10,000 Blaze," *Rand Daily Mail*, August 16, 1912.

10. "Südwestafrikanische Diamanten," *Dresdner Neueste Nachrichten*, November 19, 1913. "Deutschland," *Berliner Tageblatt*, March 22, 1913. "Schwurzeuge," *Windhuker Nachrichten*, June 19, 1914.

11. Kolmanskop Diamond Mines Meeting notes, March 6, 1911, NAN ZBU 1622, R.XIV.i.8, Band 2. See *Lüderitzbuchter Zeitung,* March 20, 1909, and December 4, 1909. "Die deutschen Diamanten und die Regie-Verträge," *Frankfurter Zeitung,* January 5, 1912. Fürstenberg's protocol of Regie board-meeting, April 4, 1912, HID, Archives of Deutsche Bank Zentrale Berlin, Sekretariat (Frankfurt), S097. Curt Pasel's memo, November 17, 1913, BAB R1001/1347. Report of Diamanten-Regie for 1912/13, HID, Archives of Deutsche Bank Zentrale Berlin, Sekretariat (Frankfurt), S097. RKA to Gottlieb von Jagow, April 2, 1913, BAB R901/789. "Hanau," *Dresdner Neueste Nachrichten,* August 17, 1913. Theodor Fasching, *Organisation* (München: Steinebach, 1914), 62. J. Neumann, "Verwendung," *Abhandlungen des Hamburgischen Kolonialinstituts,* vol. 26 (Hamburg, 1914), 121. See Bruno Simmersbach, "Bergbau," *Zeitschrift für die gesamte Staatswissenschaft* 72 (1916), 420. Solf's decree, December 30, 1912, BAB R1001/4730.

12. Nachlass Bernhard von König, BAB N 2146/114 and N 2146/128. See, e.g., protocol of board meeting, August 20, 1913, BAB R1001/1390. Curt Pasel to RKA, January 26, 1911, NAN ZBU 1613, R.XIV.f.2, Band 2. Cf. "Diamantenfrage," *Vorwärts,* March 19, 1914. See G. Glockemeier to Deutsche Diamanten-Gesellschaft, June 2, 1915, BAB R1001/1396. "Tages-Rundschau," *Frankfurter Zeitung,* April 19, 1912. Stauch to RKA, January 5, 1910, BAB R1001/1360. "Diamanten-Regie," *Reichs- und Staats-Anzeiger,* April 9, 1913.

13. See Lüderitzbuchter Minenkammer, *Umwandlung der Bruttoabgaben* (Lüderitzbucht: Lüderitzbuchter Zeitung, 1911), 1–23. See also Ludwig Kastl's memos, April 16, 1912, and May 22, 1912, BAK N1138/51. "Poorer," see "Handelsteil," *Berliner Volkszeitung,* October 14, 1910; "Steuerpolitik," *Berliner Börsen-Courier,* June 24, 1912. See Sigmund Schilder, *Entwicklungstendenzen,* vol. 2 (Berlin, 1915), 189. Walter Delsarte, *The Negro, Democracy and the War* (Detroit: Wolverine, 1919), 19. "Ausfuhrzoll auf Rohdiamanten," *Vossische Zeitung,* July 2, 1910. "Diamond Duties," *The Observer* (London), June 1, 1913.

14. Tax rate, see Dernburg to Kaiser, January 7, 1909, BAB R1001/1341. Cf. *Jahresbericht der Lüderitzbuchter Minenkammer über das Geschäftsjahr 1912* (Lüderitzbucht: Lüderitzbuchter Zeitung, 1912), 29. BAB R1001/1458a. Karl Pickel, *Selbstverwaltungsverbände* (Berlin: Schweitzer, 1916), 23. Stauch to RKA, January 5, 1910, BAB R1001/1360. Seitz to RKA, November 14, 1911, BAB R1001/1447; Seitz to Solf, February 19, 1912, BAK N1053/134. "Denkschrift über die Diamantensteuer, April 16, 1912, BAK N 1138/51. "Diamanten und Mischehen," *Berliner Volkszeitung,* May 3, 1912. "Auseinandersetzungen um die Diamanten-Abgaben (Ausfurhrzoll)," BAB R1001/1447–1452. "Steuerpolitik," *Börsen-Courier,* June 24, 1912.

15. "Bergbau," *Glückauf* 50, no. 8 (Essen, 1914): 298. "Pomona's Year," *African World and Cape-Cairo Express* 43, no. 550 (London, 1913): 135. "Net," see Karl Kucklentz, *Das Zollwesen der deutschen Schutzgebiete* (Halle: Universität Halle-Wittenberg, 1913), 48. Waldstein's speech, May 2, 1912, *Stenographische Berichte,* 1624. Max Otzen, *Diamond Taxation* (Kimberley, 1952), 10. Hence, attachment to Hintrager's decree of February 25, 1913, BAB R1001/4730. "Steuerpolitik," *Börsen-Courier,* June 24, 1912. "Diamantenprozess," *Berliner Tageblatt,* November 29, 1913, and December 1, 1913. Decree of January 12, 1913, cited in *Berliner Jahrbuch für Handel und Industrie: Bericht der Ältesten der Kaufmannschaft von Berlin, Jahrgang 1913,* vol. 1 (Berlin, 1914), 68. "Equivalent," see Report of A. C. Sutherland et al. for Administrator of SWA Protectorate, July 28, 1920, NAN BBL 45 M.104/1. Cf. Ernest Oppenheimer's memorandum, April 12, 1932, BL MS/OPP/EO/K1.11.36.

16. Johannes Bühler, *Deutsche Geschichte* (Berlin: de Gruyter, 1960), 331. See, e.g., Friedrich von Bernhardi, *Deutschland und der nächste Krieg* (Stuttgart: Cotta, 1912).

17. Rudolf Emil Martin, *Deutsche Machthaber* (Berlin: Schuster and Loeffler, 1910), 532. "Pays 2,500 Per Cent," *New York Times*, March 28, 1914. Solf to Matthias Erzberger, March 25, 1914, BAK N1053/102.

18. Reinhart Kößler, *Namibia and Germany* (Münster: Westfälisches Dampfboot, 2015), 150. Disconto-Gesellschaft in Berlin, *Geschäftsbericht für das Jahr 1910* (1911), 12. Franz Baltzer, *Kolonialbahnen* (Berlin: Göschen, 1916), 31. Cf. August Austerhoff, *Die Banken in den deutschen Kolonien* (Leipzig: Noske, 1918), 35. Deutsche Diamantengesellschaft to Solf, October 22, 1913, HID, Archives of Deutsche Bank Zentrale Berlin, Sekretariat (Frankfurt), S097.

19. Alwin Wünsche, *Die deutschen Kolonien* (Leipzig: Voigtländer, 1912), 146. "Etat des Reichskolonialamts," *Vorwärts*, March 8, 1914. Ledebour's speech, January 25, 1910, *Stenographische Berichte*, 793. See Max von Grapow, *Die deutsche Flagge im Stillen Ozean* (Berlin: Reimer, 1916), 34.

20. "Too many diamonds," see "Hobelspäne," *Der wahre Jacob* 26, no. 609 (1909): 6431. See "Dernburgs Impressionen," *Der Tag*, November 5, 1909. Carl Peters, "An Deutsch-Südwest vorbei," *Der Tag*, June 27, 1911. *Berliner Jahrbuch für Handel und Industrie: Bericht der Ältesten der Kaufmannschaft von Berlin, Jahrgang 1913*, vol. 1 (Berlin, 1914), 69. Minister für Handel und Gewerbe (Lusensky) to Bethmann Hollweg, October 13, 1911, BAB R901/787. Simmersbach, "Bergbau," 420. Erich Quiring, *Die Eisenbahnen Deutsch-Südwestafrikas und ihre Bedeutung für die wirtschaftliche Entwicklung der Kolonie* (Leipzig: Noske, 1911), 38. Cf. Ludwig Quessel to Reichstag on March 20, 1914, *Stenographische Berichte*, 8217. "Fürstenberg triumphans," *Die Zukunft* 85 (1913): 67. Speech by Gustav Noske, *Stenographische Berichte*, May 2, 1912, 1639, 1641.

21. Otto Jöhlinger, *Handelspolitik* (Berlin: Simion, 1914), 57. Karl Wehrstedt, *Die Handelspolitische Bedeutung der deutschen Kolonien* (Hildesheim: Borgmeyer, 1926), 115. "Politische Nachrichten," *Berliner Börsenzeitung*, May 3, 1912. Export figures, see Karl Dove, *Wirtschaftsstudien* (Hamburg: Westermann, 1917), 4. Figures from Carl Peters, *Zur Weltpolitik* (Berlin: Sigismund, 1911), 153, 155. Karl Radek, "Rundschau," *Die neue Zeit* 30, no. 32 (1912): 214–215.

22. *Volkswirtschaftliche Chronik für das Jahr 1912*, vol. 15 (Jena, 1913), 24. H. Jürgen Wächter, *Naturschutz in den deutschen Kolonien in Afrika* (Münster: LIT, 2008), 67, note 632. Zimmermann, *Unsere Kolonien*, 232. See Oberstleutnant Gallus, "Die Diamantvorkommen (Schluss)," *Zeitschrift für Kolonialpolitik, Kolonialrecht und Kolonialwirtschaft* 12 (1910): 946. Cf. "Deutsche Schutzgebiete," *Frankfurter Zeitung*, September 5, 1909. See S. H. Lotz, "Diamantenproduktion," *Koloniale Rundschau*, April 1912, 193–196. Emil Kreplin, *Die deutschen Diamanten und ihre Gewinnung* (Berlin: Reimer, 1914), 55.

23. "Bergbau," *Glückauf* 49, no. 10 (Essen, 1913): 366. Robert Gerstenhauer, "Südwestafrikanische Diamantenpolitik," *Jahrbuch über die deutschen Kolonien* 7 (Essen: Baedeker, 1914): 179. "Poorer outlying claims," see A. L. Hall, *Geology* (Pretoria: Government Printing and Stationery Office, 1912), 102. "Regelung der Pomonafrage," *Frankfurter Zeitung*, January 28, 1911. Cf. "Teilweise Einstellung," *Berliner Börsen-Courier*, August 14, 1911.

24. Cf. Ernest Oppenheimer to Dernburg, September 18, 1909, BAK N1130/35. "Aus Lüderitzbucht," *Lüderitzbuchter Zeitung*, May 1, 1914. *Adreßbuch für Stadt und Bezirk Lüderitzbucht (Deutsch-Südwestafrika)*, ed. Rudolf Geschke (Lüderitzbucht, 1914), 53, 60. Ernest Oppenheimer to William Honnold, June 18, 1914, Box 3, Folder 16, CCL Honnold Papers. See Ernest Oppenheimer and Alpheus F. Williams, *Diamond Deposits of German South West Africa* (Kimberley, 1914), 10–11, 13, 40, 57. Report was printed "for private circulation only" and given to a few directors of De Beers. Original contained in NAN: PB/0132.

25. This report was separate, having been produced by a German geologist, Erich Kaiser. It was cited in *Consolidated Diamond Mines of Southwest Africa, First Annual Report* (Year ending December 3, 1920), 3. *Diamantenwüste*, ed. Erich Kaiser, vol. 2 (Berlin, 1926), 339–343. On this see Hedley A. Chilvers, *The Story of De Beers* (London: Cassell, 1939), 200.

26. "Diamond Output," *New York Times*, November 18, 1913.

27. Natty Rothschild (1st Lord Rothschild) to Baron Édouard Alphonse James de Rothschild in Paris, November 7, 1913 and April 21, 1914, RAL XI/130A/7/217 and XI/130A/8/79. "Klein's Diamond Engagement Rings," *Montgomery Advertiser* (Alabama), October 22, 1913. Cf. "Deutsche Kolonialgesellschaft," *Berliner Börsen-Courier*, August 11, 1913. "Antwerp's Diamond Trade," *Wall Street Journal*, May 1, 1913. German production, 1913, see Wilhelm von Humboldt-Dachroeden, *Diamantenpolitik* (Jena: Fischer, 1915), 163. Carat total comes from statement of Walter N. Kahn, printed in House of Representatives Committee on Ways and Means, Seventieth Congress, Second Session, *Tariff Readjustment—1929*, vol. 12 (Washington, DC: Government Printing Office, 1929), 7458.

28. "Verhältnisse am Diamantenmarkte," *Frankfurter Zeitung*, March 16, 1913. Cf. Deutsche Diamanten-Gesellschaft to Solf, October 22, 1913, HID, Archives of Deutsche Bank Zentrale Berlin, Sekretariat (Frankfurt), S097. Ernest Oppenheimer to William Honnold, March 30, 1914, Box 3, Folder 16, CCL Honnold Papers. "Sights," see Protocol of Regie boardmeeting, October 11, 1913, HID, Archives of Deutsche Bank Zentrale Berlin, Sekretariat (Frankfurt), S097. "Ueber die Lage des Diamantenmarktes," *Berliner Börsen-Courier*, November 22, 1913. "Fiskus und Geschäft," *Die Zukunft* 86 (1914): 67. Julius Kaliski, "Wirtschaft," *Sozialistische Monatshefte* 22, no. 9 (Berlin 1916): 512. Wilhelm Dyes, "Bergbau," *Metall und Erz* 4, no. 3 (Halle: Knapp, 1916): 42.

29. Cf. Humboldt-Dachroeden, *Diamantenpolitik*, 163, with the understanding that the United States represented 75 percent of world demand.

30. For latter: J. Zeelander to Reichskolonialamt, February 21, 1912; I. J. Verzoken to RKA, March 10, 1912; Dr. Felix Leviticus to Solf, February 22, 1912; RKA to Hermann Strauss & Co., May 9, 1912, BAB R1001/1353. "Not in the German Reich," see Arno Jollast, "Fürstenberg triumphans," 65. "Certain members," see Humboldt-Dachroeden to Bethmann Hollweg, October 27, 1911, BAB R901/787. Fürstenberg to Meyer-Gerhard, October 12, 1913, HID, Archives of Deutsche Bank Zentrale Berlin, Sekretariat (Frankfurt), S097. "Diamantenprozess," *Berliner Volkszeitung*, October 9, 1913. Solf's address to Reichstag, March 20, 1914, *Stenographische Berichte des deutschen Reichstages*, 8157.

31. Richthofen's speech, May 2, 1912, *Stenographische Berichte des deutschen Reichstages*, 1625. Dernburg to A. A., April 23, 1913, BAB R901/789. German consulate at Johannesburg to Bethmann Hollweg, April 28, 1913, BAB R901/789. "Diamanten," *Vossische Zeitung*, May 29, 1913. Falz, *Die Idar-Obersteiner Schmuckstein-Industrie*, 172. "Diamanten," *Vossische Zeitung*, June 7, 1913. W. J. Yerby, "Diamond Output," *Department of Commerce and Labor: Daily Consular and Trade Reports*, vol. 2 (Washington, DC, 1912), 1247. Arno Jollast, "Fürstenberg triumphans," 65. Otto Jöhlinger, "Deutschlands Kolonialwirtschaft," *Koloniale Rundschau, Jahrgang 1914* (Berlin, 1914), 35. Fritz Fischer, *War of Illusions* (London: Chatto & Windus, 1975), 319. Below (Ambassador to Brussels) to Bethmann Hollweg, November 7, 1913, BAB R901/789; Hatzfeldt to Bethmann Hollweg, September 23, 1913, BAB R901/789. "Le diamant au Congo," *L'Echo de la Bourse*, October 28, 1913. Von Schnitzler (Consul at Antwerp) to Bethmann Hollweg, November 6, 1913, BAB R901/789.

32. "Chronologische Übersicht" of the Regie, undated, 1914, BAB R1001/1375. Report of Diamanten-Regie for 1912/13, HID, Archives of Deutsche Bank Zentrale Berlin,

Sekretariat (Frankfurt), S097. See "L'Officiel," *Le Soir,* May 13, 1912; "Les diamantaires," *Le Soir,* June 11, 1913. "Een kinderfeest door M. Coetermans gegeven," *Het Handelsblad* (Antwerp), December 24, 1913. "Away," see "Die 'gelbe' Saison," *Hamburger Nachrichten,* August 31, 1913. Arno Jollast, "Fürstenberg triumphans," 66. "French People Not Anxious to Have War with Germany," *Wall Street Journal,* May 5, 1913.

33. Natty Rothschild to Robert de Rothschild, Paris, September 4, 1913, RAL XI/130A/7/177. "Antwerpen," *Frankfurter Zeitung,* March 30, 1912. Attachment to letter of June 14, 1913, from Fürstenberg to Solf; RKA to Louis Coetermans, July 22, 1913, BAB R1001/1980. Report of Diamanten-Regie for 1912/13; Lotz's protocol, November 17, 1913, HID, Archives of Deutsche Bank Zentrale Berlin, Sekretariat (Frankfurt), S097. "Not going to help," see Ernest Oppenheimer to William Honnold, October 23, 1913, Box 3, Folder 16, CCL Honnold Papers. "Diamantensubmission," *Frankfurter Zeitung,* April 3, 1914.

34. "Diamond war," see "Besprechung mit den Vertretern der Förderer der Regie," November 17, 1913, BAB R1001/1390. "New Diamond Field?" *New York Times,* May 4, 1913. Cf. Colin Newbury, *The Diamond Ring* (Oxford: Oxford University Press, 1989), 189.

35. Protocol of meeting of board for *Regie,* June 6, 1913, BAB R1001/1930; "Die Antwerpener Gruppe erhält den Zuschlag auf eine Million Karat deutscher Diamanten," *Neue Preußische Zeitung,* June 7, 1913. On Koppel's group: "Deutscher Diamanten-Verband G.m.b.H.," *Von der Heydt's Kolonial-Handbuch,* ed. Julius Hellmann, vol. 8 (Berlin, 1914), 149. Albert Hahn, "De krisis in het diamant-vak," *De Notenkraker,* January 24, 1914. Natty Rothschild to Édouard Rothschild, Paris, June 11, 1913, RAL XI/130A/7/116. Cf. "Bedingungen für die Ausschreibung," *Berliner Börsen-Courier,* April 8, 1913. Cf. "Schutzgebiets-Chronik," *Windhuker Nachricthen,* July 2, 1913. "Bewerber um die deutschen Diamanten," *Frankfurter Zeitung,* May 21, 1913.

36. "Bemühungen der Regie," *Frankfurter Zeitung,* November 19, 1913. Attachment to Lotz's protocol, November 17, 1913, HID, Archives of Deutsche Bank Zentrale Berlin, Sekretariat (Frankfurt), S097. "Being the least clean," see Fürstenberg to Meyer-Gerhard, October 7, 1913, BAB R1001/1390. Rothschilds in London to Robert Philippe Gustave de Rothschild in Paris, November 20, 1913, RAL XI/130A/7/235. Ernest Oppenheimer to William Honnold, October 22 and 23, 1913, Box 3, Folder 16, CCL Honnold Papers. See protocol of meeting of *Regie*'s board of directors, August 20, 1913, BAB R1001/1390. "Paris Failures," *Wall Street Journal,* May 5, 1914. "French Financial Affairs," *Wall Street Journal,* June 20, 1914. Max Warburg to Peter Conze, October 8, 1913, BAB R1001/1390.

37. Rothschilds in London to Robert Philippe Gustave de Rothschild in Paris, November 20, 1913, RAL XI/130A/7/235. See undated *Regie* memo (c. 1914) in NAN ZBU 1613, R.XIV.f.2, Band 3. "Streit um die Diamantenregie," *Berliner Börsen-Courier,* December 6, 1913. Cf. Rathenau, *Notes and Diaries 1907–1922,* ed. Hartmut Pogge von Strandmann (Oxford: Clarendon, 1985), 182. Fürstenberg to Helfferich, November 17, 1913, HID, Archives of Deutsche Bank Zentrale Berlin, Sekretariat (Frankfurt), S097. "Bemühungen der Regie," *Frankfurter Zeitung,* November 19, 1913. "Material für die Besprechung am 17. diesen Monats in Diamantsachen," undated, BAB R1001/1347.

38. Jöhlinger, "Deutschlands Kolonialwirtschaft," 36. "Kolonialetat," *Deutsche Kolonialzeitung* 30, no. 11 (1913): 190. "Industrie und Handel," *Vorwärts,* January 14, 1914.

39. Jöhlinger, "Rundschau," *Koloniale Rundschau, Jahrgang 1914* (Berlin, 1914), 318. "Über die Verhandlungen," *Berliner Börsen-Courier,* July 18, 1914. London Rothschilds to James de Rothschild, May 12, 1914, RAL XI/130A/8/94.

40. "Diamond Trust," *New York Times,* July 18, 1914. Helfferich to Seitz, November 20, 1913, HID, Archives of Deutsche Bank Zentrale Berlin, Sekretariat (Frankfurt), S097.

41. "National," see Stauch's report, March 6, 1914, BAB R8023/217. "A new diamond trust," see "Diamanten," *Plutus: Kritische Wochenschrift für Volkswirtschaft und Finanzwesen,* October 26, 1912, 846, BAB R1001/1346. Solf's diary entry for July 29, 1912, BAK N1053/36.

42. Otto Jöhlinger, "Kolonialschulden und Kolonialanleihen," *Finanz-Archiv: Zeitschrift für das gesamte Finanzwesen* 31, no. 1 (1914): 10, note 1. Lilian Knowles and C. M. Knowles, *Economic Development of Overseas Empire,* vol. 3 (London: Routledge, 1936), 244. Captain Retzmann of SMS Strassburg to Wilhelm II, February 2, 1914, BAB R1001/1909.

43. On strike disruption: Natty Rothschild to Robert de Rothschild, January 13, 1914, RAL XI/130A/8/10. "Bent on German cooperation," see William Honnold to Dunkelsbuhler & Co., January 27, 1914, Box 75, Folder 2, CCL Honnold Papers. For negotiations, see records of German Foreign Office in BAB R 901/789–790. Ernest Oppenheimer to William Honnold, March 26, 1914, Box 3, Folder 16, CCL Honnold Papers.

44. William Honnold to Messrs. Dunkelsbuhler & Co., January 27, 1914, Box 75, Folder 2, CCL Honnold Papers. Ernest Oppenheimer to William Honnold, April 18, 1914, Box 3, Folder 16, CCL Honnold Papers. Chilvers, *Story of De Beers,* 201.

45. But see Jan Rüger, "Anglo-German Antagonism," *Journal of Modern History* 83, no. 3 (2011): 579–617. See also Ulrike Lindner, "Transnational Movements," *European Review of History* 16, no. 5 (2009): 684. Tilman Dedering, "War," *The International Journal of African Historical Studies* 39, no. 2 (2006): 280. See Horst Drechsler, *'Let Us Die Fighting': The Struggle of the Herero and Nama Against German Imperialism, 1884–1915* (London: Zed, 1980), 204. Bernhard Dernburg, "Germany and England in Africa," *Journal of the Royal African Society* 9, no. 34 (1910): 115. Louis Botha to Dernburg, March 22, 1909, BAK N1130/33.

46. See Imanuel Geiss, "Origins," in *The Origins of the First World War,* ed. H. W. Koch (London: Macmillan, 1984), 75. See P. H. S. Hatton, "Harcourt and Solf," *European Studies Review* 1, no. 2 (1971): 123.

47. Harcourt to Kühlmann, April 14, 1912, cited in Hatton, "Harcourt and Solf," 134, note 49. See Jens-Uwe Guettel, "'Between Us and the French There Are No Profound Differences,'" *Historical Reflections* 40, no. 1 (2014): 29–46. "Commercial entente," see Fritz Fischer, "World Policy," in *The Origins of the First World War,* ed. H. W. Koch (London: Macmillan, 1984), 139.

48. But see Dirk van Laak, "Kolonien," in *Das Kaiserreich transnational,* eds. Sebastian Conrad and Jürgen Osterhammel (Göttingen, 2004), 257. German consulate at Johannesburg to Bethmann Hollweg, November 6, 1913, R901/789. "Great combine," see "Über die Verhandlungen," *Berliner Börsen-Courier,* July 18, 1914. Compare Kurt Wiedenfeld, *Cartels and Combines* (Geneva: Kundig, 1927), 20. "Only a question," see Natty Rothschild to Édouard de Rothschild, Paris, April 21, 1914, RAL, XI/130A/8/79.

49. "Diamond Trust," *New York Times,* July 18, 1914. Otto Jöhlinger, "Rundschau," *Koloniale Rundschau, Jahrgang 1914* (Berlin, 1914), 318. J. Fink to Solf, January 24, 1912, BAB R1001/1353.

50. "Diamantenhandel," *Berliner Tageblatt,* August 4, 1914; "Diamantenregie," *Berliner Tageblatt,* October 20, 1914. "Strong enough," see "Diamanten," *Vossische Zeitung,* May 29, 1913.

51. See Nathaniel, 1st Lord Rothschild to James Rothschild, Paris, December 9, 1913, RAL XI/130A/7/249. "German diamond empire," see Arno Jollast, "Fürstenberg triumphans," 67.

52. "The act of delivering the fate," see "Nachdem es den Bemühungen der Regie . . ." *Frankfurter Zeitung,* November 19, 1913.

53. "Über die Verhandlungen," *Berliner Börsen-Courier,* July 18, 1914. "Rache des Herrn Fürstenberg," *Deutsche Tageszeitung,* December 17, 1913. Cf. "Erklärung des Kolonialamtes zur Diamantenfrage," *Deutsche Tageszeitung,* December 20, 1913. Perspective of producers recorded in NAN ZBU vol. 1613, R X iv, f 2, Bd. 3, Bl. 78 and 142.

11. Guns

1. Franz Oskar Karstedt, *Was war uns deutscher Kolonialbesitz?* (Berlin: Kolonialgesellschaft, 1918), 55. Cf. Smith, *German Colonial Empire,* 138. See Dirk Bönker, "Maritime Force," in *German Colonialism in a Global Age,* eds. Bradley Naranch and Geoff Eley (Durham: Duke University Press, 2014), 287. See David Killingray, 'War in Africa,' in *Companion to World War I,* ed. John Horne (Oxford: Wiley Blackwell, 2010), 112–126.

2. See Hew Strachan, *First World War,* vol. 1 (Oxford: Oxford University Press, 2003), 543–569. Gerald L'Ange, *Imperial Service* (Cape Town: Ashanti, 1991), 91. See John Phillips, "Pomona Story," *Journal-SWA Scientific Society* 36/37 (1982): 11–44. James Wilford Garner, *International Law and the World War,* vol. 1 (London: Longmans, 1920), 290. Cf. Marion Wallace, *Health, Power and Politics* (Basel: Schlettwein, 2002), 71–72. Solf's memo, October 14, 1914, BAB R1001/1375. Seitz to Lüderitzbuchter Minenkammer, August 6, 1914, BAB R1002/6. Nicolaus Henningsen, *Unserer Auslandskreuzer Ruhm und Ende 1914* (Cologne: Schaffstein, 1915), 56.

3. "Zwischenakt unserer Kolonialpolitik," *Karlsruher Tageblatt,* October 27, 1914. Colmanskop Mines Ltd., Cape Town to Kolonialgouvernement at Windhoek, October 1, 1911, BAB R1001/1349. Anonymous memo to Referat B 2, undated, BAB R1001/1375. See file marked "Versicherung der Diamanten gegen Kriegsgefahr," BAB R1001/1349.

4. Carleton Case, *Anecdotes of the Great War* (Chicago: Shrewesbury, 1916), 57. Lamar Cecil, *Wilhelm II: Emperor and Exile, 1900–1941* (Chapel Hill: University of North Carolina Press, 1996), 214.

5. Peter Rainier, *African Hazard* (London: Murray, 1940), 141. Margarethe von Eckenbrecher, *Was Afrika mir gab und nahm* (Berlin: Mittler, 1940), 165. W. S. Rayner, *How Botha and Smuts Conquered German South West* (London: Simpkin, 1916), 26; attachment to Johannes Kröger to Stauch, December 30, 1914, BAB R1001/1425. *Der Völkerkrieg,* ed. C. H. Baer, vol. 2 (Stuttgart: Hoffmann, 1914), 302. Peter William Rainier, *My Vanished Africa* (New Haven: Yale University Press, 1940), 150.

6. Attachment to Johannes Kröger to August Stauch, December 30, 1914, BAB R1001/1425.

7. Colin Newbury, *The Diamond Ring* (Oxford: Oxford University Press, 1989), 198. See NAN BBL M.68/20.

8. Protocol of Regie's board meeting, May 18, 1909, HID, Sekretariat (Frankfurt), S097. Cf. "'Titanic' Insurances," *The Economist,* April 20, 1912; "Insurance Lessons from the 'Titanic,'" *The Economist,* April 27, 1912. See J. Beenhouwer to Rough and Export Diamond Committee of Amsterdam, June 26, 1917, UKNA FO 115/2209.

9. Seitz to Lüderitzbuchter Minenkammer, August 19, 1914, BAB R1002/6. Eckenbrecher, *Was Afrika mir gab,* 166. Theodor Seitz, *Südafrika im Weltkriege* (Berlin: Reimer, 1920), 16.

10. "Diamantenhandel," *Berliner Tageblatt und Handels-Zeitung,* August 4, 1914. Lüderitzbuchter Minenkammer to Seitz, August 6 and 18, 1914; Seitz to Lüderitzbuchter Minenkammer, August 19, 1914, BAB R1002/6. Attachment on Johannes Kröger to Stauch, December 30, 1914, BAB R1001/1425. See NAN BBL 44 M.68/20. Ian van der Waag, "Major JGW Leipoldt, DSO," *Militaria* 25, no. 1 (1995): 17.

11. "There were diamonds," see J. P. Robinson, "With Botha's Army," *True Stories of the Great War,* vol. 2 (New York: Review of Reviews, 1917), 122. Eugen Kalkschmidt, "Aus der Sommeschlacht," *Illustrierte Geschichte des Weltkrieges 1914–16,* vol. 5 (Stuttgart: Verlagsgesellschaft, 1917), 268. Hans Meyer, *Kolonien* (Berlin: Mittler, 1916), 37. Cf. Heinrich Kaufmann, *Meine Erlebnisse in Deutsch-Südwestafrika* (Bonn: Schergens, 1916), 31; Gottfried Galli, *Die Deutsch-englische Auseinandersetzung* (Berlin: Bahlen, 1916), 24. Anonymous, "Diamantenproduktion," *Weltwirtschaftliches Archiv* 10 (1917): 55.

12. "British Soldiers Seek for Precious Stones," *Spokesman-Review* (Spokane), July 18, 1916. Meyer-Gerhard to Solf, October 6, 1914, BAB R1001/1375. "Ausland: Diamanten," *Metall und Erz* 4, no. 16 (Halle, 1916): 363. "Die Diamantindustrie," *Weltwirtschaftliches Archiv* 13 (1918), 35. "Mails Used to Smuggle," *Peking Gazette,* January 13, 1916.

13. Nicolaus, "Diamanten als Kapitalanlage," *Die Umschau* 20 (Frankfurt, 1916), 793. George Frederick Kunz, "Production of Precious Stones for the Year 1916," *Jewelers' Circular-Weekly* 75 (New York, 1917): 57. Vice-President of Diamond Exchange in Amsterdam to Solf, February 16, 1915, BAB R1001/1353. Cf. "Aufhebung der Vorschusspflicht," *Berliner Börsenzeitung,* August 16, 1914. "Kleine Nachrichten," *Deutsche Uhrmacher-Zeitung* 40, no. 21 (Berlin: Strauß, 1916): 289. Enclosure no. 1 in Valentine Chirol to A. Nicolson, December 4, 1914, UKNA CAB 37/122.

14. "Diamonds in U-Boat Cargo," *New York Times,* July 4, 1916. Cf. "German Diamonds," *The Observer* (London), June 25, 1916.

15. "Every selling opportunity," see report on Diamantenregie in *Berliner Börsen-Courier,* April 24, 1915. BAB R 901/791, Consulate-General in Bern, Switzerland to Bethmann Hollweg, November 1, 1915. "Les diamants industriels," *Journal de Genève,* November 4, 1917. BAB R901/791, German Consul-General at Amsterdam to Bethmann Hollweg, April 23, 1915.

16. Onyx, e.g., at funerals. Ernst Falz, *Idar-Obersteiner Schmuckstein-Industrie* (Idar: Carl Schmidt Verlag, 1926), 227. "Very good price," see Solf to Jagow, November 11, 1915, BAB R901/791. "Diamantindustrie," *Weltwirtschaftliches Archiv* 13 (1918): 35. "Nut-sized diamonds," cf. David Hamlin, "'Wo sind wir?' Orientalism, Gender and War in the German Encounter with Romania," *German History* 28, no. 4 (2010): 440–441. G. Badermann, "Glück und Niederlage Deutschlands in Diamanten," *Deutsche Goldschmiede-Zeitung* 22, no. 17–18 (1919): 104.

17. Frank Mahin's Report of August 7, 1915, *U.S. Department of Commerce, Commerce Reports,* vol. 3, year 18 (Washington, 1915), 1244.

18. See entry for Leopold Stern, *Biographical Directory of the State of New York, 1900* (New York, 1900), 466; "Freundschaft Is in New $500,000 Home," *New York Times,* June 18, 1914. See ad for firm in the *Jewelers' Circular-Weekly,* October 3, 1917, 54.

19. Nicolaus, "Diamanten als Kapitalanlage," *Die Umschau* 20 (Frankfurt, 1916): 793. Memorandum attached to Foreign Office to Cecil Spring-Rice, June 6, 1917, UKNA FO 115/2209.

20. "Diamond Black List," see "Black List Consisting of Names of Persons with Whom No Trade in Diamonds Can Be Allowed under Any Circumstances," UKNA FO 115/2209. "Approved list," see Smart to J. Joyce Broderick, November 23, 1917; Monroe to Balfour, November 29, 1917; Constantine Graham to Arthur Balfour, October 11, 1917; Graham to Balfour, October 11, 1917, UKNA FO 115/2209. "Verkauf der deutschen Diamanten in London," *Berliner Börsenzeitung,* December 6, 1916.

21. "Polished diamond guarantee," see "Industrial Diamond Guarantee, old," undated (1917), UKNA FO 115/2209. (Illegible) to Smart, November 15, 1917, UKNA FO 115/2209.

Broderick's draft of "Industrial Diamond Guarantee," November 14, 1917, UKNA FO 115/2209.

22. "Diamond runners," see "Week by Week," *Bulawayo Chronicle,* October 6, 1916. "Probleme in der Diamanten-Gesellschaft (u.a. Diebstahl, Schlägerei)," BAK N1138/55.

23. British Consul-General, New York to Secretary of State for Foreign Affairs, March 26, 1917; British ambassador at Washington, DC, to Foreign Office, April 2, 1917; British Consul-General, New York to Secretary of State for Foreign Affairs, March 26, 1917, UKNA FO 115/2209.

24. See, e.g., p. 4 of Black List, as well as the case mentioned in Constantine Graham to Arthur Balfour, May 22, 1917, UKNA FO 115/2209. J. Collie to Ludwig Kastl, May 9 and September 26, 1916, BAB R1002/2138. "Proclamation No. 88," *Official Gazette of the East Africa Protectorate* 19, no. 555 (Nairobi: HMC, 1917)" 940.

25. "Clean" associates, see British Consul-General, New York to Secretary of State for Foreign Affairs, March 26, 1917, UKNA FO 115/2209. Constantine Graham to Arthur Balfour, June 1, 1917, UKNA FO 115/2209. "Diamond Trade Conditions," *Jewelers' Circular* 77, no. 25 (New York, 1919): 57. "Hun Spies," *Sacramento Union,* December 20, 1919. Directorate of Special Intelligence (Strand House) to War Trade Intelligence Department, November 9, 1917, UKNA FO 115/2209.

26. Richard von Kühlmann, *Erinnerungen* (Heidelberg: Schneider, 1948), 279. A. C. Nelson, "Scheveningen Agency," *Supplements to Commerce Reports: Review of Industrial and Trade Conditions in Foreign Countries in 1914 by American Consular Officers,* ed. United States Department of Commerce, vol. 1 (Washington, DC, 1916), 27. "Antwerpia," see Dina Siegel, *The Mazzel Ritual* (Dordrecht: Springer, 2009), 85.

27. Scheveningen figures, see Nelson, "Scheveningen Agency," 28. George Kunz, "Precious Stones," *The Mineral Industry: Its Statistics, Technology and Trade During 1916,* vol. 25 (London, 1917), 612.

28. "Veterinarian," see Fritz Leviticus to Dr. Meyer-Gerhard, December 16, 1916, BAB R1001/1353.

29. Directorate of Special Intelligence (Strand House) to War Trade Intelligence Department, November 10, 1917; Punch, Edye & Co. to Det Forenede Dampskibs Selskab, October 17, 1917, UKNA FO 115/2209.

30. Bosenick (Consul-General at Rotterdam) to Bethmann Hollweg, September 25, 1916, BAB R1001/1347.

31. Directorate of Special Intelligence (Strand House) to War Trade Intelligence Department, November 6, 1917, UKNA FO 115/2209. For example, Alfred van den Acker to M. Felix Blom, September 14, 1917, UKNA FO 115/2209.

32. Smart to Broderick, April 2, 1917, UKNA FO 115/2209.

33. For coded messages, see, e.g., Ernest Silberfeld to Arthur Silberfeld, May 23, 1917, UKNA FO 115/2209. Foreign Office to Nosworthy, March 29, 1917; Directorate of Special Intelligence (Strand House) to War Trade Intelligence Department, November 6, 1917; Copy of "Henriette Munk" to "Bernard Munk," September 25, 1917, UKNA FO 115/2209. Cf. Directorate of Special Intelligence (Strand House) to War Trade Intelligence Department, October 31, 1917, November 1 and 3, 1917; Maurice Poser to Louis Poser, August 4, 1917, UKNA FO 115/2209.

34. Colville Barclay to Arthur Balfour, August 3, 1917, UKNA FO 115/2209. Carl Gneist to Bethmann Hollweg, June 27 and 29, 1917, BAB R1501/118541. See Marc Frey, *Der Erste Weltkrieg und die Niederlande* (Berlin: de Gruyter, 1998), 297.

35. "Diamond committees," see Lord Robert Cecil to Broderick, April 23, 1917; Broderick to Nosworthy, April 25, 1917, UKNA FO 115/2209. George Kunz, "Precious Stones," *The Mineral Industry* 26 (London, 1918), 581. "Diamond Trade Conditions," *Jew-*

elers' Circular 77, no. 25 (New York, 1919), 57. American Diamond Committee, see Monroe to Charles L. Robinson, November 22, 1917; American Diamond Committee to Broderick, November 19, 1917, UKNA FO 115/2209. "H. C. Larter Honored," *Jewelers' Circular* 85 (New York, 1922): 81.

36. "Indirectly or directly," see "Rough Diamond Guarantee, old" UKNA FO 115/2209. British ambassador at Washington, D.C., to Foreign Office, April 2, 1917, UKNA FO 115/2209.

37. "Polished Diamond Guarantee, Form no. 1, new" and "no. 1, old," undated (1917), UKNA FO 115/2209.

38. On Dutch neutrality: Kees van Dijk, *The Netherlands Indies and the Great War* (Leiden: Brill, 2007).

39. Directorate of Special Intelligence (Strand House) to War Trade Intelligence Department, October 31, 1917; Directorate of Special Intelligence (Strand House) to War Trade Intelligence Department, November 2, 1917; David Zinger to H. Zinger, September 9, 1917, UKNA FO 115/2209.

40. "Internationale Wanderversammlung der Bohringenieure und Bohrtechniker in Teplitz," *Zeitschrift für praktische Geologie*, ed. Max Krahmann, November (Berlin, 1893), 443. *Elektrotechnische Zeitschrift* 10, July (Berlin, 1889): 344. Alfred Eppler, *Der Diamant im deutschen Gewerbe und auf dem Weltmarkt* (Crefeld: Hohns, 1917), 66, 72. Paul Baer, "Die deutsch-südwestafrikanische Diamantenpolitik," *Zeitschrift für Kolonialpolitik, Kolonialrecht und Kolonialwirtschaft* 14 (1912): 782. Ernest Elva Weir, "Process of Spinning Threads of Steel," *Scientific American* 116 (New York, 1917): 278. See Johann Urbanek & Co.'s advertisement, c. 1900, Hessian State Archive, Darmstadt, Germany (hereafter HStAD) Bestand R 4 Nr. 18970. State Foreign Ministry to Reichsamt des Innern in Berlin, September 14, 1911, BAB R901/787.

41. "Diamond war," see Badermann, "Glück und Niederlage," 101. "Preiskonvention im Diamantenhandel," *Frankfurter Zeitung*, November 8, 1910.

42. See Gerd Hardach, *First World War 1914-1918* (Berkeley: University of California Press, 1977), 59. See Helmut Maier, *Forschung als Waffe*, vol. 1 (Göttingen: Wallstein, 2007), 161. See BAB R8737/691. See Nachlass Günther Karl Anton, BAB N2007/82.

43. *Die Umschau* 21 (1917): 226.

44. "Southwest Africa for the *Reich*," see "Zukunft der deutschen Diamantschleiferei," *Deutsche Goldschmiede-Zeitung* 20, no. 49-50 (Leipzig, 1917): 297-298. "L'industrie diamantaire," *L'Indépendance Belge*, February 10, 1917.

45. British Ambassador at Washington, DC, to Foreign Office, April 2, 1917; British Consul-General, New York, to Broderick, March 24, 1917, UKNA FO 115/2209. Nosworthy (British Consul-General) to Broderick, March 28 and April 26, 1917, UKNA FO 115/2209. Figures for use of abrasives, see Charles Cheape, *Family Firm to Modern Multinational* (Cambridge, MA: Harvard University Press, 1985), 94. "Scarcity, expense, and unreliability," see Howard Dunbar, "Wheel Dressing and Truing," *Machinery* 23 (New York, 1917): 895.

46. "Good quality," see report of Vice-Consul Manners, September 1914, UKNA FO 403/448. "Die Diamantindustrie," *Weltwirtschaftliches Archiv* 13 (1918): 33. Foreign Office to Nosworthy, March 29, 1917, UKNA FO 115/2209. Ginsberg (Jeweler) to A. A. for "Kriegsmetall Aktiengesellschaft," November 23, 1916; Freiherr Hans Paul von Humboldt-Dachroeden's memorandum, November 30, 1917, BAB R901/791.

47. "Germany Begging," *New York Times*, July 23, 1918.

48. "Die Deutschen sammeln Diamanten," *Bozner Nachrichten*, August 12, 1919. On living standards, see Gerd Hardach, *The First World War*, 30-34; Alan Kramer, "Blockade and Economic Warfare," *First World War*, vol. 2, ed. Jay Winter (Cambridge: Cambridge

University Press, 2014), 471; Avner Offer, *The First World War: An Agrarian Interpretation* (Oxford: Oxford University Press, 1989), 48. "Edelsteine als Zahlungsmittel," *Vossische Zeitung,* June 19, 1918.

49. "Finances: Les Belligérants," *Bulletin Quotidien de Presse Étrangère: Confidentiel* (Ministères de la Guerre et des Affaires Étrangères), January 26, 1917.

50. Entry for July 9, 1917, *Der erste Weltkrieg: Kriegstagebuch des Generals Nikolaus Ritter von Endres,* ed. Elisabeth Haug (Hamburg: BOD, 2013), 316. See Frey, *Der erste Weltkrieg,* 201–202.

51. See Frey, *Der erste Weltkrieg,* 202–203.

52. "A grave danger," see Director Schneider to Siegfried von Roedern, Reich State Secretary for Finance, August 31, 1918, BAB R3101/7620. Badermann, "Glück und Niederlage," 104.

53. "Extraordinarily strong demand," see Reichsbank Directors to Karl Helfferich, October 1, 1917, BAB R3101/7620. Credit for source to Frey, *Der erste Weltkrieg,* 202–203.

54. "Gold gab ich für Eisen," see Jürgen Stockmann, *Private Vermögensbildung mit Gold* (Wiesbaden: Springer, 1974), 48. James Watson Gerard, *Face to Face with Kaiserism* (New York: Doran, 1918), 185. "Kaiserin's Jewels," *New York Times,* July 21, 1917. Cf. Krupp von Bohlen und Halbach to Red Cross, November 25, 1916, in Willi A. Boelcke, *Krupp und die Hohenzollern in Dokumenten* (Berlin: Athenaion, 1970), 259.

55. David Werner Bloch, *Entwertung der deutschen Valuta im Weltkrieg* (Basel: Finckh, 1918), 73. "Failed to appreciate," quoted in "Germany Begging," *New York Times,* July 23, 1918. "Deutsche Männer, Deutsche Frauen," *Vorwärts,* February 18, 1917, 6. Regarding frantic message, see, e.g., "Weltkrieg drängt zur Entscheidung," *Allgemeine Rundschau* 14 (Munich 1917): 145. *Frankfurter Zeitung,* June 19, 1918. "Begs Gems and Gold," *Jewelers' Circular-Weekly,* July 24, 1918. Wilhelm Solf to Bethmann Hollweg, January 14, 1916; August Stauch to Solf, January 5, 1916, BAB R901/791.

56. "Edelsteine als Zahlungsmittel," *Vossische Zeitung,* June 19, 1918.

57. "Edelsteine als Zahlungsmittel," *Vossische Zeitung,* June 19, 1918.

58. "Inoperative," see Ernest Oppenheimer's Memorandum, April 12, 1932, BL MS/OPP/EO/K1.11.36. Zander (Deutsche Diamanten-Gesellschaft) to G. Glockemeier, April 16, 1916, BAB R1001/1350a. Lübbert to Böhmer, January 17, 1918, BAB R1001/1350. Badermann, "Glück und Niederlage," 105. Böhmer to Lübbert, December 17, 1917, BAB R1001/1350.

59. Memo concerning "Charlottenfelder AG, Emden, Diamantenfeldererwerb und—abbau in Südwestafrika, undated (1915); memo concerning "Deutsche Diamanten GmbH, Berlin," undated (1915), Secret State Archives Prussian Cultural Heritage Foundation, Geheimes Staatsarchiv Preußischer Kulturbesitz (Prussian State Archive), I. HA Rep. 120 MfHuG, C IX 1 Nr. 19 adh. 4 Bd. 1 and Bd. 2. Stefan Kanfer, *The Last Empire* (New York: FSG, 1993), 193. Cf. Ernst Fabarius, *Neue Wege der deutschen Kolonialpolitik* (Berlin: Curtius, 1916), 27. Cf. Emil Lehmann to Deutsche Bank, February 4, 1919, HID, Archives of Deutsche Bank Zentrale Berlin, Sekretariat (Frankfurt), S0103. Hermann Niess to Lübbert, January 6, 1918; Lübbert to Böhmer and Niess, January 17, 1918, BAB R1001/1350. Pomona Diamanten-Gesellschaft and Koloniale Bergbaugesellschaft to Administrator at Windhoek, January 24, 1919, BAB R1001/1350. Regarding Entente's propaganda, see Karstedt, *Kolonialbesitz,* 3. Recordkeeping, see "Geschäftsbericht der Kolonialen Bergbau-Gesellschaft [...] für [...] 1918," BAB R8127/14212.

60. "Bull market," see Ludwig Scholz, *Adjustment of German Colonial Claims* (Bern, 1918), 8. Fritz Naphtali, "Kolonisation," *Sozialistische Monatshefte* 25, no. 15 (Berlin:

Doern, 1919): 1189. Regarding Bogenfels, see Report concerning events of August 18, 1918, BAK N1138/55.

61. DKSSWA to RKA, October 3, 1919, BAB R1001/1530. Deutche Bank to DKSSWA, October 3, 1919; DKSSWA to Deutsche Bank, October 20, 1919, HID, Archives of Deutsche Bank Zentrale Berlin, Sekretariat (Frankfurt), S0103.

62. See Anthony Hocking, *Oppenheimer & Son* (New York: McGraw-Hill, 1973), 78.

63. "Diamond King," *Time Magazine,* December 9, 1957.

64. "Always on the lookout," see Ernest Oppenheimer (from London) to William Honnold, August 15, 1918, Box 4, Folder 19, CCL Honnold Papers. Cf. "Diamond Trade," *Jewelers' Circular* 77, no. 25 (New York, 1919): 57. Ron Chernow, *House of Morgan* (New York: Simon and Schuster, 1990), 350, note 12. See, finally, Theodore Gregory, *Ernest Oppenheimer* (London: Oxford University Press, 1962), 84–85. Founding documents: Supreme Court of South Africa to US Consulate at Johannesburg, Box 4, Folder 8, CCL Honnold Papers; Supreme Court of South Africa to US Consulate at Johannesburg, September 11, 1918, Box 4, Folder 10, CCL Honnold Papers.

65. Hocking, *Oppenheimer,* 87. "Aus der süfwestafrikanischen Diamantenindustrie," *Frankfurter Zeitung,* May 23, 1911. Cf. "Zukunft der südwestafrikanischen Diamantengesellschaften," *Vossische Zeitung,* November 8, 1919. See BAK N1053/62. On legal work, *Adreßbuch für Stadt und Bezirk Lüderitzbucht* (Leipzig: Koehler, 1914), 47. "Important people," see Stauch and Lübbert's "Niederschrift über die Sitzung der Hauptkommission [der Kolonialen Bergbaugesellschaft] am 21. August 1919," BAB R1001/1405. See Olga Levinson, *Diamonds in the Desert* (Cape Town: Tafelberg, 1983), 118.

66. Trading for German Colonial Corporation, compare table in Fritz Naphtali, "Kolonisation," 1189. "Foreign property," see "Kolonialanteile," *Die Bank: Monatshefte für Finanz- und Bankwesen,* ed. Alfred Lansburgh (Berlin: Bank Verlag, 1919), 703. Josef Neumann, *Freiheit der Meere* (Berlin: Kalkoff, 1917), 19.

67. "Vereinigte Diamantminen-AG in Liquidation, Lüderitzbucht-Geschäftsbericht Jan. 1921 bis Apr. 1922," BAB R2/2765.

68. "Impartially," see Walter Loeb's report, May 10, 1919, *Akten der Reichskanzlei: Kabinett Scheidemann,* vol. 1 (Boppard am Rhein: Boldt, 1971), 327–328. Protocol of meeting on March 21, 1919; "Richtlinien," c. April 17, 1919; Report by peace delegation, June 17, 1919, *Akten der Reichskanzlei: Kabinett Scheidemann,* vol. 1, 83, 180, 471. "Deutsche Nationalversammlung," *Jenaer Volksblatt,* October 14, 1919. Charles S. Maier, *Recasting Bourgeois Europe: Stabilization in France, Germany, and Italy in the Decade after World War I* (Princeton: Princeton University Press, 1975), 237.

69. See Stauch and Lübbert's memo, August 21, 1919, BAB R1001/1405. Indeed, the coming years validated such prognostications when the South African colonial government annulled longstanding rights and contracts of a German copper miner without compensation. See League of Nations, *Supplementary Report on the Work of the League since the Tenth Session of the Assembly* (Lausanne: Réunies, 1930), 22. DPG to Meyer-Gerhard, January 22, 1918; Stauch and Lübbert's "Niederschrift über die Sitzung der Hauptkommission [der Kolonialen Bergbaugesellschaft] am 21. August 1919," BAB R1001/1405.

70. Disconto-Gesellschaft in Berlin, *Geschäftsbericht für das Jahr 1919* (Berlin, 1920), 7. Lübbert to DPG, September 2, 1919, BAB R1001/1405. List of shareholders is attached to notarized protocol of DKSSWA's board meeting, held in the Deutsche Bank's *Sitzungssaal* in Berlin's Kanonenstraße, November 3, 1919, BAB R1001/1530. Cf. "Deutsche Kolonial-Gesellschaft," *Vossische Zeitung,* November 3, 1919. See Michael Coulson, *History of Mining* (Petersfield, UK: Harriman, 2012), 233. Nora von Steinmeister, *Briefe,* eds. Karl Wulff, Jr. and Monika Schotten (Hamburg: Diplomica, 2013), 48, 61.

71. Adolf Rüger, "Streben," *Drang nach Afrika*, ed. Helmuth Stoecker (Berlin: Akademie, 1991), 280. See R8127/14212 for the Berliner Handels-Gesellschaft's Sekretariat discussion of contract drafts between August Stauch, Erich Lübbert, and Walter Bredow on the one side, and H. C. Hull on the other side. See J. L. Goode, *Report on the Conditions and Prospects of Trade in the Protectorate of South-West Africa* (London: HMSO, 1920), 21. Invitation from RKA to Deutsche Kolonialgesellschaft and Deutsche Diamantengesellschaft, September 29, 1919, BAB R1001/1405. See various drafts and agreements in R8127/14212. See German ambassador to Hague to A. A., November 7, 1919, PAAA R 246.271.

72. "Anglo American Corporation of South Africa: Chairman's Speech, undated (1919), Box 4, Folder 11, CCL Honnold Papers. Theodore Gregory, *Ernest Oppenheimer*, 116. "Ausschüttung der Deutschen Kolonialgesellschaft," *Frankfurter Zeitung*, April 16, 1921. Deutsche Kolonialgesellschaft für Südwestafrika to Deutsche Bank, October 20, 1919, HID, Archives of Deutsche Bank Zentrale Berlin, Sekretariat (Frankfurt), S0103. "Deutsche Kolonialgesellschaft," *Berliner Börsen-Courier*, April 16, 1920. "Mining sovereignty," see Kurt Heinig, *Die Finanzskandale des Kaiserreichs* (Berlin: Verlag für Sozialwissenschaft, 1925), 49–50.

73. "The exit of the Germans," see "Diamantenpolitik," *Deutsche Goldschmiede-Zeitung* 22 (1919): 343; "Diamond Market Cornered," *New York Times*, December 7, 1919. See Tony Emmett, *Popular Resistance and the Roots of Nationalism in Namibia* (Basel: Schlettwein, 1999), 68.

74. Oppenheimer's agreement, see Hocking, *Oppenheimer*, 114. Duncan Innes, *Anglo American and the Rise of Modern South Africa* (New York: Monthly Review, 1984), 104. Cf. Erwin Matsch, *Internationale Politik*, vol. 1 (Wien: Böhlau, 2005), 267.

75. Leopold Grahame, "Give Back Those Colonies?" *New-York Tribune*, February 2, 1919. "A share of the trade," see Speech of Ernest Oppenheimer, undated, BL MS/OPP/EO/K1.11.37. "Land der Diamanten," *Berliner Tageblatt*, August 18, 1919. Numbers cited incidentally in Martin Eberhardt, *Zwischen Nationalsozialismus und Apartheid* (Berlin: LIT, 2007), 89. See "Diamantentraum," *Neues Wiener Journal*, February 16, 1921. "Crammed with goods," see "News From England," *Jewelers' Circular*, December 13, 1922.

76. Cf. Ernst Steiner, *Der internationale Diamantenmarkt* (Wien: Richards, 1933), 14. For a succinct overview: Edward Jay Epstein, *The Rise and Fall of Diamonds* (New York: Simon & Schuster, 1982), 76–88. "Weltgewinnung," *Deutsche Goldschmiede-Zeitung* 26 (1923): 303. Staff News Letter of J. Walter Thompson Company, no. 177 (March 24, 1927), RL, Duke University, RL.00733 Box MN8.

Conclusion

1. "World ambitions," see Paul Rohrbach, *Der deutsche Gedanke in der Welt* (Düsseldorf: Langewiesche, 1912), 191, 159–160. "Inspired more Germans," see Helmut Walser Smith, *Continuities of German History* (Cambridge: Cambridge University Press, 2008), 202.

2. Cf. Helmut Böhme, "Thesen zur Beurteilung," *Der moderne Imperialismus*, ed. Wolfgang J. Mommsen (Stuttgart: Kohlhammer, 1971), 42. Ralf Forsbach, *Alfred von Kiderlen-Wächter* (Göttingen: V&R, 1997), 473.

3. Wolfdieter Bihl, *Deutsche Quellen zur Geschichte des Ersten Weltkrieges* (Darmstadt: Wissenschaftliche Buchgesellschaft, 1991), 61–62. Fritz Fischer, *Germany's Aims in the First World War* (New York: Norton, 1967), 109, 224.

4. Theodor Wolff, *Tagebücher 1914–1919*, vol. 1 (Boppard: Boldt, 1984), 289. "A few hundreds of millions," see W. E. B. Du Bois, "African Roots of War," *Atlantic Monthly*

115 (1915): 712. "Robbers," see "Spukgeschichten," *Kladderadatsch,* vol. 72, no. 33 (Berlin, 1919), 440. "Escapades," cf. "Die deutsche Kolonialunternehmung," *Frankfurter Zeitung,* February 26, 1919.

5. "Dernburg's diamonds," see Adolph Hoffmann, *Episoden und Zwischenrufe* (Berlin: Hoffmann, 1924), 40. Kurt Tucholsky, "Kolonisatoren," *Die Weltbühne* 23, no. 29 (Charlottenburg: Jacobsohn, 1927): 98. Woodruff Smith, *Ideological Origins of Nazi Imperialism* (Oxford: Oxford University Press, 1989), 224. Cf. Klaus Hildebrand, *Vom Reich zum Weltreich* (München: Fink, 1969), 441.

6. Cf. Diary entry of July 26, 1919, Harry Graf Kessler, *Tagebücher 1918–1937,* ed. Wolfgang Pfeiffer-Belli (Frankfurt am Main: Insel, 1961), 192. Theodor Wolff, *Tagebücher 1914–1919,* vol. 1, 680, 717. Leo Haupts, *Friedenspolitik* (Düsseldorf: Droste, 1976), 361. "Rumänien und der Krieg," *Friedenauer Lokal-Anzeiger,* August 20, 1916. Felix Pinner, "Dernburg," *Die Weltbühne,* vol. 18, no. 2: 472.

7. See Annika Klein, "Hermes, Erzberger, Zeigner," in *Skandale: Strukturen und Strategien öffentlicher Aufmerksamkeitserzeugung,* eds. Kristin Bulkow and Christer Petersen (Wiesbaden: VS, 2011), 53.

8. "Wie geht es in Südwest?" *Vossische Zeitung,* July 22, 1926. "Berliner Handelsgesellschaft," *Vossische Zeitung,* April 9, 1921. Johannes Steinbach, *Siedlungsmöglichkeiten* (Berlin: Landbuchhandlung, 1928), 22. Max Chop, "Vox," *Signale für die musikalische Welt,* vol. 80, no. 42 (Berlin: Redepenning, 1922): 1171. "Koloniale Bergbau-Gesellschaft," *Berliner Adreßbuch 1918,* vol. 2 (Berlin: Scherl, 1918), 1393. Eric Rosenthal, *Shovel and Sieve* (London: Unwin, 1950), 50. "Stauchscher Farm-Konzern liquidiert," *Vossische Zeitung,* January 29, 1931. Paul Rohrbach's diary entries for August 4 and 18, 1933, BAK 408/29. Rohrbach, "Die schwarzen Diamanten von Südwest," *Hamburger Anzeiger,* September 4, 1933. "Ein Diamant wird gespalten," *Dolomiten,* August 28, 1937.

9. Lawrence G. Green, *Panther Head* (Cape Town: Paul, 1955), 76. "Tod eines alten Südwesters," *Das Echo* 51 (Berlin, 1932): 352.

10. Gustav Stresemann to Jan Smuts, October 29, 1923, *Akten der Reichskanzlei, Kabinette Stresemann I u. II,* vol. 2, eds. Karl Dietrich Erdmann and Martin Vogt (Boppard am Rhein: Boldt, 1978), 894. Reichsministerium des Innern to Landesregierungen, January 5, 1926, HStAD Bestand R 1 B Nr. 7887. Hugo Blumhagen, *Südafrika* (Hamburg: Friederichsen, 1921), 106. Friedrich Reck-Malleczewen, "Menagerieschiff," *Tagesbote* (Brno), November 25, 1933. Rochus Schmidt, "Rund um Afrika," *Berliner Börsenzeitung,* January 7, 1926. "Außerdeutsches Logenleben," *Mitteilungen aus dem Verein Deutscher Freimaurer,* vol. 2 (Leipzig: Schwabe, 1923), 168. "Nationalfestspiele in Weimar," *Berliner Tageblatt,* January 22, 1920.

11. Henry Walker, *A Doctor's Diary in Damaraland* (London: Arnold, 1917), 204. F. Maywald, "Lüderitzbucht," *Geographischer Anzeiger* 32, no. 10 (Gotha: Perthes, 1931): 294. Carl Schmidt, *Geographie der Europäersiedelungen* (Jena: Fischer, 1922), 96. "Pomona Diamanten-Gesellschaft," *Berliner Tageblatt,* September 5, 1922. "Aufwertungsmöglichkeit," *Die Uhrmacherkunst* 48, no. 49 (Halle, 1923): 545. "Zehn Jahre Deutscher Arbeiterverband," *Vorwärts,* April 6, 1929.

12. "Colonial shares," see "Die deutsche Kolonialunternehmung," *Frankfurter Zeitung,* February 26, 1919. Karl Schmidt, Bezirksamtmann Hamburg, to Regierungsrat Heilingbrunner at German Foreign Office, August 7, 1925; Nordische Bankkommandite Sick & Co. to Foreign Office, May 29, 1926, BAB R1001/6407. "Die Diamantenregie," *Swakopmunder Zeitung,* August 3, 1921. "Kleine Nachrichten," *Deutsche Uhrmacher-Zeitung* 47, no. 23 (Berlin 1923): 303. Cf. Dr. Wangemann to Emil Georg von Stauss, December 2, 1926, HID, Archives of Deutsche Bank Zentrale Berlin, Sekretariat (Frankfurt), S096. Cf. "World Scarcity of Diamonds," *American Jeweler* 39, no. 11 (1919): 430.

13. Short overview in Duncan Innes, *Anglo American and the Rise of Modern South Africa* (New York: Monthly Review, 1984), 102–113. See "Diamantenstadt," *Berliner Volks-Zeitung,* October 30, 1929. "Lived on diamonds," see "Zehn Jahre Deutscher Arbeiterverband," *Vorwärts,* April 6, 1929. See Rochus Schmidt, "Rund um Afrika," *Berliner Börsenzeitung,* January 7, 1926. Ernst Steiner, *Der internationale Diamantenmarkt* (Wien: Richards, 1933), 9.

14. "Important," see Margarethe von Eckenbrecher, *Was Afrika mir gab und nahm* (Berlin: Mittler, 1940), 319. See Olga Levinson, *Diamonds in the Desert* (Cape Town: Tafelberg, 1983), 122. On Stauch's political activities after the war, see Zedekia Ngavirue, *Political Parties* (Basel: Schlettwein, 1997), 151. Paul Leutwein, *Kolonialfrage* (Berlin: Safari, 1938), 29. See Alexander Dietz, *Handelsgeschichte,* vol. 1 (Frankfurt: Minjon, 1910), 106. "Perfect monopolies," see "Streit um Diamanten," *Bozner Tagblatt,* May 30, 1944. Steiner, *Diamantenmarkt,* 12.

15. See Martin Eberhardt, *Zwischen Nationalsozialismus und Apartheid* (Berlin: LIT, 2007), 365. Deutsches Konsulat for SWA to A. A., February 22, 1930, BAB R1001/7149. "50 Jahre Lüderitzbucht," *Salzburger Volksblatt,* May 27, 1933. "Feeding trough," see "Kolonialmandate," *Lachen links* 3, no. 16 (Berlin: Dietz, 1926): 187. Albrecht Wirth, *Völkische Weltgeschichte* (Braunschweig: Westermann, 1934), 287.

16. Cf. Nora von Steinmeister and Karl Wulff, *Briefe aus Afrika 1932–1938,* eds. Karl Wulff, Jr. and Monika Schotten (Hamburg: Diplomica, 2013), 68–69. "Hotbed," see Harald Bielfeld to Reichswirtschaftsministerium, January 19, 1939, BAB R1001/7543. Aleko Lilius, "South Africa's Desert of Diamonds," *Travel* 74, no. 6 (New York: McBride, 1940), 32. P. Bruchhausen, "Nazis in South-West Africa," *The Listener* (London), November 7, 1934. "Dark chapter," see Rohrbach, "Diamanten," *Hamburger Anzeiger,* September 4, 1933.

17. See image 116 in Reichskolonialbund, *Afrika in Farben* (München: Fichte, 1941). "Verfassungskommission," *Lüderitzbuchter Zeitung,* September 19, 1935. Report of Jewish Central Information Office, October 24, 1935, Jewish Press Agencies Collection; AR 5316; Box 1, Folder 15; Leo Baeck Institute, New York. "Not tolerated," see Lilius, "Desert of Diamonds," 32.

18. "Betrayed," "Wall Street," "Jewish circles," see Erich Kühn, "Bild der Lage," *Deutschlands Erneuerung,* vol. 4 (München: Lehmanns, 1920), 530; Ottokar Stauf von der March, *Die Juden im Urteil der Zeiten* (München: Boepple, 1921), 180; Paul Bang, *Judas Schuldbuch* (München: Volksverlag, 1919), 168; Helga Krohn, *Juden in Hamburg* (Hamburg: Christians, 1974), 204. "Jewish stockjobber," see Ernst Rademacher, *260 Revolutionshelden* (Berlin: Warthemann, 1920), 6. Gottfried Feder to Reichstag, November 13, 1926, *Stenographische Berichte,* 8115. On Feder: Thomas Weber, *Becoming Hitler* (New York: Basic, 2017), 86.

19. Rudolf Emil Martin, *Deutsche Machthaber* (Berlin: Schuster and Loeffler, 1910), 71, 75–76, 501–507, 532–533. Werner Sombart, *Die Juden und das Wirtschaftsleben* (Munich: Duncker & Humblot), 30. "Jewish problem," see Derek Penslar, *Shylock's Children* (Berkeley: University of California Press, 2001), 114–116.

20. Werner Sombart, *Händler und Helden* (Leipzig: Duncker & Humblot, 1915). Jürgen G. Backhaus, ed., *Werner Sombart (1863–1941)—Social Scientist,* vol. 1 (Marburg: Metropolis, 1996), 208. "Jewish land," see Sombart, *Die Juden,* 31.

21. See Harold James, *The Reichsbank and Public Finance in Germany* (Frankfurt: Knapp, 1985), 209. "Big capitalists," see Arthur Schumann, *Die kommunistischen Kapitalistenknechte* (München: Eher, 1932), 35. Wirth, *Völkische Weltgeschichte,* 287.

22. See Eric Kurlander, *Living with Hitler* (New Haven: Yale University Press, 2009), 167. "Jewish politicians," see Hans Diebow, *Der ewige Jude* (München: Zentralverlag der

NSDAP, 1937), 99. "Jewish interests," see Hermann Seifert, *Der Jude zwischen den Fronten* (Berlin: Eher, 1943), 171.

23. "The greatest wealth," "control of diamond mines," see Karl Fischer, "1914/15: Schicksalsweg nach Khorab," in *Die Wehrmacht*, ed. Oberkommando der Wehrmacht, vol. 2, no. 14 (Berlin: Reichskriegsministerium, 1938), 12; Kurt Schwartzkopff, "Mit unseren Fahnen," *Deutsches Nachrichtenbüro* 7, no. 107 (Berlin: Deutsches Nachrichtenbüro, 1940): 1. Heinrich Heffter, ed., *Deutsche Kolonien* (Dresden: Cigaretten-Bilderdienst, 1936), image number 143. "Lüderitzbucht," *Kladderadatsch* 92, no. 39 (Berlin: Steiniger, 1939). Götz Aly, *Hitler's Beneficiaries* (New York: Holt, 2006), 198.

24. "Rich colonial land," see "Sektflaschen," *Banater Deutsche Zeitung,* March 20, 1938. Werner vom Hofe, ed., *Die ewige Straße: Geschichtsbuch für Hauptschulen,* vol. 1 (Berlin: Schulverlag, 1944), 71.

25. See Pascal Grosse, "What Does German Colonialism Have to Do with National Socialism? A Conceptual Framework," in *Germany's Colonial Pasts,* eds. Eric Ames, Marcia Klotz, and Lora Wildenthal (Lincoln: University of Nebraska Press, 2005), 119. See Christian Stuart Davis, *Colonialism, Antisemitism, and Germans of Jewish Descent in Imperial Germany* (Ann Arbor: University of Michigan Press, 2012).

26. "Insel der Pinguine," *Berliner Tageblatt,* November 1, 1925. Sture Lagercrantz, "Lebzelter Viktor," *Anthropos* 30 (Wien: Mechitharisten, 1935): 255. "Controls," see anonymous memorandum on Consolidated Diamond Mines, undated, BL, MS/OPP/EO/K1.11.38. F. Bult to Secretary for South West Africa, January 9, 1923, NAN BBL 45 M. 124/20.

27. Eckenbrecher, *Afrika,* 320–321. "Lüderitz Bay," *Evening Star* (Washington, DC), October 18, 1928. "Diamantenindustrie," *Altonaer Nachrichten,* June 16, 1931. Konrad Olbricht, *Deutschland als Kolonialmacht* (Breslau: Handels, 1933), 25. Allan Cooper, *Ovambo Politics in the Twentieth Century* (Lanham, MD: University Press of America, 2001), 94. "Verschluckte Diamanten," *Altonaer Nachrichten,* October 7, 1931. On workers', and even bureaucratic, concerns about this machine, see letter from CHl Hahn to Deputy Commissioner of the South African Police at Windhoek, August 20, 1942. NAN IMW, Box 55, File No. A44/2/7. See Allan Cooper, "Institutionalization of Contract Labor in Namibia," *Journal of Southern African Studies* 25, no. 1 (1999): 132.

28. "Administrator von Südwest gegen Lügenmeldungen," *Deutsches Nachrichtenbüro* 6, no. 358 (Berlin: Deutsches Nachrichtenbüro, 1939): 1. Cf. German Consulate in Windhoek to German Foreign Office, August 7, 1934, BAB R1001/7540. "Upswing," see Olbricht, *Deutschland als Kolonialmacht,* 13 (italics mine).

29. Cooper, "Contract Labour in Namibia," 125. International Labour Office, *Minutes of the 25th Session of the Governing Body,* vol. 25 (Geneva, 1925), 478. "Sake of the diamonds," see Elizabeth van Maanen-Helmer, *Mandates System in Relation to Africa and the Pacific Islands* (London: King, 1929), 267. "Civilizer," see "Sir Ernest Oppenheimer Honoured," *African World* (London), October 9, 1937.

30. "Skelette entwichener Neger," *Berliner Börsenzeitung,* July 4, 1930. "Rund um Afrika," *Berliner Börsenzeitung,* January 7, 1926. "Deutsches Leben," *Hamburger Nachrichten,* June 30, 1930. P. Woodley to J. F. Herbst, September 14, 1921, *Garvey and Universal Negro Improvement Association Papers,* vol. 9 (Berkeley: University of California Press, 1995), 207. Lothar Engel, *Kolonialismus und Nationalismus* (Frankfurt: Peter Lang, 1976), 247.

31. See Susan Pedersen, *The Guardians: The League of Nations and the Crisis of Empire* (Oxford: Oxford University Press, 2015), 114. "Most sinister," see T. L. O'Reilly's report on concessions in Southwest Africa, February 1919, NAN 1/4/15/2/0, Concessions Commission of 1919, KCO 11. For contemporary legal take on diamond cartel as of 1947, see "Diamond Cartel," *Yale Law Journal* 56 no. 8 (September 1947): 1404–1419. Cf.

"Diamond Diggings Granted," *The Star* (South Africa), March 27, 1958. "Advocacy," see Speech of Ernest Oppenheimer, undated, BL, MS/OPP/EO/K1.11.37.

32. "South-West Africa," *Manchester Guardian,* September 27, 1921. Friedrich Nitschmann, *Abtretung der Kolonien* (Hamburg: Universität Hamburg, 1925), 51. Cf. Cooper, "Institutionalization of Contract Labor in Namibia," 124. "Economic standpoint," see "Aus Busch," *Berliner Tageblatt,* October 30, 1925 (italics mine).

33. The South West African Department of Economic Affairs acknowledged rumors of overmining in a report in 1985, but said "no evidence" could be found to support such a conclusion. R. McG. Miller, *Departmental Report on the Mining and Production of Diamonds at CDM (1945 to 1983)* (Windhoek, 1985), 28. This finding stood in stark contrast to that made by the Thirion Commission of South Africa.

34. "Unfit," see "Bethanie Water," *The Namibian,* March 13, 2007. "Fresh Water for Bethanie," *Namibian Sun,* October 24, 2017.

35. "Conflict diamonds," see United Nations Press Release GA/9839, December 1, 2000. https://www.un.org/press/en/2000/20001201.ga9839.doc.html

ACKNOWLEDGMENTS

In writing this book, I have drawn heavily on support from colleagues, institutions, and loved ones.

I remain indebted to David Blackbourn and Charles Maier, whose work continues to inspire me and shape my thinking.

I am also deeply grateful for various senior scholars who have read the manuscript and engaged with its structure and arguments: James T. Campbell, J. P. Daughton, Geoff Eley, Gabrielle Hecht, Isabel V. Hull, Harold James, Norman Naimark, Richard Roberts, James J. Sheehan, and Helmut Walser Smith.

In Palo Alto, Priya Satia and Jun Uchida have provided much-needed mentorship. Paula Findlen, Matthew Sommer, and Caroline Winterer have been generous chairs. Keith Baker, Rowan Dorin, Jonathan Gienapp, Kathryn Olivarius, Robert Proctor, Jessica Riskin, Paul Robinson, and Peter Stansky, among many others in the History Department, listened to presentations and offered feedback. Brenda Finkel, Burcak Keskin Kozat, and Monica Wheeler enabled my work at countless junctures. So did Maria van Buiten, who kept financial matters in order. At the Stanford Humanities Center, Roland Greene and Jenny Martinez arranged a wonderful manuscript workshop in 2020. Gil-li Vardi, in addition to lending numerous insights, helped me to secure research funding through the Stanford Institute for Innovation in Developing Economies.

I have been lucky to present portions of research for this book to groups at other universities. At Princeton, I thank hosts Jack Guenther, Harold James, Yair Mintzker, and Natasha Wheatley; at Sydney, Glenda Sluga; at Harvard, Sven Beckert, Walter Friedman, and Sophus Reinert; at Konstanz, Martin Rempe and Nikolai Wehrs; at Duke, Charles Bartlett, Rachel Brewster, and Phil Stern; at Tel Aviv, Avihay Dorfman and Alon Harel; at Berkeley, Heike Friedman and Stefan Ludwig-Hoffmann; at the German Historical Institute in Washington, Rüdiger Graf, Anne Schenderlein, Quinn Slobodian, and Heidi Tworek.

It is an honor to publish with Andrew Kinney as my editor. My appreciation extends to the rest of the team at Harvard University Press, as well as to the anonymous referees, who saved me from numerous infelicities and who helped me to revise and strengthen my manuscript.

Dr. Carolyn Taratko and Basetsana Tsuwane provided valuable assistance with research. For arranging access to records, I would like to thank Justin

Cavernelis-Frost of the Rothschild Archive in London, Jennifer Kimble of the Brenthurst Library in Johannesburg, Julia Woolcott of the Barloworld Archive in Sandton, and Dr. Martin Müller of the Deutsche Bank Historical Institute in Frankfurt.

Last but not least, I thank my family.

CREDITS

INDEX

Page numbers in *italics* refer to images.